JAPANE FROM ZERO!

George Trombley
Yukari Takenaka
Kanako Hatanaka

Japanese From Zero! Book 5
Proven Methods to Learn Japanese with Integrated Workbook

PREFACE
Japanese From Zero! is a Japanese language book series built on Japanese grammar that makes sense! Each book is crafted page by page and lesson by lesson to have relevant (and sometimes fun) Japanese conversation and sentence structure patterns that enhance the Japanese learner's ability to speak Japanese faster and understand the small nuances of Hiragana and everyday Japanese speech.

DEDICATION
This book series is dedicated and made for:

Japanese culture lovers, Japanese language learners, Japanese anime and drama watchers, Japanese beginners, JPOP music fans, people of Japanese heritage connecting to their history, and anyone planning travel to Japan!

I lived in Japan for 9 years and have been married to my Japanese wife, Yukari, for 24 years. When we began writing the Japanese From Zero series, it was out of frustration with current Japanese books on the market. I felt they were either too fast, too slow, or too complicated. Japanese has enriched my life so much and writing this series was a way to express my sincere appreciation to all that the country of Japan and the Japanese language can offer.

All of us on the Japanese From Zero! team wish you success on your road to Japanese fluency and hope this book is a solid first step!

DISTRIBUTION
Distributed in the USA, Canada, Others by:
From Zero LLC.
10624 S. Eastern Ave. #A769
Henderson, NV 89052, USA
sales@fromzero.com

Distributed in the UK & Europe by:
Bay Foreign Language Books Ltd.
Unit 4, Kingsmead, Park Farm,
Folkestone, Kent. CT19 5EU, Great Britain
sales@baylanguagebooks.co.uk

Thanks for the nice comments! We love feedback!

I'm grateful for your work... wouldn't have gotten as far as I have if I hadn't found Japanese From Zero
Jack Haveman – JFZ Discord Server

I'm definitely a fan of your teaching and your books I have all of them JFZ 1-4 and Kanji from Zero.
Hat_On_A_Fox – Discord PM

These books and this website remain my nihongo bible!
Ray_San – YesJapan.com

The books are great! I like the way everything is explained, the examples, the lessons and the reviews.
Eijioo – YesJapan.com

Japanese From Zero Book 1 and 2 are amazing books for beginners! Having tried other ways of learning Japanese from the beginning, I find that the Japanese from Zero series are incredibly user friendly.
Kurisuti.Chan – YesJapan.com

I love JFZ, because it's so so so easy to use compared to others I've tried! It's clear you put a lot of work into it and I'm very grateful. Even though I lead a busy life and can't find too much time to learn, JFZ makes it easy for me to pick up where I left off and revise what I might have forgotten. THANKS!! ☺
J. Brooks – Facebook

THANK-YOU JFZ!!!!!! I think Everything JFZ does is wonderful! It is the most helpful book I've come across!
Rukia Kuchiki – YesJapan.com

Keep up the great work and the video series on YouTube, Love the series and the books they've been a great help in my studies with my one on one teacher and I will be getting books 4&5 to complete my set.
>>GameHacKeR<< – JFZ Discord

Thank you for your videos! I'm really enjoying learning Japanese and I'm using your resources the most at the moment.
cornwagon – Discord PM

Thank you, I just finished the 2nd book and can't wait to start with the 3rd! Soon am getting my hands on the 4th!
religionflag – YesJapan.com

JFZ! is perfect. If you're a complete beginner, this book takes you through the bare basics and really helps you progress quickly. I highly recommend it.
F. Morgan – Good Reads review

The perfect Japanese textbook for young learners. One of the benefits of this book, which also slows it down, are the tangents it takes to explain the nuances of Japanese that a beginner might encounter.
Michael Richey – Tofugu.com

You really learn Japanese from zero – no prior knowledge at all required. The grammar is easy to understand.
Karl Andersson - karlandersson.se

As someone who owns the first three books, I can say the books are great.
Mastema – YesJapan.com

feedback@fromzero.com

Japanese From Zero! Book 5
– CONTENTS –

Special Thanks!

We began writing this book around 1999 or 2000. The book 5 materials were solely used for our live classes for years and then sat uncomplete for more years than I want to admit. We initially never thought to release the "Japanese From Zero!" books to the public, but we are glad we did, and we continue to be grateful for the multitudes that have learned and continue to learn Japanese with our series.

Over the last 5 years, we have deleted, rewritten, and added new information to this book. With the amazing efforts of Kanako Hatanaka, and countless discussions (fights) debating Japanese nuanced grammar with my wife, Yukari Takenaka, we finally have completed what my wife 20 years ago called, "our life work".

I want to give thanks to the students who spent over a year and a half in BETA CLASSES via Skype with Kanako and I (George) as we tested the new material in this book. Your insight was invaluable to the process and helped make book 5 what it has become! It was a pleasure to watch each of you grow your Japanese skills.

I also want to thank Alex, also known as "silt", for the artwork he provided for the book. Most of the art added to the book was during the final crunch time prior to release. Alex was super responsive and even made art on a day he told me he wouldn't be available. Alex has the perfect combination of amazing skills and a superb work ethic. Thanks!

Finally, I want to give a special thanks to Melanie Schicker who put her keen eye to finding bugs and typos in the final draft. Thanks for taking time out of your busy schedule to fix my caffeine fueled typos!

Resources

http://youtube.com/yesjapan
You can watch videos for each lesson contained in the Japanese From Zero! books. Currently we have videos for the first three books. More to come!

http://learnfz.com/JFZDiscord
Come join the official JFZ Discord and meet other students who are also studying Japanese. Drop me a line if you have a chance. Just click "George" from the member list. (I'm on the very top) (as of December 2019 I am still alive!)

http://www.reddit.com/r/JapaneseFromZero
Come join the official JFZ Discord and meet other students who are also studying Japanese. Drop a line to me if you have a chance. Just click "George" from the member list. (I am on the very top)

A

The Basics A:
Before we get started

A | From me to you 私からあなたへ

This section is not written from a big company or a marketing executive. It's from me, George, to you personally. I kindly ask that you read it before beginning this book.

● A-1. Who are you, we, and them?

The Japanese From Zero! book series is one of the most successful projects I personally have ever been involved with. People all around the world have learned Japanese with the series. I interact with many of the students on our website, Facebook, YouTube, various chat rooms, and even have personal relationships with many of the very people using these books. Due to the sheer numbers of readers however, it's not possible to meet even a fraction of these people. These people, including you, come from all walks of life, from many different countries, and certainly with many intricate life circumstances that I cannot even pretend to understand.

But there is something that, you, me, and all the other people reading these books share. It's a love for Japanese language. I doubt that the love is just for the language. Certainly Japan, as a country, the Japanese people, and the rich entertainment exported from Japan, all motivate you to keep learning.

ANYONE reading this book has been studying Japanese for years, and Japanese has become a part of their personal identity. Among your friends you are most likely, "the guy" or "the girl" that speaks Japanese. You are probably considered a genius or maybe even weird due to your interest in Japan. You have probably even visited or lived in Japan which puts you on an even higher level of uniqueness considering most people in the world never leave their own country much less learn another language. Of course, Europeans almost all learn another language and have visited other nearby countries due to the proximity. But I think it's safe to say that a large portion of Americans, Canadians, and Australians rarely leave the safety of the English-speaking world.

Just visiting another country, and even living there, doesn't however ensure that you dedicate the time needed to learn the language of that country. Honestly, I can sometimes be a jerk to people I meet in other countries, often half-joking and half-seriously I say, "shame on you" to the people I meet who haven't learned even a bit of the language after years of living in the country. It's embarrassing, and I feel that there is absolutely no valid reason not to at least know the basics of a language after just even 1 year.

So, to those of you, here, now reading this passage. I say now to you what I would say if I met you in person. Congratulations! You are indeed impressive to have come this far. I am truly proud of achievers like you. You should be very proud of yourself.

I do have one request to all of you. Please don't be a jerk like I am. You should be proud of your accomplishments, but you shouldn't claim superiority over other people or treat them as less than you simply because you learned Japanese. If anything, learning other languages should make you more understanding of people. We must understand that life is complicated, and people have circumstances, as we all do, as to why they haven't learned a language.

The elephant in the room is that my own Japanese wife of 24 years, and co-author of the Japanese From Zero! series, never really dove into speaking English. While she has organically learned more English than your typical Japanese person living in Japan, she would not be considered fluent or even close to it. Her circumstances are ... me. I was fluent in Japanese when I met her, and she didn't plan on marrying an American, much less living in an English-speaking country. It was pure circumstance that we met. One of the first things she told me was how she was never interested in English. Well... she wasn't lying. She reads Japanese books voraciously and is one of the smartest, most logical women I have ever met. Yet... she can't speak English. That doesn't change her intelligence, drive, compassion or any of the other great traits she has.

So, when you meet someone like my wife, have compassion. This is true for when you meet anyone where you have a superior skill. I ask that you keep the following Japanese saying in your head:

実るほど頭を垂れる稲穂かな
The more the rice stalk bears fruit, the lower its head hangs.

This just simply means, the greater you get, the humbler you should be.

● A-2. The benefits of learning a new language

When you are born into a language, you inherit the culture, mannerisms, and the basic way of thinking for that language. You are essentially programmed like a computer and have defined parameters. But, when you learn a different language, you gain the ability to think outside of your programming. Japanese especially has an amazing effect on your way of thinking. For example, before you knew kanji you probably didn't think as symbolically as you do now. You probably didn't think about how certain words relate to others. Kanji provides you with a mental "tagging" in your brain. When you hear certain sound combinations in an unfamiliar Japanese word, your brain breaks up the word and finds all words tagged with that sound. Often, based on the results of this tag search and the context of the conversation, you can understand or "guess" a word's meaning the first time you hear it. Until Japanese, this method of thinking probably wasn't available to you unless you studied Latin or know other Latin-based languages.

The level of politeness in Japanese society, the way Japanese tend to favor the group over the individual, has certainly also affected your interactions with other people. Your interactions with Japanese people have certainly enriched your life as much as it has mine.

I am often asked, "Why did you learn Japanese?" and "Why did you learn Korean?" and my go-to answer is always, "Because the girls are beautiful." While this is certainly true, it's not enough to sustain me for over 30 years. It's the interactions with Japanese people, and the integration of Japanese into my life, that keeps me motivated to learn more.

I am certain that my life would be only half as fun without my involvement with Japan and its culture. So, as a veteran in the thing that you love, my advice to you is to keep learning, and more importantly, keep interacting. It's completely worth the time you are expending. If you haven't already, do your best to move past just watching anime or reading manga. Make Japanese friends, then go meet those friends. Do something most people never do. Live.

● A-3. How can I really improve?

As of the writing of this passage, I, George Trombley, am 47 years old. I can honestly tell you that my Japanese is still improving even after years of simultaneous interpreting and 24 years of marriage to my wife who, as I said before, doesn't speak much English. So, don't kick yourself for not knowing it all and getting stuck from time to time. I have yet to meet a perfect speaker of ANY language.

So how can you improve your Japanese? I will tell you honestly that until I started learning Korean at age 39, I had forgotten a lot of how I learned Japanese. My pace has been fast, and I went from speaking zero Korean to having detailed conversations on religion and other heated topics completely in Korean. Granted, my sentences aren't all pretty, but I am understood, and the conversation moves forward. Now, if I could just bring my Chinese level up to my Korean level, and then my French level up to my Chinese level I would be pretty satisfied.

Because I teach Japanese, I often analyze why I have made progress in Korean so that I can relay these methods back to you and other students. Here are the top 11 techniques that I use to improve my Korean that have helped TREMENDOUSLY, that will help you with your Japanese:

1. Set the primary language on your PC to Japanese.

2. Set the language of your Facebook profile to Japanese.

3. Set your smartphone display language to Japanese.

4. Set your voice control settings, such as Siri, to Japanese (it's fun). Then talk to your phone in Japanese to set appointments and alarms. Don't give up! Eventually, you will be able to do it.

5. Listen to Japanese radio and podcasts. Try to find a lot of talk-heavy content. Do this every day for at least 30 minutes. It's okay if you don't understand. The goal of listening is to acclimate to native speaking speed, and subconsciously build up recognition of language patterns and speaking styles. Don't beat yourself up for not understanding, and if you skip a day or two it isn't the end of the world. We all get busy!

6. Find Japanese TV to watch (not just anime). This is also easy thanks to the internet.

7. Think in Japanese. Narrate what you are doing AS you do it in Japanese. For example, "I am walking", "I am trying to find my cell phone" etc.

8. Repeat new words OVER and OVER in your head. This is surprisingly effective.

9. Immediately find a place to use new concepts learned. Using new concepts helps move the concept into your long-term memory. Even if you must make something up to test a concept, do it. I purposely work on new grammar the

day that I learned it. And on the next and the day after even! This is so that I know it without thinking.

10. Text your Japanese friends daily. If you don't have friends... go make some on apps like HelloTalk. Here is a live demonstration showing how quickly you can make a Japanese friend on HelloTalk (free!): **http://learnfz.com/hellotalk**

11. Replace your news sites, and sites you visit when bored, to Japanese language sites. A site that allows Japanese users to post content is going to give you a great resource for study. What I like to do is read the title of a picture post and try to figure out what the picture will be based on what I read.

Once I added more Korean media to my life my Korean listening skills increased dramatically. When I learned Japanese, I lived in Japan and watched a LOT of Japanese TV and essentially did the same thing. Your brain is amazing at learning from its environment. So, do it a favor and give it a Japanese environment.

Okay! Now let's get cracking and learn some more Japanese!

● A-4. What should I already know?

This is the 5th book in the Japanese From Zero! series. All the lessons in this book assume you have somewhat mastered the prior books' materials. We will freely use grammar, vocabulary, and phrases taught in the prior books. In book 4 we had kanji words in the "Kanji Recognition" section that would no longer have ふりがな that we assumed you could read. However, in order to focus on the grammar, we decided to keep ふりがな for all words in this book. We figured you will get enough practice without ふりがな in the real world!

B

The Basics B:
Direct vs Natural Translation

B | New Words 新しい言葉

Nouns etc.

<ruby>直<rt>ちょく</rt>訳<rt>やく</rt></ruby>
直訳   direct translation

<ruby>意<rt>い</rt>訳<rt>やく</rt></ruby>
意訳   free / natural / liberal translation

B | Grammar and Usage 文法と使い方

● **B-1. The differences between 直訳 and 意訳**

In the prior books, when the grammar concepts were simpler, it was easy to directly translate a Japanese or English sentence. It was also very convenient for us, the book writers, and you, the student who was often asked to translate sentences for practice.

Now that we are dealing with higher level grammar, direct translation often ends up sounding weird and unnatural. And for us, the book writers, it becomes increasingly difficult to create natural sounding Japanese sentences if we are required to make the English also sound natural.

So, in order to accomplish the goal of using natural Japanese and English, we must abandon the idea that EVERY word in an English or Japanese sentence is represented in its translation.

Natural translation means you as a student will have to let go of the desire to have every word in both sentences. Your goal is to relay the Japanese into English or English into Japanese. Getting every word perfect is often not possible.

Let's see how different direct and natural translations can be:

EXAMPLE SENTENCES

1. 行ってきます。
   Direct: I will go and come back.
   Natural: I'll be back.

2. お風呂を入れたよ。
   Direct: I put it in the bath.
   Natural: I drew a bath.

3. 明日寒くなりますね。
   Direct: Tomorrow it will get cold (won't it?).
   Natural: It'll be cold tomorrow.

4. 私は百円しかないです。
   Direct: I have nothing, except 100 yen.
   Natural: I only have 100 yen.

5. 明日休みたいので、お店をお願いできませんか？
   Direct: Since I want to rest tomorrow, can I request the store?
   Natural: I want to take the day off tomorrow, do you think you can handle the store?

6. 週末は雨だから、家でゆっくりしよう。
   Direct: Since the weekend is rain, let's do it slow at the house.
   Natural: Since it's going to rain on the weekend, let's just relax at the house.

Examples 5 and 6 are particularly good at showing how bad a direct translation can be. Often a direct translation is more confusing.

So, keep your mind open and be ready for translations where some words are added in the translation or even removed to keep the sentences natural.

● B-2. What is more important? Level 5 or 1 grammar

In higher level books you often learn a more nuanced way to say something learned in earlier books. However, it would be a mistake to assume that the advanced version of a similar concept should be used because it's more "advanced". Concepts taught in the higher levels tend to have restrictions on when they can be used and are often only used in certain circumstances or when trying to convey a certain feeling. The most widely used grammar will be taught in the earlier books and are certainly more important than nuanced grammar taught later. Your Japanese will sound much better when using grammar that matches the situation based on nuance.

● B-3. Grammar VS Vocabulary

As I learned Japanese, then eventually wrote the Japanese From Zero! series and created hundreds of Japanese teaching videos on YouTube, my opinion on whether grammar or vocabulary is more important has changed. I eventually came to the following realizations:

1. Grammar is useless without words.
2. Words are useless without grammar.

In the end you will know tens of thousands of words, but only a few hundred grammar patterns exist. I personally lean towards thinking grammar is most important. My years as a simultaneous interpreter taught me that you could sometimes get away without knowing a word. However, if you didn't understand a grammar pattern you would be completely stuck.

Despite what I just said, when I was interpreting, I would almost never get stuck on grammar as there are fewer grammar than words to know. It was always a word that made or broke a translation.

One word means a lot
Once I was interpreting for a criminal lawyer representing a young Japanese man who had committed a crime at a large musical festival. I was hired to update his parents in Japan via a phone call. Everything was going great until the parents asked:

検察官は何と言っていますか。What is the けんさつかん saying?

I had never heard the word けんさつかん, but it was close enough to 警察官 (けいさつかん) "police" to make me feel like I had misheard it, so I just interpreted it as, "police officer". The next time, it came up, I was certain it wasn't police officer, but I knew from the context that it was a *person* and that they had an important role, so to be safe, I used the generic term "they". I was lucky that the American lawyer eventually used the word "prosecutor". I immediately made the connection, and when interpreting the word "prosecutor", which I previously had not known, I used けんさつかん. There are quite a few examples of me stumbling into a word like this and surviving the encounter. But making up grammar on the fly, I feel is less easy to do since you can't rely on kanji knowledge and the part of the sentence that relays meaning is not known.

But you can't use grammar without words, and you can't do much with words without grammar. As a result, they are both equally important.

C — The Basics C:
Missing Kanji

From the teacher...

PLEASE READ: Skip this lesson if you completed book 4 **published** after 2019.

C — New Kanji 新しい漢字

In the new revision of book 4, we re-grouped kanji into logical groups to make learning them easier. The new ordering shifted 40 kanji down to *book 4*, and 40 up to *book 5*.

If you used book 4 published prior to 2020, the 40 kanji in this lesson might be new to you. Please review them before Lesson 1. The other 40 kanji from book 4's prior ordering are now taught in book 5, so you should already know them.

Notes:
1. When possible, the 40 kanji listed here are grouped in logical groups.
2. The kanji number, in the black box, are from the revised order, and left for reference.

C — Kanji Grouping - Adjectives

86	木	13 画	enjoyable; comfort; ease

	くんよみ	たの(しい、しむ)
	おんよみ	ラク、ガク

楽しい (たの・しい) enjoyable   楽しむ (たの・しむ) to enjoy oneself
音楽 (おん・がく) music   楽器 (がっ・き) musical instrument
気楽 (き・らく) comfortable   楽勝 (らく・しょう) easy victory

90	夕	6 画	many; much; multiple

	くんよみ	おお(い)
	おんよみ	タ

多い (おお・い) many   多め (おお・め) more than average
多分 (た・ぶん) probably   多数 (た・すう) majority
多少 (た・しょう) more or less   多才 (た・さい) talented

92	日	8画	bright; light; clear		
		くんよみ	あ(かり)、あか(るい、るむ、らむ)、あ(ける、く、くる、かす)、あき(らか)		
		おんよみ	メイ、ミョウ		

明るい (あか・るい) bright 不明 (ふ・めい) unknown, unidentified
明らか (あき・らか) obvious 明朝 (みょう・ちょう) tomorrow morning
明ける (あ・ける) to dawn 明日 (あした) tomorrow

明 | | | | | | | | |

94	大	4画	big; fat; thick		
		くんよみ	ふと(い、る)		
		おんよみ	タイ、タ		

太い (ふと・い) think, fat 太鼓 (たい・こ) drum
太る (ふと・る) to get fat 太平洋 (たい・へい・よう) Pacific Ocean
太陽 (たい・よう) sun 丸太 (まる・た) log

太 | | | | | | | | |

95	糸	11画	narrow; thin; fine		
		くんよみ	ほそ(い、る)、こま(か、かい)		
		おんよみ	サイ		

心細い (こころ・ぼそ・い) lonely 細かい (こま・かい) small, minute, delicate
細い (ほそ・い) fine, thin 細道 (ほそ・みち) narrow path; narrow lane
細菌 (さい・きん) bacterium 細心 (さい・しん) meticulous; careful

細 | | | | | | | | |

96	、	3画	round; ball		
		くんよみ	まる、まる(い、める)		
		おんよみ	ガン		

丸い (まる・い) round, circular 丸顔 (まる・がお) round face
丸ごと (まる・ごと) whole 弾丸 (だん・がん) bullet
丸太 (まる・た) log 丸める (まる・める) to roll up; to make round

丸 | | | | | | | | |

97	長	8画	long; far; chief									
			くんよみ	なが(い)								
			おんよみ	チョウ								
			校長 (こう・ちょう) principal			身長 (しん・ちょう) height (people)						
			長い (なが・い) long			長方形 (ちょう・ほう・けい) rectangle						
			長所 (ちょう・しょ) merit			成長 (せい・ちょう) growth; development						
			長									

C Kanji Grouping - Body related

148	イ	7画	body; style									
			くんよみ	からだ								
			おんよみ	タイ、テイ								
			体 (からだ) body			体力 (たい・りょく) physical strength						
			体育 (たい・いく) gymnastics			体温 (たい・おん) body temperature						
			体裁 (てい・さい) appearance			全体 (ぜん・たい) whole; entirety						
			体									

151	頁	16画	head									
			くんよみ	あたま、かしら								
			おんよみ	トウ、ズ、ト								
			頭 (あたま) head			六頭 (ろく・とう) six (large) animals						
			頭痛 (ず・つう) headache			頭金 (あたま・きん) down payment						
			先頭 (せん・とう) head; lead			頭文字 (かしら・も・じ) initials; capital letter						
			頭									

152	毛	4画	hair; fur									
			くんよみ	け								
			おんよみ	モウ								
			毛布 (もう・ふ) blanket			髪の毛 (かみ・の・け) hair on the head						
			毛皮 (け・がわ) fur, skin			羽毛 (う・もう) feathers; plumage; gown						
			毛糸 (け・いと) knitting wool			羊毛 (よう・もう) wool						
			毛									

C Kanji Grouping - Family and People

138	又	4画	friend

くんよみ	とも
おんよみ	ユウ

友情 (ゆう・じょう) friendship   親友 (しん・ゆう) close friend
友達 (とも・だち) friend   友人 (ゆう・じん) friend
旧友 (きゅう・ゆう) old friend   悪友 (あく・ゆう) bad company; buddy

友											

142	父	4画	father

くんよみ	ちち
おんよみ	フ

父 (ちち) my father   父兄 (ふ・けい) parental guardian
父親 (ちち・おや) father   父母 (ふ・ぼ) father and mother; parents
祖父 (そ・ふ) grandfather   神父 (しん・ぷ) Catholic priest; minister

父											

143	母	5画	mother

くんよみ	はは
おんよみ	ボ

母 (はは) my mother   乳母車 (う・ば・ぐるま) baby carriage
母親 (はは・おや) mother   母国語 (ぼ・こく・ご) native tongue
祖母 (そ・ぼ) my grandmother   祖父母 (そ・ふ・ぼ) grandparents

母											

144	儿	5画	elder brother

くんよみ	あに
おんよみ	ケイ、キョウ

兄 (あに) elder brother   義理の兄 (ぎり・の・あに) brother-in-law
兄弟 (きょう・だい) siblings   兄弟子 (あに・で・し) senior apprentice
兄姉 (けい・し) brother and sister   兄弟分 (きょう・だい・ぶん) buddy, sworn brother

兄											

145	女	8画	elder sister

	くんよみ	あね
	おんよみ	シ

姉 (あね) my elder sister　　　　お姉さん (お・ねえ・さん) elder sister
姉妹 (し・まい) sisters　　　　義理の姉 (ぎ・り・の・あね) one's sister-in-law
姉貴 (あね・き) elder sister　　　姉妹都市 (し・まい・と・し) sister cities

146	弓	7画	younger brother

	くんよみ	おとうと
	おんよみ	テイ、ダイ、デ

兄弟 (きょう・だい) sibling　　　　弟 (おとうと) my younger brother
弟子 (で・し) disciple; follower　　弟さん (おとうと・さん) other's younger brother
師弟 (し・てい) teacher and student　弟分 (おとうと・ぶん) friend treated as brother

147	女	8画	younger sister

	くんよみ	いもうと
	おんよみ	マイ

妹 (いもうと) my younger sister　　妹さん (いもうと・さん) other's younger sister
姉妹 (し・まい) sisters　　　　実妹 (じつ・まい) (biological) younger sister
義妹 (ぎ・まい) sister-in-law　　弟妹 (てい・まい) younger brother and sister

C | Kanji Grouping - Verbs

99	⻌	10画	pass; go to and from

	くんよみ	とお(る、す)、かよ(う)
	おんよみ	ツウ、ツ

通う (かよ・う) to commute　　　通勤 (つう・きん) commuting to work
通り道 (とお・り・みち) path　　通学 (つう・がく) commuting to school
通夜 (つ・や) funeral wake　　　通る (とお・る) to go by; to pass through

100	走	7 画	run		
			くんよみ	はし(る)	
			おんよみ	ソウ	

走る (はし・る) to run 代走 (だい・そう) substitute runner
走者 (そう・しゃ) runner 逃走 (とう・そう) get-away, escape
競走 (きょう・そう) race 滑走路 (かっ・そう・ろ) runway

走									

101	止	8 画	walk; step; rate		
			くんよみ	ある(く)、あゆ(む)	
			おんよみ	ホ、ブ、フ	

散歩 (さん・ぽ) a walk 歩行者 (ほ・こう・しゃ) pedestrian
歩く (ある・く) to walk 歩道 (ほ・どう) sidewalk; walkway
歩み (あゆ・み) step; progress 歩む (あゆ・む) to walk; to go on foot

歩									

103	木	7 画	come; next; since		
			くんよみ	く(る)、きた(る、す)	
			おんよみ	ライ	

未来 (み・らい) future 来年 (らい・ねん) next year
来る (く・る) to come 来客 (らい・きゃく) houseguest
来たる (き・たる) next; coming 将来 (しょう・らい) future (usually near)

来									

109	士	7 画	sell		
			くんよみ	う(る、れる)	
			おんよみ	バイ	

売る (う・る) to sell 発売 (はつ・ばい) sale; release (for sale)
売れる (う・れる) to be famous 商売 (しょう・ばい) business, trade
売り手 (う・り・て) seller 売上高 (うり・あげ・だか) sales; amount sold

売									

110	貝	12 画	buy

	くんよみ	か(う)
	おんよみ	バイ

買う (か・う) to buy	売買 (ばい・ばい) trade
買い手 (か・い・て) buyer	買収 (ばい・しゅう) buy-out
買い物 (か・い・もの) shopping	購買 (こう・ばい) purchase; procurement

買										

113	言	14 画	read

	くんよみ	よ(む)
	おんよみ	ドク、トク、トウ

読む (よ・む) to read	音読 (おん・どく) read aloud
読書 (どく・しょ) reading	読解 (どっ・かい) reading comprehension
読者 (どく・しゃ) reader	句読点 (く・とう・てん) punctuation mark

読										

131	用	5 画	business; errand; use

	くんよみ	もち(いる)
	おんよみ	ヨウ

使用 (し・よう) use	用心 (よう・じん) care, precaution
用事 (よう・じ) errands	用いる (もち・いる) to make use of
用意 (よう・い) preparation	急用 (きゅう・よう) urgent business

用										

133	小	6 画	hit; appropriate; this / that

	くんよみ	あ (たる、てる)
	おんよみ	トウ

お弁当 (お・べん・とう) lunch box	手当て (て・あ・て) benefit; medical care
当たる (あ・たる) to hit; strike	当然 (とう・ぜん) natural; as a matter of course
当番 (とう・ばん) on duty	当日 (とう・じつ) appointed day; very day

当										

135	目	8 画	direct; soon; honestly

	くんよみ	ただ(ちに)、なお(す、る)
	おんよみ	チョク、ジキ

正直 (しょう・じき) honest　　　　直接 (ちょく・せつ) direct
直す (なお・す) to repair　　　　　直角 (ちょっ・かく) right angle
直る (なお・る) to be repaired　　直ちに (ただ・ちに) immediately

直									

134	氵	9 画	live; life

	くんよみ	none
	おんよみ	カツ

活動 (かつ・どう) activity　　　　活火山 (かつ・か・ざん) active volcano
生活 (せい・かつ) living, life　　　食生活 (しょく・せい・かつ) eating habits
活躍 (かつ・やく) great efforts　　活ける (い・ける) to arrange (flowers in a vase)

活									

C Kanji Grouping - Communication Verbs

111	耳	14 画	hear; listen to; ask

	くんよみ	き(く、こえる)
	おんよみ	ブン、モン

聞く (き・く) to hear; to ask　　　聞こえる (き・こえる) to be heard; to be audible
聞き手 (き・き・て) listener　　　　聞き取り (き・き・と・り) listening comprehension
新聞 (しん・ぶん) newspaper　　　前代未聞 (ぜん・だい・み・もん) unheard-of

聞									

112	言	7 画	say; speak; word

	くんよみ	い(う)、こと
	おんよみ	ゲン、ゴン

言う (い・う) to say　　　　　　　言い訳 (い・い・わけ) excuse; explanation
言葉 (こと・ば) word　　　　　　　遺言 (ゆい・ごん) testament; will
言語 (げん・ご) language　　　　　方言 (ほう・げん) dialect

言									

114	言	13 画	story; conversation; talk		
	くんよみ	はな(す)、はなし			
	おんよみ	ワ			

話 (はなし) talk, story　　　話す (はな・す) to talk
噂話 (うわさ・ばなし) gossip　　話題 (わ・だい) topic; subject
会話 (かい・わ) conversation　　昔話 (むかし・ばなし) old tale; folk tale

121	竹	12 画	answer; reply		
	くんよみ	こた(え、える)			
	おんよみ	トウ			

答え (こた・え) answer; reply　　答える (こた・える) to answer; to reply
口答え (くち・ごた・え) back-talk　口答 (こう・とう) oral answer
応答 (おう・とう) reply; response　即答 (そく・とう) immediate reply

127	刀	4 画	part; portion; segment		
	くんよみ	わ(ける、かれる、かる、かつ)			
	おんよみ	ブン、フン、ブ			

五分 (ご・ふん) five minutes　　分割 (ぶん・かつ) division; splitting
分ける (わ・ける) to separate　　分かる (わ・かる) to understand; to grasp
気分 (き・ぶん) mood　　　　　　分かれる (わ・かれる) to split; to divide

137	矢	8 画	knowledge		
	くんよみ	し(る)			
	おんよみ	チ			

知る (し・る) to know　　　　　お知らせ (お・し・らせ) news, information
知恵 (ち・え) wisdom　　　　　　知的 (ち・てき) intellectual
知識 (ち・しき) knowledge　　　　知人 (ち・じん) acquaintance; friend

C | Kanji Grouping - Plants and Animals

122	鳥	14画	cry; sing; howl

くんよみ	な(く、る、らす)
おんよみ	メイ

鳴く (な・く) to cry (animal)　鳴る (な・る) to ring; to sound
鳴き声 (な・き・ごえ) roar　鳴らす (な・らす) to ring; to chime; to beat
悲鳴 (ひ・めい) fearful cries　耳鳴り (みみ・な・り) ringing in the ear

鳴

153	肉	6画	meat

くんよみ	none
おんよみ	ニク

筋肉 (きん・にく) muscle　鶏肉 (とり・にく) chicken meat
肉屋 (にく・や) butcher　牛肉 (ぎゅう・にく) beef
豚肉 (ぶた・にく) pork　肉親 (にく・しん) blood relationship

肉

155	馬	10画	horse

くんよみ	うま、ま
おんよみ	バ

馬 (うま) horse　馬小屋 (うま・ご・や) stable
馬力 (ば・りき) horsepower　出馬 (しゅつ・ば) running (for election)
乗馬 (じょう・ば) horse riding　競馬 (けい・ば) horse racing

馬

157	鳥	11画	bird

くんよみ	とり
おんよみ	チョウ

鳥 (とり) bird　鳥肌 (とり・はだ) goose bumps
小鳥 (こ・とり) small bird　白鳥 (はく・ちょう) swan
七面鳥 (しち・めん・ちょう) turkey　鳥居 (とり・い) Shinto shrine archway

鳥

158	米	6 画	rice			

	くんよみ	こめ
	おんよみ	ベイ、マイ

お米 (お・こめ) uncooked rice	日本米 (に・ほん・まい) Japanese rice
渡米 (と・べい) going to U.S.A.	米国 (べい・こく) America
玄米 (げん・まい) brown rice	新米 (しん・まい) new rice; first rice crop

米											

159	麦	7 画	wheat; barley			

	くんよみ	むぎ
	おんよみ	バク

麦 (むぎ) wheat, barley	麦茶 (むぎ・ちゃ) barley tea
麦芽 (ばく・が) malt	麦わら帽子 (むぎ・わら・ぼう・し) straw hat
小麦粉 (こ・むぎ・こ) wheat flour	大麦 (おお・むぎ) barley (Hordeum vulgare)

麦											

Vocabulary Builder:
Groups A, B, C, D

In the "Vocabulary Builder" sections, we will introduce words that might be used in the following lessons. They are commonly used words that might be beneficial to know. You shouldn't feel the need to memorize them before moving on but at least take a glance. Most likely you will see a word you have heard in conversation.

■ Group A: Words with repeating sounds

ぼろぼろ	battered; beat-up; shabby
まあまあ	so-so; good enough; decent; fairly; pretty;
ぽとぽと	trickle down in thick drops (Onomatopoeia)
次々	one after another
くたくた	exhausted; worn out
なかなか	quite; rather; easily; very; by no means; fairly
ワンワン	woof-woof; ruff-ruff
ガチャガチャ	the sound of metal clamoring
ドキドキ	heart beating fast (due to being excited or nervous)

■ Group B: Japanese dishes

しゃぶしゃぶ	thinly sliced beef dipped in boiling water
すき焼き	thin slices of beef, cooked with vegetables in a table-top cast-iron pan
肉じゃが	meat and potato stew
焼きそば	fried noodles (similar to Chow Mein)
お好み焼き	savory pancake with various ingredients
たこ焼き	octopus dumplings
ハンバーグ	Hamburg steak; Salisbury steak
納豆	natto (fermented soybeans)

Words introduced on this page shouldn't require much for you to learn them since they are all borrowed from English.

■ Group C: "AS IS" borrowed words

These words are used exactly like their English counterparts.

クローゼット (closet)

ヘッドフォン (headphone)

イヤホン (ear phones)

テスラ (Tesla)

クラスメート (classmate)

メッセージ (message)

アレルギー (allergy)

サイレン (siren; horn)

メンバーズカード (member's card)

■ Group D: Katakana words that require explanations

These words are made with English but might not be understood without explanation.

パソコン (personal computer)
(PC / Mac / Linux) shortened from パーソナル・コンピューター.

ノートパソコン (laptop computer)
(PC / Mac / Linux) shortened from ノートブック・パーソナル・コンピューター

ガス (gas)
Not for a car, but for an oven to cook food on.

ライン (LINE)
A popular messaging app in Japan.

クラクション (car horn / horn)
Named after horn manufacturer Klaxon.

スマホ (smartphone)
This is a short version of スマートフォン and is used much more than the original word.

| 15 PAGES | 5 USAGE SECTIONS | 29 NEW WORDS |

1

Lesson 1:
Even Though...

From the teacher...

The のに grammar taught in this lesson isn't the only time you will learn about のに. Near the end of the book, it will come up again for a completely different grammar.

1 | New Words 新しい言葉

Nouns etc.

相手 (あいて)	companion; partner; opponent	点 (てん)	point; mark; spot
気温 (きおん)	air temperature	大都市 (だいとし)	big city; large city
(お)世話 (せわ)	looking after; help; aid; assistance	へそくり	secret savings
何とか (なん)	somehow; one way or another	違い (ちが)	difference
卒業式 (そつぎょうしき)	graduation ceremony	文化 (ぶんか)	culture
自信 (じしん)	confidence; self-assurance	節約 (せつやく)	savings; economizing

Adjectives

しょうがない	hopeless; can't be helped	珍しい (めずら)	unusual; rare

Adverbs

きっと	surely; certainly; most likely	真剣に (しんけん)	seriously; earnestly
あまりにも	too much; excessive; too	一度も (いちど)	not even once
朝早く (あさはや)	early in the morning		

Connectors

それとも	**or perhaps**	そうしたら	**and then**

Verbs

ふりをする	to act as; to pretend like	落ち込む (おこ)	to feel down
別れる (わか)	to break up; to separate; to part from	困る (こま)	to be troubled/bothered
どきどきする	to have one's heart beat rapidly	汗をかく (あせ)	to sweat
出てくる (で)	to come out; to appear; to turn up	汗が出る (あせ で)	to sweat

1 | Japanese Living 日本の暮らし

● Heating and Cooling in Japan

エアコン is a borrowed and also shortened word for "air conditioner" and can heat up or cool air depending on settings. In the United States it's very common to have "central air" where the entire house or one floor is heated or cooled.

Often there will be a small エアコン unit in certain rooms of a house. Some rooms might not have any cooling unit. Of course, this depends on the house and when it was built. 冷房 (れいぼう) and クーラー on the other hand are just cooling units which cannot produce heat.

We commonly call a cooler box for storing drinks a "cooler" in America, however in Japan this would be a クーラーボックス and never just クーラー. クーラー is really just the borrowed word for 冷房. THIS BEING SAID... Japanese people will freely use these words not really knowing there is any difference.

The word 暖房 (だんぼう) is the opposite of 冷房 (れいぼう) and means "heating". If you say ヒーター, however those are typically small electric heaters used to warm your feet etc. In America a "stove" is something we cook on, but in Japan this word means "heater". ストーブ can come in mainly three types, oil 石油 (せきゆ), propane 灯油 (とうゆ) and just electric 電気 (でんき). Now you probably know more about Japanese heaters than you thought you ever would!

● 電気代節約 electricity savings

せつやく means "saving" or "economizing". Electricity in Japan is considered quite expensive by Japanese people, so there is much effort made to use less electricity to save money. For example, new air conditioner units in Japan have a 電気代 (でんきだい) button, that when clicked informs you how much money was spent for the current cooling. It's also common to unplug appliances such as microwaves, toasters, or rice cookers etc. when not in use to prevent those appliances from using electricity.

● 水道代節約 water bill savings

In Japan, to save water, Japanese families will often share the same bath water. To keep the water clean they wash before entering the tub. The water will be drained after the last family members bathes for the day, and sometimes the water is used another day or even sent to the laundry machine through a connected hose. Of course, if the water somehow gets dirty it will be drained early and replaced.

● 食費節約 food cost savings
<small>しょく ひ せつ やく</small>

Around 6 o'clock in the evening many Japanese supermarkets discount pre-cooked food items that can't be sold the next day. Many Japanese people, who don't have time to cook, scoop up these discounted items after work. If you want to save, don't be late!

● 交通費節約 transportation cost savings
<small>こう つう ひ せつ やく</small>

American society is built around roads. It's common to tell someone cross streets when giving directions. Japanese society, especially in the cities, is built around train stations. How far a certain business is from a train station can make or break that business. Many advertisements for apartments and stores use the distance from the train station as a key selling point. Many people living in Tokyo and other large areas don't own a car due to the high cost of maintaining a car in the city. Even households that own a car will often walk or ride a bicycle to save money. You will see large areas for bicycle parking around most Japanese train stations. Japanese bicycles are so common, that in Japan many people even pay for bicycle insurance. The insurance is not expensive, usually under 50 USD per family per year. Some policies cover up to 1 billion yen or around 900,000 USD. (NOTE: These numbers are for 2019.)

1 | New Expressions 新しい表現

1. そうなんだけど / そうなんですけど
   That's true but... / That is the case but...
   This is used when agreeing but clarifying the reasons.

2. どうする？
   What will you / we do?
   どうした means "What happened?" and どうしよう？ means "What should I do?"

3. あれ？
   Huh? What the...
   あれ expresses the feeling that something isn't as it should be, like when you search your pocket for your keys, but they aren't there.

1 Verb Usage 動詞の使い方

V-1	ふりをする	to act like; to pretend	する
	1. (noun) の ふりをする	act like (noun)	
	2. (な adjective) な ふりをする	act like (な adjective)	
	3. (informal verb / い adjective) ふりをする	act like (informal verb / い adjective)	

With many grammar patterns, you need to know how to use them with nouns, adjectives, and verbs. With Japanese, we also have い adjectives versus な adjectives.

EXAMPLE SENTENCES

1. 日本人のふりをしました。(noun)
   I acted like a Japanese person.

2. 先生のことが好きじゃないけど、好きなふりをしました。(な adjective)
   I don't like the teacher, but I pretended that I liked him.

3. 若いふりをしました。(い adjective)
   I acted like I was young.

4. 日本語が分からないふりをしました。(verb phrase)
   I acted like I don't understand Japanese.

In the prior examples everything is past tense, but we can change する to any form.

EXAMPLE SENTENCES

1. 日本人のふりをしません。(noun)
   I don't act like a Japanese person.

2. 先生のことが好きじゃないけど、好きなふりをします。(な adjective)
   I don't like the teacher, but I pretend that I like him.

3. もう若いふりができません。(い adjective)
   I can't act like I'm young anymore.

4. 日本語が分からないふりをしたくないです。(verb phrase)
   I don't want to act like I don't understand Japanese.

5. 病気のふりをして、会社を休みました。
   I pretended to be sick and took time off from work.

> In English, 会社 sometimes sounds more natural as "work" rather than "company".

6. うちの子は学校が嫌なふりをしているけど、本当は好きです。
   Our child is pretending school is unpleasant, but she really likes it.

7. 忙しいふりをしないで、手伝って下さい。
   Don't act like you are busy, help me please.

8. 友達はよく、寝たふりをしています。
   My friend often acts like he's sleeping.

V-2 | 落ち込む | to feel down | regular

EXAMPLE SENTENCES

1. 最近、落ち込んでいます。
   Recently I have been feeling down.

2. 落ち込まないで、頑張りましょう。
   Let's not get down and do our best.

V-3 | 別れる | to break up; to separate; to part from | いる/える

1. (someone) と別れる | to part from (someone)

EXAMPLE SENTENCES

1. 卒業式でクラスメートと別れるのは、寂しいです。
   Separating with classmates at the graduation ceremony is sad.

> 聞いてくれなかった is more natural in English as "didn't agree".

2. 別れたいと言ったけど、彼女は聞いてくれなかった。
   I said I wanted to break up, but my girlfriend didn't listen to me.

3. 別れる時は、泣くより笑ったほうがいいです。
   It's better to laugh than cry when breaking up.

4. 10年飼っていた犬と別れるのは、辛かったです。
   It was rough to split with the dog I was raising for 10 years.

V-4	こま 困る	to be troubled; to be bothered	regular
	1. (thing) に こまる	having trouble with (thing)	
	2. (て form、くてform) こまる	troubled due to (adj / verb phrase)	
	3. (noun) で こまる	troubled due to (noun phrase)	

Japanese people use こまる frequently for whenever they are in a difficult position. Always translating it to "be troubled" will make for unnatural English sentences.

EXAMPLE SENTENCES

> 生活にこまる is not as heavy as it sounds. It just means you had trouble "making ends meet".

1. 若い時は、生活に困っていました。
   When I was young, I had trouble making ends meet.

2. 娘がずっと泣いて、本当に困りました。
   My daughter cried so long, I really didn't know what to do.

3. 友達の家があまりにも汚くて、困りました。
   I was really bothered my friend's house was so dirty.

> It really doesn't feel natural in English to say, "troubling things", so we used "problems" instead.

4. 海外旅行で困ったことはありますか。
   Have you ever had problems on a trip abroad?

You can say こまる by itself in casual conversation to refuse a request, or let someone know their action is a problem for you.

EXAMPLE CONVERSATION

1. **Casual conversation between friends.**

   A: 明日、アメリカに帰るよ。

   B: ええ！ 困る！

   A: 何で？ 先週、話してたでしょう？

   B: そうなんだけど。。。明日、友達に会ってほしかったの。

   A: I am returning to America tomorrow.

   B: What! This is a problem! (I will be troubled)

   A: Why? We talked about it last week, right?

   B: This is true but... tomorrow I wanted you to meet my friend.

V-5	どきどきする	to have one's heartbeat rapidly	する

This is used when the heart is beating rapidly due to being nervous, scared or excited.

EXAMPLE SENTENCES

1. 明日、日本に行くから、どきどきしています。
   I am excited because I am going to Japan tomorrow.

> どきどき is sometimes written in katakana.

2. テストの時、いつもドキドキして、あまりよくできません。
   When I take a test, I always get nervous and I can't do it that well.

> Here, よく means "well". With あまり it means, "so well/that well"

V-6	出てくる	to come out; to appear; to turn up	くる irregular

1. (somewhere) から出てくる	comes out from (somewhere)

EXAMPLE SENTENCES

1. 妹が怒っていて、部屋から出てきません。
   My younger sister is mad, so she won't come out of her room.

2. 私の友達が今晩、テレビに出てきますよ。
   My friend will appear on TV this evening.

3. 財布をなくして、もう見つからないと思ったのに、今日出てきました。
   I lost my wallet and although I thought it wouldn't ever be found, it turned up today.

V-7	汗をかく	to sweat (due to activity)	regular
	汗が出る	to sweat (naturally)	いる/える

For natural phenomena, such as hot weather, use 汗が出る. With a purposed action, such as playing sports, use 汗をかく. But, even Japanese people often mix the usage.

EXAMPLE SENTENCES

1. 私はテニスをする時、汗をかきます。
   I sweat when I play tennis.

2. 汗をかいたら、水をたくさん飲みます。
   I drink a lot of water when I sweat.

3. 天気が暑い時、汗が出ます。
   I sweat when the weather is hot.

4. 夏に汗が凄く出るから、シャワーをよくします。
   Because I sweat a ton in summer, I often shower.

1 Grammar and Usage 文法と使い方

● 1-1. 何とか + verbs (to handle something)

なんとか by itself means "somehow" or "one way or another". It's put in front of a verb to say that you will make that action happen via some unspoken method.

EXAMPLE SENTENCES

1. 今日は忙しいけど、何とか時間を作ります。
   I am busy today, but I will make time one way or another.

2. 給料は少ないですが、何とかお金が貯められました。
   My pay is not much, but I somehow was able to save money.

何とかなる explains what happened. 何とかする explains what YOU or someone did.

何とかなる	It will get handled somehow
何とかする	I will handle it somehow

EXAMPLE SENTENCES

1. 困っていたけど、何とかなりました。
   I was troubled, but it all worked out.

   > The situation cleared up naturally or an unnamed person handled it.

2. 困っていたけど、何とかしました。
   I was troubled, but I figured it out.

   > The speaker took action to fix the situation.

EXAMPLE CONVERSATION

1. **Casual conversation between a mother and a child**

   A: 明日はテストがあるのに、どうして何もしていないの？
   B: 大丈夫。何とかなるよ。
   A: 何とかなるじゃないでしょう！何とかするの！
   B: 分かったよ。じゃあ、今から勉強する。

   A: Why aren't you doing anything, even though there is a test tomorrow?
   B: It's okay. It will all work out.
   A: It's not going to "all work out!" You make it work out!
   B: I understand. Ok then, I will study from now.

● **1-2. Using のに (even though, despite) with verbs and い adjectives**

[noun] なのに	even though it's a [noun]
[な adjective] なのに	even though it's [な adjective]
[い adjective] のに	even though it's [い adjective]
[informal verb] のに	even though [verb / verb phrase]

のに can mean "even though", "despite the fact", and "although". It's used to say even though the situation is this, this thing is happening. Notice in the following examples のに is added directly after ALL tenses of the い adjective.

EXAMPLES (い ADJECTIVES)

1. 難しいのに   even though it's difficult
2. 難しかったのに   even though it was difficult
3. 難しくないのに   even though it isn't difficult
4. 難しくなかったのに   even though it wasn't difficult

In the next examples, we use "I" as the pronoun. However, this is only because English requires a pronoun. The pronoun could have been "he", "she", "they" etc.

EXAMPLES (VERBS)

1. 食べるのに   even though (I) eat / will eat
2. 食べたのに   even though (I) ate
3. 食べないのに   even though (I) don't eat / won't eat
4. 食べなかったのに   even though (I) didn't eat
5. 食べているのに   even though (I) am eating
6. 食べていないのに   even though (I) am not eating
7. 食べたいのに   even though (I) want to eat
8. 食べたかったのに   even though (I) wanted to eat
9. 食べたくないのに   even though (I) don't want to eat

EXAMPLE SENTENCES (VERBS AND い ADJECTIVE)

1. 今日は暑いのに、田中さんはセーターを着ています。
   Even though it's hot today, Mr. Tanaka is wearing a sweater.

2. フランス語を三年前から勉強しているのに、まだ話せません。
   Even though I've been studying French from 3 years ago, I still can't speak it.

● **1-3. Using のに (even though, despite) with nouns and な adjectives**

な is required before のに after nouns or な adjectives in the present / positive tense.

EXAMPLES (NOUNS IN PRESENT / POSITIVE TENSE)

1. アメリカ人なのに   even though (he) is American
2. 週末なのに   even though it's the weekend
3. 大都市なのに   even though it's a large city

EXAMPLES (な ADJECTIVES IN PRESENT / POSITIVE TENSE)

1. 静かなのに   even though it's quiet
2. 便利なのに   even though it's convenient
3. きれいなのに   even though it's pretty

Anytime you make the noun or な adjective past tense or negative the な is no longer used.

EXAMPLES (NOUNS IN PAST OR NEGATIVE TENSE)

1. アメリカ人じゃないのに   even though (he) is not American
2. アメリカ人だったのに   even though (he) was American
3. アメリカ人じゃなかったのに   even though (he) wasn't American

EXAMPLES (な ADJECTIVES IN PAST OR NEGATIVE TENSE)

1. 静かじゃないのに   even though it's not quiet
2. 静かだったのに   even though it was quiet
3. 静かじゃなかったのに   even though it wasn't quiet

EXAMPLE SENTENCES

1. 授業は明日なのに、宿題がまだ終わっていません。
   Even though my class is tomorrow, I haven't finished my homework yet.

2. 南さんはきれいなのに、彼がいません。
   Even though Miss Minami is beautiful, she doesn't have a boyfriend.

3. 昨日は休みだったのに、遊びに行けませんでした。
   Even though yesterday was my day off, I was not able to go to play.

● 1-4. Trying to do something 〜てみる

When you want to try something, you can use this handy pattern て form + みる.

> ## (verb て form) + みる
> ## to try to (verb)

〜てみる is conjugated just like 見る (to see). However, it's written in hiragana.

EXAMPLES

1. 作ってみる (みます)   will try to make
2. 作ってみた (みました)   tried to make
3. 作ってみたい (みたいです)   want to try to make
4. 作ってみたかった (みたかったです)   wanted to try to make

EXAMPLE SENTENCES

1. 海外で英語を教えてみたいです。
   I would like to try to teach English abroad.

2. すき焼きは簡単だと聞いたので、一度作ってみました。
   Since I heard sukiyaki was easy (to make), I tried to make it once.

3. ずっと落ち込んでいたけど、頑張ってみることにしました。
   For a long time, I was feeling down, but I decided to try to do my best.

EXAMPLE CONVERSATION

1. **Conversation between friends**

   A: 今度、お好み焼きを食べてみませんか。

   B: いいですね。私たちだけですか。

   This で is covered in book 4 section 12-11.

   A: じゃあ、妹さんにも聞いてみて下さい。3人で行きましょう。

   A: How about we eat okonomiyaki next time?

   B: Sounds good. Just us?

   A: Hmmm, (try to) ask your younger sister. Let's go with the 3 of us.

RELATED GRAMMAR

Japanese From Zero! ④ Section 12-11. Using で with amounts

● 1-5. Verb + 〜たりしますか (Do you ever~)

〜たりする makes a sentence softer or subtle when compared to standard 〜ますか.

EXAMPLE SENTENCES

1. アメリカに帰ったりしますか。
   Do you ever go back to America?

2. 友達と飲みに行ったりしますか。
   Do you ever go drink with your friends?

3. 日本の文化の違いに困ったりしませんか。
   Don't you ever get troubled by differences in Japanese culture?

> This たりする is used for "representative action lists" showing a sample of actions.

Casual conversation between friends

A: 東京の生活はどう？

B: 楽しいよ。学校の休みの日は、ショッピングをしたり、友達とカラオケをしたりしてる。

A: 青森のお母さんに電話したりする？

B: 最近はしない。たくさん勉強したり、友達と遊んだりして、
電話するのを忘れてしまうんだ。

A: How is life in Tokyo?

B: It's fun. On my school's days off, I do things like shopping and sing karaoke with friends.

A: Do you ever call your mother in Aomori?

B: I don't recently. Because I'm studying a lot and playing with friends,
I end up forgetting to call.

Polite conversation between company workers

> ではありません is a more formal way to say じゃない and is often used in the workplace.

A: 明日の予定は会議ですか。

B: 会議ではありません。明日は工場に行ったり、報告書を書いたりします。

A: 工場に行く時、食事が出たりしますか。

B: 出る時と出ない時がありますが、明日は出ます。

> 出る means "to come out", but the English is more naturally translated as "to be provided"

A: Are the plans for tomorrow a meeting?

B: It isn't a meeting. Tomorrow we are going to the factory or writing reports.

A: When going to the factory, are meals ever provided?

B: Sometimes they are, sometimes they aren't, but tomorrow it's provided.

RELATED GRAMMAR

Japanese From Zero! ④ Section 9-8. The たり verb form

1 | Practice and Review 練習と復習

● Mini Conversation ミニ会話 J → E

Try translating the entire conversation before looking at the translation below.

1. Casual conversation between husband and wife

A: あれ？クローゼットからお金が出てきた！

B: え？ 誰のかな。

A: 知らないふりしないで。これは、へそくりでしょう！

B: ごめん。お願いだから、返してくれる？

> お願いだから is similar to "I beg you please" in English.

A: Hmm? Money turned up from (in) the closet.

B: What? I wonder whose it is.

A: Don't pretend like you don't know. This is your secret savings, right?

B: Sorry. I beg you (please), can you please give it back to me?

2. Polite conversation between neighbors

A: 最近、暑くなりましたね。

B: そうですね。家の窓を開けているのに、汗が出ますね。

A: 私の家は暑くて、一週間前からエアコンをつけていますよ。

B: あ、本当ですか。うちは電気代を節約してるので、まだ一度もつけていません。

A: Recently, it sure has gotten hot.

B: Yes. Despite having the house windows open, you sweat.

A: Our house is so hot that we have been turning on (using) the AC from one week ago.

B: Oh really? We've been saving on our electric bill, so we haven't used it even once.

3. Casual conversation between friends

A: 彼はご飯を食べている時、いつも携帯を見てる。

B: そう？ 全然話さないの？

A: うん。私が話をしているのに、全然聞いてくれない。

B: 困ったね。なら、ラインで「こっちみて」とメッセージを送ってみてよ。(笑)

> (笑) comes from 笑う (わらう) to laugh. It's similar to LOL in English when texting.

A: My boyfriend always looks at his cell phone when eating dinner.

B: Really? He doesn't speak at all?

A: Yes. Even though I'm talking, he doesn't listen at all.

B: That's troubling. If so, try sending him a message on LINE that says, "look at me." LOL

NOTE: In conversation #3, B asks, "He doesn't speak at all?" In English, it doesn't matter if we ask "Does he speak?" or "Does NOT he speak?" We always answer as if the question was "Does he speak?" This is grammatically incorrect in English, but habitually we ignore this.

In Japanese, you either agree or disagree with the question. So, if it is asked "He doesn't talk to you? in the negative and you answer "YES," it means "Yes, he does NOT talk" because you are disagreeing with the question. If you answer "NO," it means "No, he does talk". This is a common point of confusion when English and Japanese speakers interact.

● **Mini Conversation ミニ会話 E → J**

Try translating the entire conversation before looking at the translation below.

1. **Polite conversation between neighbors**

   A: Can you hear the barking of the dog early in the morning?
   B: Yes. It's because it barks from around 5 o'clock every morning, it troubles me.
   A: It's so loud I'm also troubled. Nothing but a constant "woof woof".
   B: I want them to handle it somehow.

   A: 朝早く、犬の鳴き声が聞こえますか。
   B: はい。毎朝 5 時ごろから鳴くから、困っています。
   A: うるさくて私も困っています。ずっとワンワン鳴いていますね。
   B: 何とかしてほしいですね。

2. **Polite conversation between friends**

   A: I'm coming in. (literally, "I will be a nuisance.") Oh? Where is your cat?
   B: He's most likely under the bed.
   A: Ah, he came out. I can see his head.
   B: Even though normally he never comes out, this is rare.

   > It might sound unnatural to use "even though" this way in English.

   A: おじゃまします。あれ、猫はどこですか。
   B: きっと、ベッドの下にいるでしょう。
   A: ああ、出てきましたよ。頭が見えました。
   B: いつもは出てこないのに、珍しいですね。

3. Casual conversation between friends

A: I'm feeling down now.

B: What happened?

A: Even though I was finally able to go on a date with Hana, we already broke up.

B: Oh, that's rough. But you should try to talk to her again.

A: 今、落ち込んでる。

B: どうしたの？

A: やっと花さんとデートできたのに、もう別れた。

B: それは辛いね。でも、もう一度、話をしてみたほうがいいよ。

● Short Dialogue

Aiko is talking about her breakup to her friend.

あいこ	「今日、彼と別れた。」
友達	「え？本当？結婚すると思ってたのに、どうしたの？」
あいこ	「あの人、若いふりをしていたけど、本当は50歳だった！私はまだ21歳なのに！」
友達	「50歳のどこがだめなの？」
あいこ	「もし結婚して、すぐ子供が生まれたら、子供が10歳になった時には、彼はもう60歳だよ！おじいちゃんの年だよ。」
友達	「う～ん。それはそうだね。」
あいこ	「おじいちゃんと子供のお世話を毎日するのは嫌。」
友達	「嫌だよね。誰かいい人いないかなぁ。」

> You can end a sentence with のに when the context is known in casual conversation.

> かな can be かなぁ (small あ) to lengthen it out showing more thinking.

1 Kanji Lesson 1:
台組画番点語

From the teacher...

This lesson groups kanji that can be used as counters or suffixes.

1 How This Book Works

Each of the Kanji Lessons in this book teach 6-8 new kanji. When possible, the kanji are grouped into logical groups. Memorizing the readings for each kanji is a common method of learning, however we suggest instead you learn common words using the new kanji such as in (G) of new kanji introduced. The side result of learning these words will be learning how the kanji are read.

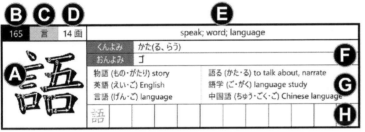

(H) Boxes are provided to practice writing the new kanji. When typing kanji, you only need to be able to recognize the kanji.

While learning to write isn't as important as in the past, writing the kanji may make it easier for you to remember them.

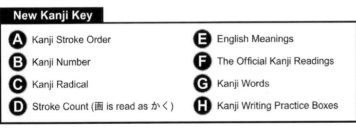

New Kanji Key

Ⓐ Kanji Stroke Order
Ⓔ English Meanings
Ⓑ Kanji Number
Ⓕ The Official Kanji Readings
Ⓒ Kanji Radical
Ⓖ Kanji Words
Ⓓ Stroke Count (画 is read as かく)
Ⓗ Kanji Writing Practice Boxes

(A) Stroke order is important when writing. If proper stroke order isn't followed, it's possible your kanji will look "off" from the way it should look.

(F) くんよみ are the native "Japanese" readings, while おんよみ are based on the original "Chinese" sound of the kanji when it was introduced into Japan. The sounds often do not match current Chinese. The hiragana inside parenthesis are the kanji readings (like furigana but in brackets) and are not part of the kanji words.

1 | New Kanji 新しい漢字

NOTE: The kanji number is continued from the kanji introduced in books 3 and 4.

160	口	5画	stand; basis; platform

くんよみ	none
おんよみ	ダイ、タイ

二台 (に・だい) two (machinery)	台風 (たい・ふう) typhoon
台所 (だい・どころ) kitchen	舞台 (ぶ・たい) stage (theatre)
台本 (だい・ほん) script (TV etc.)	台湾 (たい・わん) Taiwan

台

161	糸	11画	group; team; construct; assemble; association

くんよみ	く(む)、くみ
おんよみ	ソ

番組 (ばん・ぐみ) program (e.g.TV)	組み立てる (く・み・た・て・る) to assemble
組 (くみ) group	組合 (くみ・あい) association, union
組織 (そ・しき) organization	組み込み (く・み・こ・み) included (in product etc.)

組

162	田	8画	picture; painting; drawing; stroke (of kanji etc.)

くんよみ	none
おんよみ	カク、ガ

映画 (えい・が) movie	画面 (が・めん) screen (TV, phone)
画像 (が・ぞう) image	計画 (けい・かく) plan
画家 (が・か) painter, artist	画数 (かく・すう) stroke count (in character)

画

163	田	12画	number; turn; watch; guard

くんよみ	none
おんよみ	バン

一番 (いち・ばん) first, number one	番号 (ばん・ごう) number (phone etc.)
交番 (こう・ばん) police box	定番 (てい・ばん) standard; routine
番犬 (ばん・けん) watchdog	三番目 (さん・ばん・め) third (in sequence)

番

164	灬	9 画	dot; mark; points	
			くんよみ	none
			おんよみ	テン

点

交差点 (こう・さ・てん) intersection
満点 (まん・てん) perfect score
点数 (てん・すう) score

欠点 (けっ・てん) flaw; weak point; defect
百点 (ひゃく・てん) 100 points
終点 (しゅう・てん) last stop (train, bus etc.)

点

165	言	14 画	speak; word; language	
			くんよみ	かた(る、らう)
			おんよみ	ゴ

語

物語 (もの・がたり) story
英語 (えい・ご) English
言語 (げん・ご) language

語る (かた・る) to talk about, narrate
語学 (ご・がく) language study
中国語 (ちゅう・ごく・ご) Chinese language

語

1 ⏐ Kanji Culture 漢字の文化

● 「点」to mean "item" or "piece"

点 can be used to count more than points on a test. It's also used by store clerks when counting products while talking to the customer, and counting works of art.

For example, at a store you have, 3 pencils (本 counter), 2 erasers (個 counter), and 1 notebook (冊 counter) at the register. After scanning them, the staff might confirm:

> 1. 全部で6点ですね。   Altogether, it's 6 items, right?

Using 点 to count conveys a sense of politeness. Japanese ads for products might also use 点 to say, ３点で、なんと３００円！(3 items for, wow, 300 yen!). It would be strange as a customer to say, "give me 6 items" using 点 at the store, but it isn't wrong to say, "I have 6 items for sale".

Mercari (メルカリ) is a popular selling site.

> 2. メルカリで6点を出品しています。   I have 6 items for sale on Mercari.

1 | Words You Can Write 書ける言葉

Write the following words using the kanji that you have just learned.

組合 (くみあい) association; guild; union

組	合								

点火 (てんか) ignition; set fire to

点	火								

三組 (さんくみ) three groups

三	組								

画家 (がか) painter; artist

画	家								

三画 (さんかく) three strokes

三	画								

言語 (げんご) language

言	語								

一番 (いちばん) first; number one

一	番								

番組 (ばんぐみ) program

番	組								

百点 (ひゃくてん) 100 points

百	点									

交番(こうばん) police box

交	番									

点数 (てんすう) score

点	数									

語る (かたる) talk; recite

語	る									

語学 (ごがく) language study

語	学									

当番 (とうばん) being on duty; duty

当	番									

台本 (だいほん) script; scenario

台	本									

土台 (どだい) foundation; base; basis

土	台									

天文台 (てんもんだい) astronomical observatory

天	文	台								

1 | Kanji Drills 漢字ドリル

● **1. Writing counters and suffixes in kanji**

Look at the following pictures and write appropriate counters/suffixes in kanji.

1. 100 points

2. three strokes

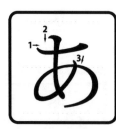

3. number one

4. four groups

5. Korean language

6. two cars

7. five fingers

8. three computers

● **2. Fill in the Kanji**

Fill in the appropriate kanji in the blanks for each sentence.

1.   こうえんで ___つけた さいふを ___ ___ にとどけました。

み
こう ばん

I dropped off the wallet I found in the park at the police box.

2.　パズルを ＿＿ み＿＿わせるのは ＿＿しいですね。

             _く   _あ   _{たの}

Putting together a puzzle sure is fun.

3.　「＿＿」というかん ＿＿ は、＿＿ ＿＿ ＿＿ですよね。

  _{もり}   _じ   _{じゅう} _に _{かく}

The MORI kanji has 12 strokes, right?

4.　＿＿よう ＿＿は ＿＿ ＿＿で そうじ＿＿ ＿＿です。

  _{げつ}   _び   _{がっ} _{こう}   _{とう} _{ばん}

On Monday, I am on cleaning duty at school.

5.　＿＿ ＿＿ がわるかったので、ふゆ ＿＿みにべん＿＿します。

  _{てん} _{すう}   _{やす}   _{きょう}

Because my score was bad, I will study on (during) winter break.

6.　＿＿ ＿＿ ＿＿で ＿＿ を ＿＿いました。

  _に _{ほん} _ご   _{うた}   _{うた}

I sang a song in Japanese.

7.　＿＿ は＿＿ を＿＿ ＿＿もっています。

  _{ちち} _{くるま}   _に _{だい}

My father owns two cars.

1 Workbook 1: Workbook Activities

1 Usage Activities 文法アクティビティー

● ### 3. Reading comprehension

Translate the following on a separate piece of paper or type in an electronic device.

日本での生活

Moving to a new place is a struggle but learning a new language at the same time is an even bigger challenge.

---

❶ 私は日本に五年、住んでいます。

❷ 最初は日本語が分からなかったから、日本人と話す時はどきどきして、よく汗をかいていました。

❸ 言いたい事が言えないから、落ち込んだりしました。

❹ 相手の言っている事が分からないのに、分かったふりをしました。

❺ だから、私は真剣に勉強してみることにしました。

❻ 言葉が出てこない時は、先生や友達に教えてもらいました。

❼ 電車に乗っている時は、ずっとヘッドフォンで日本の音楽を聴いていました。

❽ 毎日、日本のテレビ番組を見たり、漫画を読んだりもしました。

❾ そうしたら、少し自信が出てきました。

❿ 言いたい言葉がすぐ出てきた時は、すごく嬉しいです。

⓫ 間違えた時は落ち込まないで、しょうがないと思うことにしています。

⓬ まだ会話で困ることはありますが、いつも何とかなっています。

⓭ 今やっと、日本での生活が楽しいと思えます。

⓮ 「聞くは一時の恥、聞かぬは一生の恥」ですね。

> This proverb means, "To ask is a moment's shame, but not to ask is an everlasting shame."

聞くは一時の恥、聞かぬは一生の恥

Asking is a temporary shame,
not asking is a lifetime shame.

● 4. Reading comprehension questions

Translate the questions about the reading comprehension then answer in Japanese.

1. この人は、どうしてどきどきしていましたか。

　　Translation: _____

　　Answer: _____

2. この人は、どんな時に落ち込んでいましたか。

　　Translation: _____

　　Answer: _____

3. どうして分かったふりをしていたと思いますか。

　　Translation: _____

　　Answer: _____

4. この人は一生懸命勉強をしましたか。

　　Translation: _____

　　Answer: _____

5. この人はどうやって日本語を勉強しましたか。二つ、教えて下さい。

　　Translation: _____

　　Answer: _____

6. この人は日本語がペラペラになりましたか。

Translation: _____

Answer: _____

● 5. Fill in the blanks

Fill in the missing part based on the English sentence.

1. _____のに、テストでいい点を取りました。

   Even though I didn't study at all, I got a good score on the test.

2. _____のに、言葉が出てきません。

   Even though I want to talk with Yuko, the words don't come out.

3. 彼女に_____会えるから、_____。

   I am excited because I can finally see (meet) her.

4. 昨日買った靴を_____。

   I tried on the pair of shoes I bought yesterday.

5. 何_____。

   I will try to handle it somehow.

● 6. Question and Answer

Answer the following questions as if they are being asked to you.

1. 時々、落ち込んだりしますか。

_____

2. 誰と別れた時、さびしかったですか。

_____

3. 寝たいのに、寝られないのは、どんな時ですか。

_____

4. 何月ごろから、クーラーをつけますか。

_____

5. 大都市で何がしてみたいですか。

_____

● 7. Translation
Translate the following sentences into Japanese.

1. When I'm in trouble, I always figure out a way to handle it.

_____

2. Please turn on the air conditioner since I'm sweating.

_____

3. There are a lot of people coming out of the (concert) hall.

_____

4. I will seriously try to find a job.

_____

5. I can't speak Korean well even though I know a lot of words.

_____

● **8. Visual clue questions**
Look at the picture, make a complete Japanese sentence with のに <u>including</u> the provided English.

かのじょ

1. Even though my older brother is good looking...

_____

2. Even though it's tough...

_____

3. Even though it's Friday...

_____

Test Time!

4. Even though he is taking a test...

_____

5. Even though I went to the customer's house...

_____

1 | Answer Key 答え合わせ

Short Dialogue (translation)

Aiko	Today I broke up with my boyfriend.
Friend	What? Really? (even though) I thought you were going to get married. What happened?
Aiko	He (that person) pretended he was young, but he was really 50 years old! Even though I am still 21 years old.
Friend	What (what part / where) of 50 years old isn't good?
Aiko	If we got married and had children right away, when the child turned 10, he would already be 60! That's the age of a grandfather (old man).
Friend	Hmmm. Yeah that's right.
Aiko	I wouldn't want to take care of an old man and a baby every day. (Taking care of an old man and a baby every day is awful.)
Friend	That is awful, right! I wonder if there isn't some good person (out there).

1. Writing counters and suffixes in kanji (answers)

1. 百点（ひゃくてん）　2. 三画（さんかく）　3. 一番（いちばん）　4. 四組（よんくみ）

5. かんこく語（ご）　6. 二台（にだい）　7. 五本（ごほん）　8. 三台（さんだい）

2. Fill in the kanji (answers)

1. こうえんで 見つけた さいふを 交番にとどけました。
2. パズルを組み合わせるのは楽しいですね。
3. 「森」というかん字は十二画ですよね。
4. 月よう日は学校でそうじ当番です。
5. 点数がわるかったので、ふゆ休みにべん強します。
6. 日本語で歌を歌いました。
7. 父は車を二台もっています。

3. Reading comprehension (translation)

❶ I have been living in Japan for 5 years.
❷ In the beginning I didn't understand Japanese, so when I spoke to Japanese people, my heart beat was fast and I often sweated.
❸ I sometimes got down because I couldn't say what I wanted to say.
❹ Even though I didn't understand what the other person was saying, I acted as if I understood.
❺ So, I decided to seriously study.
❻ When the words didn't come out, I had my teachers and friends help me.
❼ When I was on the train, I was always listening to Japanese music on my headphones.
❽ Every day I did things like watching Japanese TV and reading comic books.
❾ Upon doing so, a bit of confidence appeared. (I got a bit confident.)
❿ When what I wanted to say came out immediately, I was really happy.
⓫ When I made a mistake, I have decided not to get down and to think it can't be helped.
⓬ There are still things I am troubled with in conversation, but it always works out somehow.
⓭ Now finally, I am able to think life in Japan is enjoyable.
⓮ It's "Asking is a temporary shame, not asking is a lifelong shame." isn't it?

4. Reading comprehension questions (answers)

1. Translation: Why was this person's heart throbbing?
   Answer(s):   最初は日本語が分からなかったからです。

2. Translation: During which times was this person feeling down?
   Answer(s):   言いたい事が言えない時、落ち込んでいました。

3. Translation: Why do you think he acted like he understood?
   Answer(s):   分からないと言いたくないからです。/ シャイだからです。

4. Translation: Did this person study hard?
   Answer(s):   はい、しました。

5. Translation: How did this person study Japanese? Please tell two (ways).
   Answer(s):   電車の中でヘッドフォンで日本の音楽を聴いていました。
   毎日、日本のテレビ番組を見ました。漫画を読んだりしました。

6. Translation: Did this person become fluent in Japanese?
   Answer(s):   いいえ。でも、会話は何とかなっています。

5. Fill in the blanks (answers)

1. 全然勉強しなかったのに、テストでいい点を取りました。
2. ゆうこさんと話したいのに、言葉が出てきません。
3. 彼女にやっと会えるから、どきどきしています。
4. 昨日買った靴をはいてみました。
5. 何とかしてみます。

6. Question and Answer (answers may vary)

1. Do you sometimes feel down/get depressed?
   はい、よく落ち込みます。/ いいえ、あまり落ち込みません。

2. Who, when you [broke up with / separated from] them, were you sad?
   (When you [broke up with / separated from] who...)
   昔の彼女と別れた時、さびしかったです。/ 母と別れた時です。

3. What kind of times (When) can't you not sleep even though you want to sleep?
   暑い時です。/ 何か考えている時、寝られません。

4. Around what month do you turn on the cooler?
   7月ごろから、つけます。/ ここは暑いので、5月ごろからです。

5. What do you want to try (to do) in a large city?
   モールで買い物がしてみたいです。/ 観光して、写真をたくさんとりたいです。

7. Translation (answers)

1. 困った時は、いつも何とかします。

2. 汗をかいているから、エアコンをつけて下さい。

3. 会場からたくさんの人が出てきています。

4. 真剣に仕事を探してみます。

5. 言葉をたくさん知っているのに、韓国語がよく話せません。

8. Visual clue questions (sample answers)

1. 兄はかっこいいのに／お兄ちゃんはハンサムなのに

    ～性格が悪いです。(his personality is bad)

    ～彼女がいません。(he doesn't have a girlfriend)

2. つらいのに／大変なのに

    ～がんばって階段を上がりました。(he did his best and climbed up the stairs)

    ～階段を使いました。(he used the stairs)

3. 金曜日なのに

    ～仕事がまだたくさんあります。 (he still has lots of work)

    ～まだ家に帰れません。(he can't go home yet)

4. テストをしているのに

    ～遊んでいます。(he is playing)

    ～何も書いていません。(he hasn't written anything)

5. お客さんの家に行ったのに

    ～いませんでした。(they weren't there)

    ～誰も出て来ませんでした。(nobody came out)

Vocabulary Builder:
Groups E and F

■ Group E: nature and weather

<ruby>地震<rt>じ しん</rt></ruby>	earthquake
<ruby>余震<rt>よ しん</rt></ruby>	after quake; aftershock
<ruby>震度<rt>しん ど</rt></ruby>	Japanese earthquake scale
<ruby>火山<rt>か ざん</rt></ruby>	volcano
<ruby>活火山<rt>かつ か ざん</rt></ruby>	active volcano
<ruby>津波<rt>つ なみ</rt></ruby>	tsunami, tidal wave
<ruby>洪水<rt>こう ずい</rt></ruby>	flood
<ruby>竜巻<rt>たつ まき</rt></ruby>	tornado, twister
<ruby>雪崩<rt>な だれ</rt></ruby>	avalanche
<ruby>台風<rt>たい ふう</rt></ruby>	typhoon
ハリケーン	hurricane

■ Group F: season related

<ruby>季節<rt>き せつ</rt></ruby>	season
<ruby>天気予報<rt>てん き よ ほう</rt></ruby>	weather forecast
<ruby>梅雨<rt>つゆ</rt></ruby>	rainy season
<ruby>雨漏り<rt>あま も</rt></ruby>	roof leak
<ruby>大雨<rt>おお あめ</rt></ruby>	heavy rain
<ruby>吹雪<rt>ふ ぶき</rt></ruby>	snow storm; blizzard
どしゃぶり	heavy~ (rain)

> This season starts in southern Japan, 沖縄 (おきなわ) in early May then continues north to the mainland, 本州 (ほんしゅう) where it rains almost daily from early June to mid-July.

> This is similar to "raining cats and dogs".

2

| 15 PAGES | 5 USAGE SECTIONS | 21 NEW WORDS |

Lesson 2:
Natural Disasters

From the teacher...

This lesson will help you learn natural disaster related conversation which is common in Japan due to the location of Japan. (more in the Living in Japan section)

2 New Words 新しい言葉

Nouns etc.

ひ がい 被害	damage; injury; harm		えいきょう 影響	influence; effect
ほう ほう 方法	method; process; manner; way		しな ぎ 品切れ	out of stock
こう じょう 工場	factory; plant; mill; workshop		りょう 量	amount; quantity
れつ 列	line; queue; row; column		かん こう きゃく 観光客	tourist; visitor
つう がく 通学	school commute		てい きゅう び 定休日	fixed day off

Adverbs

とく 特に	especially; in particular	しばらく	for a while; awhile

Verbs

お 起きる	to occur; to happen; to arise		うご 動く	to move; to run
ちゅう い 注意する	to be careful; to pay attention; to warn		ふん か 噴火する	to erupt; to spout
ふ 降る	to rain; to snow; to fall		ふ 増える	to increase; to grow
えいぎょう 営業する	to do business; to be open (stores etc.)		ふ 増やすす	to increase; to grow
こわ 怖がる	to be afraid			

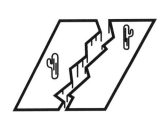

2 | Japanese Living 日本の暮らし

Japan sits on a geological region called, "the ring of fire", which means there are regular earthquakes which can lead to tsunami (tidal waves) and still many active volcanoes. Also, every year there are large typhoons that often cause much havoc as they pass.

Due to the frequency of earthquakes furniture is often secured to the wall or floor with brackets to prevent it from tipping over or moving and injuring or killing someone in the house during an earthquake. Many Japanese register their phone numbers to get early warning voice notices on their phone of an impending earthquake or tsunami. Often elementary schools are set up as emergency shelters that are stocked with food and water.

After the large earthquake followed by a tsunami and nuclear meltdown disaster in March of 2011 that was responsible for over 15,000 deaths, Japanese people were reminded of how they must be vigilant against such disasters. The sales of "disaster preparedness kits" sky rocketed. Common items in the kit are canned food, water, toothbrushes, face masks, flashlights, rechargeable batteries, blankets, raincoats, heating pads, tape (to stop bleeding), anti-bacterial gel, and gloves.

The kits are normally stored in near the main entrance of the house so as to be easily picked up when escaping during a disaster.

2 | Verb Usage 動詞の使い方

V-1	起_おきる	to occur; to happen; to arise	いる/える
	1. (event) が起きる	(event) occurs	

In Book 2, we learned that 起きる means "to wake up". As we learn in this lesson 起きる also means "to occur" and "to happen."

EXAMPLE SENTENCES

1. 私たちの間では、色々な問題が起きています。
   Between us, a variety of problems are occurring.

2. もう地震が起きてほしくないですね。
   I don't want earthquakes to occur anymore.

V-2	注意する	to warn; be cautious; be careful; pay attention	する
	1. (person, thing) に注意する	to warn a (person, thing)	

Depending on the circumstances, 注意をする can be used to warn somebody or also to say caution will be taken.

EXAMPLE SENTENCES

1. この道を運転する時は、注意した方がいいです。
   When you drive this road, you should be careful.

2. 私は上司と話す時、いつも言葉に注意します。
   When I talk to my boss, I am always careful with my words.

V-3	降る	to fall; to come down (rain, snow etc.)	regular
	1. (rain, snow etc.) が降る	(rain, snow etc.) falls	

EXAMPLE SENTENCES

1. 昨日からずっと雨が降っていますね。
   It's been raining continually since yesterday.

2. 去年の冬は、あまり雪が降りませんでした。
   Last winter it didn't snow that much.

3. 運動会の日に雨降るかなぁ。
   I wonder if it will rain on sports day.

> The small あ is used to lengthen the sound for かな.

V-4	動く _{うご}	to move, to run (work)	regular

1. (thing, person) が動く	(thing, person) moves / works

EXAMPLE SENTENCES

1. 今、お腹の赤ちゃんが動いた！
   My baby (in my stomach) moved now!

2. 最近、私のパソコンがちゃんと動かない。
   Recently, my computer doesn't work properly.

3. 車が動かないので、見ていただけますか。
   My car doesn't run, so could you please take a look at it?

> 動く is sometimes used to say something is broken (when in negative form). This is normally for things that have moving parts.

V-5	噴火する _{ふん か}	to erupt (volcano)	する

1. (something) が噴火する	(something) erupts

EXAMPLE SENTENCES

1. 今でも噴火する火山は「活火山」といいます。
   Volcanoes that erupt even now are called "active volcanoes."

2. もう噴火しない火山は「死火山」といいます。
   Volcanoes that no longer erupt are called "extinct volcanoes."

3. 富士山が噴火したら、東京はどうなるでしょうか。
   If Mt. Fuji erupts, what will happen to Tokyo?

V-6	営業する _{えい ぎょう}	(to run a business; to be in operation (open)	する

1. (a store etc.) を営業する	to run (a store etc.)

1. このデパートは、午前10時から午後8時まで営業しています。
   This department store is open from 10 in the morning to 8 at night.

2. うちの店は、地震が起きた日は営業できませんでした。
   Our store couldn't operate the day the earthquake happened.

---

3. この店は火曜日が定休日ですが、今週の火曜日は、珍しく営業します。
This store's fixed closed day is Tuesday, but this Tuesday it will be unusually open.

Shops and restaurants in Japan often have a sign on the door that says 営業中 which means "we are open".

V-7	増える	to increase; to grow in numbers (DESCRIPTIVE)	いる/える
	1. (something) が増える	(something) increases	

	増やす	to increase; to grow in numbers (ACTION)	Regular
	1. (something) を増やす	to increase (something)	

EXAMPLE SENTENCES

1. 最近、仕事の量が増えました。
Recently my workload has increased.

2. 日本のアニメは、全世界でファンが増えています。
All over the world, (the number of) Japanese anime fans are increasing.

3. 痩せたいなら、運動量を増やしましょう。
If you want to lose weight, let's increase the amount of exercise.

4. 仕事を始めたから、貯金を増やしたいです。
Because I started to work, I want to increase my savings.

V-8	怖がる	to be afraid to; to fear; to be frightened	regular
	1. (something) を怖がる	to be afraid to (something)	

EXAMPLE SENTENCES

1. 怖がらないでください。
Don't be afraid.

2. うちの犬は、台風を怖がります。
Our dog is afraid of typhoons.

3. 怖がっているふりをしないで下さい。
   Don't act like you are frightened.

4. 妹は去年までプールに入るのを怖がっていましたが、今はもう大丈夫です。
   My younger sister was afraid of entering the pool until last year, but now she is okay.

When talking about your own fears, use the [something]が こわい pattern.
怖がる is used ONLY for people other than yourself.

EXAMPLE Q&A

1. 何を怖がっているんですか。   **What are you scared of?**

   あの犬が怖いんです。   I am scared of that dog over there.

   高い所が怖いんです。   I am afraid of heights.

2   Grammar and Usage 文法と使い方

● **2-1. Confirmation and Reasons 〜(な)んです**
As with any grammar, you have to know how the grammar works with nouns, い adjectives, な adjectives, and verbs.

ALWAYS USE
verbs, nouns, and
all adjectives → んです

EXCEPT WITH
present (positive) tense
nouns and な adjectives → なんです

Everything except positive present tense nouns and な adjectives use んです.

EXAMPLES (NOUNS)

1. 面接なんです。   It's an interview.
2. 面接じゃないんです。   It's not an interview.
3. 面接だったんです。   It was an interview.

EXAMPLES (な ADJECTIVES)

1. 必要なんです。   It is necessary.
2. 必要じゃないんです。   It's not necessary.
3. 必要じゃなかったんです。   It wasn't necessary.

EXAMPLES (い ADJECTIVES)

1. 冷たいんです。   It's cold. (to the touch)
2. 冷たくないんです。   It isn't cold.
3. 冷たかったんです。   It was cold.

EXAMPLES (VERBS)

1. 増えているんです。   It's increasing.
2. 増えていないんです。   It isn't increasing.
3. 増えなかったんです。   It didn't increase.

(な)んです has a few uses. The first we will learn is when asking for confirmation or providing a reason. For example, you saw your classmate packing her backpack in the middle of the day at school. You want to know if she is going home or not.

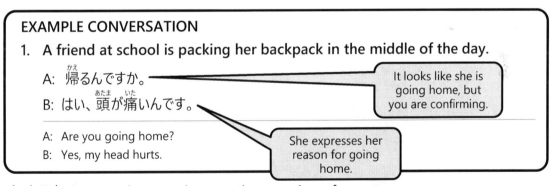

EXAMPLE CONVERSATION

1. **A friend at school is packing her backpack in the middle of the day.**

   A: 帰るんですか。   *It looks like she is going home, but you are confirming.*

   B: はい、頭が痛いんです。   *She expresses her reason for going home.*

   A: Are you going home?
   B: Yes, my head hurts.

(な)んです changes the tone, but not the meaning of a sentence.

EXAMPLE CONVERSATIONS

1. **Upon noticing a friend's child studying for a test...**

   A: いつ、テストがあるんですか。(A is assuming B has a test.)
   B: 明日なんです。

   A: When do you have a test?
   B: It's tomorrow.

2. **Upon seeing a neighbor that owns a car is standing at the bus stop...**

A: どうして車を運転しないんですか。

B: 奥さんが使っているんです。

> A is assuming B can drive.

A: How come you aren't driving?

B: My wife is using the car.

3. **Upon hearing a friend is going to Kyoto...**

A: どうして京都へ行くんですか。

B: 京都のお寺が好きなんです。

> A knows B is going to Kyoto and is curious why.

A: How come you are going to Kyoto?

B: I like the temples of Kyoto.

4. **Upon seeing a friend crying...**

A: どうしたんですか。

B: お腹が痛いんです。

> Watch any drama or anime and (な)ん will show up in many conversations.

A: What happened?

B: My stomach hurts.

● 2-2. Using 〜(な)んです when emphasizing

When you want to show a bit of emotion or emphasis, you can use 〜(な)んです.

EXAMPLE Q&A

1. 日本の夏はどうですか。   How is summer in Japan?

   蒸し暑いんです。   It is so muggy.

   寒いんですよ。   It's so cold.

2. 赤ちゃんは元気ですか。   Is your baby fine?

   はい、大きくなったんですよ。   Yes. She has gotten <u>so</u> big!

   元気いっぱいなんです。   She is <u>so</u> full of energy.

3. テストはどうでしたか。   How was your test?

   100点だったんです。   I got 100 points!

   全然だめだったんです。   It wasn't good at all.

● ## 2-3. The difference between (な)んです and から

Both から and (な)んです can be used to state a reason. Imagine someone asks you:

> なんで、新しい車を買わないんですか。(Why won't you buy a new car?)

You can answer with から or んです as follows:

EXAMPLE SENTENCES

1. お金がないんです。   It's that I don't have money.
2. お金がないからです。   It's because I don't have money.

The more Japanese you know, the more you should be able to use more nuanced sentences to better fit a situation. However, this is normally learned through usage and not something easily learned by reading a textbook such as this.

That being said, if you use either からです or (な)んです, both convey the same thing. However, the tone of the sentence changes:

〜からです

からです is a fact based reason. It's clearly and unambiguously stating a reason. The stated reason is in the open. In some situations, it can feel direct.

〜(な)んです

(な)んです conveys more emotion and emphasis. It also sounds softer than から and is more indirect and ambiguous. The reason is understood, but not directly stated.

EXAMPLE Q&A (COMPARE THE ANSWERS)

1. なんで仕事を休んだんですか。   **Why did you take a day off from work?**
   子供が病気だったんです。   It's that my child was sick.
   子供が病気だったからです。   Because my child was sick.

2. なんでテスト勉強しないんですか。   **Why aren't you studying for the test?**
   やりたくないんです。   It's that I don't want to do it.
   やりたくないからです。   Because I don't want to do it.

RELATED GRAMMAR

Japanese From Zero! ② Lesson 10-3 Connecting sentences with から
Japanese From Zero! ② Lesson 11-4 The question words なぜ and なんで

● **2-4. Doing two actions at once using the ながら extension**

With ながら, you can say, "I was watching TV <u>while</u> I did my homework."

"while doing" pattern ~ながら				
verb type	**verb**		**い form**	**while~**
regular **い form + ながら**	いく →	いき →	いきながら	(while going)
	のる →	のり →	のりながら	(while riding)
	あらう →	あらい →	あらいながら	(while washing)
いる/える **minus る + ながら**	たべる →	たべ →	たべながら	(while eating)
	ねる →	ね →	ねながら	(while sleeping)
	みる →	み →	みながら	(while watching)
irregulars etc.	する →	し →	しながら	(while doing)
★ As a shortcut, just replace ます with ながら from the ます form of any verb.				

In English, "while" can be in front of the entire statement, or in between both actions. However, in Japanese, ながら is always attached to the first action. The second action of the statement is considered the MAIN action.

> **(1st action) い form + ながら + (2nd action)**
> **while doing (1st action), I (2nd action any tense)**

The tense of the second action always determines the entire tense of the sentence.

EXAMPLE SENTENCES

1. 食べながら、勉強します。 I will study while eating.
2. 食べながら、勉強したいです。 I want to study while eating.
3. 食べながら、勉強しました。 I studied while eating.
4. 食べながら、勉強すると思う。 I think I will study while eating.

EXAMPLE SENTENCES (PART 2)

1. わたしはよくテレビを見ながら、勉強します。
   I often study while watching TV.

2. 音楽を聞きながら、本を読むのは難しいです。
   It is difficult to read a book while listening to music.

3. 運転しながら、携帯電話で話さないで下さい。
   Please don't talk on the cell phone while driving.

📖 もっと詳<ruby>く<rt>わ</rt></ruby>しく… More Details ℹ️

The differences between あいだ and ながら
ながら is attached to an action, あいだ is a period of time.

EXAMPLE SENTENCES

1. 大学に行きながら、仕事をしています。
   I work while going to school. (action)

2. 大学に行っている間、仕事もしました。
   During the time I went to school, I also worked. (time period)

When using ながら, the first and second action MUST be done by the same person. With あいだ, the first and second action can be different people.

3. 私は音楽を聴きながら、料理をします。
   I cook while listening to music.

4. 私が音楽を聴いている間、母は料理します。
   My mom cooks while I'm listening to music.

5. 私は運転しながら、スマホを見ません。
   I don't look at my smartphone while driving.

6. 私が運転している間、友達はスマホを見ています。
   My friend looks at their smartphone while I'm driving.

RELATED GRAMMAR

Japanese From Zero! ④ Section 13-3. Using あいだ to mean "while～ing"

● **2-5. Adding background information with が and けど**

We have learned that having が and けど after a sentence means, "but" or "however". These types of sentences are used to show some sort of contrast.

EXAMPLE SENTENCES (CONTRAST)

1. 東京に行ったけど、大阪には行かなかったです。
   I went to Tokyo, but I didn't go to Osaka.

2. 日本人はよく緑茶を飲みますが、アメリカ人はあまり飲まないと思います。
   Japanese people often drink green tea, but I think Americans don't drink it that much.

Sometimes けど or が is used to show a result that is different from what is expected.

> **EXAMPLE SENTENCE (DIFFERENT RESULTS THAN EXPECTED)**
>
> 1. 日本に１０年間住んだけど、日本語が全然話せないです。
>
>   I lived in Japan for 10 years, <u>but</u> I don't speak Japanese at all.
>
>   The expectation is that after 10 years you should speak Japanese pretty well.

There are times where が and けど simply mark "background information" and aren't used to show any contrast or different expectations. In these cases, since there isn't an English equivalent, が or けど are not translated.

> **EXAMPLE SENTENCES (BACKGROUND INFORMATION)**
>
> 1. 私の妹は日本に住んでるんだけど、日本の有名な会社で働いています。
>
>   My youngest sister lives in Japan, she works for a famous Japanese company.
>
>   The fact that the younger sister is living in Japan is just background/supporting information and has no relation to her working at the Japanese company.
>
> 2. 友達にプレゼントを買いたいんだけど、何がいいかな。
>
>   I want to buy a present for my friend, I wonder what's good.
>
>   Here if you translate けど into "but", it sounds weird, so we leave it out of the translation.
>
> 3. 昨日、日本から帰ってきましたが、本当に疲れました。
>
>   Yesterday I got back from Japan, I am really tired.
>
>   If you translate が into "but", then the expected sentence would be "but I'm not tired at all".

RELATED GRAMMAR

Japanese From Zero! ④ Section 6-7. Connecting sentences with が

2 | Practice and Review　練習と復習

● 1. Mini Conversation ミニ会話 J → E
Try translating the entire conversation before looking at the translation below.

1. Polite conversation between friends

A: この間、津波が起きて大変でしたね。大丈夫でしたか。
B: はい、大丈夫でした。林さんは？
A: うちは津波の心配はないんですが、どしゃぶりの雨で近所に被害が出ましたね。
B: そうですか。これからも注意しましょう。

> Calling someone by their name instead of saying あなた is common.

A: The tsunami the other day was rough. Were you okay?
B: Yes, I was okay. How about you?
A: We don't worry about tsunami, but due to the downpour of rain, there was damage.
B: I see. Let's be careful from now on.

2. Polite conversation between friends

A: 昨日、スーパーに行ったら、品切れの物がたくさんありました。
B: ああ。それは地震の影響ですね。
A: ガスが使えなくて、料理ができないですから。
B: 食べる物がなくなるのは、困りますね。

A: Yesterday when I went to the supermarket, there were a lot of things sold out.
B: Ahh. That's the effect of the earthquake.
A: Right, you can't cook because gas can't be used.
B: It's a problem when they run out of things to eat.

3. Casual conversation between Japanese and non-Japanese friends

A: 日本の電車はいつも人がいっぱいだね。
B: うん。今は通勤と通学の時間だから、特に多いよ。
A: スーツケースを持ってる人もたくさんいるね。
B: そうだね。外国からの観光客が増えたから。

A: There are always a lot of people on Japanese trains.
B: Yeah, there are especially a lot since it's work and school commute time.
A: There are also a lot of people with suitcases.
B: You are right. That's because of an increased number of tourists from abroad.

● 2. Mini Conversation ミニ会話 E → J

Try translating the entire conversation before looking at the translation below.

1. Casual conversation between friends

A: Did you see the weather report?

B: Yeah. There's a typhoon coming tomorrow.

A: Right. I wonder if school will be off.

B: Maybe. I hope there isn't any big damage.

A: 天気予報を見た？

B: うん。明日は台風が来るんだね。

A: そう。学校が休みになるかな。

B: 多分ね。大きな被害が出なかったらいいね。

2. Polite conversation between two husbands

A: The earthquake yesterday was scary, huh?

B: Yes, it was. Our kid is still frightened.

A: Since it was such a big earthquake, that can't be helped.

B: Yes. Today he went to school while being cautious.

A: 昨日の地震は怖かったですね。

B: そうですね。うちの子はまだ怖がっているんです。

A: 大きい地震だったから、しょうがないですよ。

B: ええ。今日は注意しながら、学校へ行きました。

3. Casual conversation between siblings

A: Did you buy me a new cell phone today?

B: No. I went to the store, but they were sold out.

A: What? Really? That's not good. My current one is broken.

B: It's okay, I'll loan you mine for a bit.

A: 今日、新しい携帯電話を買ってくれた？

B: ううん。お店に行ったけど、品切れだった。

A: ええ、本当？困るなあ。今のは壊れてるんだ。

B: しばらく私のを貸してあげるから、大丈夫。

● 3. Short Dialogue

Hiroshi is talking about the supermarket that he owns to his friend.

友達	「最近、お店はどうですか。」
ひろし	「忙しいですよ。今年は去年より暑いので、冷たい物がよく売れています。」
友達	「夏休みに入ったら、もっとお客さんが増えますね。」
ひろし	「はい。毎日夏休みの間は夜12時まで営業しています。夜はアルバイトの子が頑張ってくれています。」
友達	「実は、うちの息子がアルバイトを探しているんです。もし人が必要なら、息子をお願いできませんか。」
ひろし	「いいですよ。今は家内が家のことをしながら、レジの仕事を手伝ってくれているんです。だから、息子さんが来てくれたら嬉しいです。」

2 · Kanji Lesson 2: 羽週曜才毎半

From the teacher...

Continuing from Lesson 1, this lesson introduces kanji that can be used as counters and suffixes.

2 | New Kanji 新しい漢字

| 166 | 羽 | 6画 | feather; wing |

| くんよみ | は、はね |
| おんよみ | ウ |

一羽 (いち・わ) one bird — 羽毛 (う・もう) feathers, down
羽 (はね) wing, feather — 羽織 (は・おり) Haori (Japanese overgarment)
羽布団 (はね・ぶ・とん) down quilt — 羽ばたく (は・ばたく) to flap (wings)

| 167 | 辶 | 11画 | week |

| くんよみ | none |
| おんよみ | シュウ |

今週 (こん・しゅう) this week — 週刊誌 (しゅう・かん・し) weekly magazine
毎週 (まい・しゅう) every week — 週末 (しゅう・まつ) weekend
来週 (らい・しゅう) next week — 一週間 (いっ・しゅう・かん) one week

| 168 | 日 | 18画 | day of the week |

| くんよみ | none |
| おんよみ | ヨウ |

日曜日 (にち・よう・び) Sunday — 水曜日 (すい・よう・び) Wednesday
曜日 (よう・び) day of the week — 火曜日 (か・よう・び) Tuesday
月曜日 (げつ・よう・び) Monday — 何曜日 (なん・よう・び) What day of the week?

169	才	3 画	genius; wit; talent; ability		
			くんよみ	none	
			おんよみ	サイ	
			一才 (いっ・さい) one year old		才能 (さい・のう) ability
			多才 (た・さい) talented		漫才 (まん・ざい) comedy duo
			天才 (てん・さい) genius		英才 (えい・さい) gifted person; brilliance

170	母	6 画	every; each		
			くんよみ	none	
			おんよみ	マイ	
			毎回 (まい・かい) every time		毎月 (まい・つき) every month
			毎年 (まい・とし) every year		毎朝 (まい・あさ) every morning
			毎日 (まい・にち) every day		毎晩 (まい・ばん) every night

171	十	5 画	half; middle		
			くんよみ	なか(ば)	
			おんよみ	ハン	
			二時半 (に・じ・はん) 2:30		半島 (はん・とう) peninsula
			半ば (なか・ば) middle		半額 (はん・がく) half price
			半分 (はん・ぶん) half		一時間半 (いち・じ・かん・はん) 1 hour and a half

2 | Kanji Culture 漢字の文化

● **The difference between 才 and 歳**

Officially, the kanji used to represent age, 歳 (years old), is taught in junior high school. However, since there are many strokes in 歳, a simpler kanji, 才 is used as 略字 (an abbreviation)/代用漢字 (a substitution). This makes it easier for younger children to write their ages. They switch to the more complicated kanji after learning how to write it.

● **Every ~ (day of week) 毎**

Although it isn't part of the 常用漢字 (common use kanji), a commonly used reading for 毎 is ごと. It can be added after a weekday in the place of 日 to mean "every~".

EXAMPLE SENTENCES

1. 日曜毎に図書館で日本語の勉強会があります。
   Every Sunday, there is a Japanese study meetup at the library.

2. 火曜と木曜毎、ジムで筋トレをトレイナーとしています。
   Every Tuesday and Thursday, I weight train at the gym with a trainer.

---

2 | Words You Can Write　書ける言葉

Write the following words using the kanji that you have just learned.

羽毛 (うもう) feather (down)

羽	毛								

二羽 (にわ) two birds (or rabbits)

二	羽								

毎週 (まいしゅう) every week

毎	週								

先週 (せんしゅう) last week

先	週								

五才 (ごさい) five years old

五	才								

天才 (てんさい) genius

天	才										

毎日 (まいにち) every day

毎	日										

半分 (はんぶん) half

半	分										

半日 (はんにち) a half day

半	日										

月曜日 (げつようび) Monday

月	曜	日						

水曜日 (すいようび) Wednesday

水	曜	日						

金曜日 (きんようび) Friday

金	曜	日						

2 Workbook 2: Workbook Activities

2 | Kanji Drills 漢字ドリル

● 1. Writing counters and suffixes in kanji

Look at the following pictures and answer each question using this lesson's kanji.

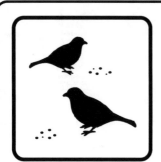

1. 鳥は何羽いますか。

_____

2. 6月は何週間、ありますか。

_____

3. 6月4日は何曜日ですか。

_____

ひろこさん
けん君

5 ½ yrs old   14 yrs old

4. けん君は何才ですか。

_____

5. ひろこさんは何才ですか。

_____

● **2. Fill in the Kanji**
Fill in the appropriate kanji in the blanks for each sentence.

1.　　　　う　　もう　　　　　　よん　まん　えん
　　この ＿＿ ＿＿ ぶとんは、＿＿ ＿＿ ＿＿ しました。
　　This feather (down) quilt cost 40,000 yen.

2.　　せん　しゅう　　くるま　　なお
　　＿＿ ＿＿、＿＿を＿＿ してもらいました。
　　I had my car fixed last week.

3.　　　ど　　よう　　び　　　　よう　　　　　　きん　よう　　び
　　＿＿ ＿＿ ＿＿は＿＿ じが あるから、＿＿ ＿＿ ＿＿は どう？
　　Since I have things to do on Saturday how about Friday?

4.　　　　　に　　じゅう　ろく　さい
　　わたしは、＿＿ ＿＿＿＿＿＿ ＿＿に なりました。
　　I turned 26 years old.

5.　　　　　く　　がつ　なか　　あ
　　じゃあ、こんどは＿＿ ＿＿ ＿＿ばに＿＿ いましょう。
　　Ok then, let's meet next time in the middle of September.

6.　　まい　とし　　いもうと　　　　　に　ほん　　　かえ
　　＿＿ ＿＿、＿＿といっしょに ＿＿ ＿＿に ＿＿ ります。
　　Every year I return to Japan (together) with my younger sister.

7.　　まい　しゅう　にち　よう　び　　さかな　　　　い
　　＿＿ ＿＿＿＿＿＿ ＿＿ ＿＿に ＿＿つりに ＿＿ きます。
　　Every Sunday I go fishing.

2 | **Usage Activities 文法アクティビティー**

● 3. Reading comprehension
Translate the following on a separate piece of paper or type in an electronic device.

おおさか の じしん
大阪の地震   *Shaking the ground is only one of the things that happen in Japan when an earthquake disrupts life.*

❶ 日本は、活火山が 100以上ある国で、2017年には 2000以上の地震が起きました。

❷ 2018年に、大阪で震度 6 の地震が起きました。

❸ この地震はこれまでの地震より小さいですが、被害は大きかったです。

❹ その理由の一つは、大都市で起きたことです。

❺ 次は、地震が起きた時間でした。

❻ 朝8時ごろだったので、通勤や通学をしている人に大きい影響が出ました。

❼ その日は電車が動かなくなったので、タクシー乗り場に長い列ができました。

❽ 帰る方法がなくて、歩いて帰る人もたくさんいました。

❾ いろんな影響で、会社や工場も営業できなくなりました。

❿ ひどい所では、しばらくガスや電気が使えなかったんです。

⓫ 最初の 2 、3 日は、コンビニが品切れにもなりました。

2，3日
（にさんにち）means "two or three days".

⓬ 地震の後は余震を怖がって、寝られない人がたくさんいました。

⓭ みんなは次の地震を心配しながら、生活しています。

● 4. Reading comprehension questions
After translating the following questions about the reading comprehension into English, answer in Japanese below.

1. どうして大阪の地震は被害が大きかったんですか。理由を 2 つ書いて下さい。

Translation: _____

Answer: _____

2. 日本人は普通、通勤や通学にタクシーを使いますか。

Translation: _____

Answer: _____

3. どうして歩いて帰ったんですか。

Translation: _____

Answer: _____

4. 地震の後は、全部の家のガスや電気が使えませんでしたか。

Translation: _____

Answer: _____

5. 地震の後、どんな物がすぐ品切れになると思いますか。

Translation: _____

Answer: _____

6. 大きい地震の後に、何がよく来ますか。

Translation: _____

Answer: _____

● **5. Fill in the blanks**
Fill in the missing part based on the English sentence.

1. ここは＿＿＿＿＿＿＿＿＿＿＿＿＿＿んです。

    There are a lot of tourists here.

2. 私^{わたし}のおばあちゃんは＿＿＿＿＿＿＿＿＿＿＿＿んです。

    My grandmother can't move by herself.

3. 何<sup>なに</sup >を＿＿＿＿＿＿＿＿＿＿＿＿んですか。

    What are you scared of?

4. 昔^{むかし}の＿＿＿＿＿＿＿＿＿＿＿＿、窓^{まど}の外^{そと}を見^みていました。

    I was looking out the window while recalling old days.

5. 先生^{せんせい}の話^{はなし}を＿＿＿＿＿＿＿＿＿＿＿、ペンをかばんに入^いれました。

    While listening to what my teacher was saying, I put my pen in my bag.

● **6. Question and Answer**
Answer the following questions as if you were directly asked.

1. あなたの住^すんでいる国^{くに}に、火山^{かざん}がありますか。

    ＿＿＿＿＿＿＿＿＿＿＿＿＿＿＿＿＿＿＿＿＿＿＿＿

2. あなたの町^{まち}で大雨^{おおあめ}で被害^{ひがい}が起^おきたことがありますか。

    ＿＿＿＿＿＿＿＿＿＿＿＿＿＿＿＿＿＿＿＿＿＿＿＿

3. 近所^{きんじょ}のレストランは、何時^{なんじ}ごろまで営業^{えいぎょう}していますか。

    ＿＿＿＿＿＿＿＿＿＿＿＿＿＿＿＿＿＿＿＿＿＿＿＿

4. 何^{なに}をしながら、日本語^{に ほん ご}を勉強^{べん きょう}しますか。

_____

5. あなたは、いつもどんなことに注意^{ちゅう い}していますか。

_____

● 7. Translation

Translate the following sentences into Japanese.

1. I was troubled because my car didn't work.

_____

2. You should be careful when you walk this street.

_____

3. After the big earthquake happened, we decided to stay at home for 2 or 3 days.

_____

4. I couldn't buy a laptop computer because it was out of stock. (sold out)

_____

5. You should wear a raincoat when it's raining.

_____

● **8. Visual clue questions**

Look at the picture, translate the question on the first line, then answer in Japanese using 〜(な)んです grammar pattern.

1. 何をするのが好きですか。

_____

_____

2. よく何をしますか。

_____

_____

3. 誰が怖いですか。

_____

_____

4. 去年、何がありましたか。

_____

_____

5. お店はどうですか。

_____

_____

2 | Answer Key 答え合わせ

Short Dialogue (translation)

Friend	How is the store recently?
Hiroshi	It's busy. Since it's hotter this year than last, cold things are selling well.
Friend	Once summer vacation starts, you'll get more customers.
Hiroshi	Yes. Every day during summer vacation, we are open until 12 at night. At night the part-time staff is working hard.
Friend	Actually our son is looking for a part-time job. If you need people, can I ask that you consider my son?
Hiroshi	Sure. My wife is helping with the register work while doing housework. So I would be happy if your son could come.

1. Writing counters and suffixes in kanji (answers)

1. 二羽、います。
2. 五週間、あります。
3. 木曜日です。
4. 五才半です。
5. 十四才です。

2. Fill in the kanji (answers)

1. この羽毛ぶとんは、四万円しました。
2. 先週、車を直してもらいました。
3. 土曜日は用じがあるから、金曜日は どう？
4. わたしは、二十六才に なりました。
5. じゃあ、こんどは九月半ばに会いましょう。
6. 毎年、妹といっしょに日本に帰ります。
7. 毎週日曜日に魚つりに行きます。

3. Reading comprehension (translation)

❶ Japan is a country with over 100 active volcanoes, and in 2017 over 2,000 earthquakes occurred.
❷ In 2018, there was a scale 6 (on the Japanese earthquake scale) earthquake in Osaka.
❸ This earthquake was smaller than earthquakes up until now, but the damage was big.
❹ One of the reasons for this is it occurred in a big city.
❺ Next is the time that the earthquake occurred.
❻ Since it was 8 in the morning, there was a large effect on people commuting to school and work.
❼ On that day, since the trains stopped running, long lines formed at the taxi stands.
❽ Having no way to return home, there were a lot of people walking home.
❾ Due to various effects (of the earthquake), companies and factories became unable to operate.
❿ In the bad places, gas and electricity became unusable for some time.
⓫ For the first 2 to 3 days, convenience stores also ran out of goods.
⓬ Fearing aftershocks after the earthquake, there were a lot of people that couldn't sleep.
⓭ Everyone is living while worrying about the next earthquake.

4. Reading comprehension questions (sample answers)

1. Translation: How come there was a lot of damage for the Osaka earthquake? Write 2 reasons.

   Answer(s):   大阪は大都市だからです。

   地震が通勤と通学の時間に起きたからです。

---

2. Translation: Do Japanese people normally use taxis to commute to school and work?

   Answer(s):   いいえ、使いません。

   いいえ、地震で電車が止まったから、使いました。

---

3. Translation: Why did they walk home?

   Answer(s):   帰る方法がなかったからです。

   電車が動かなくて、タクシー乗り場に長い列ができていたからです。

---

4. Translation: After the earthquake, were all houses unable to use gas and electricity?

   Answer(s):   いいえ、全部じゃないです。

   被害がひどい所だけです。

---

5. Translation: Which type of items do you think will sell out immediately after an earthquake?

   Answer(s):   水やパンだと思います。

   すぐ食べられる物だと思います。

---

6. Translation: What often follows a large earthquake?

   Answer(s):   余震が来ます。

   津波が来ると思います。

5. Fill in the blanks (answers)

1. ここはたくさんの観光客がいるんです。／ここは観光客が多いんです。／ここは観光客がたくさんいるんです。
2. 私のおばあちゃんは一人で動けないんです。／ 私のおばあちゃんは自分で動けないんです。
3. 何を怖がっているんですか。
4. 昔のことを思い出しながら、窓の外を見ていました。
5. 先生の話を聞きながらペンをかばんに入れました。

6. Question and Answer (sample answers)

1. Are there volcanoes in the country that you live in?

   はい、あります。／ いいえ、ないと思います。

2. Has there been any damage from heavy rain in your town?

はい、あります。 ／ いいえ、今_{いま}までありません。

3. How late are restaurants in your neighborhood open until?

10時_じごろまで営業_{えいぎょう}しています。 ／ 24時間_{じかん}、営業_{えいぎょう}しています。

4. What do you do while studying Japanese?

音楽_{おんがく}を聴_ききながら、勉強_{べんきょう}します。 ／ 何_{なに}もしません。

5. What do you always pay attention to?

車_{くるま}の運転_{うんてん}に注意_{ちゅうい}をしています。／ お金_{かね}の使_{つか}い方_{かた}に注意_{ちゅうい}しています。／ 食_たべる物_{もの}に注意_{ちゅうい}しています。

7. Translation (answers)

1. 車_{くるま}が動_{うご}かなかったから、困_{こま}りました。
2. この道_{みち}を歩_{ある}く時_{とき}は、注意_{ちゅうい}したほうがいいです／注意_{ちゅうい}して下_{くだ}さい。
3. 大_{おお}きい地震_{じしん}が起_おきた後_{あと}、2、3日_{にち}は家_{いえ}にいることにしました。
4. 品切_{しなぎ}れだったので、ノートパソコンが買_かえませんでした。
5. 雨_{あめ}が降_ふっている時_{とき}、レインコートを着_きたほうがいいです。

8. Visual clue questions (answers)

(answers may vary)

1. (甘_{あま}い物_{もの}を)食_たべるのが好_すきなんです。

2. よく 泳_{およ}ぐんです。／よく 水泳_{すいえい}するんです。

3. 社長_{しゃちょう}(ボス)が怖_{こわ}いんです。

4. 火山_{かざん}が噴火_{ふんか}したんです。

5. 忙_{いそが}しいんです。／お客_{きゃく}さんが多_{おお}いんです。

Vocabulary Builder:
Groups G, H, I, J

■ Group G: people

社会人 しゃ かい じん	working adult
社員 しゃ いん	employee
正社員 せい しゃ いん	full employee; full-time worker
同僚 どう りょう	co-worker
上司 じょう し	boss; chief; superior
社長 しゃ ちょう	company president
部下 ぶ か	junior staff; follower
受付(係) うけ つけ がかり	receptionist

■ Group H: Japanese house areas (Part 1)

玄関 げん かん	entrance; front door area
居間 い ま	living room
寝室 しん しつ	bedroom
和室 わ しつ	Japanese-style room
洋室 よう しつ	Western-style room
畳 たたみ	tatami mat; Japanese straw floor coverings
襖 ふすま	fusuma (Japanese sliding screen)
靴箱 くつ ばこ	shoebox

Words introduced on this page shouldn't require much for you to learn them since they are all borrowed from English.

■ Group I: "AS IS" borrowed words

These words are used exactly like their English counterpart.

フローリング　(flooring)

マット (floor mat / mat)

メートル (meter)

ドアベル (doorbell)

カーペット　(carpet)

フィート　(feet) (measuring word)

ストレス (stress)

■ Group J: Katakana words that require explanation

These words require some explanation despite being derived from English.

English words with マイ for "my" added in front of them show that a person has pride in the item that they have purchased or are in the process of paying down a loan. This is not for things that are merely being rented.

マイホーム (my own house)

マイカー (my own car)

マイペース (a pace that works for me)

This translates to "my pace", but Japanese use it to describe how a person does things in their own time. For example, they might say, "He is my pace", but that doesn't mean that "he is the same speed as me". It means "he does something when he wants to, without regard for other peoples' pace".

マイブーム (thing I am into right now)

This is made from the English words "my boom" to denote something a person is really interested in at the moment.

| 3 | 21 PAGES | 6 USAGE SECTIONS | 30 NEW WORDS |

Lesson 3:
Others Wants and the Five Senses

3 New Words 新しい言葉

Nouns etc.

蚊 (か)	mosquito		暮らし (く)	living; day-to-day life
田舎 (いなか)	countryside; back-country		匂い (にお)	smell; aroma; odor
実家 (じっか)	one's parents' home		袋 (ふくろ)	bag; packet
人材 (じんざい)	manpower; human resources		ほこり	dust
あちこち	here and there; all over the place		さっき	a little while ago
救急車 (きゅうきゅうしゃ)	ambulance		ふた	lid; cover; cap
扇子 (せんす)	Japanese folding fan		(お)鍋 (なべ)	a pan; a pot
最新 (さいしん)	the newest; the latest		白板 (はくばん)	whiteboard
襖 (ふすま)	traditional Japanese sliding door			

> ホワイトボード is also commonly used.

Adjectives

無理(な) (むり)	unreasonable; impossible; overdoing
懐かしい (なつ)	nostalgic; bring back memories

Adverb

まず	first (off all); to start with

Verbs

たまる	to collect; to save; to pile up		離れる (はな)	to be separated; to be apart
開ける (あ)	to open		開く (ひら)	to open
閉める (し)	to close; to shut		閉じる (と)	to close; to shut
置く (お)	to place; to put		鳴る (な)	to ring

Connectors

そこで	so; accordingly; now; therefore		なぜなら	the reason is; because

3　Japanese Living 日本の暮らし

This section is FULL JAPANESE. Look up words you don't know. The English translation is provided below.

● 部屋のサイズ (Room Sizes)

畳は、床に敷くマットのことで、表面がイグサで編みこまれています。和室には通常、たたみが敷かれています。それに対して、洋室はカーペットやフローリングです。日本の家には、和室と洋室の両方のタイプの部屋が見られます。日本では、部屋の広さを畳の数で表します。畳を数える時は、「畳」と書いて「じょう」と言います。洋室には畳がないことから、「畳」ではなく、「帖(じょう)」という漢字が代わりに使われます。畳のある和室には、どちらの漢字も使えますが、畳があることで「畳」を使うことが多いようです。

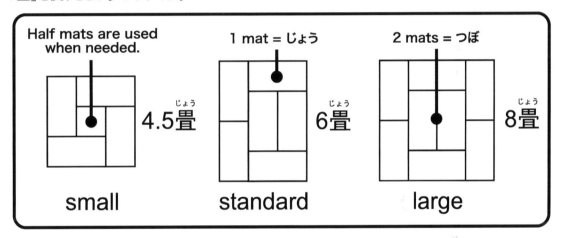

畳の大きさは、日本の地域によって違いますが、サイズはだいたい３フィート×６フィート(１メートル×２メートル)です。家の広告では、部屋のサイズは「帖(畳)」で、そして家全体は「坪」数で表されます。一坪は、畳2畳分ぐらいの大きさです。

たたみ is a mat laid on floors with a surface woven out of straw. In わしつ (Japanese-style rooms), たたみ mats normally cover the floor, whereas ようしつ (Western-style rooms) have carpeting or wooden floors. In Japanese homes, both types of rooms can be seen. In Japan, the size of a room is represented by the amount of tatami mats. The counter for tatami mats is written with the kanji 畳 (たたみ), but it is read as じょう. The 帖 (じょう) kanji is used instead of 畳 for western-style rooms since there are no たたみ mats. Japanese-style rooms with たたみ mats can use either kanji, but it seems that using 畳 kanji is common.

Although the size of 1 tatami varies depending on the region in Japan, the size is roughly 3 feet by 6 feet (1 meter by 2 meters). When advertising, the size of rooms tend to be counted in じょう while the entire house is counted in つぼ which is the size of two tatami mats.

● Shoeboxes

靴箱 sounds like it might be the box shoes come in when you buy them, however this actually is the place in the entrance of a Japanese home where shoes are stored. Shoes that are used daily are often left in the 玄関 (entrance area), so they can easily be put on when leaving the house, but other shoes are put in the 靴箱.

げた

In olden times, Japanese people wore wooden shoes similar to sandals called 下駄, so 靴箱 is also referred to as 下駄箱. As for what the box is called when you buy shoes, that is just a 靴の箱. To sound trendy, stores selling 靴箱 often refer to them as the borrowed word, シューズボックス.

---

3 | Word Usage 言葉の使い方

W-1	暮らし	living; day-to-day life

暮らし by itself means "living", but is often combined with other nouns.
When combined with other nouns、くらし changes to ぐらし。

アパート暮らし (apartment living)　　一人暮らし (living alone)
貧乏暮らし (living poor)　　　　　　　田舎暮らし (country living)
都会暮らし (city living)　　　　　　　その日暮らし (living day by day; scraping by)

EXAMPLE SENTENCES

1. 大学生になってから、一人暮らしを始めました。
   After becoming a college student, I began living alone.

2. 田舎暮らしより、都会暮らしのほうが楽しいです。
   City living is more enjoyable than country living.

3. マイホームを買うまで、アパート暮らしをしています。
   Until I buy my own home, I am living in an apartment.

○○暮らしをする makes
the verb "living in ○○"

3 | Verb Usage 動詞の使い方

V-1	たまる	to collect; to save; to pile up (DESCRIPTIVE)	regular
	1. (something) がたまる	(something) piles up	

たまる is only used to describe a "build up" and not the action of "saving".

EXAMPLE SENTENCES

1. 父はストレスがたまっているんです。
   My father is stressed. (stress is built up)

2. ほこりがたまっているから、掃除をしましょう。
   Let's clean since the dust has collected.

3. お風呂のお湯がたまりましたか。
   Has the hot water in the bath filled up?

RELATED VERB(S)

Japanese From Zero! ④ V12-8. ためる (to save)

 もっと詳しく… More Details ⓘ

Different kanji for たまる and ためる based on item type
Depending on intent, either 貯 or 溜 is used for the た part of たまる (to save).

If you are collecting/saving money or items used similarly to money such as points or stamp cards, or even paid vacation days, then 貯まる・貯める is used. All other items use 溜まる・溜める.

EXAMPLE SENTENCES

1. お金を貯めています。
   I am saving money.

2. お風呂にお湯を溜めました。
   I filled the bathtub with hot water.

3. お金が貯まりました。
   Money has accumulated.

4. お風呂にお湯が溜まりました。
   The bathtub has filled with hot water.

To avoid confusion, you can just use hiragana like Japanese people often do. After all, you can't use the wrong kanji if you aren't using kanji. ☺

V-2	離<ruby>はな</ruby>れる	to separate; to be apart; to leave	いる/える
	1. (something) を／と／から離れる	to be apart from (something)	

Whether you use を, と or から to mark the thing or place you are separating from, the meaning is the same.

EXAMPLE SENTENCES

1. 実家<ruby>じっか</ruby>を離<ruby>はな</ruby>れてから、もう十年<ruby>じゅうねん</ruby>になります。
   It's already been 10 years since I left my home. (parent's home)

2. 転勤<ruby>てんきん</ruby>するので、東京<ruby>とうきょう</ruby>から離<ruby>はな</ruby>れることになりました。
   Since I am transferring, I'm going to leave Tokyo.

3. 家族<ruby>かぞく</ruby>と離<ruby>はな</ruby>れた所<ruby>ところ</ruby>に住<ruby>す</ruby>んでいるので、よくメールをしています。
   Since I live away from my family, I often e-mail them.

V-3	置<ruby>お</ruby>く	to place; to put	regular
	1. (something) を (location) に置く	to place (something) in/on (location)	

EXAMPLE SENTENCES

1. どこにリモコンを置<ruby>お</ruby>いたの？
   Where did you put the remote control?

2. テーブルの上<ruby>うえ</ruby>に置<ruby>お</ruby>いた鍵<ruby>かぎ</ruby>を取<ruby>と</ruby>って下<ruby>くだ</ruby>さい。
   Please get the keys that I put on the table.

> かぎ (key) is modified by テーブルのうえにおいた (put on the table). "Modifying with verbs" is introduced in Book 4 Lesson 3.

3. コンピューターの近<ruby>ちか</ruby>くに飲<ruby>の</ruby>み物<ruby>もの</ruby>を置<ruby>お</ruby>かないでください。
   Please don't place drinks near the computer.

V-4	鳴<ruby>な</ruby>る	to ring	regular
	1. (something) が鳴る	(something) rings	

鳴<ruby>な</ruby>る is used with electronic devices such as pagers, telephones and also bells.

EXAMPLE SENTENCES

1. ドアベルが壊れているから、今は鳴りません。
   The doorbell is broken, so it doesn't ring now.

2. 誰かの携帯が鳴っています！消してください！
   Someone's cell phone is ringing! Please turn it off!

V-5	開ける	to open (ACTION)	いる/える
	1. (thing)を あける	to open (thing)	

	閉める	to close; to shut (ACTION)	いる/える
	1. (thing)を しめる	to close a (thing)	

あける (to open) is used when removing something covering the opening of things which have *open space inside,* such as buildings, boxes, bags, and bottles etc.

しめる (to close), the opposite of あける, is used to seal off or cover up the opening of things that have *open space inside,* such as buildings, boxes, bags, and bottles etc.

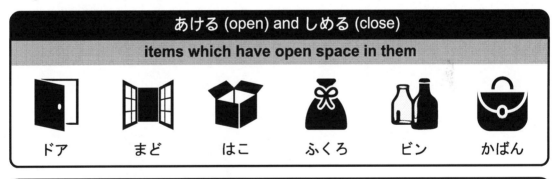

あける (open) and しめる (close)

items which have open space in them

ドア　　まど　　はこ　　ふくろ　　ビン　　かばん

EXAMPLE SENTENCES

1. 窓を開けました。 | I opened the window.
2. 窓を閉めました。 | I closed the window.
3. ドアを開けてください。 | Please open the door.
4. ドアを閉めてください。 | Please close the door.
5. このビンを開けてくれますか。 | Will you open this bottle for me?
6. このビンを閉めてくれますか。 | Will you close this bottle for me?

EXAMPLE CONVERSATION

1. **Conversation between friends.**

   A: 窓を開けたら、気持ちがいいですね。

   B: でも、蚊が入るから、閉めましょう。

   > ～ましょう is being used as a softly worded command.

   A: It would feel nice if we opened the window.

   B: But since the mosquitos will come in, close it.

V-6	開く	to open; to unseal (ACTION/DESCRIPTIVE)	regular
	1. (thing)を ひらく	to open (thing)	

	閉じる	to close; to shut (ACTION/DESCRIPTIVE)	regular
	1. (thing)を とじる	to close a (thing)	

ひらく (to open) is used when opening items that are folded or pressed together such as umbrellas, books etc. These items do not have any open space inside.

とじる (to close) is used to close items that were originally folded or pressed together such as umbrellas, books etc. Doors and windows can use BOTH sets of verbs.

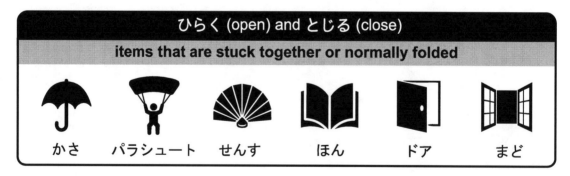

ひらく (open) and とじる (close)
items that are stuck together or normally folded

かさ　　パラシュート　　せんす　　ほん　　ドア　　まど

ひらく and とじる are interesting because they can be both an ACTION using を and a DESCRIPTION using が.

ドアを開きました。 — ACTION
I opened the door.

ドアが開きました。 — DESCRIPTION
The door opened.

EXAMPLE SENTENCES

1. 家の中で傘を開かないでください。
Please don't open the umbrella inside.

2. 風でドアが開いてしまいました。
The door opened due to the wind.

3. テストの時は本を閉じましょう。
Close your books when we test.

4. パラシュートが開かなかったら大変です。
If the parachute doesn't open, it will be bad.

5. 外は寒いので窓を閉じてください。
Please close the window since it's cold outside.

6. ダイエットしてるからデザートメニューを閉じた。
Because I'm dieting, I closed the dessert menu.

EXAMPLE CONVERSATIONS

1. **Conversation between a teacher and a student.**

A: 森田さん、教科書の 65ページを開きましたか。

B: すみません。まだ開いていません。

A: Morita, did you open the textbook to page 65?

B: Sorry, I haven't opened it yet.

2. **Conversation between a Japanese person and a foreigner.**

A: この扇子は、どうやって閉じるんですか。

B: こうやって閉じるんですよ。

A: How do you close this Japanese folding fan?

B: You close it like this.

もっと詳しく… More Details

Why can doors and windows use both forms of open and close?
Doors and windows are special because they aren't only covering up the opening of a room or open space, but they are also "stuck" to the window or door frame.

「窓をあける」= Remove the item covering up the opening of the room.
「窓をひらく」= Open the window that is "stuck" to the window frame.

Opening and closing non-physical things
ひらく is good for opening non-physical things such as windows on a computer or a website. You can even "open your heart". Of course closing a window or website uses とじる, however, closing your heart uses another version of close using the same kanji, 閉ざす (とざす) which isn't used for many other situations.

3 | Grammar and Usage 文法と使い方

● 3-1. Using 〜っぱなし (leaving something on; keep ...-ing)

By adding ~っぱなし to the い form of a verb, you can say that an action is continuing without stopping, for example someone talking non-stop.

For some actions っぱなし can just mean something was left in a state, like a door being left open. っぱなし sounds negative, and is often used when complaining.

constantly; non-stop; without break ~っぱなし					
regular い form + っぱなし	たつ すわる	→ →	たち すわり	→ →	たちっぱなし (standing without break) すわりっぱなし (sitting constantly)
いる/える minus る + っぱなし	たべる あける	→ →	たべ あけ	→ →	たべっぱなし (eating non-stop) あけっぱなし (left open)
irregulars etc.	する	→	し	→	しっぱなし (doing non-stop)
★ As a shortcut, just replace ます with っぱなし from the ます form of any verb.					

EXAMPLES

置きます (to put; to place)　　　置きっぱなし (leave behind)

つけます (to turn on)　　　　　つけっぱなし (left on)

しゃべる (to talk)　　　　　　しゃべりっぱなし (talk non-stop)

歩く (to walk)　　　　　　　歩きっぱなし (walk without break)

EXAMPLE SENTENCES

1. ドアが開けっぱなしだから、閉めて下さい。
   Please close the door since it's been left open.

2. 体育の時間は、走りっぱなしだったね。
   We were running constantly during gym, weren't we?

3. 財布が置きっぱなしなのは、よくないですよ。
   It's not good to leave your wallet out in the open.

EXAMPLE CONVERSATION

1. **Conversation between office workers**

A: 私は本当に会議が嫌いです。

B: どうして？

A: 社長がいつも、しゃべりっぱなしだからです。

A: I really dislike meetings.

B: How come?

A: Because the president always talks non-stop.

● **3-2. She said, he said 〜んだって、〜って**

When talking about something YOU want, you use ほしい and たい form.

EXAMPLE SENTENCES

1. 新しいアイフォンがほしいです。
   I want a new iPhone.

2. 沖縄に旅行したいです。
   I want to travel to Okinawa.

However, in Japanese culture, people commonly avoid speaking with certainty about other people. So a Japanese person will often avoid saying "he wants to _____" or "she wants a _____". Instead they relay what they heard, or what they observed. One common method is just to relay what the person themselves said.

EXAMPLE SENTENCES

1. お母さんは新しいアイフォンがほしいと言いました。
   Mom said she wants a new iPhone.

2. お父さんは沖縄に旅行したいと言いました。
   Dad said he wants to travel to Okinawa.

〜と言いました can be a bit "stiff" when speaking casually, so to sound more natural, use the んだって or just って ending. The ん shows emphasis or emotion.

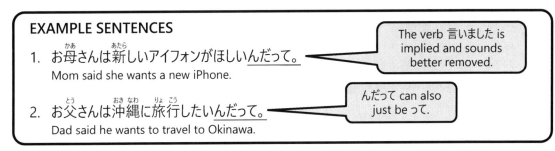

EXAMPLE SENTENCES

1. お母さんは新しいアイフォンがほしいんだって。
   Mom said she wants a new iPhone.

   The verb 言いました is implied and sounds better removed.

2. お父さんは沖縄に旅行したいんだって。
   Dad said he wants to travel to Okinawa.

   んだって can also just be って.

We can also ask questions in this form. NOTE: This is ONLY used with good friends!

1. 今、なんて？
   What did you/he/she say just now?

   > なんだって can also be said, but can sound a bit arrogant as it shows a bit of disbelief. Such as "WHAT DID YOU SAY!". なんて (no っ) is a better choice for standard conversation with friends.

2. だれだって？ だれって？
   Who did you/he/she say it is?

3. いつ日本に行くんだって？
   When did you/he/she say they were going to Japan?

EXAMPLE CONVERSATIONS

1. **Conversation between friends at a party.**

   A: まりちゃんは今日来るって言ってた？

   B: ううん。来ないんだって。

   A: どうして？
   B: 気分が悪いって。

   A: Did Mari say she was coming today?
   B: No, she said she isn't coming.
   A: Why?
   B: She said she isn't feeling good.

んだって means you heard the information directly from the person being talked about. In later lessons, we will learn that そうです and みたいです can be based on observation or what we have heard about the person.

RELATED GRAMMAR

Japanese From Zero! ① Section 6-3. Wanting and not wanted
Japanese From Zero! ③ Section 4-2. いう (to say)
Japanese From Zero! ⑤ Section 2-2. Using 〜(な)んです when emphasizing

● **3-3. Using って to say, "what do you mean?"**

って can also be said after a phrase or word to ask "what do you mean by that?" The って can also imply many other questions such as who, where etc.

> (phrase or word) って?
> **What do you mean by (phrase or word)?**

EXAMPLE CONVERSATIONS:

1. **Informal conversation between friends**

   A: 来週、マークの家に遊びに行く。

   B: マークって、誰？

   A: 昔の友達だよ。

   A: I am going to Mark's house next week.
   B: Who is Mark?
   A: An old friend.

2. **Informal conversation between a foreigner and a Japanese person**

   A: 歴史の授業が難しい・・・

   B: 歴史って？

   A: Historyのことだよ。

   A: REKISHI class is difficult...
   B: What is REKISHI?
   A: It's "history".

3. **Polite conversation between a foreigner and a Japanese person**

   A: 「トトロ」の曲を聴いたことがありますか。

   B: 「トトロ」って？

   A: 有名な日本の映画です。

   A: Have you ever listened to the "Totoro" song?
   B: What's "Totoro"?
   A: It's a famous Japanese movie.

● **3-4. What someone else wants 〜がる (adjectives)**

〜がる is used to directly relay what other people feel. Similar to こわがる, ほしい becomes the verb ほしがる. Many adjectives can drop い and add がる to make a verb.

EXAMPLES (い ADJECTIVES)

欲しい (I want) → 欲しがる (other person wants)

怖い (I am scared/it is scary) → 怖がる (other person is scared)

暑い (I am hot/it is hot) → 暑がる (other person is hot)

寂しい (I am lonely) → 寂しがる (other person is lonely)

When using a 〜がる verb the object marker を marks any object.

うちの犬は、いつも私が食べている物を欲しがります。
Our dog always wants what I am eating.

EXAMPLE SENTENCES

1. 彼はお金持ちだから、何も欲しがりません。
   Because he is rich, he doesn't want anything.

   > As you can see, ほしがる can be conjugated like any other verb.

2. 竹中先生はもっと広い白板を欲しがっています。
   Miss Takenaka (teacher) wants a wider whiteboard.

   > ます form shows a "tendency", but ています form shows the "current state".

3. うちの子は私が近くにいなかったら、寂しがります。
   When my child isn't close to me, he is sad.

4. 弟は夜、クーラーをつけなかったら、暑がります。
   My little brother feels hot if we don't turn on the cooler at night.

It's important to note that adjectives that use がる are limited to feelings. がる can't be just added to any adjective.

な adjectives can also simply add がる when talking about other people.

EXAMPLES (な ADJECTIVES)

嫌 (disagreeable; unpleasant) → 嫌がる (disagreeable for another person)

残念 (I feel unfortunate) → 残念がる (other person feels unfortunate)

迷惑 (I am bothered) → 迷惑がる (other person is bothered)

📖 もっと詳（くわ）しく… More Details

Types of people...
Some がる verbs are commonly used to describe people with certain tendencies.

怖（こわ）がり (one who scares easily) 　　暑（あつ）がり (one who easily gets hot)
寂（さみ）しがり (one who easily gets lonely) 寒（さむ）がり (one who easily gets cold)

1. 女性（じょせい）の多（おお）くは寒（さむ）がりです。
   Many women tend to easily feel cold.

屋さん (やさん) is normally added after a person's job. Someone who runs a book store is a 本屋さん (ほんやさん) and a real estate agent is a 不動産屋さん (ふどうさん やさん). So you might hear や or やさん added to the words above.

● 3-5. What someone else wants 〜がる (たい form verbs)

All たい form verbs can be changed into がる form to express another person's wants.

EXAMPLES
食（た）べたい (I want to eat) 　　→　食（た）べたがる (someone wants to eat)
来（き）たい (I want to come) 　　→　来（き）たがる (someone wants to come)
歩（ある）きたい (I want to walk) →　歩（ある）きたがる (someone wants to walk)

EXAMPLE SENTENCES

1. 主人（しゅじん）は会社（かいしゃ）から帰（かえ）ったら、ビールを飲（の）みたがります。
   When my husband comes home from work, he wants to drink beer.

   > 〜たがります is used for "habitual" wants.

2. 日本（にほん）の話（はなし）をしたら、アメリカ人（じん）の友達（ともだち）は日本（にほん）へ行（い）きたがりました。
   When I talked about Japan, my American friend wanted to go to Japan.

3. 子供（こども）が夏休（なつやす）みにハワイへ旅行（りょこう）したがっています。
   My children want to travel to Hawaii on summer break.

   > ている form shows the "current state".

4. 姉（あね）が仕事（しごと）を辞（や）めたがっていますが、今（いま）は無理（むり）だと思（おも）います。
   My older sister wants to quit her job, but I think it's impossible right now.

RELATED GRAMMAR

Japanese From Zero! ③ Section 9-5. The たい verb form

● 3-6. Describing what you feel using 〜がする

We already know words like きこえる (to be able to hear) and みえる (to be able to see). Using NOUN + がする we can make a grammar pattern in Japanese that relays feelings from each of your five senses. The first three follow the same pattern.

聴覚 (ちょうかく) (hearing)	
〜音がする (to hear a sound)	変な音がする (to hear a strange sound)
〜声がする (to hear voices)	変な声がする (to hear a strange voice)

EXAMPLES

雨の音がする	hear the rain
台所で包丁の音がする	hear the sound of a knife in the kitchen
お母さんの声がする	hear my mother's voice
鳥の鳴き声がする	hear birds singing

EXAMPLE CONVERSATION

1. **Conversation between friends at a haunted house.**

   A: お化け屋敷に来たのは、初めてだね。

   B: そうだね。あ！何かあそこで音がしてる！

   > The sound hasn't stopped so we use ている form to show that it is ongoing.

   A: 音じゃなくて、人の声じゃない？

   B: ほんとだ。誰かが泣いてる。怖い〜！

   > In casual speaking, dropping う from ほんとう is common.

   A: It's your first time coming to a haunted house.

   B: Yeah. Ah! I hear a sound over there!

   A: Isn't it a person's voice, not a sound?

   B: You're right. Someone is crying. Scary!

味覚 (みかく) (taste)	
〜味がする (to taste)	変な味がする (to have a strange taste)

EXAMPLES

醤油の味がする	to taste like soy sauce
懐かしい味がする	to taste nostalgic
ひどい味がする	to taste awful/disgusting

EXAMPLE CONVERSATION

1. **Conversation between a couple.**

   A: はい、ハンバーグができたよ。食べてみて。

   B: うわあ、おいしそうだね。いただきます。

   A: 私が好きな納豆とキムチをいっしょに入れてみたの。どう？

   B: う〜ん。色んな味がするね。お水、ください。。。

   A: The Salisbury steak is done. Try it.

   B: Wah, looks delicious. Let's eat. (I will receive)

   A: I put my favorite natto and kimchi in it. How is it?

   B: Hmm. I taste many flavors. Give me some water please.

もっと詳しく… More Details ⓘ

Taste of mother???

Japanese refer to "mother's cooking" as ママの味 or お母さんの味. It has nothing to do with taking a bite out of or licking your mother's arm to taste her.

EXAMPLE SENTENCE

1. お母さんの味が一番です。
   Mom's cooking is the best.

臭覚 (しゅうかく) (smell)

〜においがする (to smell)　　　変なにおいがする (to smell a strange smell)

EXAMPLES

コーヒーのにおいがする (smells of coffee)　　変なにおいがする (smells strange)

いいにおいがする (smells sweet and good)　　魚のにおいがする (smells of fish)

EXAMPLE CONVERSATION

1. **Conversation between friends.**

   A: この喫茶店、タバコのにおいがしますね。

   B: そうですね。違う所に行きましょうか。

   A: This coffee shop smells like cigarettes.

   B: Yeah. How about we go to a different place.

もっと詳しく… More Details ⓘ

There are two kanji for におい.
匂い for good smells, and 臭い for bad.

臭い can also be read as、くさい to mean "smelly". When used as "odor" it's always read におい. To be safe you can always just use hiragana.

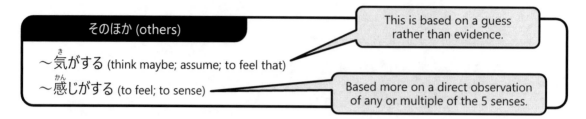

そのほか (others)

〜気<ruby>気<rt>き</rt></ruby>がする (think maybe; assume; to feel that)
〜<ruby>感<rt>かん</rt></ruby>じがする (to feel; to sense)

> This is based on a guess rather than evidence.

> Based more on a direct observation of any or multiple of the 5 senses.

Both of these have slight nuance differences as you can see. They are often used interchangeably by Japanese natives. But let's explore the differences. We have covered hearing, taste, and smell. Sight, and touch do not directly use the がする pattern, however <ruby>気<rt>き</rt></ruby> (spirit; mind; heart) and <ruby>感<rt>かん</rt></ruby>じ (feeling; sense; impression) can be used with がする to cover multiple senses. 気がする is very close to と<ruby>思<rt>おも</rt></ruby>う.

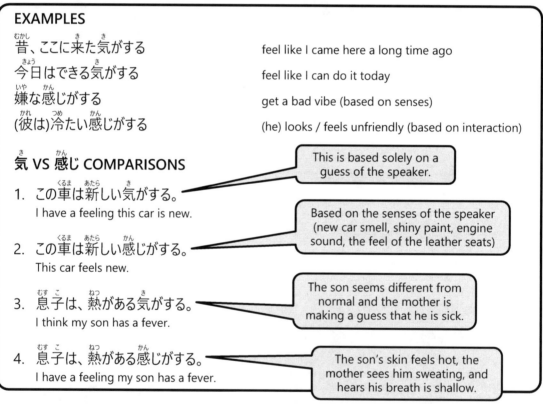

EXAMPLES

<ruby>昔<rt>むかし</rt></ruby>、ここに<ruby>来<rt>き</rt></ruby>た<ruby>気<rt>き</rt></ruby>がする   feel like I came here a long time ago

<ruby>今日<rt>きょう</rt></ruby>はできる<ruby>気<rt>き</rt></ruby>がする   feel like I can do it today

<ruby>嫌<rt>いや</rt></ruby>な<ruby>感<rt>かん</rt></ruby>じがする   get a bad vibe (based on senses)

(<ruby>彼<rt>かれ</rt></ruby>は)<ruby>冷<rt>つめ</rt></ruby>たい<ruby>感<rt>かん</rt></ruby>じがする   (he) looks / feels unfriendly (based on interaction)

<ruby>気<rt>き</rt></ruby> VS <ruby>感<rt>かん</rt></ruby>じ COMPARISONS

1. この<ruby>車<rt>くるま</rt></ruby>は<ruby>新<rt>あたら</rt></ruby>しい<ruby>気<rt>き</rt></ruby>がする。
   I have a feeling this car is new.

> This is based solely on a guess of the speaker.

2. この<ruby>車<rt>くるま</rt></ruby>は<ruby>新<rt>あたら</rt></ruby>しい<ruby>感<rt>かん</rt></ruby>じがする。
   This car feels new.

> Based on the senses of the speaker (new car smell, shiny paint, engine sound, the feel of the leather seats)

3. <ruby>息子<rt>むすこ</rt></ruby>は、<ruby>熱<rt>ねつ</rt></ruby>がある<ruby>気<rt>き</rt></ruby>がする。
   I think my son has a fever.

> The son seems different from normal and the mother is making a guess that he is sick.

4. <ruby>息子<rt>むすこ</rt></ruby>は、<ruby>熱<rt>ねつ</rt></ruby>がある<ruby>感<rt>かん</rt></ruby>じがする。
   I have a feeling my son has a fever.

> The son's skin feels hot, the mother sees him sweating, and hears his breath is shallow.

1. **Conversation between a company president and his employee.**

   A: <ruby>森田<rt>もり た</rt></ruby><ruby>君<rt>くん</rt></ruby>、<ruby>今日<rt>きょう</rt></ruby><ruby>面接<rt>めん せつ</rt></ruby>した<ruby>女<rt>おんな</rt></ruby>の<ruby>子<rt>こ</rt></ruby>はどうだった?

   B: はい。<ruby>学校<rt>がっ こう</rt></ruby>の<ruby>成績<rt>せい せき</rt></ruby>はよかったんですが、おとなしい<ruby>感<rt>かん</rt></ruby>じがしました。

   A: そう。じゃあ、<ruby>受付<rt>うけ つけ</rt></ruby>の<ruby>仕事<rt>し ごと</rt></ruby>は<ruby>難<rt>むずか</rt></ruby>しいかな。

   B: まだ<ruby>分<rt>わ</rt></ruby>かりません。もう<ruby>一度<rt>いち ど</rt></ruby><ruby>面接<rt>めん せつ</rt></ruby>した<ruby>方<rt>ほう</rt></ruby>がいい<ruby>気<rt>き</rt></ruby>がします。

A: Morita, how was the girl that did the interview today?

B: Yes. Her grades were good in school, but she seemed quiet.

A: I see. Well then, I wonder if it would be difficult for her to do receptionist work.

B: I'm not sure yet. I feel like it would be better to do another interview.

📖 もっと詳しく… More Details ⓘ

The difference between おもう (to think) and かんじる (to feel)

かんじる is based on your direct experience using the five senses. おもう can also be based on experience, however it can also be just for an opinion without a fact or when talking about something you guess or imagine in a certain way.

外は寒いと感じます。

> You went outside and felt cold air on your skin.

外は寒いと思います。

> You are actually outside or are inside just saying what you think about what you see.

父の仕事は大変だと感じます。

> You are actually looking at your father working.

父の仕事は大変だと思います。

> You actually saw your father working, OR you heard about his work from someone.

3 | Practice and Review　練習と復習

● 1. Mini Conversation ミニ会話 J → E

Try translating the entire conversation before looking at the translation below.

1. Polite conversation between friends

A: 昨日、家に帰ったら、1階の窓が開けっ放しだったんです。

B: 閉めるのを忘れたんですか。

A: いいえ。それから、2階で変な音がしたんです。

B: ええ！どろぼうですか。

A: いいえ。おばあちゃんが遊びに来ていたのを忘れていました。

A: When returning home yesterday, (I saw) the first-floor window was left open.

B: Did you forget to shut it?

A: No. And also, I heard a strange sound on the second floor.

B: What! A thief?

A: No. I had forgotten that my grandma had come to hang out.

2. Polite conversation between a foreigner and a Japanese mother

A: いい匂いがしますね。何を作っているんですか。

B: すき焼きです。豆腐やお肉や野菜がお鍋に入っているんですよ。

A: 私の家族はきっと食べたがりますね。

B: じゃあ、皆でいっしょに食べませんか。

A: Something smells good. What are you making?

B: It's sukiyaki. Tofu, meat, and vegetables are in a pot.

A: My family surely would want to eat it.

B: Well, how about we all eat together?

3. Casual conversation between boyfriend and girlfriend (named Aki)

A: あきちゃんのことは昔から知っている気がする。

B: ええ、本当？嬉しいな。

うれしい = happiness in the moment
しあわせ = long-term happiness

A: もう離れたくない。これからもずっと一緒にいてくれる？

B: ちょっと待って。それ、プロポーズ？

A: I feel like I've known you from a long time ago.

B: What really? That makes me happy.

A: I don't want to leave you anymore. Will you be with me from now on forever?

B: Hang on. Is that a proposal?

● 2. Mini Conversation ミニ会話 E → J

Look at the English conversations and see if you can figure out the Japanese.
Try to translate the entire conversation first before looking at the translation.

1. Polite conversation between friends at work

A: The president (of the company) today, has been continually mad.

B: He's got a lot of stress.

A: Is it perhaps because everyone's using their smartphones even though it's not lunch break?

B: I don't know. But he did say he wanted good people.

A: 今日の社長は、怒りっぱなしですね。

B: ストレスがたまっているんですよ。

A: 昼休みじゃないのに、皆がスマホを使うからでしょうか。

B: 分かりません。でも、いい人材がほしいと言っていましたよ。

2. Casual conversation between siblings

A: Do you know about the keys that were here?

B: No. Did you lose them?

A: I've been looking all over the place, but they're not there.

B: Ah, I think I just saw them in the entrance (of the house).

A: ここにあった鍵を知らない？

B: ううん。なくしたの？

A: あちこち探しているんだけど、ないの。

B: あ、さっき玄関で見た気がする。

3. Casual conversation between actors

A: I can finally go back home (parent's home) next month. I am really looking forward to it.

B: Where is your home?

A: It's in Aomori prefecture. Since it's far, I really don't return so much.

B: My home (parent's home) is also far. Go and have a good time.

A: 来月、やっと実家へ帰れます。すごく楽しみです。

B: 実家はどちらですか。

A: 青森県です。ここから遠いので、なかなか帰れないんです。

B: 私の実家も遠いんです。楽しんできてください。

● 3. Short Dialogue

A mother is visiting her son's apartment for the first time.

お母さん	「おじゃまします。けんちゃんのアパートに入るの、初めて。」
息子	「どうぞ。ちょっと汚いけど。。。」
お母さん	「変な匂いがする。何の匂い？」
息子	「きっと昨日の晩ご飯の匂いだよ。テーブルに置きっぱなしなんだ。」
お母さん	「じゃあ、窓を開けましょう。くさいよ。」
息子	「蚊が入るから、開けたくないよ。窓はいつも閉めっぱなしなんだ。」
お母さん	「ええ！それはだめでしょう。何とかしようよ。」
息子	「僕はこれでいいの！」

3 Kanji Lesson 3:
東西南北方角

We have collected kanji related to directions in this lesson.

3 | New Kanji　新しい漢字

172	木	8 画	east		
			くんよみ	ひがし	
			おんよみ	トウ	
			中東 (ちゅう・とう) Middle East		東日本 (ひがし・に・ほん) east Tokyo
			東 (ひがし) east		東洋 (とう・よう) orient
			東京 (とう・きょう) Tokyo		東北 (とう・ほく) north-east
			東		

173	西	6 画	west		
			くんよみ	にし	
			おんよみ	セイ、サイ	
			東西 (とう・ざい) east and west		西海岸 (にし・かい・がん) west coast
			西 (にし) west		関西 (かん・さい) the Kansai region
			西日 (にし・び) the setting sun		西洋 (せい・よう) the west; Western world
			西		

174	十	9 画	south		
			くんよみ	みなみ	
			おんよみ	ナン、ナ	
			南 (みなみ) south		南米 (なん・べい) South America
			南西 (なん・せい) southwest		南北 (なん・ぼく) north and south
			南極 (なん・きょく) South pole		南国 (なん・ごく) southern country
			南		

175	ヒ	5画	north			
北		くんよみ	きた			
		おんよみ	ホク、ボク			
		北 (きた) north		南北戦争 (なん・ぼく・せん・そう) (US) civil war		
		北米 (ほく・べい) North America		北極 (ほっ・きょく) north pole		
		敗北 (はい・ぼく) defeat		北欧 (ほく・おう) Northern Europe		

176	方	4画	direction; side			
方		くんよみ	かた			
		おんよみ	ホウ、ポウ			
		方向 (ほう・こう) direction		作り方 (つく・り・かた) how to make		
		方法 (ほう・ほう) method		日本の方 (に・ほん・の・かた) Japanese person		
		方言 (ほう・げん) dialect		方面 (ほう・めん) direction; district; area		

177	角	7画	horns; angle; corner			
角		くんよみ	かど、つの			
		おんよみ	カク			
		三角 (さん・かく) triangle		角度 (かく・ど) angle		
		街角 (まち・かど) street corner		角 (つの) horns		
		角 (かど) corner		四角 (し・かく) square (shape)		

3 │ Kanji Culture 漢字の文化

● 北 symbolizes "defeat"

南 (south) was originally considered the direction of entrances, and 北 (north) represented the opposite. The Japanese word for "defeat", 敗北 contains 北 which the direction one's back faces one's away from the entrance meaning that you are escaping or running away.

3 | Words You Can Write　書ける言葉

中東 (ちゅうとう) Middle East

中	東									

西日 (にしび) west sun, setting sun

西	日									

南口 (みなみぐち) south exit

南	口									

北口 (きたぐち) north exit

北	口									

南北 (なんぼく) north and south

南	北									

北西 (ほくせい) northwest

北	西									

方言 (ほうげん) dialect

方	言									

四角 (しかく) square

四	角									

方角 (ほうがく) direction

方	角										

行き方 (いきかた) directions

行	き	方								

東西南北 (とうざいなんぼく) north; south; east and west

東	西	南	北								

3 Workbook 3: Workbook Activities

3 | Kanji Drills 漢字ドリル

● **1. Directions**
Write appropriate kanji in the boxes below.

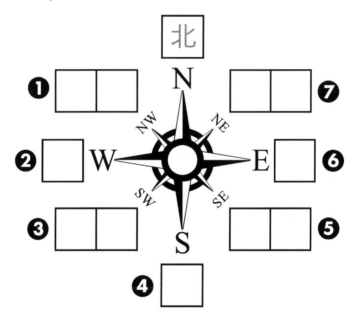

● **2. Fill in the Kanji**
Fill in the appropriate kanji in the blanks for each sentence.

1. 　ひがし　　ほう　　　　　やま
　　___の ___ にきれいな___ が ありますよ。

　　In the direction of the east, there is a pretty mountain.

2. 　　　さい　　すう　　げつ　　　　は　　　ひ　　おお
　　かん___ は ___ か___ かん、___れの___が ___かった。

　　For several months, the Kansai area has had many sunny days.

3. ___ ___ 、えきの___ ___ で___ いましょう。
あ した　　　　きた ぐち　　あ

Let's meet at the north exit of the station tomorrow.

4. ___ ___ には___ くの___ ___が あります。
に ほん　　おお　　ほう げん

Japanese has many dialects.

5. あの ___ を___ に まがって___ さい。
かど　　みぎ　　　くだ

Please turn right at that corner over there.

6. ___ ___ は___の___ ___に ありますよ。
がっ こう　みなみ　ほう がく

School is in the southern direction.

7. このどうろは、___ ___ に___っています。
なん ぼく　　はし

This road runs north to south.

3 | Usage Activities 文法アクティビティー

● 3. Reading comprehension
Translate the following on a separate piece of paper or type in an electronic device.

狭い家

A family can have many struggles. But even this happy event is troubling for this couple.

❶ 僕と奥さんは、7年前に結婚してから、ずっとアパート暮らしをしています。

❷ 今の暮らしには、問題が色々あります。

❸ まず、このアパートは駅に近いので、いつも電車の音がしています。

❹ 次に、3階に住んでいるんですが、エレベーターがなくて困っています。

❺ なぜなら、奥さんのお腹には赤ちゃんがいて、階段を上がるのが大変だからです。

❻ それから、6歳の息子がずっと自分の部屋をほしがっています。

❼ そこで、僕たちは家を買うことにしました。

❽ 僕たちは、3LDKの家がいいと思っています。

❾ 不動産屋さんに見せてもらった家は、キッチンが4帖、リビングが12帖、そして6帖の寝室が3つありました。

❿ 寝室は全部フローリングなんですが、和室よりいい気がします。

⓫ 小さい子供がいたら、すぐに畳や襖をだめにしてしまうからです。

⓬ 奥さんはその家に決めたがっています。

⓭ 僕は本当はリビングが18帖ぐらいほしいんですが、奥さんには勝てません。

⓮ 家族がもう一人増える前に、マイホームを買いたいと思います。

● 4. Reading comprehension questions
Translate the questions about the reading comprehension then answer in Japanese.

1. この人のアパートは、どんなところが便利ですか。

Translation: _____

Answer: _____

2. アパートのどんなところに困っていますか。

   Translation: _____

   Answer: _____

3. 家を買うことになった一番の理由は何ですか。

   Translation: _____

   Answer: _____

4. 不動産屋さんと見に行った家は、何部屋ありましたか。

   Translation: _____

   Answer: _____

5. この家族には、どうして洋室のほうがいいんですか。

   Translation: _____

   Answer: _____

6. この人はこの家を買うと思いますか。それはどうしてですか。

   Translation: _____

   Answer: _____

● 5. Fill in the blanks

Fill in the missing part based on the English sentence.

1.　娘 は＿＿＿＿＿＿＿＿＿＿＿＿＿＿＿います。
   <small>むすめ</small>

   My daughter wants some "takoyaki" (octopus dumplings).

2.　今、＿＿＿＿＿＿＿＿＿＿＿＿＿しました。
   <small>いま</small>

   Just now, I heard strange voices.

3.　このコーヒーは＿＿＿＿＿＿＿＿＿＿＿します。

   This coffee smells good.

4.　玄関のドアが＿＿＿＿＿＿＿＿＿＿＿＿＿。
   <small>げん かん</small>

   The front door has been left open.

5.　あのおじいさんは＿＿＿＿＿＿＿＿＿＿と思います。
   <small>おも</small>

   I think that old man over there wants to sit down.

● 6. Question and Answer

Answer the following questions as if they were asked to you.

1.　高校生はどんな物をほしがりますか。
   <small>こう こう せい</small>　　　　　　<small>もの</small>

   ＿＿＿＿＿＿＿＿＿＿＿＿＿＿＿＿＿＿＿＿＿＿＿＿＿＿

2.　あなたの友達は何をしたがっていますか。
   <small>とも だち</small>　<small>なに</small>

   ＿＿＿＿＿＿＿＿＿＿＿＿＿＿＿＿＿＿＿＿＿＿＿＿＿＿

3.　誰かの財布が喫茶店のテーブルに置きっぱなしだったら、どうしますか。
   <small>だれ</small>　<small>さい ふ</small>　<small>きっ さ てん</small>　　　　　<small>お</small>

   ＿＿＿＿＿＿＿＿＿＿＿＿＿＿＿＿＿＿＿＿＿＿＿＿＿＿

4. 誰と離れたくないですか。

_____

5. あなたの家で、どんな音がしますか。

_____

● **7. Translation**

Translate the following sentences into Japanese.

1. The rice cooker has been left on.

_____

2. My father wants to leave the big city.

_____

3. I was standing all day today.

_____

4. I hear a strange sound in the kitchen.

_____

5. I feel like that teacher is kind.

_____

● 8. Visual clue questions

Look at the picture, translate the question on the first line, then answer in Japanese.

1. 何の音がしますか。

_____

おかあさん

2. どんな味がしますか。

_____

_____

3. 友達は何をほしがっていますか。

_____

_____

4. 二人は何をしたがっていますか。

_____

_____

5. この人はいつも何をしていますか。(use the っぱなし pattern)

_____

_____

3 | Answer Key 答え合わせ

Short Dialogue (translation)

Mother	Sorry to disturb. It's my first time entering your apartment.
Son	Come on in, it's a bit dirty.
Mother	There's a strange smell. What's this smell?
Son	It's probably the smell of last night's dinner. I left it on the table.
Mother	Well, let's open the window. It smells.
Son	I don't want to open it since the mosquitoes will come in. I always leave the windows closed.
Mother	What! That's not good. Try to figure something out. (soft command)
Son	I'm fine with this!

1. Directions (answers)

1. 北西   2. 西   3. 南西   4. 南   5. 南東   6. 東   7. 北東

2. Fill in the kanji (answers)

1. 東の方にきれいな山がありますよ。
2. かん西は数か月かん、晴れの日が多かった。
3. 明日、えきの北口で会いましょう。
4. 日本には多くの方言が あります。

5. あの角を右にまがって下さい。
6. 学校は南の方角に ありますよ。
7. このどうろは、南北に走っています。

3. Reading comprehension (translation)

❶ Since getting married seven years ago, my wife and I have been living in an apartment.
❷ There are many problems with our current day-to-day living.
❸ First, since the apartment is near the train station, there is always the sounds of trains.
❹ Next, we live on the 3rd floor and we are troubled that there isn't an elevator.
❺ The reason why is, because going up the stairs is hard as my wife is pregnant.
❻ And also, my 6-year-old son has been wanting his own room for a long time.
❼ Therefore, we decided to buy a house.
❽ We think a 3LDK-house is good.
❾ The house that we had the realtor show us has a 4-tatami-mat kitchen, a 12-tatami-mat living room, and three 6-tatami-mat bedrooms.
❿ All of the bedrooms have flooring, but I think it's better than a Japanese-style room.
⓫ Because, if we had small children, they would damage the tatami mats or sliding doors right away.
⓬ My wife wants to decide on (choose) that house.
⓭ I really want a living room that is 18-tatami-mats big, but I can't win against my wife.
⓮ Before our family increases by one, I want to buy our own home.

4. Reading comprehension questions (answers)

1. Translation: What part of this person's apartment is convenient?

   Answer(s):   A) 駅に近いところが便利です。

   B) 駅に近いのが便利です。

2. Translation: What part of the apartment is troubling?

   Answer(s):   A) エレベーターがないところに困っています。

   B) 奥さんのお腹に赤ちゃんがいるのに、エレベーターがないので困っています。

   C) 息子さんが自分の部屋がないところです。

3. Translation: What is the biggest reason they decided to buy a house?

   Answer(s):   A) 家族がもう一人増えるからです。B) もうすぐ赤ちゃんが生まれるからです。

4. Translation: How many rooms did the house have that they went to see with the realtor?

   Answer(s):   A) 三部屋ありました。

5. Translation: Why is a western-style room better for this family?

   Answer(s):   A) 和室だったら、子供がたたみやふすまをだめにするからです。

   B) 和室はたたみやふすまがあって、子供がだめにしてしまうからです。

6. Translation: Do you think this person will buy this house? Why is that?

   Answer(s):   A) はい、思います。もうすぐ赤ちゃんが生まれますから。

   B) 買うと思います。家族がもう一人増える前に買いたがっていますから。

5. Fill in the blanks (answers)

1. 娘はたこ焼きをほしがっています。

2. 今、変な声がしました。

3. このコーヒーはいい匂いがします。

4. 玄関のドアが開けっ放しです。

5. あのおじいさんは座りたがっていると思います。

6. Question and Answer (answers may vary)

1. What type of things do high school students want?
   新しい携帯をほしがります。／ お金や洋服をほしがると思います。

2. What is your friend wanting to do?
   アルバイトをしたがっています。／ 一日中、寝たがっています。／ 私は友達がいません。

3. What would you do if someone left their wallet on a cafe table?
   盗みます。／お金だけ取ります。／喫茶店の人に渡します。／交番に届けます。

4. With whom do you not want to separate?
   家族と離れたくないです。／ 今の友達と離れたくないです。

5. What sounds are there in your house?
   車の音がします。／ 人の話し声がします。

7. Translation (answers)

1. 炊飯器がつけっぱなしです。

4. 台所で変な音がしました。

2. 父が大都市を離れたがっています。

5. あの先生は親切な感じがする。

3. A) 今日、一日中立ちっぱなしでした。B) 今日、一日中立っていました。

8. Visual clue questions (answers)

1. What sound do you hear? / 雨の音がします。

2. What flavor do you taste? / お母さんの味がします。

3. What does your friend want? / 友達はアイスクリームをほしがっています。

4. What do the two want to do? / 二人は別れたがっています。

5. What is this person always doing? / この人は働きっぱなしです。

Vocabulary Builder:
Groups K and L

■ Group K: money related

お小遣い	pocket money; allowance
保険料	cost of insurance
残業	overtime
税金	tax
割引券	discount coupon or ticket
消費税	consumption tax
輸入税	import taxes
バブル崩壊	bubble economy burst

> After World War II, Japan saw great economic gains until the "bubble" economy burst with a strong downturn beginning in March 1991 to October 1993. This period is referred as バブル崩壊 and was the start of the so called, "Lost 20 years".

■ Group L: entertainment words

オーディション	audition
セリフ	lines (in a TV show / movie)
本番	main take; live take
台本	script
俳優	actor; actress
男優	actor
女優	actress
監督	director

16 PAGES	4 USAGE SECTIONS	16 NEW WORDS

4

Lesson 4:
Action in a certain way

---

4 | New Words 新しい言葉

Nouns etc.

せい	fault; because; due to	順番 (じゅんばん)	turn (in line); order of things
平日 (へいじつ)	weekday	外車 (がいしゃ)	foreign car
対策 (たいさく)	countermeasure, step	人気 (にんき)	popular; popularity
予約 (よやく)	appointment; reservation; booking	工事 (こうじ)	construction
地下鉄 (ちかてつ)	underground train; subway	割引券 (わりびきけん)	discount ticket; voucher

Verbs

残る (のこ)	to remain; to be left	残す (のこ)	to leave behind
失敗する (しっぱい)	to mess up; to make a mistake	成功する (せいこう)	to succeed
残業する (ざんぎょう)	to work overtime	期待する (きたい)	to expect; to anticipate

---

4 | Japanese Living 日本の暮らし

This section is FULL JAPANESE. Look up words you don't know. The English translation is provided below.

● **Japanese hair salons are heaven! 日本(にほん)のヘアサロンは天国(てんごく)です！**

女性(じょせい)が行(い)くのは美容院(びよういん)、美容室(びようしつ)、とヘアサロンです。男性(だんせい)が行(い)く所(ところ)は散髪屋(さんぱつや)もしくは理髪店(りはつてん)と呼(よ)ばれています。おしゃれな若(わか)い男性(だんせい)もヘアサロンに行(い)きます。

ヘアサロンでは、お客様(きゃくさま)を確保(かくほ)するためにポイントカードを出(だ)しています。例(たと)えば、1000円(えん)ごとにスタンプを1個(こ)押(お)して、たまったら割引(わりびき)してもらえたりします。ヘアカットをする時(とき)は、シャンプーからスタイリングまで丁寧(ていねい)にしてくれます。肩(かた)をマッサージしてくれる店(みせ)も多(おお)いです。カットやパーマをしている間(あいだ)に読(よ)めるように、大抵(たいてい)目(め)の前(まえ)に雑誌(ざっし)が2,3冊(さつ)、用意(ようい)されています。

料金は、もちろん住んでいる町によりますが、4000円〜5000円ぐらいです。あまり技術やサービスを求めない人には、お手軽なヘアサロンもあって、2500円前後でカットしてもらえます。

忙しいサラリーマン向けの理髪店も人気です。駅前や駅のホームにあって、待ち時間も外に表示されています。髪を切る時間は10分程度でタイマーを使っています。安くて早いのが助かります。

Woman go to びよういん (beauty parlor), びようしつ (beauty parlor), and ヘアサロン. The places that men go are called, さんぱつや or りはつてん. Fashion-conscious young men also go to ヘアサロン.

In order to retain customers, ヘアサロン have point cards. For example, you can get a discount after collecting stamps for each 1,000 yen spent. When getting a haircut, service includes shampooing and even styling. Many places will also give a shoulder massage. While getting a cut or a perm, 2 or 3 magazines are usually prepared for your reading and placed in front of you.

The cost, of course depends on the town you live in, but will be around 4,000~5,000 yen. For people not desiring technique or service, there are also reasonable ヘアサロン that will give you a cut for around 2,500 yen.

りはつてん (barber shops) geared towards the busy salaried men are also popular. These are located in front of train stations or on the station platform and have wait times listed outside. Cutting hair takes around 10 minutes and a timer is used. It helps to be cheap and fast.

4 | Verb Usage 動詞の使い方

V-1	期待(を)する	to expect, to anticipate	する
	1. (something)を期待する	to expect (something)	

EXAMPLE SENTENCES

1. 誕生日にたくさんのプレゼントを期待しています。
   I am expecting a lot of presents on my birthday.

2. 彼氏は今日のデートで初キスを期待しています。
   My boyfriend is expecting a first kiss on today's date.

3. 私は料理が下手だから、おいしいものを期待しないでください。
   Because my cooking is unskilled, don't expect anything delicious.

> 初 (はつ) is used to mean "first". Such as 初デート (first date)

> ファーストキス is also commonly said instead of 初キス.

📖 もっと詳しく… More Details ⓘ

きたいする only works when something "good" is expected.
In English, we freely use "expect" in a variety of situations.

I didn't expect to meet you here today.
I didn't expect to get a gift on my birthday.

However, 期待する is used when "anticipating" or "looking forward" to something. Therefore, if you say, 期待しなかった, it means that you didn't expect much "good" out of the situation in discussion.

✖ ここであなたに会うことを期待しなかった。

Although this sentence feels correct, because it translates to, "I didn't expect to meet you here", in Japanese 期待する is not used for "unexpected events".

This might create an awkward situation when meeting a person that you like in an unexpected place. In such a case it's better simply to use:

✔ ここであなたに会えると思わなかった。
    I didn't think I would be able to meet you here.

This has the assumed meaning of, "but happily it happened".

1. この旅行で富士山が見られると思わなかった。
    I didn't expect to be able to see Mt. Fuji on this trip.

2. あなたのような美人と結婚できると思わなかった。
    I didn't expect to be able to marry a beautiful person like you.

3. 私の息子が本を最後まで読めると思わなかった。
    I didn't expect my son to be able to read a book until the end.

4. 初めて会った時、あなたが日本語を話せると思わなかった。
    When I first met you, I didn't think you were able to speak Japanese.

5. うるさい飛行機の中で寝られると思わなかった。
    I didn't expect to be able to sleep on the loud airplane.

V-2	失敗 (を)する しっぱい	to fail	する
	1. (something)に失敗する	to fail at (something)	

	成功 (を)する せいこう	to succeed	する
	1. (something)に成功する	to succeed at (something)	

When you fail or succeed at a certain task, that task is marked with に.

EXAMPLE SENTENCES

1. 失敗をすることは恥ずかしくないです。
   It's not embarrassing to make a mistake.

2. このオーディションに失敗できません。
   I can't mess up this audition.

   > キロ is short for either キログラム or キロメーター depending on the context.

3. ダイエットに成功しました。
   I succeeded on my diet.

4. 毎日トレーニングをして、やっと1キロを5分で走ることに成功しました。
   I trained every day and finally succeeded at running 1 kilometer in 5 minutes.

A huge mistake can be called 大失敗 and a great success is 大成功.

V-3	残る のこ	to remain; to be left (DESCRIPTIVE)	regular
	1. (something)が残る	(something) remains	

残る is a DESCRIPTIVE verb describing the state of something, as in "one is left".

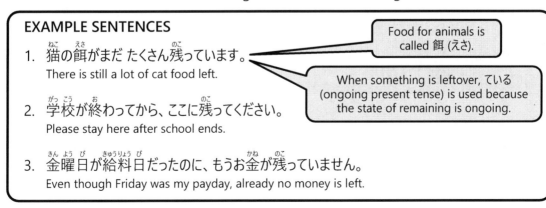

EXAMPLE SENTENCES

1. 猫の餌がまだ たくさん残っています。
   There is still a lot of cat food left.

   > Food for animals is called 餌 (えさ).

   > When something is leftover, ている (ongoing present tense) is used because the state of remaining is ongoing.

2. 学校が終わってから、ここに残ってください。
   Please stay here after school ends.

3. 金曜日が給料日だったのに、もうお金が残っていません。
   Even though Friday was my payday, already no money is left.

The ている form is used to show the ongoing state. Notice how the meaning changes when not in the ている form.

EXAMPLE Q&A

Future tense form

1. 食べ物が残りますか。

いいえ、残りません。

はい、残ると思います。

Will any food be left?
No, there won't be any left.
Yes, I think there will be some left.

Ongoing present tense form

2. 食べ物が残っていますか。

いいえ、残っていません。

はい、たくさん残っています。

Is there any food left?
No, there isn't any left.
Yes, there is a lot left.

V-4	残す	to leave (behind); to save (ACTION)	regular
	1. (something)を 残す	to leave (something)	

残る describes the STATE, whereas 残す is the ACTION of leaving something.

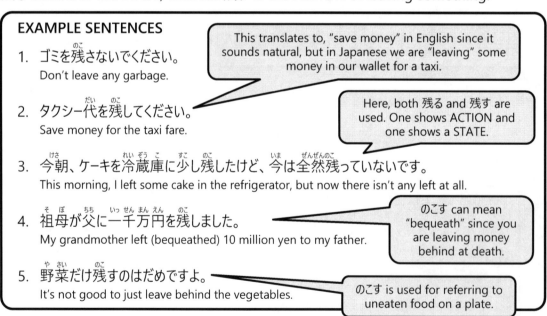

EXAMPLE SENTENCES

1. ゴミを残さないでください。
   Don't leave any garbage.

> This translates to, "save money" in English since it sounds natural, but in Japanese we are "leaving" some money in our wallet for a taxi.

2. タクシー代を残してください。
   Save money for the taxi fare.

> Here, both 残る and 残す are used. One shows ACTION and one shows a STATE.

3. 今朝、ケーキを冷蔵庫に少し残したけど、今は全然残っていないです。
   This morning, I left some cake in the refrigerator, but now there isn't any left at all.

> のこす can mean "bequeath" since you are leaving money behind at death.

4. 祖母が父に一千万円を残しました。
   My grandmother left (bequeathed) 10 million yen to my father.

5. 野菜だけ残すのはだめですよ。
   It's not good to just leave behind the vegetables.

> のこす is used for referring to uneaten food on a plate.

| V-5 | 残業(を)する
ざん ぎょう | to work overtime | する |

The 残 in 残業 is the same kanji in 残る (to remain) and 業, common in work related words, means "work". So, "working overtime" is "to do remaining work".

残業する doesn't take any objects or subjects. It's just something that you do.

> **EXAMPLE SENTENCES**
> 1. 金曜日に残業をしました。
>   I worked overtime on Friday.
>
> 2. 毎日、残業をする日本人が多いです。
>   There are a lot of Japanese people who work overtime every day.
>
> 3. 今日、残業をした人たちは明日、早く来なくてもいいです。
>   The people who worked overtime today, don't have to come in early tomorrow.

4 | Word Usage 言葉の使い方

| W-1 | 本番
ほん ばん | performance; live take |

本番 (actual thing) is used for performance related tasks. For example, if you are strong or weak during the live performance compared to practice, you can say #1.

> **EXAMPLE SENTENCES**
> 1. 大丈夫、私は本番に強いです。
>   It's okay. I will be strong during the actual performance.
>
> 2. 彼は本番に弱いです。
>   He's weak during the actual performance.
>
> 3. 練習の時はよく失敗したけど、本番では失敗しなかった。
>   I often made mistakes when practicing, but I didn't mess up during the live take.

After rehearsals, the producer will announce the "real take" by shouting 本番！

| W-2 | 真~
 ま | directly~; right~ |

By adding 真 in front of a location noun, you can say "DIRECTLY in front" etc.

EXAMPLES

ん is required.

真ん前 (right in front; right before)   真後ろ (right behind; directly behind)

真上 (right above; directly overhead)   真下 (right below; directly underneath)

真横 (right beside; just beside)

You can never say 真右 and 真左, instead you can say すぐ右 (immediate right) and すぐ左 (immediate left).

EXAMPLE SENTENCES

1. 私の家の真ん前に学校があるから、平日に子供たちの声がします。
   There's a school right in front of my house, so on weekdays you can hear the sound of children.

2. このデパートの真下に、地下鉄が走っています。
   The subway runs directly below this department store.

3. わたしの真後ろで、順番を待ってください。
   Wait for your turn directly behind me.

W-3	人気 にんき	popular; popularity
1. (someone)に 人気がある		to be popular with (something)
2. 人気のある (item / person)		a popular (item / person)

You can say something or someone is popular by just using 人気です (is popular). However, 人気 is commonly paired with 人気がある or 人気のある.

EXAMPLE SENTENCES

1. ちひろさんは、人気のある女の子です。
   Chihiro is a popular girl.

2. 私の弟は、クラスの女の子に人気があります。
   My younger brother is popular with the girls in class.

4 | Grammar and Usage 文法と使い方

● 4-1. In order to, so that 〜ように

You can add ように after non-past tense verbs to say that an action will be done with a certain goal in mind. It defines the intention of the following verb phrase.

EXAMPLE SENTENCES

1. 失敗しないように、頑張ります。
   I will do my best to not fail.

2. 日本に行けるように、お金を貯めます。
   I will save money so that I can go to Japan.

3. 虫が来ないように、窓を閉めました。
   So that bugs wouldn't come, I closed the window.

4. 汚くならないように、毎日 机をきれいにします。
   So that it doesn't become dirty, I clean my desk every day.

5. 風邪をひかないように、ジャケットを着ました。
   I put on a jacket in order to not catch a cold.

● 4-2. To become able to 〜ようになる

ように + なる shows a new ability or a change in a prior status.
The potential form (can/can't do form) is often used but isn't required.

(informal form verb) + ようになる

This often translates to "I can ~ now", or "Now I can ~". Consider this scenario:

You were unable to travel to Las Vegas, but now you can.

A: ラスベガスで遊ぼう！

B: ええ？行けるの？

A: はい。今、行けます。 ✘ ← Read why this is wrong on the next page.

A: Let's hang out in Las Vegas.
B: What? You can go?
A: Yes. I can go now.

In a direct translation, "I can go now", is 今、行けます。 This means the person is ready to go *now*. With ~ように we can also infer about the past and future.

いま vs ように (I can go now.)			
What do we know about the situation?	**PAST** —	**NOW** —	**FUTURE** ➡
いま、いける。	(unknown)	can go	(unknown)
いける ように なった。	couldn't go	can go	can go

EXAMPLE SENTENCES

1. 日本に行けるようになりました。
   I can go to Japan now.

   > This implies that before they were not able to go, but now something made "going to Japan" possible.

2. 私の妹がお箸を使えるようになりました。
   My younger sister can use chopsticks now.

3. 最近、監督はよく怒るようになりました。
   Recently, the director often gets angry.

   > Implying that the director didn't used to get mad, but NOW he does.

4. ジェフさんは、去年より日本語が上手に話せるようになりました。
   Jeff can now speak Japanese more skillfully than last year.

5. あの女優は彼と別れたせいで、よく休むようになりました。
   That actress takes a lot of days off now due to breaking up with her boyfriend.

~ようになる can also be conjugated into various forms.

EXAMPLE SENTENCES

1. 日本語が話せるように<u>なりたい</u>。
   I <u>want to be</u> able to speak Japanese.

2. 日本語が話せるように<u>なりたかった</u>。
   I <u>wanted to be</u> able to speak Japanese.

3. 日本語が話せるように<u>なりませんでした</u>。
   I <u>didn't become</u> able to speak Japanese.

4. 日本語が話せるように<u>なりましょう</u>。
   <u>Let's become</u> able to speak Japanese.

5. 日本語が話せるように<u>なってください</u>。
   Please <u>become</u> able to speak Japanese.

● 4-3. せい fault, because, due to

せい is used with nouns, verbs, and adjectives to show the fault or reason a certain circumstance has occurred. The circumstance is considered unwanted or negative. The grammar changes slightly whether the reason is an adjective, noun, or verb.

Type	English Pattern	Japanese Pattern
noun	fault of (noun)	(person)のせい
noun	due to (noun), (result) happened	(noun)のせいで(result)
い adj.	due to (い adjective), (result) happened	(い adjective)せいで(result)
な adj.	due to (な adjective), (result) happened	(な adjective)なせいで(result)
verb	due to (verb), (result) happened	(verb)せいで(result)

EXAMPLE SENTENCES (DUE TO NOUN, FAULT)

1. あなたのせいです。
   It's your fault.

2. 彼女と別れたのは、私のせいです。
   It's my fault I broke up with my girlfriend.

3. ジョージのせいだと思う！
   I think it's George's fault!

4. 誰のせいですか。
   Whose fault is it?

In the following examples, we show complete REASON + RESULT sentences.

EXAMPLE SENTENCES (NOUNS + RESULT)

1. 薬のせいで胃が痛くなった。
   Due to the medicine, my stomach hurts.

2. あなたのせいで遅れた。
   Because of you, I was late.

3. 台風のせいで屋根が壊れた。
   Because of the typhoon, the roof broke.

4. 交通事故のせいで保険料が上がりました。
   Because of the traffic accident, my insurance rates rose.

With い adjectives, の is not used. Just add せいで directly after the adjective.
な adjectives also don't use の but require な instead. Add なせいで after the adjective.

EXAMPLE SENTENCES (ADJECTIVES + RESULT)

1. 家が汚いせいで、ゴキブリがたくさんいる。
   Due to the house being dirty, there are a lot of cockroaches.

2. 工事の音がうるさいせいで、寝られないんです。
   Due to the sounds of construction being loud, I can't sleep.

3. 輸入関税が高いせいで、外車は高いです。
   Due to import taxes being expensive, foreign cars are expensive.

4. セリフが複雑なせいで、その俳優は思い出せなかった。
   Due to the lines being complicated, the actor couldn't recall them.

5. 彼は英語が下手なせいで、いい仕事が見つからなかった。
   He wasn't able to find a good job due to his English being poor.

When verb phrases are in front of せいで, they become the reason for an unwanted result. The verb phrase should be in casual/informal form.

EXAMPLE SENTENCES (VERB PHRASE + RESULT)

1. 同僚が休んだせいで、残業した。
   Because my co-worker was off, I worked overtime.

2. あなたが動いたせいで、写真を撮るのに失敗した。
   I messed up taking the photo because you moved.

> You can just add the cause of an allergy in front of アレルギー without any particles.

3. 会場に犬がいるせいで、犬アレルギーの子供が入れないです。
   Due to dogs being in the exhibition center, children with allergies can't enter.

4. 英語ができないせいで、アメリカに行った時は困りました。
   Due to not being able to speak English, I was troubled when I went to America.

● **4-4. Nouns made from verbs**

Quite a few nouns are derived using just the い form of verbs.

Verb	English	Noun	English
帰^{かえ}ります	to return	帰^{かえ}り	return
休^{やす}みます	to take a break	休^{やす}み	break; day off
生^うまれます	to be born	生^うまれ	birthplace
読^よみます	to read	読^よみ	reading (how to read)
行^いきます	to go	行^いき、行^ゆき	the way; going; bound for
感^{かん}じます	to feel	感^{かん}じ	feeling; sense; impression
話^{はな}します	to speak; to talk	話^{はなし}	talk; speech; story

話 in this case is not spelled 話し.

EXAMPLE SENTENCES

1. 今日^{きょう}は帰^{かえ}りが早^{はや}かったです。
   Today my return was early.

2. この漢字^{かんじ}は読^よみがたくさんあります。
   This kanji has a lot of readings.

3. ５月^{がつ}には休^{やす}みが多^{おお}いです。
   I have a lot of days off in May.

4. 私^{わたし}はフロリダ生^うまれです。
   I was born in Florida. / I'm from Florida.

Many, if not all, of the する verbs are standalone nouns when する is removed.

Verb	English	Noun	English
勉強^{べんきょう}する	to study	勉強^{べんきょう}	studies
練習^{れんしゅう}する	to practice	練習^{れんしゅう}	practice
注文^{ちゅうもん}する	to order	注文^{ちゅうもん}	order
失敗^{しっぱい}する	to make a mistake	失敗^{しっぱい}	mistake; failure
期待^{きたい}する	to expect	期待^{きたい}	expectation

EXAMPLE SENTENCES

1. お母_{かあ}さんの私_{わたし}への期待_{きたい}は大_{おお}きいです。
   My mother's expectations towards me are high (big).

> Japanese uses おおきい (big) instead of たかい (high) for expectations.

2. 私_{わたし}は最近_{さいきん}、仕事_{しごと}で失敗_{しっぱい}が多_{おお}いです。
   Recently, I have made many mistakes at work.

3. 日本語_{にほんご}をしゃべる練習_{れんしゅう}がもっと必要_{ひつよう}です。
   I need more practice speaking Japanese.

> On trains etc., an area name followed by 行き means, "bound for (area)". However, it's often read as ゆき. So bound for Tokyo can be 東京行き (とうきょうゆき).

4. 大阪行_{おおさかゆ}きの新幹線_{しんかんせん}は多_{おお}いんですが、青森行_{あおもりゆ}きは少_{すく}ないです。
   There are many trains bound for Osaka, however there are few bound for Aomori.

NOTE: If you are just saying, "the way to go", then 行き is read as いき.

4 | Practice and Review　練習と復習

● 1. Mini Conversation ミニ会話 J → E
Try translating the entire conversation before looking at the translation below.

1. Polite conversation between friends
A: 田中君_{たなかくん}が怒_{おこ}っています。私_{わたし}のせいです。
B: え！どうしたんですか。
A: 田中君_{たなかくん}がごはんを作_{つく}ってくれたけど、ほとんど残_{のこ}しました。
B: それは怒_{おこ}るでしょうね。

A: Tanaka is mad. It's my fault.
B: What? What happened?
A: Tanaka made dinner for me, most of it remained. (I didn't eat all of it)
B: Yeah, that would certainly make one mad. (Yeah... that would do it.)

2. Casual conversation between friends with strict parents
A: ぼくは親_{おや}にあまり期待_{きたい}してほしくない。
B: どうして？けん君_{くん}は成績_{せいせき}がよくて、スポーツもできるでしょう？
A: できがいい子供_{こども}にはプレッシャーがあるんだ。
B: そうかあ。じゃ、あまりがんばらないでね。

A: I don't want my parents to expect much of me.

B: Why? Your grades are good, and you can play sports, too, right?

A: There is pressure on children who do well.

B: Ah I see. Well then, don't try too hard.

3. Mixed conversation between friends

A: 今、うちの犬が動物病院にいるの。

B: 本当？何があったんですか？

A: となりの犬とけんかしたせいで、足に怪我をしたんだ。だから、今は歩けないの。

B: そうなんですか。。。早く歩けるようになったらいいですね。

A: Our dog is at the animal hospital right now.

B: Really? What happened?

A: Due to a fight with the dog next door, he injured his foot. So, now he can't walk.

B: Is that so... It would be good if he could walk again soon. (I hope he can...)

4. Polite conversation between co-workers

A: もう夜7時ですね。でも、まだ仕事がたくさん残ってます。

B: 残業しますか。それとも、仕事を残して帰りますか。

A: 明日は休みたいから、今、しますよ。

B: 分かりました。

A: It's already 7 o'clock. But there is still a lot of work left.

B: Will you work overtime? Or perhaps, will you leave it and go home?

A: I want to take tomorrow off, so I'll do it now.

B: Got it.

● 2. Mini Conversation ミニ会話 E → J

Try translating the entire conversation before looking at the translation below.

1. Polite conversation between friends

A: Won't you meet with me on the way back from school?

B: Today I... I am going to clean my house.

A: What? Don't you always keep it clean?

B: Yes, that's true, but due to my younger brother being here, my house got dirty.

A: I see. That's tough.

A: 今日、学校の帰りに会いませんか。

B: 今日はちょっと。。。家の掃除をするんです。

A: あれ、いつもきれいにしてるじゃないですか。

B: そうなんだけど、弟が来ているせいで、家の中がきたなくなりました。

A: そうですか。大変ですね。

2. Polite conversation between non-Japanese speakers in Japanese

A: Recently, I've became able to speak Japanese.

B: That's amazing. What did you do to get good?

A: I made Japanese friends, then made it so we only spoke in Japanese.

B: That's nice. Because I'm shy, I can't speak a lot.

A: 最近、日本語が話せるようになりました。

B: すごいですね。どうやって上手になりましたか。

A: 日本人の友達を作って、日本語だけで話すようにしました。

B: いいですね。わたしはシャイなせいで、あまり話せません。

3. Casual conversation between actors

A: Tomorrow we have a movie audition (right?)

B: Yeah. Let's do our best to not mess up (okay?)

A: Yeah. Let's practice a lot until the actual performance.

B: Yeah, true. So, we don't forget our lines, from now let's practice! (Let's start now)

A: 明日は映画のオーディションがあるね。

B: うん。失敗しないようにがんばろうね。

A: うん。本番までにたくさん練習しよう。

B: そうだね。セリフを忘れないように、今から練習しよう！

● 3. Short Dialogue
A customer and a receptionist are talking at a hair salon.

お店の人　「いらっしゃいませ。今日はどうなさいますか。」

お客さん　「今日はカットとカラーをお願いします。」

お店の人　「かしこまりました。お客様、メンバーズ・カードはございますか。」

お客さん　「いいえ、ありません。今日が初めてなので。」

お店の人　「メンバーの方は、ポイントがためられます。1000円で1ポイントです。
　　　　　10ポイントたまったら、割引券が使えるようになります。」

お客さん　「それはいいですね。今日から使えますか。」

お店の人　「はい、もちろんです。」

お客さん　「じゃあ、お願いします。」

4 Kanji Lesson 4:
風雪星雲海谷岩

From the teacher...

This lesson contains kanji that are related to nature.

4 | New Kanji 新しい漢字

178	風	9画		wind; breeze
	くんよみ		かぜ、かざ	
	おんよみ		フウ、フ	

突風 (とっ・ぷう) gust of wind　　風船 (ふう・せん) balloon
風 (かぜ) wind　　風景 (ふう・けい) scenery; landscape
風情 (ふ・ぜい) appearance　　北風 (きた・かぜ) northern wind

風 | | | | | | | | | | |

179	雨	11画		snow
	くんよみ		ゆき	
	おんよみ		セツ	

初雪 (はつ・ゆき) first snow　　積雪 (せき・せつ) accumulation of snow
雪 (ゆき) snow　　雪だるま (ゆき・だるま) snowman
雪国 (ゆき・ぐに) snow country　　雪道 (ゆき・みち) snow-covered road

雪 | | | | | | | | | | |

180	雨	12画		cloud
	くんよみ		くも	
	おんよみ		ウン	

雨雲 (あま・ぐも) a rain cloud　　雲海 (うん・かい) a sea of clouds
雲 (くも) cloud　　入道雲 (にゅう・どう・ぐも) a bank of clouds
雷雲 (らい・うん) thunder cloud　　星雲 (せい・うん) nebula; galaxy

雲 | | | | | | | | | | |

181	日	9画	star		
			くんよみ	ほし	
			おんよみ	セイ	
			星座 (せい・ざ) constellation	流れ星 (なが・れ・ぼし) shooting star	
			星空 (ほし・ぞら) starry sky	惑星 (わく・せい) planet	
			火星 (か・せい) Mars	星占い (ほし・うらな・い) astrology; horoscope	

星 | | | | | | | | | | | |

182	氵	9画	ocean		
			くんよみ	うみ	
			おんよみ	カイ	
			海外 (かい・がい) abroad, overseas	海辺 (うみ・べ) beach side	
			海水 (かい・すい) sea water	海抜 (かい・ばつ) height above sea-level	
			海軍 (かい・ぐん) navy	東海岸 (ひがし・かい・がん) the east coast	

海 | | | | | | | | | | | |

183	谷	7画	valley		
			くんよみ	たに	
			おんよみ	コク	
			渓谷 (けい・こく) canyon	谷底 (たに・そこ) bottom of the valley	
			谷 (たに) valley	死の谷 (し・の・たに) Death Valley (national park)	
			谷間 (たに・ま) ravine; cleavage	峡谷 (きょう・こく) ravine; gorge	

谷 | | | | | | | | | | | |

184	山	8画	boulder; rock		
			くんよみ	いわ	
			おんよみ	ガン	
			岩 (いわ) rock	溶岩 (よう・がん) lava	
			岩場 (いわ・ば) cliff	砂岩 (さ・がん) sandstone	
			岩石 (がん・せき) rock	花崗岩 (か・こう・がん) granite (rock)	

岩 | | | | | | | | | | | |

4 | Kanji Culture 漢字の文化

● **What does "a person on the clouds" mean?**

There is a Japanese phrase 雲^{くも}の上^{うえ}の人^{ひと} which means, "a person on top of the clouds". This is someone so amazing they can't be touched or caught up with. It doesn't mean they are dead or in heaven.

> **EXAMPLE SENTENCES**
> 1. ケイティ・レデッキーは、水泳選手^{すいえいせんしゅ}にとって雲^{くも}の上^{うえ}の人^{ひと}です。
>   For swimmers, Katie Ledecky is untouchable.

● **What does "a star is broken" mean?**

The phrase 星^{ほし}が割^われる literally means, "the star will break". In actual usage 星^{ほし} is a "criminal" and the phrase means "we will find out who did it".

> **EXAMPLE SENTENCES**
> 1. やっと星^{ほし}が割^われたぞ！
>   We finally figured out who did it!

4 | Words You Can Write 書ける言葉

風力 (ふうりょく) wind power

風	力								

風車 (ふうしゃ) windmill

風	車								

台風 (たいふう) typhoon

台	風								

大雪 (おおゆき) heavy snow

大	雪									

雨雲 (あまぐも) a rain cloud

雨	雲									

星空 (ほしぞら) starry sky

星	空									

火星 (かせい) Mars

火	星									

海水 (かいすい) sea water

海	水									

谷川 (たにがわ) valley river

谷	川									

岩石 (がんせき) rock

岩	石									

日本風 (にほんふう) Japanese style

日	本	風							

日本海 (にほんかい) Sea of Japan

日	本	海							

4 Workbook 4:
Workbook Activities

4 | Kanji Drills 漢字ドリル

● **1. Reading practice**
Write FURIGANA above or below the underlined kanji words.

1. 日本海で星空をながめました。

2. 風が強い時に、大雪がふりました。

3. この谷間には、岩石がたくさんあります。

4. 海水を飲むと、しょっぱいですよ。

5. 今日は雲が多くて、星が見えません。

● **2. Fill in the kanji**
Fill in the appropriate kanji in the blanks for each sentence.

1. ___ が___ いから、そとで あそぶのは やめましょう。
    Let's stop playing outside because the wind is strong.

2. ___ さいときは よく___ がっせんを しました。
    When I was small (young), I often had snow fights.

3. あの ___ きい___ ___ が ___えますか。
    Can you see that big rain cloud?

4. ここは ___ ___ らしが いいから、___ ___ がよく___える。
<small>み は　　　　　　　　ほし ぞら　　　み</small>

Because the view is good here, you can see the starry sky very well.

---

5. きょ ___ 、___に ___ ___ いきました。
<small>ねん　　うみ　さん　かい</small>

Last year, I went to the ocean three times.

---

6. むかしは ___ ___と、よく___や___ に___きました。
<small>ちち おや　　　　　やま　たに　い</small>

Long ago, I would often go to the mountain and valley with my father.

---

7. ___ ___ ___に ___ のぼりを しました。
<small>ど よう び　　いわ</small>

I went rock climbing on Saturday.

▌**4** ▏ **Usage Activities 文法アクティビティー**

● **3. Reading comprehension**

Translate the following on a separate piece of paper or type in an electronic device.

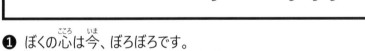

| 大変な人生
<small>たい へん　じん せい</small> | *Maybe you have some advice for this poor guy.*
Nothing seems to be going right for him! |

❶ ぼくの心は今、ぼろぼろです。
<small>こころ いま</small>

❷ 大学生活はまあまあ楽しくて、友達もたくさんいました。
<small>だい がく せい かつ　　　　　た の　　　とも だち</small>

❸ 女の子にもとても人気があって幸せでした。
<small>おんな こ　　　　　にん き　　　　しあわ</small>

❹ 問題は、大学を卒業してからです。
<small>もん だい　　だい がく　そつ ぎょう</small>

❺ 社会人になってからは、上司のせいで、ほとんど毎日残業をしています。
<small>しゃ かい じん　　　　　　じょう し　　　　　　　　　まい にち ざん ぎょう</small>

❻ それに、同僚が会社から遠いところに住んでいるせいで、一緒に飲みに行くこともできません。
<small>どう りょう かい しゃ　　　と お　　　　す　　　　　　　　いっ しょ　の　　　い</small>

❼ 僕が住んでいるマンションは、台風が来たせいで、ぽとぽと雨漏りがします。
<small>ぼく す　　　　　　　　　　　　たい ふう き　　　　　　　　あま も</small>

❽ マンションの真ん前で工事をしているせいで、休みの日もゆっくり寝られません。
<small>ま まえ こう じ　　　　　　　　　やす ひ　　　　　　　ね</small>

❾ 最近は、交通事故のせいで、車の保険料も上がりました。
<small>さい きん　こう つう じ こ　　　　くるま ほ けん りょう あ</small>

❿ 次々に問題が出てきて、くたくたです。
<small>つぎ つぎ もん だい で</small>

⓫ あ〜あ。どうしたら、彼女ができるようになるんでしょうか。
<small>かの じょ</small>

⓬ いつになったら、大きい家に住めるようになるんでしょうか。
<small>おお うち す</small>

❸ 僕はまた幸せになれるんでしょうか。
❹ 誰か、教えてください！

● 4. Reading comprehension questions

Translate the questions about the reading comprehension then answer in Japanese.

1. この人は、今の生活を楽しんでいますか。

   Translation: _____

   Answer: _____

2. 大学では、どうして幸せでしたか。

   Translation: _____

   Answer: _____

3. 誰のせいで、毎日残業をしていますか。

   Translation: _____

   Answer: _____

4. どうしてマンションで雨漏りがしますか。

   Translation: _____

   Answer: _____

5. 何のせいで、車の保険料が上がりましたか。

   Translation: _____

   Answer: _____

6. この人は今、何がほしいと言っていますか。

Translation: _____

Answer: _____

● 5. Fill in the blanks
Fill in the missing part based on the English sentence.

1. 私の_____のせいで、映画が見えないです。

   Because of the person sitting directly in front of me, I can't see the movie.

2. _____せいで、次の日の朝は起きられませんでした。

   Because I worked overtime, I couldn't get up next morning.

3. お皿にある物を全部_____、がんばって下さい。

   Please try your best so that you can eat everything on the plate.

4. _____ようになりました。

   I no longer mess up during the actual performance.

5. 日曜日に_____ようになりました。
   I can now take days off on Sunday.

● 6. Question and Answer
Answer the following questions as if they were directly asked to you.

1. テストに失敗したことがありますか。あるなら、どんなテストだったんですか。

_____

2. あなたの冷蔵庫に食べ物が残っていますか。あるなら、何がありますか。

_____

3. レストランで食べ物を残したことがありますか。あるなら、どんな食べ物を残しましたか。

_____

4. 休みは何曜日ですか。

_____

5. あなたは本番の時と練習の時と、どちらが強いですか。

_____

● 7. Translation

Translate the following sentences into Japanese.

1. Going is easy but returning is tough.

_____

2. I'm not expecting anything on my birthday.

_____

3. Because of the traffic accident, I was late for work.

_____

4. The kanji 上 has a lot of readings.

_____

5. On my day off, I leave the TV on all day.

_____

● 8. Visual clue questions

Make a ～ようになりました sentence based on the provided picture, then translate the sentence you made on the next line.

1. ～ようになりました。

_____

_____

2. ～ようになりました。

_____

_____

3. ～ようになりました。

_____

_____

4. ～ようになりました。

_____

_____

5. ～ようになりました。

_____

_____

4 | Answer Key 答え合わせ

Short Dialogue (translation)

Store clerk	Welcome. How may I help you? (What will you be doing today?)
Customer	Today I would like a cut and coloring please.
Store clerk	Certainly. Do you have a member's card?
Customer	No, I don't. Since today it's my first time here.
Store clerk	Members are able to collect points. With 1,000 yen you get 1 point.
	When you have collected 10 points, you will be able to use a discount coupon.
Customer	That's great. Can I use it from today?
Store clerk	Yes. Of course.
Customer	Well then, I would like a member's card please.

1. Reading practice (answers)

1. 日本海で星空をながめました。
2. 風が強い時に、大雪がふりました。
3. この谷間には、岩石がたくさんあります。
4. 海水を飲むと、しょっぱいですよ。
5. 今日は雲が多くて、星が見えません。

2. Fill in the kanji (answers)

1. 風が強いから、そとであそぶのは やめましょう。
2. 小さいときはよく雪がっせんを しました。
3. あの大きい雨雲が見えますか。
4. ここは見晴らしがいいから、星空がよく見える。
5. きょ年、海に三回 いきました。
6. むかしは父親と、よく山や谷に行きました。
7. 土曜日に岩のぼりを しました。

3. Reading comprehension (translation)

❶ My heart is completely destroyed right now.
❷ My college life was fairly enjoyable, and I had a lot of friends.
❸ I was even popular with girls and was happy.
❹ The problems started after I graduated college.
❺ Since becoming a working adult, I have worked overtime almost every day because of my boss.
❻ Also due to my co-workers living far from the company, I also can't go drinking with them.
❼ The apartment where I live has rain leaks because of the typhoon passing.
❽ Due to the construction directly in front of the apartment, I can't even relax on my days off.
❾ Recently, due to a car accident, the cost of my car insurance also rose.
❿ I am exhausted because of problem after problem coming up.
⓫ Ahh. What can I do to get a girlfriend?

⓬ When will it be that I will be able to live in a large house?
⓭ Can I become happy again?
⓮ Somebody help me please!

4. Reading comprehension questions (answers)

1. Translation: Is this person enjoying his current life?

    Answer(s):   いいえ、楽しんでいません。

2. Translation: Why was he happy in college?

    Answer(s):   女の子にとても人気があったからです。

    まあまあ楽しくて、友達もたくさんいたからです。

3. Translation: Who's fault is it that he has to work overtime every day?

    Answer(s):   上司のせいです。

4. Translation: How come the apartment is leaking when it rains?

    Answer(s):   台風が来たせいです。

5. Translation: Due to what did his car-insurance cost rise?

    Answer(s):   交通事故のせいです。

6. Translation: What is this person saying that he wants now?

    Answer(s):   彼女と大きい家がほしいと言っています。

    幸せがほしいと言っています。

5. Fill in the blanks (answers)

1. 私の真ん前に座っている人のせいで映画が見えないです。
2. 残業したせいで、次の日の朝は起きられませんでした。
3. お皿にある物を全部食べられるように、がんばって下さい。
4. 本番で失敗しないようになりました。
5. 日曜日に休めるようになりました。／日曜日に休みが取れるようになりました。

6. Question and Answer (answers may vary)

1. Have you ever failed a test? If you have, what type of test was it?

はい、あります。数学のテストでした。/ はい、一回だけ失敗しました。日本語のテストでした。

いいえ、ありません。/ いいえ、私は誰よりも頭がいいから、一度も失敗したことがないです。

2. Is there any food left in the refrigerator? If there is any, what is there?

はい、(たくさん)残っています。おにぎりと納豆があります。

いいえ、(あまり)残っていません。

3. Have you ever left food behind at a restaurant? If you have, what type of food did you leave behind?
    はい、あります。よく野菜を残します。／ はい、あります。嫌いな物をいつも残します。

    いいえ、いつも全部食べます。/ いいえ、何も残しません。

4. What day of the week is your day off?
    土曜日と日曜日です。/ 休みは決まっていません。/ 休みがないです。

5. When are you strong, at the time of the actual performance, or at the time of practicing?
    本番の方が強いです。/ 練習の方が強いです。

    どちらも弱いです。/ どちらも強いです。/ 本番も練習も強いです。/ 本番も練習も弱いです。

7. Translation (answers)

1. 行きは簡単だけど、帰りは大変です。／ 行くのは簡単ですが、帰るのは大変です。

2. 誕生日に何も期待していません。

3. 交通事故のせいで、仕事に遅れました。

4. 「上」という漢字は、読みがたくさんあります。

5. 休みの日は、一日中テレビをつけっぱなしです。／休みの日は、一日中テレビをつけています。

8. Visual clue questions (answers)

1. ギターがひけるようになりました。

2. 英語が話せるようになりました。

3. (車が)運転できるようになりました。

4. スプーンで食べられるようになりました。／食べられるようになりました。

5. 歩けるようになりました。／立てるようになりました。

5

| 17 PAGES | 8 USAGE SECTIONS | 22 NEW WORDS |

Lesson 5:
Unintended Actions

From the teacher...

Some of the words in this lesson might be strange like "hay" and "farmer," but they are used in the workbook area reading comprehension, so don't ignore them. 😊

5 | New Words 新しい言葉

Nouns etc.

ある日 <small>ひ</small>	one day; a certain day	ぬいぐるみ	stuffed animal
追いかけっこ <small>お</small>	chase game; game of tag	約束 <small>やく そく</small>	a promise
雌牛 <small>め うし</small>	female cow	パンの耳 <small>みみ</small>	bread crust
お百姓 <small>ひゃくしょう</small>	farmer	住所 <small>じゅう しょ</small>	address
干草 <small>ほし くさ</small>	hay	画面 <small>が めん</small>	screen; picture

Adverbs

その代わり <small>か</small>	instead; in return; alternatively
二度と <small>に ど</small>	never again; ever again (always used with negative verb)

Verbs

噛み切る <small>か き</small>	to bite off	腐る <small>くさ</small>	to spoil; to turn rotten
渡す <small>わた</small>	to hand; to pass; to give	しまう	to put away; put an end to
忘れる <small>わす</small>	to forget	入れる <small>い</small>	to put into; to put inside
あくびをする	to yawn		

Adjectives

賢い <small>かしこ</small>	wise; clever; smart
偉い <small>えら</small>	good! great!

Connector

すると	thereupon; with that

5 | Word Usage 言葉の使い方

W-1	ある日 (ひ)	one day

Unspecified, but some day in particular. ある can also be used in front of other nouns to say "a certain~ (noun)" or "one~ (noun)"

EXAMPLES
1. ある夏の日 (なつ・ひ)
   one summer day
2. ある人 (ひと)
   someone; a certain person
3. ある所 (ところ)
   a certain place
4. あるおばあさんの話 (はなし)
   one old lady's story

EXAMPLE SENTENCES
1. ある人から、武田さんが引っ越したと聞きました。
   I heard from someone that Takeda-san was going to move.
2. ある所では、台風でガスが三日間、使えませんでした。
   In some places, gas couldn't be used for three days due to the typhoon.

5 | Verb Usage 動詞の使い方

V-1	噛み切る (か・き)	to bite off	いる/える exception
1. (something) を噛み切る		to bite off (something)	

EXAMPLE SENTENCES
1. 犬がぬいぐるみの耳を噛み切りました。
   The dog bit off the ear of a stuffed animal.
2. お菓子の袋を開ける時、口で噛み切らないで下さい。
   When you open the snack bag, please don't bite it off with your mouth.
3. このお肉は噛み切れないですね。
   I cannot bite off this meat.

V-2	渡す (わた)	to hand; to hand over; to pass; to give	regular

1. (somebody)に (something) を渡す	to hand (something) to (somebody)

Depending on what sounds natural in English, 渡す translates to, "hand over", "pass", "give" or any other similar English that has the same core meaning of 渡す.

EXAMPLE SENTENCES

> を and に appear in different order from sentence #1. This is okay if the particles move with the words.

1. これをスミスさんに渡して下さい。
   Please hand this over to Mr. Smith.

2. 竹中さんにこの割引券を渡したほうがいいです。
   You should hand this discount coupon over to Takenaka.

3. 森さんが遊びにくるので、紙に住所を書いて、渡しました。
   Mr. Mori is coming to hang out, so I wrote my address on paper and gave it to him.

📖 もっと詳しく… More Details

The difference between わたす and あげる

渡す and あげる both mean "to give". あげる is used to imply a change of ownership of the object being given. 渡す can mean a change in ownership AND it also refers to the changing of location of the object from one person to another. It all depends on the context.

There are clear cases where only 渡す should be used.

1. 先生にこの手紙を渡してね。
   Give this letter to the teacher.

> Even though this has "give" in the translation, we are just "handing" the letter to the teacher.

2. バトンを次のランナーに渡した。
   I gave (handed) the baton to the next runner.

3. 伊藤君にほうきを渡して、掃除してもらった。
   I handed the broom to Ito and had him clean.

If you are giving something to someone as a present, あげる is a much better choice of verb.

RELATED VERB(S)

Japanese From Zero! ④ Section 3-2. あげる (to give)

V-3	忘れる (わす)	to forget	いる/える

1. (place)に (thing)を忘れる — to forget (thing) at a (place)

EXAMPLE SENTENCES

1. 家に財布を忘れました。
   I forgot my wallet at my house.

2. 教室を出る時、教科書を忘れないで下さい。
   Don't forget your textbook when you leave the classroom.

📖 もっと詳しく… More Details ⓘ

Particle usage with わすれる

に and で can both mean, "at" in English, so it's easy to mix them up.

CORRECT ✔

1. 財布を家に忘れました。
   I forgot my wallet at home.

> に is perfect for saying WHERE you forgot a particular item.

WRONG ✘

2. 財布を家で忘れました。
   I forgot my wallet (while) at home.

> で marks EVENT LOCATION. So, instead of saying where you left the wallet, you are saying where you were when you forgot.

These sentences are both correct.

3. 玄関で靴を脱ぐのを忘れました。
   I forgot to take my shoes off at the front door.

> PERFECT! You use で to mark WHERE you were when you forgot.

4. 友達の家に靴を忘れました。
   I forgot my shoes at my friend's house.

> PERFECT! You use に to mark the location of your forgotten shoes.

V-4	あくびをする	to yawn	する

EXAMPLE SENTENCES

1. あくびをしてるけど、昨日ちゃんと寝たの？
   So... you are yawning, did you sleep well yesterday?

2. 会議であくびをしないように、コーヒーをたくさん飲みました。
   So that I wouldn't yawn at the meeting, I drank a lot of coffee.

V-5	入れる <small>い</small>	to put into; to put inside	いる/える

1. (thing)を (place)に いれる	to put (thing) into (place)

EXAMPLE SENTENCES

1. コーヒーをもう少し入れて下さい。
   <small>すこ　い　　　くだ</small>
   Please add (put) a little more coffee.

2. 昼ご飯はいつもこの黄色い袋に入れます。
   <small>ひる　はん　　　　　き いろ　ふくろ　い</small>
   I always put my lunch into this yellow bag.

3. 毎日六時に、赤ちゃんをお風呂に入れることにしています。
   <small>まい にち ろく じ　　あか　　　　　　ふ ろ　い</small>
   I make it a rule to give my baby a bath at 6 o'clock every day.

4. お茶を入れました。
   <small>ちゃ　い</small>
   I put on some tea.

 Japanese people use お茶を入れる to mean, "make tea".

 "Give a bath" can never be おふろを あげる.

📖 もっと詳しく… More Details ⓘ
<small>くわ</small>

Fun with 入る (to enter), 入れる (to put in), and 入れる (to be able to enter)
<small>はい　　　　　　　　　い　　　　　　　　　　　　　　　　はい</small>

Because the kanji 入 (to enter) is used in similar verbs, it's easy to get confused. This should remind you that context is very important.

1. お風呂に入る。 <small>ふ ろ　はい</small> to take a bath	2. お風呂に入れる。 <small>ふ ろ　い</small> to give a bath	3. お風呂に入れる。 <small>ふ ろ　はい</small> to be able to take a bath

EXAMPLE SENTENCES

4. お父さんは今朝、お風呂に入りました。
   <small>とう　　　けさ　　　ふ ろ　はい</small>
   Father took a bath this morning.

5. お父さんは今朝、赤ちゃんをお風呂に入れました。
   <small>とう　　　けさ　あか　　　　　　ふ ろ　い</small>
   Father gave the baby a bath this morning.

6. 時間があったから、今朝お風呂に入れました。
   <small>じ かん　　　　　　　けさ　ふ ろ　はい</small>
   Because I had time, I was able to take a bath this morning.

7. 私は赤ちゃんとお風呂に入りたかったけど、時間がないから入れなくて、その代わり、
   <small>わたし　あか　　　　　　ふ ろ　はい　　　　　　　　じ かん　　　　　　はい　　　　　　　か</small>
   奥さんが赤ちゃんをお風呂に入れました。
   <small>おく　　　　あか　　　　　　ふ ろ　い</small>
   I wanted to take a bath with the baby, but since I had no time I couldn't go in, so instead, my wife gave the baby a bath.

RELATED VERB(S)

Japanese From Zero! ④ V-1. 入る (to enter)

V-6	腐る (くさ)	to spoil; to turn rotten	regular

1. (thing)が腐る — (thing) spoils

EXAMPLE SENTENCES

1. 冷蔵庫の中の食べ物が腐りました。
The food in the refrigerator became spoiled.

2. 冷蔵庫の中の食べ物が腐っています。
The food in the refrigerator is spoiled.

> Notice the minor nuance difference. くさりました means "became spoiled" while くさっています means "is spoiled".

3. この鶏肉は腐ってると思う。
I think this chicken is spoiled.

> Don't forget that ~ている (present ongoing tense) often drops the い to become just てる.

4. 臭いけど、このヨーグルトはまだ腐ってないです。
It smells bad, but this yogurt isn't spoiled yet.

V-7	しまう	to put away	regular

1. (place)に (thing)をしまう — to put away (thing) in (place)

EXAMPLE SENTENCES

1. 本をしまって下さい。
Please put away your books.

> In the KANSAI area, "to put away" is なおす. However, しまう will be understood.

2. 洗濯物をしまいますから、手伝って下さい。
I am going to put away the laundry, so please help me.

3. 牛乳が腐らないように、冷蔵庫にしまってください。
Please put away the milk in the refrigerator so that it doesn't spoil.

5 | Grammar and Usage 文法と使い方

● 5-1. Using しまう when an action was carried out to the end

しまう is added to the て form of a verb. It shows an action was carried out to the end. Notice how using てしまう changes the nuance of the sentence.

EXAMPLE SENTENCES

1. 本を読みました。
   I read a book.

   → 本を読んでしまいました。
   I read the entire book.

2. 一人でピザを食べました。
   I ate pizza by myself.

   → 一人でピザを食べてしまいました。
   I finished eating the (entire) pizza by myself.

● 5-2. Using てしまう when things happen unconsciously

てしまう is also used when something occurred without thinking.

EXAMPLE SENTENCES

1. 笑ってしまいました。
   Before I knew it, I laughed.

2. 転んでしまいました。
   I accidentally tripped.

3. 泣いてしまいました。
   Before I knew it, I cried.

   "accidentally" is only used to show change in nuance.

● 5-3. Using てしまう for unintended actions or circumstances

てしまう also shows a sense of regret for unintended or unplanned outcomes.

EXAMPLE SENTENCES

1. ああ...バスが行ってしまいました。
   Dang it, the bus left.

2. ダイエットをしているのに、また チョコレートを食べてしまった。
   Oops! Even though I'm on my diet, I ate chocolate again.

てしまう also shows inevitable truths or outcomes that can't be stopped.

3. 人間はいつか死んでしまいます。
   Humans die in the end someday. / Humans eventually die sometime.

4. 娘が大学に行ってしまったので、家が静かになりました。
   Since my daughter ended up going to college, the house is quiet now.

● **5-4. Using てしまう to show intention or a threat of a future action**

When a threat is conveyed in English, we normally use different tone of voice or add stress to certain words to relay the threat. しまう is the equivalent in Japanese.

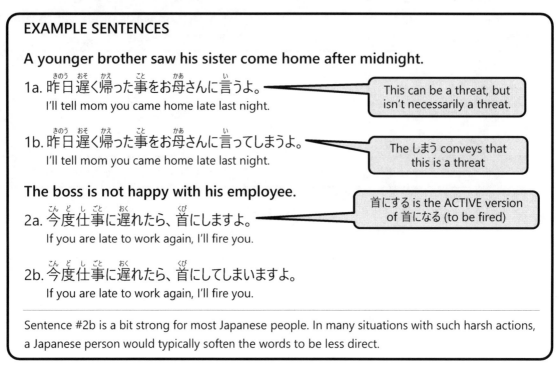

EXAMPLE SENTENCES

A younger brother saw his sister come home after midnight.

1a. 昨日遅く帰った事をお母さんに言うよ。

I'll tell mom you came home late last night.

> This can be a threat, but isn't necessarily a threat.

1b. 昨日遅く帰った事をお母さんに言ってしまうよ。

I'll tell mom you came home late last night.

> The しまう conveys that this is a threat

The boss is not happy with his employee.

2a. 今度仕事に遅れたら、首にしますよ。

If you are late to work again, I'll fire you.

> 首にする is the ACTIVE version of 首になる (to be fired)

2b. 今度仕事に遅れたら、首にしてしまいますよ。

If you are late to work again, I'll fire you.

Sentence #2b is a bit strong for most Japanese people. In many situations with such harsh actions, a Japanese person would typically soften the words to be less direct.

● **5-5. てしまう with other forms**

A verb in the てしまう form just like any verb can be conjugated into various forms.

EXAMPLES

食べてしまってください。
Please finish eating it.

食べてしまいたいです。
I want to finish eating it.

食べてしまいませんか。
Why don't we finish eating it?

食べてしまいましょう。
Let's eat it all.

食べてしまってもいいですか。
Is it okay if I eat the rest of this?

食べてしまったほうがいいです。
You should eat the rest of this.

● 5-6. てしまう informal / casual version

The informal form of てしまう is ちゃう. When て form ends in で, then use じゃう.

EXAMPLES

動<small>うご</small>いてしまう	→	動<small>うご</small>いちゃう		開<small>あ</small>けてしまう	→	開<small>あ</small>けちゃう
困<small>こま</small>ってしまう	→	困<small>こま</small>っちゃう		もらってしまう	→	もらっちゃう
読<small>よ</small>んでしまう	→	読<small>よ</small>んじゃう		休<small>やす</small>んでしまう	→	休<small>やす</small>んじゃう
来<small>き</small>てしまう	→	来<small>き</small>ちゃう		してしまう	→	しちゃう

This next conversation shows てしまう used in a variety of ways in one conversation. Also, since the conversation is between mother and daughter, it uses casual form.

EXAMPLE CONVERSATION

1. **Casual conversation between a mother and her daughter**

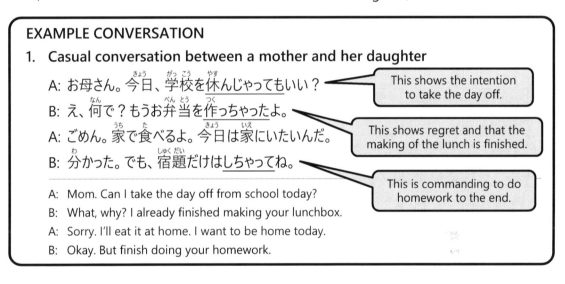

   A: お母さん。今日、学校を休んじゃってもいい？ — *This shows the intention to take the day off.*

   B: え、何で？もうお弁当を作っちゃったよ。 — *This shows regret and that the making of the lunch is finished.*

   A: ごめん。家で食べるよ。今日は家にいたいんだ。

   B: 分かった。でも、宿題だけはしちゃってね。 — *This is commanding to do homework to the end.*

   A: Mom. Can I take the day off from school today?
   B: What, why? I already finished making your lunchbox.
   A: Sorry. I'll eat it at home. I want to be home today.
   B: Okay. But finish doing your homework.

● **5-7. The と If-Then statement**

The と IF-THEN statement is often used for stating things that happen *naturally*, such as "if the temperature drops, ice turns to water" and *instructions*, such as "if you push this button, it will turn on".

> ## (condition) と、result
> ## With this (condition), this will happen.

As with the たら IF-THEN form, the と IF-THEN form can also mean either "IF" or "WHEN" depending on the context of the sentence.

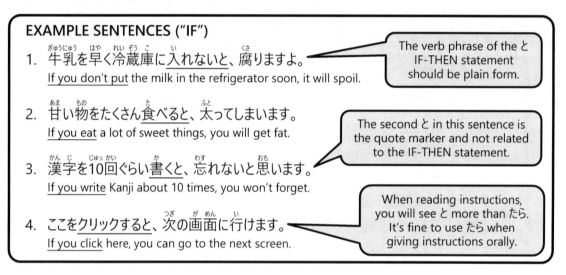

EXAMPLE SENTENCES ("IF")

1. 牛乳を早く冷蔵庫に入れないと、腐りますよ。
   If you don't put the milk in the refrigerator soon, it will spoil.

   The verb phrase of the と IF-THEN statement should be plain form.

2. 甘い物をたくさん食べると、太ってしまいます。
   If you eat a lot of sweet things, you will get fat.

   The second と in this sentence is the quote marker and not related to the IF-THEN statement.

3. 漢字を10回ぐらい書くと、忘れないと思います。
   If you write Kanji about 10 times, you won't forget.

   When reading instructions, you will see と more than たら. It's fine to use たら when giving instructions orally.

4. ここをクリックすると、次の画面に行けます。
   If you click here, you can go to the next screen.

Certain situations are always translated as WHEN in English. Ultimately the situation decides how to best translate an IF-THEN statement as IF or WHEN.

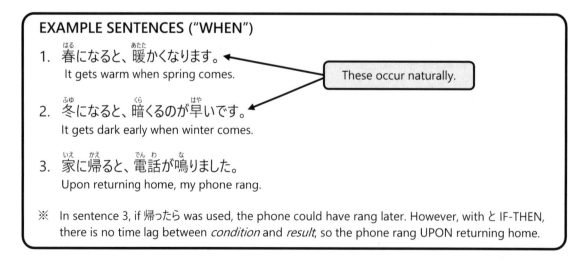

EXAMPLE SENTENCES ("WHEN")

1. 春になると、暖かくなります。
   It gets warm when spring comes.

   These occur naturally.

2. 冬になると、暗くなるのが早いです。
   It gets dark early when winter comes.

3. 家に帰ると、電話が鳴りました。
   Upon returning home, my phone rang.

※ In sentence 3, if 帰ったら was used, the phone could have rang later. However, with と IF-THEN, there is no time lag between *condition* and *result*, so the phone rang UPON returning home.

📖 もっと詳しく… More Details ℹ

The differences between と and たら

と has a few restrictions on usage that たら doesn't.

と is NEVER followed by commands, requests, invitation or suggestions.

CORRECT ✔

1. 起きたら、電話してください。
   Call me when you wake up.

2. いい天気だったら、出かけよう。
   Let's go out if the weather is good.

3. 病気だったら、休んだ方がいいよ。
   You should rest if you are sick.

WRONG ✘

起きると、電話してください。
Commands are NOT used with と IF-THEN

いい天気だと、出かけよう。
Invitations are NOT used with と IF-THEN

病気だと、休んだ方がいい。
Suggestions are NOT used with と IF-THEN

と can be used when giving an opinion. With たら, the opinion is directly aimed at the person you are speaking to. With と, it sounds softer like a general opinion.

DIRECTED AT PERSON

1. たばこを吸ったら、だめですよ。
   You shouldn't smoke. (it's bad for you)

2. このコートを着たら、暖かいですよ。
   You should wear this coat. (you'll be warm)

INDIRECT

3. たばこを吸うと、だめですよ。
   It's not good to smoke.

4. このコートを着ると、暖かいですよ。
   It's warm if you wear this coat.

RELATED GRAMMAR

Japanese From Zero! ④ Section 11-4. If-then statements using なら
Japanese From Zero! ④ Section 11-5. If-then statements using たら

● 5-8. Real life versus textbook sentences

In this lesson, you learned quite a few things that てしまう can do. It's quite possible you feel overwhelmed. After all, てしまう is used to convey all the following:

1. Regretful actions
2. Showing completed actions
3. Unconscious actions
4. Unintended consequences
5. Threat of future actions

You might be worried that not knowing which version is being used will lead to an epic misunderstanding with your Japanese friends, or worse, your boss at work.

In reality, <u>USING</u> Japanese is often much easier than <u>LEARNING</u> Japanese.
In textbooks, sentences are designed to show the basic concept of a new grammar point, and therefore often lack the clarity of context contained in a real-life conversation. Furthermore, in a real-life conversation, more words are added to the sentence that make the intent obvious.

NEUTRAL (nuance unknown)

Without a tone of voice or any words to help with context, we can only assume what the intention of the speaker was in this sentence:

> 飲んでしまいました。
>
> I drank (it).

Without any context, this means "I drank", but perhaps the person didn't want to drink since they have a drinking problem. Tone of voice, and other situational facts, would make it clear they were regretting a drink. In a real conversation though, there will often be more clues even beyond the situational context.

Regretful actions

By simply adding a regretful tone or a Japanese audible sigh, regret is understood.

> ああ、飲んでしまいました。
>
> Ah... I drank.

Showing completed actions

Since something like "drinking" (alcohol) can be a problem, in a real conversation, if a Japanese person wanted to say, "I drank <u>all</u> of it", they would add a supporting word like ぜんぶ (all).

> 全部、飲んでしまいました。
>
> I drank it all.

Unconscious actions

Unconscious action is also normally accompanied with context in real conversation.

> パーティーが楽^{たの}しくて、いつもより飲^のんでしまいました。
> The party was so fun, I drank more than usual.

Unintended consequence

In a real conversation, it would also be obvious that てしまう was used to show an unintended consequence since there would be surrounding context showing it.

> ジュースをあそこに置^おくと、犬^{いぬ}が飲^のんでしまうよ。
> If you put your juice there, the dog will drink it.

Threat of future action

A threat using てしまう would also easily be understood due to the situation and surrounding words. Although perhaps it might be weird to use drinking juice as a threat, we will use the same verb 飲む as a threat for consistency of our examples.

In the following example, an older sister who is babysitting her younger sister is threatening that she will drink her sister's favorite juice if she doesn't finish her homework. The younger sister doesn't want this, so to her it is a viable threat.

> 宿題^{しゅくだい}をしないと、あなたのジュースを飲^のんでしまうよ！
> If you don't do your homework, I will drink your juice!

5 | Practice and Review　練習と復習

● 1. Mini Conversation ミニ会話 J → E

Try translating the entire conversation before looking at the translation below.

1. **Polite conversation between co-workers**

    A: ここにあった切手を知りませんか。

    B: 全部、使ってしまいました。だめでしたか。

    A: いいけど、今度、新しいのを買って下さいね。

    B: ごめんなさい。明日、買いに行きます。

    A: Do you know of the stamps that were here?

    B: I used them all. Was that a bad thing?

    A: It's okay, but please buy some new one's next time.

    B: I am sorry. I will go to buy some tomorrow.

2. **Informal conversation between a married couple**

    A: 今日、大家さんに家賃を渡してくれた？

    B: あっ、忘れた！明日するよ。

    A: どうしていつも忘れるの？大家さんは一階にいるから、毎日会うでしょう。

    B: うん...。でも、忘れてしまう。

    A: Did you give our rent to the landlord today?

    B: Oh, I forgot! I will do it tomorrow.

    A: How come you always forget? You see him every day because he is on the first floor.

    B: Yeah... but I forget before I know it.

3. **Informal conversation between a husband and a wife**

    A: ただいま。

    B: おかえりなさい。出張はどうだった？

    A: うん、よかったよ。お腹が空いた！何かある？

    B: 実はないの。あなたがいないと、私は料理をしないでしょう。だから、冷蔵庫にある食べ物が全部腐ってしまったの。

A: I am home!

B: Hi! (Welcome home) How was your business trip?

A: Yeah, it was good. I am hungry! Is there anything (any food)?

B: Actually, nothing. You know I don't cook when you aren't home. So, all the food in the fridge went bad (before I knew it.)

4. Informal conversation between a strict mother and a son

A: ちょっと出かけてくるよ。

B: 「ちょっと」って、どこに行くの？

A: すぐそこだよ。晩ご飯の前に帰ってくるよ。

B: 夜7時になったら、ドアを閉めてしまうよ！分かった？

A: I'm going to go out for a bit.

B: A "bit"? Where are you going?

A: Just over there. I'll be back before dinner.

B: Once it's 7pm, I'll be shutting the door! You got it?

● 2. Mini Conversation ミニ会話 E → J

Look at the English conversations and see if you can figure out the Japanese.
Try to translate the entire conversation first before looking at the translation.

1. Polite conversation between friends

A: I gave the puppy I was raising to a friend, but the puppy ended up coming back to my house.

B: It sure is an intelligent dog. How many months old is he now?

A: He has become six months old. I am troubled because he always returns.

A: 飼っていた子犬を友達にあげたんですが、その子犬が家に戻ってきてしまったんです。

B: かしこい犬ですね。今、何ヶ月ですか。

A: 六か月になりました。いつも戻ってくるから、困りますよ。

2. Polite conversation between co-workers

A: What's wrong? You don't have any energy, huh?

B: Since I forgot my girlfriend's birthday, she's mad.

A: Well then, buy her a present right away.

B: Actually, now I don't have any money and can't buy anything until payday.

A: I see. Well, that's hopeless.

A: どうしましたか？ 元気がないですね。

B: 彼女の誕生日を忘れてしまったから、彼女が怒っているんです。

A: じゃあ、すぐにプレゼントを買ってあげましょうよ。

B: 実は今、お金がなくて、給料日まで何も買えないんですよ。

A: そうですか。じゃあ、しょうがないですね。

3. Informal conversation between a father and son

A: I don't want to eat spinach.

B: If you don't eat vegetables, you can't get big.

A: Instead of that, I will eat a lot of potatoes.

B: No, because potatoes and spinach are not the same.

A: Well then, I will eat a little.

A: ほうれん草を食べたくない。

B: 野菜を食べないと、大きくなれないよ。

A: その代わり、じゃがいもをたくさん食べるよ。

B: だめ。じゃがいもとほうれん草は同じじゃないから。

A: じゃあ、少しだけ食べるよ。

4. Polite conversation between college students

A: I always get hungry when I am studying.

B: I also can't study if I don't eat chocolate.

A: But since I am dieting, I can't eat anything.

B: That's great. I can't do that! (dieting)

A: 勉強をしている時、いつもお腹が空きます。

B: 私もチョコレートを食べないと、勉強ができません。

A: でも、僕はダイエットをしているから、何も食べられないんです。

B: えらいですね。私はできません。

● 3. Short Dialogue

Mrs. Takada tends to buy too many things at stores.

高田さん　「西本さん・・・私は本当にだめな人間です。」

西本さん　「どうしてですか。」

高田さん　「私はデパートに行くと、いつも要らない物を買ってしまいます。」

西本さん　「それは私も時々、ありますよ。」

高田さん　「スーパーに行く時も同じです。たくさん買うけど、料理をあんまりしないから、食べ物が腐ってしまうんです。」

西本さん　「そうですか。じゃあ、行く前に買い物リストを作るといいですよ。」

高田さん　「う～ん・・・。私は多分、その買い物リストを忘れてしまいますね。」

西本さん　「ははは。書いてから、すぐカバンに入れたら忘れないですよ。」

高田さん　「カバンに入れるのも忘れると思います。」

西本さん　「それじゃ、しょうがないですね。」

5

Kanji Lesson 5:
家寺門店園場

From the teacher...

The kanji in this lesson are related to places and buildings.

5 | New Kanji 新しい漢字

185	宀	10 画	house

	くんよみ	いえ、や、うち
	おんよみ	カ、ケ

家 (いえ、うち) house　　　　家賃 (や・ちん) rent
家族 (か・ぞく) family　　　　貸家 (かし・や) house for rent
家来 (け・らい) servant　　　　屋根 (や・ね) roof

家									

186	寸	6 画	temple

	くんよみ	てら
	おんよみ	ジ

お寺 (お・てら) temple　　　　山寺 (やま・でら) mountain temple
神社 (じんじゃ) shrine　　　　金閣寺 (きん・かく・じ) Golden Pavilion temple
禅寺 (ぜん・でら) zen temple　　清水寺 (きよ・みず・でら) Kiyomizu temple

寺									

187	門	8 画	gate

	くんよみ	かど
	おんよみ	モン

校門 (こう・もん) school gate　　　門松 (かど・まつ) New Year's pine decoration
正門 (せい・もん) main gate　　　門限 (もん・げん) curfew; closing time
門 (もん) gate　　　　　　　　専門家 (せん・もん・か) expert; specialist; pundit

門									

188	广	8画	store; a shop		
			くんよみ	みせ	
			おんよみ	テン	
			お店 (お・みせ) store; a shop	支店 (し・てん) branch store	
			店員 (てん・いん) clerk	100 店舗 (ひゃく・てん・ぽ) 100 stores	
			店長 (てん・ちょう) shop manager	喫茶店 (きっ・さ・てん) coffee shop; cafe	

189	□	13画	garden		
			くんよみ	その	
			おんよみ	エン	
			公園 (こう・えん) park	花園 (はな・その) flower garden	
			園児 (えん・じ) kindergarten pupil	国立公園 (こく・りつ・こう・えん) National park	
			園芸 (えん・げい) gardening	遊園地 (ゆう・えん・ち) amusement park	

190	土	12画	place; location		
			くんよみ	ば	
			おんよみ	ジョウ	
			会場 (かい・じょう) assembly hall	工場 (こう・じょう) factory	
			場所 (ば・しょ) place	現場 (げん・ば) location; scene of a crime	
			場面 (ば・めん) scene, setting	穴場 (あな・ば) little-know good place	

5 | Kanji Culture 漢字の文化

● Same kanji parts, same reading

The following three kanji characters look complicated; however, they have something in common. They all have a variation of 「袁」 in them. Sometimes the way a kanji is read in the おんよみ (Chinese reading) is solely based on the parts used to make them. In this case, despite having completely different meanings, all three of these kanji share the same おんよみ of エン.

EXAMPLES

1. 園 (garden; place)   公園 (park); 動物園 (zoo)

2. 遠 (distant; far)   永遠 (eternity); 遠足 (excursion)

3. 猿 (monkey)   犬猿の仲 (cats and dogs); 猿人 (ape man)

5 | Words You Can Write かける言葉

大家 (おおや) landlord

大	家									

画家 (がか) painter; artist

画	家									

山寺 (やまでら) mountain temple

山	寺									

校門 (こうもん) school gate

校	門									

正門 (せいもん) main gate

正	門									

お店 (おみせ) store; a shop

お	店									

店長 (てんちょう) shop manager

店	長									

花園 (はなぞの) flower garden

花	園									

田園 (でんえん) rural districts

田	園									

会場 (かいじょう) assembly hall; meeting place

会	場									

場合 (ばあい) case; situation

場	合									

家計 (かけい) family finances

家	計									

作家 (さっか) author; novelist; artist

作	家									

入門 (にゅうもん) entering an institution; beginning training

入	門									

売店 (ばいてん) stand; stall; booth; kiosk; store

売	店									

5 Workbook 5: Workbook Activities

5 | Kanji Drills 漢字ドリル

● 1. Reading practice

Write FURIGANA above the underlined kanji words.

1. 家の近じょにお寺があります。

2. 学校の校門は、8 時 45 分にしまります。

3. 一つ目の信号を右にまがると、小さいお店があります。
   <small>しんごう</small>

4. 明日、コンサート会場で会いましょう。

5. あの公園には、きれいな花園がありますよ。
   <small>こう</small>

● 2. Fill in the kanji

Fill in the appropriate kanji in the blanks for each sentence.

1. ___ ___ 、 ___ ___ さんに ___ ちんを はらいました。
   <small>せん げつ　おお や　　　や</small>

   Last month, I paid the owner the rent.

2. お ___ ___ に お___ に ___ きました。
   <small>しょう がつ　　　てら　　い</small>

   I went to a temple on New Year's Day.

3. ___ と___ ___ のまえで___ うことに なっています。
   <small>はは　こう もん　　　あ</small>

   It's decided that I'm meeting my mother in front of the school gate.

4. <ruby>おとうと</ruby> ___は、お___<ruby>みせ</ruby> で おもちゃを ___<ruby>か</ruby>いました。

My little brother bought toys at the store.

5. こう ___ で ___<ruby>えん</ruby>を ___<ruby>ほん</ruby>むのが すきです。<ruby>よ</ruby>

I like reading books at the park.

6. ___<ruby>しち</ruby> ___<ruby>がつ</ruby> ___<ruby>よっ</ruby> ___<ruby>か</ruby> に、あの_____<ruby>かい</ruby> <ruby>じょう</ruby>でコンサートが ある。

On July 4th, there is a concert at that meeting hall.

7. ___<ruby>うち</ruby> から ___<ruby>ちか</ruby> くのお___<ruby>てら</ruby>までは、___<ruby>ある</ruby>いて___ ___<ruby>じっ</ruby>です。<ruby>ぷん</ruby>

It's 10 minutes by foot to the nearby temple from our house.

5 | Usage Activities 文法アクティビティー

● 3. Reading comprehension

Translate the following on a separate piece of paper or type in an electronic device.

| ネズミの尻尾 | *You might learn some valuable negotiation skills from the poor guy who lost his tail in this story.* |

❶ ある日、猫とねずみが追いかけっこをしている時、猫がねずみのしっぽを噛み切ってしまいました。

❷ 「しっぽを返してよ。」と、ねずみがびっくりして言いました。

❸ でも、猫はしっぽを返してくれません。

❹ 「しっぽを返してほしいなら、雌牛のところへ行って、ミルクをもらってきて。」と猫は怖い顔で言いました。

❺ ねずみは、雌牛のところへ行きました。

❻ 「ぼくにミルクを下さい。猫にあげないと、しっぽが戻らない。」

❼ 「だめだめ。ミルクがほしいなら、お百姓のところへ行って、干し草をもらってきて。」

❽ ねずみはお百姓のところへ行きました。

❾ 「ぼくに干し草を下さい。干し草がないと、ぼくのしっぽが戻らない。」

❿ 「だめだめ。ほし草がほしいなら、肉屋へ行って、お肉をもらってきて。」

⓫ ねずみは肉屋へ行きました。

⓬ 「ぼくに お肉を下さい。お肉がないと、ぼくのしっぽが戻らない。」

⓭ 「だめだめ。お肉がほしいなら、パン屋へ行って、パンをもらってきて。」

⓮ ねずみはパン屋へ行きました。

⓯ 「ぼくにパンを下さい。パンがないと、ぼくのしっぽが戻らない。」

⓰ すると、パン屋がこう答えました。

⓱ 「いいですよ。その代わり、もう、うちの小麦を食べないで。」

⓲ 「はい、二度とあなたの小麦を食べません。約束します。」と答えました。

⓳ ねずみはパンを肉屋に、お肉をお百姓に、干し草を雌牛に、ミルクを猫に渡して、やっとしっぽを返してもらいました。

● 4. Reading comprehension questions

Translate the questions about the reading comprehension then answer in Japanese.

1. 猫はどうしてねずみのしっぽを返してくれませんか。

   Translation: _____

   Answer: _____

2. ねずみはどこにミルクをもらいに行きましたか。

   Translation: _____

   Answer: _____

3. ねずみはどこに干し草をもらいに行きましたか。

   Translation: _____

   Answer: _____

4. ねずみはどうしてパン屋に行きましたか。

   Translation: _____

   Answer: _____

5. ねずみはパン屋に何をあげましたか。

   Translation: _____

   Answer: _____

6. ねずみはどんな性格だと思いますか。

Translation: _____

Answer: _____

● 5. Fill in the blanks
Fill in the missing part based on the English sentence.

1. 牛乳が_____。

    The milk spoiled (before I knew it.)

2. お百姓さんから_____ました。

    I accidentally lost the address I got from the farmer.

3. _____きます。

    I'm going on a business trip (and come back).

4. 年を_____、お肉が_____。

    When you grow old, you can't bite off meat.

5. _____、いつも_____をしてしまいます。

    If I watch a boring movie, I always end up yawning.

● 6. Question and Answer
Answer the following questions.

1. いつも家の鍵をどこに置きますか。

    _____

2. 日本茶を入れたことがありますか。

    _____

3. 仕事をしている時、あくびをしてしまいますか。

_____

4. 何歳ごろ、一人で出かけるようになりましたか。

_____

5. 何をすると、元気になりますか。

_____

● 7. Translation
Translate the following sentences into Japanese.

1. If you turn right here, there is a post office on your left.

_____

2. Eating vegetables is good for you. (lit: If you eat vegetables, it is good.)

_____

3. Smoking cigarettes isn't good for you. (lit: If you smoke, it is no good.)

_____

4. Due to the typhoon, the window broke (unfortunately).

_____

5. I'm going to go make a phone call to my boss (and come back).

_____

● 8. Visual clue questions

Look at the picture and complete the Japanese sentence using てしまう form.
Then translate the entire sentence into English on the next line.

1. 寒くなったせいで、

_____

_____

2. パーティーが楽しかったから、

_____

_____

3. お腹が空いていたので、

_____

_____

4. 大きい音にびっくりして、

_____

_____

5. 卒業式で皆と別れた時、

_____

_____

5 | Answer Key 答え合わせ

Short Dialogue (translation)

Takada	Nishomoto... I really am a failed human.
Nishimoto	Why?
Takada	When I go to the department store, I always end up buying things I don't need.
Nishimoto	That also happens to me too.
Takada	When I go to the supermarket, it's the same. I buy a lot, but since I don't cook, the food ends up spoiling.
Nishimoto	I see. Well then, it would be good if you make a shopping list before you go.
Takada	Hmmm... I would probably end up forgetting that shopping list.
Nishimoto	Ha-ha. You won't forget it if you put it in your bag immediately after writing it.
Takada	I think I will forget to put it in my bag.
Nishimoto	Well then, it's hopeless.

1. Reading practice (answers)

1. 家の近じょにお寺があります。
2. 学校の校門は、8時45分にしまります。
3. 一つ目の信号を右にまがると、小さいお店があります。
4. 明日、コンサート会場で会いましょう。
5. あの公園には、きれいな花園がありますよ。

2. Fill in the kanji (answers)

1. 先月、大家さんに家ちんを はらいました。
2. お正月にお寺に 行きました。
3. 母と校門のまえで会うことに なっています。
4. 弟は、お店でおもちゃを買いました。
5. こう園で本を読むのが すきです。
6. 七月四日に、あの会場でコンサートが ある。
7. 家から近くのお寺までは、歩いて十分です。

3. Reading comprehension (translation)

❶ One day, when a cat and a mouse were chasing each other, the cat ended up biting off the mouse's tail.
❷ The mouse was surprised and said, "Give my tail back to me".
❸ But the cat wouldn't give it back.
❹ The cat said with a scary face, "If you want your tail back, go to the female cow's place, go and get me some milk."
❺ The mouse went to the female cow's place.
❻ "Please give me some milk. If I don't give it to the cat, I won't get my tail back."
❼ "No, No. If you want some milk, go to the farmer's place and get me some hay."
❽ The mouse went to the farmer's place.
❾ "Please give me some hay. If I don't get some hay, I won't get my tail back."
❿ "No, no. If you want some hay, go to the butcher and get me some meat."
⓫ The mouse went to the butcher.

⑫ "Please give me some meat. If I don't get some meat, I won't get my tail back."
⑬ "No, no. If you want some meat, go to the bakery and get me some bread."
⑭ The mouse went to the bakery.
⑮ "Please give me some bread. If I don't get some bread, I won't get my tail back."
⑯ With that, the baker answered this way.
⑰ "Ok sure. In return, don't eat our wheat anymore."
⑱ The mouse answered, "Yes, I won't eat your wheat ever again. I promise."
⑲ The mouse handed bread to the butcher, meat to the farmer, hay to the female cow, milk to the cat and finally had his tailed returned to him.

4. Reading comprehension questions (answers)

1. Translation: Why won't the cat return the mouse's tail?
   Answer(s):   ミルクがほしいからです。
   ねずみにミルクをもらってきてほしいからです。

2. Translation: Where did the mouse go to get milk?
   Answer(s):   雌牛のところです。

3. Translation: Where did the mouse go to get hay?
   Answer(s):   お百姓のところです。

4. Translation: Why did the mouse go to the bakery?
   Answer(s):   肉屋が「お肉がほしいなら、パン屋へ行ってパンをもらってきて」と言ったからです。
   肉屋にパンを渡すからです。

5. Translation: What did the mouse give to the bakery?
   Answer(s):   何もあげませんでした。

6. Translation: What type of personality do you think the mouse has?
   Answer(s):   えらい子だと思います。
   やさしくて、一生懸命だと思います。

5. Fill in the blanks (answers)

1. 牛乳が腐ってしまいました。
2. お百姓さんからもらった住所をなくしてしまいました。
3. 出張に行ってきます。
4. 年を取ると、お肉がかみきれません。
5. つまらない映画を観ると、いつもあくびをしてしまいます。

6. Question and Answer (answers may vary)

1. Where do you always put your house key?
   かばんの中に入れています。/　玄関に置いています。/ いつもテーブルに置きます。

2. Have you ever made Japanese tea?

はい、あります。 / いいえ、ありません。

3. Do you yawn when you work?

はい、時々してしまいます。 / いいえ、あまりしません。

4. Around what age did you become able to go out by yourself?

13歳ごろです。 / 中学に入ってからです。 / 高校生になってからです。

5. What, if you do it, energizes you?

ごはんを食べると、元気になります。 / 友達に会うと、元気になります。

7. Translation (answers)

1. ここを右に曲がると、左に郵便局があります。

2. 野菜を食べると、体にいいです。/ 野菜を食べると、いいですよ。

3. たばこを吸うと、体によくないです。/ たばこを吸うと、よくないですよ。

4. 台風のせいで、窓が壊れてしまいました。

5. 上司に電話をしてきます。

8. Practice (answers)

1. Due to it getting cold,

病気になってしまいました。(I got sick.)

2. Because the party was fun,

たくさん飲んでしまいました。(I drank a lot.)

3. Since I was hungry,

一人で全部食べてしまいました。(I ate it all by myself.)

4. Being surprised at the loud (big) sound,

赤ちゃんが起きてしまいました。(the baby woke up.)

赤ちゃんが泣いてしまいました。(the baby cried.)

5. When I left everyone at the graduation ceremony,

泣いてしまいました。(I cried.)

寂しくなってしまいました。(I became sad.)

Vocabulary Builder:
Group M

■ Group M: (time related word) + 中

The following words are used for deadlines.

_{きょう じゅう}
今日中(に)   by today; before the day is over ──┐ 中 is pronounced
_{らい しゅう ちゅう}   as じゅう.
来週中(に)   by the end of next week
_{こん げつ ちゅう}
今月中(に)   by the end of this month; later this month
_{がつ ちゅう}
12月中(に)   by the end of December ──┐ 中 is pronounced
_{ねん ない}   as ちゅう.
年内(に)   by the end of the year

NOTE: For 来週中 and 今月中, there are some people who say 中 as じゅう.

The following words are used for periods of time.

_{いち にち じゅう}
一日中   all day long
_{いちねんじゅう}
一年中   all year long
_{ひとばんじゅう}
一晩中   all night long
_{ねん じゅう}
年中   throughout the year
_{ねん じゅう む きゅう}
年中無休   always open (entire year no rest)

6

| 19 PAGES | 5 USAGE SECTIONS | 27 NEW WORDS |

Lesson 6:
Passive Verb Form

6 New Words 新しい言葉

Nouns etc.

いたずら	trick; mischief	堤 (つつみ)	bank; embankment; dike
日頃 (ひ ごろ)	every day; routinely	外出 (がいしゅつ)	outing; trip; going out
突然 (とつ ぜん)	all of a sudden	弱点 (じゃくてん)	a weak point; weakness
世の中 (よ なか)	the world	方言 (ほう げん)	dialects
田んぼ (た)	a rice field	金属 (きん ぞく)	metal
池 (いけ)	a pond	行い (おこな)	action; behavior; conduct
農作物 (のう さく ぶつ)	crops; agricultural produce	人間 (にん げん)	human(s)

Adjectives

頭がいい (あたま)	smart	正直(な) (しょうじき)	honest
素直(な) (す なお)	obedient; amenable; straightforward	新鮮(な) (しん せん)	fresh

Adverb

さり気なく (げ)	casually; incidentally

Verbs

音を立てる (おと た)	to make a sound	拾う (ひろ)	to pick up
驚く (おどろ)	to be surprised	引っ張る (ひ ぱ)	to pull
騙す (だま)	to fool; trick; deceive	飛び込む (と こ)	to jump in
騙される (だま)	to be fooled; tricked; deceived	投げる (な)	to throw

音を立てる
(おと た)

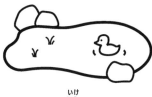

池
(いけ)

素直(な)
(す なお)

6 | Culture Clip カルチャー クリップ

● **Japan's cute and scary mythical creature**

The 河童 (カッパ) is a mythological creature that most Japanese people are familiar with. Although there are various versions of the カッパ legend, it's normally depicted as a green creature about the size of a child with a mischievous personality.

The distinguishing physical feature of カッパ is a plate storing water on the top of its head. It's said that if the plate runs out of water, the カッパ will weaken and perhaps die. For this reason, it usually lives near rivers. It's believed that カッパ will pull animals and humans into the river and suck the blood, internal organs, or the breath out of its victim. Not all カッパ are evil. They also appear in stories as cute characters that even befriend humans.

The true origin of カッパ may not be known, but one popular belief is that it was invented to prevent children from swimming in rivers alone. Children frightened of カッパ will most likely not enter the river alone. Therefore, there is less of a chance that they will drown. Another origin theory is that カッパ came from a giant salamander species living in Japan's rivers.

● **Japan's oldest national sport**

相撲 (すもう) has been in Japan for over 1,500 years in a variety of evolving forms.

In both pro sumo and international sumo, the rules are simply to force your opponent out of the ring or make them touch the ground with any part of the body other than the soles of the feet. Punching, gouging, and kicking are prohibited, but slapping and tripping are allowed. It is legal to grab the まわし (sumo belt) anywhere around the waist, but not in the groin area. Hair-pulling is also banned. (Source: usasumo.com)

The verb to take part in a sumo wrestling match is 相撲を取る. Since する is used in so many sports, people often say 相撲をする also. Both verbs are okay to use.

6 | Word Usage 言葉の使い方

W-1 | ～物(もの) | **thing; object; stuff; item**

Unlike English, Japanese distinguishes between physical and non-physical "things". 物(もの) is only used for physical items. 物(もの) can be part of a word or used alone.

EXAMPLES

忘(わす)れ物(もの)	forgotten item; lost property	(thing that was forgotten)
残(のこ)り物(もの)	leftovers	(remaining things)
入(い)れ物(もの)	case; container; holder	(thing to put things into)
食(た)べ物(もの)	food	(thing to eat)
着物(きもの)	Kimono	(thing to wear)
怖(こわ)い物(もの)	scary things	(adjective (scary) + thing)
甘(あま)い物(もの)	sweets	(adjective (sweet) + thing)

W-2 | ～者(もの) | **person; someone of that nature**

者(もの), also read as しゃ or じゃ, means "a person," and coincidentally has the same sound as 物(もの). However unlike 物(もの), 者(もの) is never used alone, but is integrated with the word.

EXAMPLES

いたずら者(もの)	mischief maker	(mischief + person)
怠(なま)け者(もの)	lazy person; idler	(lazy + person)
保護者(ほごしゃ)	parents; legal guardian	(protect + person)
働(はたら)き者(もの)	hard worker	(work + person)
担当者(たんとうしゃ)	person in charge	(in charge + person)
科学者(かがくしゃ)	scientist	(science + person)
忍者(にんじゃ)	ninja	(conceal + person)

NOTE: 者 (もの) should only be used for predefined person types. When creating new types or undefined people, 人 (ひと) should be used.

変な人 (へん・ひと) — a strange person	面白い人 (おも・しろ・ひと) — interesting person

W-3	～事 (こと)	thing; matter; event; circumstance; situation

事, also read as ごと (こと), is used when talking about non-physical things. It's often part of a word, but it can also be used alone when modified with adjectives or verbs.

EXAMPLES

昔の事 (むかし・こと)	things that have happened a long time ago
心配事／心配な事 (しん・ぱい・ごと／しん・ぱい・こと)	one's worries; things to worry about
うれしい事 (こと)	things that make someone happy
めずらしい事 (こと)	rare event; unusual case
出来ない事 (で・き・こと)	things (I) can't do; things unable to be done

RELATED GRAMMAR

Japanese From Zero! ④ Section 4-1. Section "Talking about things with こと"

W-4	日頃 (ひ・ごろ)	habitually; always; on a daily basis

日頃 (ひ・ごろ) is used as a の-adjective meaning, "daily", "everyday", or "routine" etc.

EXAMPLE SENTENCES

1. 日頃の食事は、健康的にしたいです。(ひ・ごろ・しょく・じ・けん・こう・てき)
   I want to make my daily meals healthy.

2. 早く日頃の生活に戻りたいです。(はや・ひ・ごろ・せい・かつ・もど)
   I want to quickly return to my routine life.

3. テストで悪い点を取ってから、日頃の勉強は大事だと分かりました。(わる・てん・と・ひ・ごろ・べん・きょう・だい・じ・わ)
   After getting a bad score on a test, I understood that daily studying is important.

日頃 is also used as an adverb like いつも and 毎日. It's common to use the ている form
and 日頃 together in a sentence since 日頃 shows currently ongoing actions.

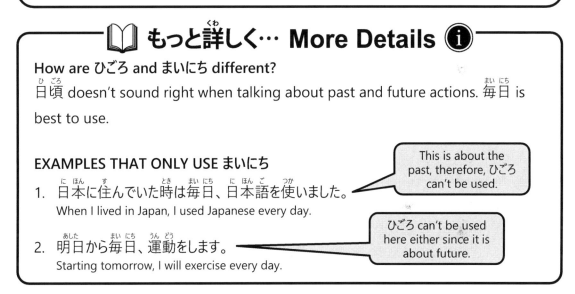

EXAMPLE SENTENCES

1. 私は日頃シャワーだけですが、昨日はお風呂に入りました。
   I <u>always</u> just take a shower, but yesterday I took a bath.

2. 日頃、運動をしていないから、階段を上るのが辛いです。
   Since I don't <u>routinely</u> exercise, it's hard to climb stairs.

   > 日頃から and 日頃 alone have the same meaning. It would be strange to say "from" in the English translation.

3. 私たちの娘は日頃から本番のテストに強いです。
   Our daughter is <u>always</u> good on the actual test.

📖 もっと詳しく… More Details ⓘ

How are ひごろ and まいにち different?

日頃 doesn't sound right when talking about past and future actions. 毎日 is
best to use.

EXAMPLES THAT ONLY USE まいにち

1. 日本に住んでいた時は毎日、日本語を使いました。
   When I lived in Japan, I used Japanese every day.

   > This is about the past, therefore, ひごろ can't be used.

2. 明日から毎日、運動をします。
   Starting tomorrow, I will exercise every day.

   > ひごろ can't be used here either since it is about future.

W-5 | 素直 (すなお) | **obedient; honest; meek; straightforward**

すなお is usually used to evaluate other people objectively and not yourself. It
describes a personality or attitude that doesn't easily oppose other people or
criticism. Someone who is すなお holds back their real feelings and doesn't upset the
other person. Being called すなお is not considered a negative trait in Japan.

When a child is すなお, you could say they "listen to their parents". If a person is
すなお, they probably take criticism well.

When すなお refers to objects or concepts, it means they are not fancy, but very straightforward without peculiarities.

EXAMPLE SENTENCES

1. 家の子は素直で、よく勉強する子です
   My child listens and studies well.

2. あの人は、素直な文章を書きますね。
   That person writes really straightforward compositions.

3. もっと素直に言うことを聞いてほしいです。
   I want you to listen to what I say with less fighting back.

> Here すなお + に makes an adverb modifying the verb いう (to say)

RELATED GRAMMAR

Japanese From Zero! ③ Section 12-5. Making adverbs with な adjectives

📖 もっと詳しく… More Details ⓘ

The difference between すなお and しょうじき (honest)
Even though すなお is sometimes translated as "honest," it's quite different from しょうじき. Being しょうじき means you say what you think is true REGARDLESS of how the other person feels. Being しょうじき may cause friction with other people.

Since すなお can be translated as "honest", it's easy to think you can use either しょうじき or すなお in similar situations. However, this is not the case.

When すなお is used to describe how someone is with other people, it means they HIDE their true feelings. HOWEVER, when it's for themselves, it means they stop hiding their true feelings and become "honest" with themselves.

1. 私は素直になれなくて、彼と別れました。
   Not being able to be honest about my feelings, I broke up with my boyfriend.

2. 正直に言うと、行きたくないです。
   Honestly speaking, I don't want to go.

すなお wouldn't be used in sentence #2 because the person is being honest and as a result possibly causing friction, which is the opposite of what すなお means.

6 | Verb Usage 動詞の使い方

V-1	音を立てる	to make a sound	いる/える

音 means sound. 立てる means "to make" and it can be used in sentences like「計画を立てる」to make or "formulate" a plan.

> **EXAMPLE SENTENCES**
>
> 1. 日本ではラーメンを食べる時、音を立ててもいいです。
>   In Japan it is okay to make noise (to slurp) when you eat ramen.
>
> 2. みんなが寝ているから、音を立てないで下さい。
>   Everyone is sleeping, so please don't make any noise.

V-2	驚く	to be surprised	regular
1. (thing) に驚く		to be surprised by (thing)	
2. (reason) で驚く		to be surprised because of (reason)	

に、で、から、ので、and ~くて can all be used to show the reason for being surprised. 驚く shows a bit more shock than びっくりする.

> **EXAMPLE SENTENCES**
>
> 1. みんなは、あの大きい音に驚きました。
>   Everyone was surprised <u>by</u> that big sound.
>
> 2. トムさんの彼女がきれいで驚きました。
>   I was surprised <u>because</u> Tom's girlfriend is so beautiful.
>
> 3. 日本にたくさんの方言があるので、驚きました。
>   I was surprised <u>since</u> there are many dialects in Japan.
>
> 4. あなたの家が遠くて、驚きました。
>   I was surprised your house was so far.

V-3	飛び込む（と　こ）	to jump in	regular

1. (place) に飛び込む	to jump into (place)

EXAMPLE SENTENCES

1. 子猫はいつも、箱に飛び込みたがっています。
   The kitten always wants to jump into a box.

2. プールに飛び込みました。
   I jumped into the pool.

V-4	投げる（な）	to throw	いる/える

1. (thing) を投げる	to throw a (thing)

EXAMPLE SENTENCES

1. 物を投げると、危ないですよ。
   It's dangerous to throw things.

2. 犬にボールを投げて下さい。
   Please throw the ball to the dog.

V-5	拾う（ひろ）	to pick up	regular

1. (thing) を拾う	to pick up a (thing)

EXAMPLE SENTENCES

1. あのごみを拾ってくれますか。
   Will you pick up that garbage over there for me?

2. 腰が痛くて、床にある物が拾えません。
   I can't pick up things on the floor since my lower back is hurt.

V-6	引っ張る（ひ　ぱ）	to pull	regular

1. (thing) を引っ張る	to pull a (thing)

EXAMPLE SENTENCES

1. コンピューターのコードを引っ張らないで下さい。
   Please don't pull the computer's cords.

2. 髪を引っ張ったら、痛いよ。
   It hurts when you pull my hair.

V-7	騙<ruby>す<rt>だま</rt></ruby>	to fool; to trick; to deceive (ACTIVE)	regular
	1. (someone) を騙す	to trick (someone)	

	騙<ruby>される<rt>だま</rt></ruby>	to be fooled or tricked (PASSIVE)	いる/える
	1. (someone) に騙される	to be tricked by (someone)	

We will sneak in some grammar here using the ACTIVE and PASSIVE verbs introduced above. Assuming that YOU are the topic, an ACTIVE verb is something YOU do. A PASSIVE verb is something that ANOTHER does to you.

EXAMPLES

<ruby>友達<rt>とも だち</rt></ruby>を<ruby>騙<rt>だま</rt></ruby>す。
to trick a friend

<ruby>友達<rt>とも だち</rt></ruby>に<ruby>騙<rt>だま</rt></ruby>される。
to be tricked by a friend

EXAMPLE SENTENCES

As with all verbs, the default pronoun is "I" when making a statement unless a prior topic has been established.

1. <ruby>友達<rt>とも だち</rt></ruby>を<ruby>騙<rt>だま</rt></ruby>しました。
   I tricked my friend.

2. <ruby>友達<rt>とも だち</rt></ruby>に<ruby>騙<rt>だま</rt></ruby>されました。
   I was tricked by my friend.

As a command, now the topic becomes YOU.

3. <ruby>友達<rt>とも だち</rt></ruby>を<ruby>騙<rt>だま</rt></ruby>さないでください。
   Please don't trick your friend.

4. <ruby>友達<rt>とも だち</rt></ruby>に<ruby>騙<rt>だま</rt></ruby>されないでください。
   Please don't get tricked by your friend.

The subject can also be a third person when marked with が.

5. ジョージが<ruby>友達<rt>とも だち</rt></ruby>を<ruby>騙<rt>だま</rt></ruby>しました。
   George tricked his friend.

6. ジョージが<ruby>友達<rt>とも だち</rt></ruby>に<ruby>騙<rt>だま</rt></ruby>されました。
   George was tricked by his friend.

Let's look at some more complicated examples.

7. <ruby>兄<rt>あに</rt></ruby>はマジックが<ruby>上手<rt>じょう ず</rt></ruby>で、<ruby>今<rt>いま</rt></ruby>でもよく<ruby>騙<rt>だま</rt></ruby>されます。
   Because my older brother is good at magic, I am often fooled even now.

8. <ruby>家族<rt>か ぞく</rt></ruby>を<ruby>騙<rt>だま</rt></ruby>さないほうがいいです。
   You shouldn't deceive your family.

9. <ruby>昔<rt>むかし</rt></ruby>は<ruby>騙<rt>だま</rt></ruby>したり、<ruby>騙<rt>だま</rt></ruby>されたりしました。

A long time ago, I used to trick and be tricked by people.

6 ｜ Grammar and Usage 文法と使い方

● 6-1. A thing called..., A place called... etc.

という is used when explaining names of places and things unknown by the listener.

> (name) という (item, place etc.)
> an (item, place etc.) called (name)

EXAMPLE SENTENCES

1. 私は「はしかみ」という町に住んでいます。
   I live in a town called "Hashikami".

2. ここに「としお」という男の人がくるから、もうちょっと待って下さい。
   A man named (called) Toshio is coming here, so please wait a little longer.

3. 昨日、友達と「トトロ」という映画を見ました。
   I saw a movie called "Totoro" with my friend yesterday.

RELATED GRAMMAR

Japanese From Zero! ③ Section 4-6. The particle と with the verb いう (to say; to tell)

● 6-2. The beginning of an action ~しはじめる

By adding はじめる to a verb root (ます form minus ます), you can say, "to begin to~".

EXAMPLES

1. 考え始める
   to begin to think (consider)

2. 節約し始める
   to start to save money

3. 腐り始める
   to begin to go bad (rot)

4. 成功し始める
   to start to succeed

NOTE: Sentence 1 and 2 are ACTIONS, while 3 and 4 are DESCRIPTIVE sentences. This grammar pattern ALWAYS uses 始める regardless of the verb being an ACTION or DESCRIPTIVE. 始まる should NEVER be used.

EXAMPLE SENTENCES

1. 5年前に日本語を勉強し始めました。
   I started studying Japanese 5 years ago.

2. 先週から、ジムに行き始めました。
   Since last week, I started going to the gym.

RELATED GRAMMAR

Japanese From Zero! ③ Section 8-5. The difference between はじまる and はじめる

3. 赤ちゃんが歩き始めました。
   My baby has just started walking.

● **6-3. Three ways something can end**

Three distinctive verbs used to signal the end of an action.

~ (が) おわる (~ will end)	(describing task completion state)
~ (を) おえる (I will end ~)	(making an effort to finish task)
~ (を) やめる (I will quit ~)	(ending a task before completion)

Each of the following examples shows that the homework is no longer being worked on. However, the current state of the homework, and how the work on it was ended is different depending on the verb used.

EXAMPLE SENTENCES

1. 宿題が終わりました。   My homework is finished.
   In this sentence, the speaker is describing that the homework is done. It's certain that the speaker took action to finish the homework, but that fact isn't directly stated when using おわる.

2. 宿題を終えました。   I finished my homework.
   In this sentence, the speaker specifically is stating "I finished" by using おえる. It's a stronger statement than おわる because it shows intention and effort.

3. 宿題を止めました。   I quit doing my homework.
   やめる is used to show an action quit before completion. Perhaps the speaker quit doing the homework out of frustration. This is like giving up.

NOTE: In English, we commonly say, "I finished my homework." however, it's much more common in Japanese to say "My homework is finished." as in sentence 1.

RELATED VERB(S)

Japanese From Zero! ④ Lesson 7 V-2. やめる (to stop; to quit)
Japanese From Zero! ③ Lesson 8 V-4. おわる (to end; to finish)

📖 もっと詳しく… More Details ⓘ

The difference between おわる (to end; to finish) and おえる (to end; to finish)
Since おえる, is an ACTIVE verb, it should only be used when it's possible for someone to take action to make something "end".

CORRECT ✔

1. 夏が終わりましたね。
    Summer is over.

WRONG ✘

2. 夏を終えましたね。
    I ended summer.

Summer is a natural event and isn't something that can be ended, unless you have invented a way to change weather OR are the ruler of the universe.

CORRECT ✔

3. オリンピックが終わりました。
    The Olympics are over.

WRONG ✘

4. オリンピックを終えました。
    I ended the Olympics.

You can't use おえる unless you are the host of the event and are speaking about how you ended the Olympics at the closing ceremonies.

● **6-4. The ending of an action ~しおえる, ~しおわる**

Just like we can have (VERB ROOT) + はじめる, we can also have (VERB ROOT) + おえる and おわる。

EXAMPLE SENTENCES

1. 仕事をし終えたら、電話しますね。
    Once I finish my work, I will call you.

2. レポートが書き終わったら、すぐメールします。
    When the report is finished (being written), I will email it right away.

3. この小説を読み終えるのは、時間がかかるでしょう。
    To finish reading this novel, it will take a lot of a time I bet.

4. 若い時に自分がやりたい事をやり終えたいです。
    I want to complete the things I want to do while I'm young.

● 6-5. Passive verb form ～られる

Many verbs are ACTIVE, which means the speaker or subject is "doing" the action. When an action is done to the speaker or subject, it is "passive". Verbs can be made into PASSIVE form using the following pattern.

Verb type	Plain form		Passive form	
Regular verbs (**あ** form + **れる**)	騙す	to trick	騙される	to be tricked
	聞く	to ask	聞かれる	to be asked
	笑う	to laugh	笑われる	to be laughed at
いる/える verbs (remove る) + **られる**	見る	to look	見られる	to be looked at
	食べる	to eat	食べられる	to be eaten
	忘れる	to forget	忘れられる	to be forgotten
Irregular verbs	する	to do	される	to have done to
	来る	to come	来られる	to be visited

Once you have your passive form, it's conjugated as if it's an いる/える verb.

EXAMPLE SENTENCES

> The "doer" of the action is always marked with に when passive forms are used.

1. 小さい魚が大きい魚に食べられました。
   The small fish was eaten by the big fish.

2. 私の日記がお兄さんに読まれてしまいました。
   My diary was read by my older brother.

3. アルツハイマーのせいで、おじいさんに忘れられた。
   Due to Alzheimer's, I was forgotten by my grandfather.

4. 家の子は今日、先生に怒られたから、泣いています。
   My child is crying because he got scolded by a teacher today.

5. 日本に住んでいたことを話すと、いつも驚かれるんですよ。
   When I say that I used to live in Japan, people are always surprised.

6. 日本人と飲みに行くと、よく「酒に飲まれるな」と言われます。
   When you go drinking with Japanese people, I am often told, "don't get drunk by the liquor".

NOTE: You might have noticed that in some cases (いる/える verbs and くる), the potential form of the verb is exactly the same as the passive form.

Verb type	Passive form		Potential form	
Regular verbs **(NOT THE SAME)**	騙される	to be tricked	騙せる	to be able to trick
	聞かれる	to be asked	聞ける	to be able to ask
	笑われる	to be laughed at	笑える	to be able to laugh
いる/える verbs **(THE SAME)**	見られる	to be looked at	見られる	to be able to see
	食べられる	to be eaten	食べられる	to be able to eat
	忘れられる	to be forgotten	忘れられる	to be able to forget
Irregular verbs **(DEPENDS)**	される	to have done to	できる	to be able to do
	来られる	to be visited	来られる	to be able to come

The context of the conversation, and the particles used should make it easy to know which form is intended.

EXAMPLE SENTENCES

1. 昔の彼女に忘れられました。   I was forgotten by my old girlfriend.
2. 昔の彼女を忘れられました。   I was able to forget my old girlfriend.

3. コンサートでアーティストに見られた。   I was looked at by the artist at the concert.
4. コンサートでアーティストが見られた。   I was able to see the artist at the concert.

RELATED GRAMMAR

Japanese From Zero!③ Section 13-6. Changing regular verbs into the potential verb form
Japanese From Zero!③ Section 13-7. Changing いるえる verbs into the potential verb form

📖 もっと詳しく… More Details ⓘ

Being inconvenienced by an action

The passive verb form can be used when the speaker is inconvenienced or disturbed by the resulting action.

1. 妹にケーキを食べられた。

   My cake was eaten by my younger sister! / My sister ate my cake!

2. 今日は雨に降られました。

   I got caught in the rain today. / Today it rained on me.

3. お母さんに友達からのメールを読まれた。

   E-mails from my friend were read by my mother. / My mother read e-mails from my friend.

EXAMPLE CONVERSATION

1. Conversation between high school classmates

A: 今日、学校の休み時間に携帯を使っていたら、先生に取られた。
B: え～、休み時間なのに取られたんだ。後で返してくれるの？
A: うん。でも、学校の帰りまで返さないって言われた。
B: うちの高校は厳しいからね。

A: Today, when I was using my phone at school during a break, it got taken away by a teacher.
B: What... even though it was break they took it away? Will they return it later?
A: Yeah. But I was told they wouldn't return it until I left to go home from school.
B: Well our high school is strict.

2. Conversation between a husband and a wife

A: 今日は雨に降られて、大変だったよ。
B: え？会社に傘を持って行かなかったの？
A: 同僚の一人に貸してあげたんだ。新しいスーツを着てたから。
B: そう。優しいのはいいけど、自分の事も考えてね。

A: I got rained on today and it was rough.
B: What? Didn't you bring an umbrella to work?
A: I loaned it to a co-worker. Because he was wearing a new suit.
B: I see. It's good that you are kind, but please think of yourself.

6 | Practice and Review　練習と復習

● 1. Mini Conversation ミニ会話 J → E

Try translating the entire conversation before looking at the translation below.

1. **Formal conversation between friends**

> This が is NOT "but", and as taught in lesson 2 is just used to show background information.

A: 聞いてください。いい話が飛び込んできたんです。

B: どんな話ですか。

A: 映画のオーディションがあるんですが、日本人を探しているんですよ！

B: それはすごいですね。何という映画ですか。

A: まだ分かりません。でも、やってみたいです！

A: Listen. Some good news jumped into my lap.

B: What news?

A: There is a movie audition, and they are looking for Japanese people!

B: That's amazing! What's the name of the movie?

A: I don't know yet. But I want to try it!

2. **Formal conversation between parents**

> 中学 1 年 is the first year of "junior high" which makes the son a "7th grader".

A: 最近、うちの息子が野球をし始めました。

B: へえ〜。いいことですね。

A: まだ中学1年生なので、試合に出られないんです。

B: 練習が辛くて、辞める子も多いでしょう？

A: はい。でも、息子は頑張っていますよ。

B: えらいですね。来年、期待できますね。

A: My son started playing baseball recently.

B: Wow, that's good.

A: Since he's still a 7th grader, he isn't able to play in a game.

B: A lot of kids quit because the practice is so hard.

A: Yes. But my son is doing his best.

B: He's great. We can look forward to next year.

3. **Polite conversation between two neighbors**

A: 林さんという人を知っていますか。

B: はい、あの一人暮らしのおじいさんですよね。

A: そうです。最近、悪い人に騙されて、お金を取られたと聞きました。

B: お年寄りを騙す人が多くなった気がします。ひどい世の中ですね。

A: Do you know Hayashi-san?

B: Yes, it's that old man who lives alone, right?

A: That's right. I heard recently he got scammed by a bad person and got his money taken.

B: I feel like there are more people tricking the elderly now. It's a terrible world.

● 2. Mini Conversation ミニ会話 E → J

Look at the English conversations and see if you can figure out the Japanese.
Try to translate the entire conversation first before looking at the translation.

1. **Casual conversation between a mom and a son**

A: Hiroshi, don't be making noise and stuff since it's already late at night.

B: Ok. Is everyone already sleeping?

A: Yeah. Grandpa's been sleeping all day due to a cold.

B: I see. What about Dad?

A: Dad's exhausted after working overtime.

B: It's rough for everyone, huh.

A: ひろし、もう夜遅いから、音を立てたりしないで。

B: 分かったよ。みんな、もう寝てるの？

A: うん。おじいちゃんは風邪で、一日中寝てる。

B: そうか。お父さんは？

A: お父さんは残業して、くたくたなの。

B: みんな大変だね。

2. **Polite conversation between neighbors**

A: I got a cat last week. (I started raising a cat from last week.)

B: Did you buy it at the pet shop?

A: No. It jumped in from the kitchen window.

B: What?! That must have surprised you.

A: 先週から、猫を飼い始めました。

B: ペットショップで買ったんですか。

A: いいえ。台所の窓から飛び込んできたんです。

B: ええ！それは驚いたでしょう。

3. Casual conversation between friends

A: Today was a horrible day.

B: What happened?

A: I had a fight with a classmate, my hair was pulled, and after that I got a warning from my teacher.

B: Really? Didn't you get injured?

A: Yeah. But my mother found by a call from school, and I got in big trouble (got mad at)

B: That's rough. But it can't be helped. Those kinds of days happen (exist).

A: 今日は嫌な一日だったよ。

B: 何かあったの？

A: クラスメートとけんかして、髪の毛を引っぱられて、その後、先生に注意された。

B: ほんとう? 怪我はしなかった？

A: うん。でも、学校から電話でお母さんに知られてしまって、すごく怒られた。

B: 大変だったね。でも、しょうがない。そんな日もあるよ。

● **3. Short Dialogue**

Two young girls are talking about what they want to do in near future.

京子:　「春美ちゃん、私、最近、大学でビジネスを勉強し始めたの。」

春美:　「へえ～、すごいね。どこの大学？」

京子:　「東南大学という所。仕事をしながら勉強してるよ。」

春美:　「それじゃあ、遊ぶ時間がなくなってしまうね。」

京子:　「うん、でも、卒業したら、お給料が上がるから、頑張るよ。」

春美:　「京子ちゃんは偉いね。私は今、何もしていないから、お母さんに
　　　　だめな娘だと思われてるよ。」

京子:　「これから、どうするの？」

春美:　「実は、知り合いがアルバイトを見つけてくれたから、そこで働きながら、
　　　　やりたいことを見つけようと思ってる。」

京子:　「春美ちゃんならできるよ。頑張ってね。」

6 Kanji Lesson 6:
原里野道地池

From the teacher...

We continue in this lesson with kanji related to places and land.

6 | New Kanji 新しい漢字

191	厂	10 画	source; origin; meadow

くんよみ	はら
おんよみ	ゲン

原因 (げん・いん) cause, reason	原始人 (げん・し・じん) primitive man
野原 (の・はら) field	原材料 (げん・ざい・りょう) raw materials
原子 (げん・し) atom	原価 (げん・か) original price (not marked up)

原									

192	里	7 画	village; hometown

くんよみ	さと
おんよみ	リ

海里 (かい・り) nautical mile	里帰り (さと・がえ・り) visiting one's parents
郷里 (きょう・り) home town	里子 (さと・ご) foster child
里親 (さと・おや) foster parents	万里の長城 (ばん・り・の・ちょう・じょう) Great Wall

里									

193	里	11 画	field; plains

くんよみ	の
おんよみ	ヤ

野原 (の・はら) field	野菜 (や・さい) vegetable
野球 (や・きゅう) baseball	野牛 (や・ぎゅう) buffalo
野良猫 (の・ら・ねこ) stray cat	野生 (や・せい) wild

野									

194	辶	12 画	road; street; way		
			くんよみ	みち	
			おんよみ	ドウ、トウ	
			近道 (ちか・みち) shortcut		道路 (どう・ろ) road
			道 (みち) way, street		北海道 (ほっ・かい・どう) Hokkaido (prefecture)
			道具 (どう・ぐ) implement		水道 (すい・どう) water supply
			道		

195	土	6 画	ground; soil; land		
			くんよみ	none	
			おんよみ	チ、ジ	
			地下 (ち・か) underground		地面 (じ・めん) ground
			地図 (ち・ず) map		地域 (ち・いき) region; area
			地球 (ち・きゅう) earth		地震 (じ・しん) earthquake
			地		

196	氵	6 画	pond		
			くんよみ	いけ	
			おんよみ	チ	
			池 (いけ) pond		電池 (でん・ち) battery
			泥池 (どろ・いけ) mud pond		リチウムイオン電池 (でん・ち) lithium ion battery
			貯水池 (ちょ・すい・ち) reservoir		太陽電池 (たい・よう・でん・ち) solar cell
			池		

6 | Kanji Culture 漢字の文化

● **Why is the kanji 池 (pond) used for "batteries"?**

「池」has the a meaning of "pond" but also means, "reservoir", which can be defined as a way to store water, or a supply or source of something. "Battery", which is written 電 (electricity) 池 (reservoir), it means a "pond / reservoir of electricity"

 電 ＋ 池

6 | Words You Can Write   書ける言葉

草原 (そうげん) grasslands; meadow

草	原								

野原 (のはら) field

野	原								

里親 (さとおや) foster parents

里	親								

分野 (ぶんや) area

分	野								

近道 (ちかみち) shortcut

近	道								

地下 (ちか) underground

地	下								

地元 (じもと) local

地	元								

里子 (さとご) foster child

里	子								

野生 (やせい) wild (e.g. animals)

野	生								

水道 (すいどう) water supply; waterway

水	道								

地上 (ちじょう) above ground; surface; earth

地	上								

北海道 (ほっかいどう) Hokkaido

北	海	道						

里帰り (さとがえり) visiting one's parents

里	帰	り						

池田さん (いけださん) Mr. (Ms.) Ikeda

池	田	さ	ん					

6 Workbook 6: Workbook Activities

6 Kanji Drills 漢字ドリル

● 1. Pick the correct kanji
Circle the correct kanji and write FURIGANA above it.

1. 夏休みに（ 里・野 ）帰りしようと思っています。

2. 電（ 地・池 ）が切れてしまいました。

3. うちの息子が（ 野・里 ）球を始めました。

4. 道にまよったので、（ 地・池 ）図を見てみましょう。

5. ここは（ 里・草 ）原が広がっていて、きれいですね。

● 2. Fill in the kanji
Fill in the appropriate kanji in the blanks for each sentence.

1. ＿＿ は ＿＿ ＿＿ を ＿＿り＿＿ りました。
   いぬ　　そう　げん　　はし　まわ

   The dog ran around the meadow.

2. ＿＿ ＿＿ りを ＿＿しんで＿＿ て＿＿さい。
   さと　がえ　　　たの　　　き　　くだ

   Enjoy the visit to your parents.

3. ＿＿ さいを＿＿ べないと、＿＿ に よくないですよ。
   や　　　　た　　　　　からだ

   If you don't eat vegetables, it isn't good for your body.

4. この ＿＿は ＿＿ が＿＿いから やめましょう。
   みち　　　くるま　おお

   Let's quit (get off) this road since there are many cars.

5. ___ ___ のデパートの___ ___には、いろんな___ べものが あります。

に ほん　　　　　　　　ち か　　　　　　　た

In the bottom (underground) of Japanese department stores, there are a variety of foods.

6. あの ___ きい___ には、___ が いますよ。

おお　　いけ　　さかな

There are fish in that big pond over there.

7. むかしはよく、___ ___で___ だちと ___きゅうを しました。

の　はら　　とも　　　　　や

A long time ago, I often played baseball with my friends in the field.

6 | Usage Activities 文法アクティビティー

● 3. Reading comprehension
Translate the following on a separate piece of paper or type in an electronic device.

カッパとお爺さん
じい

This story may teach you a valuable lesson the next time you meet a mythical creature in Japan.

❶ 日本の「はちなみ」という所に、「白水包み」という池があります。
に ほん　　　　　　　　　　　　ところ　　　　はく すい つつ　　　　　　いけ

❷ 昔、この池の中にはカッパが住んでいました。
むかし　　いけ なか　　　　　　　　す

❸ このカッパは大変ないたずら者で、よく農作物を食べたり、道具を壊したりしたので、近所のお
たい へん　　　　　もの　　　　のう さく ぶつ た　　　　　どう ぐ こわ　　　　　　　　　きん じょ
百姓さんが困っていました。
ひゃくしょう　　こま

❹ ある夏の日、頭がよくて有名なおじいさんが田んぼで草を取っていました。
なつ ひ あたま　　　　ゆう めい　　　　　　　　た　　　　くさ と

❺ すると、そこへ突然カッパが来て、「おじいさん、頑張っているね。ちょっと休んで、ぼくと相撲を
とつ ぜん　　　き　　　　　　　　　　がん ば　　　　　　　やす　　　すもう
取りませんか。」と、おじいさんに言いました。
と　　　　　　　　　　　い

❻ 日頃、カッパの力が強いことをよく聞いているおじいさんは、池の中に引っぱられたら大変だと
ひ ごろ　　　ちから つよ　　　　き　　　　　　　　いけ なか ひ　　　　たい へん
思いました。
おも

❼ 「今日中に、田んぼの草を取ってしまいたい。早く終わったら、相撲を取るから、手伝って下さ
きょう じゅう た　　　くさ と　　　　　　はや お　　　すもう と　　　て つだ くだ
い。」と、おじいさんは、どきどきしながら答えました。
こた

❽ カッパは素直に、おじいさんと田んぼの草を取り始めました。
す なお　　　　　　　　　た　　くさ と はじ

❾ 田んぼの草が、2、3本だけになった時、おじいさんはさり気なく聞きました。
た　　くさ　　　　ほん　　　　　とき　　　　　　げ き

❿ 「カッパさんたちは、世の中に怖い物はないでしょうね。」
よ なか こわ もの

⓫ すると、カッパは「ぼくたちは、ガチャガチャという金属の音が大嫌いだ」と答えました。
きん ぞく おと だい きら こた

⓬「そうですか。人間は、新鮮な魚が嫌いです。カッパさんは金属の音ですか」とカッパに言いながら、おじいさんは道にあった鉄の道具を取って、ガチャガチャと音を立てました。

⓭ 大嫌いな音に驚いたカッパは、池に飛び込んで、泳いでいる魚をおじいさんのいる田んぼへ投げ始めました。

⓮ おじいさんは魚を全部拾って、家に帰りました。

⓯ 騙されたカッパは、自分の弱点を知られたから、二度と人間に会わなくなりました。

● 4. Reading comprehension questions

Translate the questions about the reading comprehension then answer in Japanese.

1. 「いたずら者」はどんな事をする人ですか。

   Translation: _____

   Answer: _____

2. カッパに会った時、おじいさんは何をしていましたか。

   Translation: _____

   Answer: _____

3. カッパはどうしておじいさんに「相撲を取りませんか」と言いましたか。

   Translation: _____

   Answer: _____

4. おじいさんは、どうしてどきどきしましたか。

   Translation: _____

   Answer: _____

5. カッパは、どうしておじいさんに魚を投げましたか。

Translation: _____

Answer: _____

6. 結局、おじいさんはカッパに何をしてもらいましたか。（二つ）

Translation: _____

Answer: _____

● 5. Fill in the blanks
Fill in the missing part based on the English sentence.

1. _____、泣いてしまいました。

   I felt sorry, so I cried (before I knew it.)

2. 夜、音を_____、近所の人に_____。

   I made noise at night, so the neighbors got mad at me.

3. 「一番」_____に行きたいんです。

   I want to go to the restaurant called "Ichiban."

4. 日本に「100円ショップ」_____を知っています。

   I know there are interesting stores called "100-yen shop" in Japan.

5. 人に_____より_____ほうが辛いですね。

   It's more painful to trick someone than to be tricked.

● **6. Question and Answer**
Answer the following questions as if they are being asked to you.

1. 外でごみを拾ったりしますか。

_____

2. 人に騙されたことがありますか。

_____

3. 最近、何をし始めましたか。

_____

4. 普通、何時に晩ご飯を食べ終えますか？

_____

5. 「ハチ公」という犬を見たことがありますか。

_____

● **7. Translation**
Translate the following sentences into Japanese.

1. Do you know the Japanese restaurant called "Tokyo"?

_____

2. The kappa got mad and started making sounds.

_____

3. It was so loud outside that I couldn't sleep at all. (use the くて form)

_____

4. My stuffed animal's ear was bitten off by my dog.

_____

5. My wallet was taken at the train station.

_____

● 8. Verb Conjugation Chart
Complete the following chart.

A) Regular Verbs	Plain Form	Potential form	Passive Verb Form
to make	つくる	つくれる	つくられる
to recall	おもいだす		
to listen	きく		
to wear (hats etc.)	かぶる		

B) いる・える Verbs	Plain Form	Potential form	Passive Verb Form
to eat	たべる	たべられる	たべられる
to quit	やめる		
to forget	わすれる		
to throw	なげる		

C) Irregular Verbs	Plain Form	Potential form	Passive Verb Form
to do	する		
to come	くる		

● 9. Bonus Practice
Change the following sentences into the passive verb form similar to below.

> **ORIGINAL:** 妹 はテレビを壊しました。(My sister broke the TV.)
>
> **PASSIVE:** テレビは 妹 に壊されました。(The TV was broken by my younger sister.)

1. 田中さんは私の名前を忘れていました。

_____

2. 悪い人はいい人を騙します。

_____

3. お母さんはぬいぐるみを捨てました。

4. けんちゃんは私のケーキを食べました。

5. 赤ちゃんは私の髪の毛を引っ張りました。

6. 先生は生徒に怒りました。

7. 私がパーティーに来たから、田中さんはびっくりしました。

8. 広田さんは、池田さんの大事な物を壊しました。

6 | Answer Key 答え合わせ

Short Dialogue (translation)

Kyoko:	Harumi, I recently started studying business at college.
Harumi:	Really, that's amazing. Which college?
Kyoko:	A place called Tounan College. I'm studying while I work.
Harumi:	If that's the case, you won't have much time to enjoy yourself.
Kyoko:	Yeah, but I'm going to work hard because when I graduate my pay will go up.
Harumi:	You are great, Kyoko. I'm not doing anything now, so I'm thought of as a bad daughter by my mother. (My mother thinks I'm a bad daughter.)
Kyoko:	What are you going to do from this point?
Harumi:	Actually... an acquaintance of mine found me a part time job, so I think I want to find something I want to do while I work there.
Kyoko:	(If it's you) You can do it. Do your best.

1. Pick the correct kanji (answers)

1. 夏休みに里帰りしようと思っています。

2. 電池が切れてしまいました。

3. うちの息子が野球を始めました。
4. 道にまよったので、地図を見てみましょう。
5. ここは草原が広がっていて、きれいですね。

2. Fill in the kanji (answers)

1. 犬は草原を走り回りました。
2. 里帰りを楽しんで来て下さい。
3. 野さいを食べないと、体に よくないですよ。
4. この道は車が多いから、やめましょう。
5. 日本のデパートの地下には、いろんな食べものが あります。
6. あの大きい池には、魚が いますよ。
7. むかしはよく、野原で友だちと野きゅうを しました。

3. Reading comprehension (translation)

❶ There is a pond called "Hakusui tsutsumi" in a place called Hachinami, Japan.
❷ A long time ago, a Kappa lived in this pond.
❸ The neighborhood farmers were troubled since this kappa was such a mischief-maker and often did such things as eating crops and breaking tools.
❹ One summer day, an old man, who was well known for his brightness, was weeding the rice field.
❺ Whereupon, suddenly the kappa showed up there and said to him, "Old man, you are working very hard, why don't you take a break and do some sumo with me?"
❻ The old man, who had daily heard a lot about the powerful kappa, thought that it would be horrible if the kappa pulled him into the pond.
❼ "I want to finish weeding the rice field by the end of the day. If I end early, I will do sumo, so please lend me a hand." The old man answered while his heartbeat rapidly.
❽ The kappa started weeding the rice field with the old man without complaints.
❾ When there were only a few weeds left, the old man casually asked the kappa.
❿ "I bet kappas have nothing to be afraid of in the world, right?"
⓫ Thereupon the kappa answered, "We hate the clanking sound of metal."
⓬ "Is that so. Humans dislike fresh fish. You dislike the sound of metal clattering..." the old man said to the kappa as he picked up a metal tool which was on the street and made the clattering sound.
⓭ The kappa, surprised at the sound he hates, jumped into the pond and began throwing swimming fish into the rice field where the old man was.
⓮ The old man picked up all the fish and returned home.
⓯ The tricked kappa, having had his weakness found out, never met with humans ever again.

4. Reading comprehension questions (answers)

1. Translation:　What type of things do "mischief-makers" do?
   Answer(s):　いたずらや悪い事をする人です。/人を困らせる人です。

2. Translation:　What was the old man doing when he met the kappa?
   Answer(s):　田んぼで草を取っていました。

3. Translation:　Why did the kappa say to the old man, "Won't you do sumo with me?"
   Answer(s):　いたずらをしたかったからです。
   　　　　　　池の中に引っぱりたかったからです。

4. Translation: Why was the old man's heart beating fast?

   Answer(s): カッパが怖いからです。

   池の中に引っぱられるのが怖いからです。

5. Translation: Why did the kappa throw fish at the old man?

   Answer(s): 人間は魚が嫌いだと思ったからです。

   嫌いな魚を投げて、びっくりさせたかったからです。

6. Translation: In the end, what did the kappa do for the old man? (two)

   Answer(s): 田んぼの草を取ってもらいました。そして、魚をもらいました。

5. Fill in the blanks (answers)

1. かわいそうで、泣いてしまいました。／かわいそうだったから、泣いてしまいました。
2. 夜、音を立てて、近所の人に怒られました。
3. 「一番」というレストランに行きたいんです。
4. 日本に「100円ショップ」というおもしろい店があるのを知っています。
5. 人に騙されるより騙すほうが辛いですね。

6. Question and Answer (answers may vary)

1. Do you ever pick up garbage outside?
   はい、します。/いいえ、しません。

2. Have you ever been tricked/deceived by anyone?
   はい、あります。/いいえ、ありません。

3. What have you begun to do recently?
   ジムに行き始めました。/何も始めていません。

4. What time do you normally finish eating dinner?
   7時ごろに終えます。/8時ごろに食べ終えます。

5. Have you ever seen the dog called "Hachiko?"

   はい、あります。/見たことはないけど、聞いたことはあります。

7. Translation (answers)

1. 「東京」という日本(食)のレストランを知っていますか。
2. かっぱは怒って、音を立て始めました。
3. 外がうるさくて、全然寝られませんでした。
4. 私のぬいぐるみの耳が犬に噛み切られました。
5. 私の財布が駅で取られました。／盗まれました。

8. Verb Conjugation Chart

A) Regular Verbs	Plain Form	Potential form	Passive Verb Form
to make	つくる	つくれる	つくられる
to remember	おもいだす	おもいだせる	おもいだされる
to listen	きく	きける	きかれる
to wear (hats etc.)	かぶる	かぶれる	かぶられる

B) いる・える Verbs	Plain Form	Potential form	Passive Verb Form
to eat	たべる	たべられる	たべられる
to quit	やめる	やめられる	やめられる
to forget	わすれる	わすれられる	わすれられる
to throw	なげる	なげられる	なげられる

C) Irregular Verbs	Plain Form	Potential form	Passive Verb Form
to do	する	できる	される
to come	くる	こられる	こられる

9. Bonus Practice (answers)

1. 私の名前は田中さんに忘れられていました。

2. いい人は悪い人に騙されます。

3. ぬいぐるみはお母さんに捨てられました。

4. 私のケーキはけんちゃんに食べられました。

5. 私の髪の毛は赤ちゃんに引っ張られました。

6. 生徒は先生に怒られました。

7. 私がパーティーに来たから、田中さんにびっくりされました。

8. 池田さんの大事な物は、広田さんに壊されました。

Vocabulary Builder:
Groups N and O

■ Group N: "AS IS" borrowed words

These words are used exactly like their English counterparts.

リサイクル	recycling
カン	a can
エネルギー	energy

■ Group O: Katakana words that require explanation

These words are made with English, but might not be understood without explanation.

アルミ	aluminum
ペットボトル	plastic bottle

> PET stands for "polyethylene terephthalate".

7

| 16 PAGES | 4 USAGE SECTIONS | 26 NEW WORDS |

Lesson 7:
Have to do

7 | New Words 新しい言葉

Nouns etc.

環境 かんきょう	environment	決まり き	a rule
考え かんが	an idea	粗大ごみ そ だい	oversized or bulky trash
資源 し げん	natural resources	家具 か ぐ	furniture
空き缶 あ かん	empty can	塾 じゅく	cramming school
～など	etc.; or something	体重 たいじゅう	weight (for body)
～用 よう	for the use of ～	平気 へい き	all right; fine; OK
レジ袋 ぶくろ	plastic shopping bag received at a store register		

Adjectives

細かい こま	small; fine; detailed	厳しい きび	strict; severe; rigid; intense
もったいない	wasteful; too good; more than one deserves		

Adverbs

別々に べつ べつ	apart; separately; severally	平気で へい き	without hesitation
かなり	considerably; quite		

Active Verbs

集める あつ	to collect	燃やす も	to burn
減らす へ	to decrease; to diminish	節約する せつ やく	to economize; to save

Descriptive Verbs

集まる あつ	to collect	燃える も	to burn; to be fired up
減る へ	to decrease; to diminish		

7 | Word Usage 言葉の使い方

| W-1 | ～用 (よう) | for the use of ～; used for ～; made for ～ |

用 is attached to the end of a noun. It's often used on product packaging.

女性用 (じょせいよう) (for women)

男性用 (だんせいよう) (for men)

iPhone用 (アイフォンよう) (for iPhone)

個人用 (こじんよう) (for personal use)

大人用 (おとなよう) (for adults)

PC用 (ピーシーよう) (for PC)

EXAMPLE SENTENCES

1. 女性用 (じょせいよう) のお手洗い (てあら) は、あちらにございます。
   There is a ladies' room over there.

   > ございます is a formal verb that replaces あります.

2. これをプレゼント用 (よう) にしてもらえますか。
   Can you please make this a present? (Can you please wrap this as a gift?)

   > Both #1&2 are often heard at department stores.

3. 私 (わたし) は、個人用 (こじんよう) の携帯 (けいたい) と仕事用 (しごとよう) の携帯 (けいたい) を持 (も) っています。
   I have a personal (use) and a work (use) cell phone.

| W-2 | 体重 (たいじゅう) | weight (for body) |

体重 (たいじゅう) is only used for the weight of a living body, such as a human or pet. For all other weights, 重 (おも) さ can be used.

EXAMPLE SENTENCES

1. この本 (ほん) の重 (おも) さは、1キログラムです。
   The weight of this book is 1 kilogram.

   > 体重を量る means "to measure a body weight."

2. ヘリコプターに乗 (の) る前 (まえ) に、体重 (たいじゅう) を量 (はか) ります。
   You will be weighed before boarding the helicopter.

3. 女性 (じょせい) に体重 (たいじゅう) を聞 (き) くと失礼 (しつれい) です。
   It's rude to ask a woman her weight.

4. このお米 (こめ) は、10キロの重 (おも) さがあります。
   This rice has a weight of 10 kilograms.

W-3	〜なし	without~
	1. 〜なしに (action)	に makes an adverb
	2. 〜なしで (action)	で shows how an action is done
	3. 〜なしの (action)	の makes an adjective

なし comes from ない (not any) and it is added to a noun to say "without~" or "no~".

EXAMPLES

1. 冗談なし
   without joking; no joke

2. 休みなし
   without a break; no break

3. 残業なし
   without overtime; no overtime

4. 決まりなし
   without a rule; no rule

EXAMPLE SENTENCES

1. 今日は、昼ご飯なしです。
   I have no lunch today.

   > なし can be used alone.

2. 冗談なしに仕事を辞めたいです。
   No joking, I (seriously) want to quit my job.

3. 先月は、三週間休みなしで働きました。
   Last month, I worked three weeks without a day off.

4. これは消費税なしの値段ですか。
   Is this the price without consumption tax?

   > 消費税 is similar to a "sales" or VAT tax.

冗談なしに仕事を
辞めたいです

7 | Verb Usage 動詞の使い方

V-1

集める あつ	to collect; to gather (ACTION)	いる/える

1. (place) に (something) を集める　　　　　　to gather (something) in (place)

EXAMPLE SENTENCES

1. 空き缶を集めて、ごみ箱に捨てましょう。
あ　かん　あつ　　　　　ばこ　す
Let's collect and throw the empty cans into the garbage can.

2. 私のいとこは切手を集めています。
わたし　　　　　きっ　て　あつ
My cousin collects stamps.

V-2

集まる あつ	to collect; to gather (DESCRIPTIVE)	regular

1. (something) が (place) に集まる　　　　　(something) collects in (place)

EXAMPLE SENTENCES

1. 何でしょう。あそこにたくさんの人が集まっていますね。
なん　　　　　　　　　　　　　　　ひと　あつ
What is it? A lot of people are gathering over there.

2. コンサートホールに三千人、集まりました。
さん　ぜん　にん　あつ
Three thousand people gathered at the concert hall.

V-3

燃やす も	to burn (ACTION)	regular

1. (something) を燃やす　　　　　　　　　to burn (something)

EXAMPLE SENTENCES

1. 日本の田舎では秋に落ち葉を燃やします。
に　ほん　いなか　　　あき　お　ば　も
Fallen leaves are burned in autumn in the Japanese countryside.

2. プラスチックは燃やさない方がいいです。
も　　　　　ほう
You shouldn't burn plastic.

3. おじいちゃんは、昔よくゴミを外で燃やしていました。
むかし　　　　　そと　も
Our grandfather used to often burn trash outside.

V-4	燃える (も)	to burn; to get fired up (DESCRIPTIVE)	いる/える
	1. (something) が燃える	(something) burns	
	2. (something) に燃える	to be on fire with (something)	

EXAMPLE SENTENCES

1. 今日(きょう)は、燃(も)えるごみの日(ひ)ですよ。
   Today is burnable trash day.

   > Japan has certain days when different classifications of trash are put on the curb for collection.

2. ヒーターが倒(たお)れたせいで、近所(きんじょ)の家(いえ)が燃(も)えました。
   A neighborhood house burned due to a tipped over heater.

3. 私(わたし)は最近(さいきん)、漢字(かんじ)の勉強(べんきょう)に燃(も)えています。
   I am really on fire with my kanji study recently.

📖 もっと詳(くわ)しく… More Details ℹ

Burnable and non-burnable trash

Japan requires residents to separate their trash into various types of recyclables when putting trash out at their home. When throwing away trash in public, the minimal separation will be "burnable" or "non-burnable" trash.

In Japanese, to say "can be burned" or "burnable" you would say 燃(も)やせる and for "can't be burned" or "non-burnable", 燃(も)やせない could be used. But when referring to "burnable" or "non-burnable" trash, these forms are not used. Instead the following forms, even though grammatically incorrect, will be used.

燃(も)えるゴミ (burnable trash)   *literally "to get burned trash"
燃(も)えないゴミ (non-burnable trash)   *literally "to not get burned trash"

In other trashy news, often ゴミ is written in カタカナ even though it isn't 外来語(がいらいご) (foreign-origin word). One theory as to why is that カタカナ stands out making it easier to read when combined with other words. This is despite ごみ being correct.

V-5	減る	to decrease; to diminish (DESCRIPTIVE)	regular
	1. (something)が減る	(something) will diminish	

減る is used to describe the lowering of an amount of something that can be counted or measured. It can also be used to lower the amount of responsibility, or risk, etc.

Just a friendly reminder, a descriptive verb isn't something that can be "done" by someone. Instead a descriptive verb happens and merely describes a situation.

> **EXAMPLE SENTENCES**
>
> 1. リサイクルをすると、ゴミが減ります。
>   If we recycle, garbage will decrease.
>
> 2. 最近、体重が少し減りました。
>   I have lost some weight recently.
>
> 3. 仕事を変えてから、収入がかなり減りました。
>   Since changing my job, my income has considerably decreased.

V-6	減らす	to decrease; to diminish; to lower (ACTION)	regular
	1. (something) を減らす	to decrease (something)	

減らす is the action of lowering an amount of something that can be counted or measured. It can also be used to lower the amount of responsibility, or risk, etc.

Again, a friendly reminder that an action verb is something that someone does to make happen.

> **EXAMPLE SENTENCES**
>
> 1. 今日から食べる量を減らしました。
>   Starting today, I lowered the amount of food I eat.
>
> 2. お給料が減らされました。
>   My pay was lowered.
>
>   > へらされる is the passive form of へらす. The particle を changes to が when it is in the passive form.
>
> 3. 残業時間を減らしていただけますか。
>   Can you please lower my overtime hours?
>
>   > ていただけますか is more polite than てくれますか.

V-7	節約する <small>せつ やく</small>	to save; to economize	する
	1. (things) を節約する	to save or economize (something)	

This verb does not mean, "to save" in the sense of stockpiling a certain item.
節約する is the action of not wasting money, resources, or time.

EXAMPLE SENTENCES

This means you are cutting down overall living expenses.

1. 今月は大変だから、節約します。
   <small>こん げつ　　たい へん　　　　　　せつ やく</small>
   I'm going to cut down on spending because this month is hard (tight).

2. 家で仕事をしたら、時間が節約できます。
   <small>いえ　し ごと　　　　　じ かん　せつ やく</small>
   If you work at home, you can save on time.

This is economizing the COST, but not the resource itself.

3. 電気代を節約したいけど、なかなかできません。
   <small>でん き だい　せつ やく</small>
   I want to save on the cost of electricity, but it can't easily be done.

4. 資源を節約しないと、いつか問題になります。
   <small>し げん　せつ やく　　　　　　　　もん だい</small>
   If we don't save our natural resources, it will become an issue someday.

もっと詳しく… More Details ⓘ
<small>くわ</small>

節電 (せつでん) (saving electricity) and 節水 (せっすい) (saving water)

While you can say 水を節約する (conserve water) or 電気を節約する (conserve electricity), there are specific words for both.

EXAMPLE SENTENCES

1. 節電しないと、夏は電気代が高くなります。
   <small>せつ でん　　　　　なつ　でん き だい　たか</small>
   If we don't conserve electricity, our summer electric bill will be expensive.

2. シャワーをずっと浴びていないで、節水してください。
   <small>あ　　　　　　　せっ すい</small>
   Please don't continually shower, and conserve water.

7 | Grammar and Usage 文法と使い方

● 7-1. Must do, なければ なりません and ないと いけません

This verb form is used to say that something is equivalent to "must be", "has to be", or "needs to be". It's made by adding なければ なりません or ないと いけません to the あ form of regular verbs or after dropping the る of いる/える verbs.

EXAMPLES

1. 行かなければなりません
   have / must / need to go

2. 歩かなければなりません
   have / must / need to walk

3. 捨てなければなりません
   have / must / need to throw away

4. 食べなければなりません
   have / must / need to eat

5. 聞かないといけません
   have / must / need to listen

6. 集めないといけません
   have / must / need to collect

7. 入れないといけません
   have / must / need to put it in

8. 節約しないといけません
   have / must / need to save money

EXAMPLE SENTENCES

1. 学校では、先生の言う事を聞かなければなりません。
   At school you have to listen to what the teacher says.

2. 来年の七月にドイツに出張に行かなければなりません。
   I have to take a business trip to Germany next July.

   > ～ないといけない can be shortened to just ないと in casual conversations.

3. 野菜は体にいいから、食べないといけません。
   You need to eat vegetables because they are good for you.

4. 今スマホを使いたいけど、映画館にいるから我慢しないと。
   I want to use my smartphone, but since I am in a movie theatre I have to hold back.

5. 今日、しないといけないことは何でしょうか。
   What are the things we need to do today?

6. 遊びたいけど、やらないといけないことが多いから遊べないです。
   I want to hang out, but I can't because I have many things I need to do.

📖 もっと詳（くわ）しく… More Details ⓘ

The difference between なければ なりません and ないと いけません
Honestly speaking, there are no big differences between these. Japanese people will freely mix and match each one without being able to clearly explain the differences.

なければならない does sound a bit more serious, probably due to the amount of syllables. ないといけない is more commonly used because it's easier to say.

しなければならない
Used when something should be done because it objectively lines up with the rules, customs, or expectations of society.

Mixed phone conversation with an office worker and an impatient friend
A: 後（あと）30分で映画（えいが）が始（はじ）まるよ！早（はや）く行（い）こう！
B: いいえ。仕事（しごと）は5時（じ）までです。5時（じ）までいなければなりません。

A: The movie is starting in 30 minutes! Let's go soon!
B: No. Work is until 5:00. I have to be here until 5:00.

なければ ならない is used because B "must" stay at work because it's the expectation of society that he/she does so.

しないといけない
Used when something should be done voluntarily that the speaker thinks subjectively is unpleasant or undesirable to do.

Casual conversation between classmates
A: 今日（きょう）、学校（がっこう）が終（お）わったら、遊（あそ）びに行（い）かない？
B: 今日（きょう）はだめ。塾（じゅく）に行（い）かないといけない。

> Japanese students often go to special after school classes to "cram study" for specific subjects.

A: When school is over today, do you want to go do something?
B: I can't do today. I have to go to after-school classes.

ないと いけない is used because B "must" do something despite it being undesirable.

● 7-2. Question word extensions か、も、でも

You can add か, も, でも to many question words to make new useful words.

Question word	か	も	でも
なに what	なにか something	なにも nothing	なんでも anything
だれ who	だれか somebody	だれも nobody	だれでも anybody
いつ when	いつか someday	いつも always	いつでも anytime
どれ which	どれか one of them	どれも none of them every one of them	どれでも any one of them
いくつ how many	いくつか several	いくつも many	いくつでも any amount
どこ where	どこか somewhere	どこも nowhere everywhere	どこでも anywhere everywhere
なんじ what time	none	none	なんじでも any time

EXAMPLE SENTENCES

1. いつか、イタリアに行きたいです。
   I want to go to Italy <u>someday</u>.

2. 今朝六時半に学校に行ったけど、まだ誰もいなかった。
   I went to school at 6:30 this morning, but there was <u>nobody</u> there yet.

3. どれもおいしそうですね。
   <u>Every one</u> of them looks delicious.

4. ホットドッグだったら、いくつでも食べられます。
   If it's a hotdog, I can eat it <u>a lot</u> (any amount).

5. お腹が空いてるから、レストランはどこでもいいです！
   Because I'm hungry, <u>any</u> restaurant is okay!

> For natural sounding English, you can remove parts of the translation. Here, "anywhere" would be weird.

● 7-3. In the middle of something (noun + 中〔ちゅう〕)

ちゅう means "in the middle of~ ", "during~", "while~", or "currently~" in English. 中 is added after certain nouns, especially nouns used to make a する verb, to say you are in the middle of doing that action. Here are some common ~中 words.

Word	Meaning
電話中〔でんわちゅう〕	currently on the phone
勉強中〔べんきょうちゅう〕	in the middle of studying / studying
運転中〔うんてんちゅう〕	driving / in the middle of driving
仕事中〔しごとちゅう〕	working / during work
考え中〔かんがえちゅう〕	thinking / in the middle of thinking
食事中〔しょくじちゅう〕	eating / in the middle of eating
工事中〔こうじちゅう〕	under construction

EXAMPLE SENTENCES

1. 仕事中〔しごとちゅう〕に私〔わたし〕に電話〔でんわ〕をしないで下〔くだ〕さい。

   Please don't call me while I am working.

   > に is added to make the 中 word a time.

2. 授業中〔じゅぎょうちゅう〕、先生〔せんせい〕にたくさん質問〔しつもん〕をしました。

   I asked a lot of questions to the teacher during class.

   > に is sometimes removed and replaced with a small pause.

3. この道〔みち〕は工事中〔こうじちゅう〕だから、通〔とお〕れません。

   We can't get through because this road is under construction.

4. 北海道〔ほっかいどう〕に行〔い〕くか、沖縄〔おきなわ〕に行〔い〕くか考え中〔かんがえちゅう〕です。

   I am considering going to Hokkaido or going to Okinawa.

5. 旅行中〔りょこうちゅう〕に風邪〔かぜ〕を引〔ひ〕いてしまいました。

   During my trip, I ended up catching a cold.

● 7-4. Within a time frame (time period + 中^{ちゅう})

ちゅう is added after certain time words such as 今日^{きょう}、来週^{らいしゅう} to say "within" or "during" that period. Depending on the words, 中 is read as ちゅう or じゅう.

NOTE: に is added to show a limited time period or deadline.	
午前中^{ご ぜん ちゅう}に	by the end of the morning / before morning's end
今日中^{きょう じゅう}に *	by the end of today / by the end of the day
今週中^{こん しゅう ちゅう}に	by the end of this week
夏中^{なつ じゅう}に *	by the end of summer
今年中^{こ とし じゅう}に *	by the end of the year *Must always be じゅう

EXAMPLE SENTENCES

1. 今日中^{きょう じゅう}に東京^{とうきょう}に戻^{もど}ります。

    I will go back to Tokyo by the end of today.

2. 来週中^{らい しゅう ちゅう}に返事^{へん じ}をください。

    Please answer me by the end of next week.

RELATED GRAMMAR

Japanese From Zero! ⑤
Vocabulary Builder: Group M
(time related word) + 中

NOTE: Without time marker に, the words mean "the entire" time period.	
午前中^{ご ぜん ちゅう}	all morning / the entire morning
今日中^{きょう じゅう}	all day / the entire day
今週中^{こん しゅう ちゅう}	all week / the entire week
夏中^{なつ じゅう}	all summer / the entire summer
今年中^{こ とし じゅう}	all year / the entire year

EXAMPLE SENTENCES

1. 今年中^{こ とし じゅう}は休^{やす}みなしで、営業^{えい ぎょう}します。

    I will be open for business, without a break, the entire year.

2. 夏中^{なつ じゅう}はアルバイトに燃^もえました。

    I was on fire at my part time job all summer.

EXAMPLE CONVERSATIONS

1. **Formal Conversation between a receptionist and a salesman**

A: あのう、横田不動産の杉本と申しますが、森田社長はいらっしゃいますか。

B: 申し訳ございません。社長は、ただいま会議中でございます。

A: いつ会議が終わりますか。

B: 午前中に終わりますので、それからになります。

A: Umm, I am Sugimoto from Yokota Real Estate, is president Morita here?

B: I apologize. The president is currently in the middle of a meeting.

A: When will the meeting end?

B: It will finish by the end of the morning, so it will be after that.

📖 もっと詳しく… More Details ⓘ

Signboards that commonly use 中

When visiting Japan, you will see many signs ending with 中. Here are some common ones you might see.

1) 営業中   (えいぎょうちゅう)   OPEN FOR BUSINESS

This sign means you can go inside the shop or restaurant.

2) 準備中   (じゅんびちゅう)   GETTING READY; COMING SOON

This sign is a roundabout way of saying, we are not open.

3) 募集中   (ぼしゅうちゅう)   〜WANTED; NOW HIRING

This sign by itself means "NOW HIRING", but it can also be used with other words. テナント募集中 means a building is looking for tenants, アルバイト募集中 means "part-time worker wanted", a cram school with 生徒募集中 on its window would be "now accepting students".

4) 清掃中   (せいそうちゅう)   BEING CLEANED

This one is easy enough to understand. You can't enter if you see this sign.

7 | Practice and Review　練習と復習

● 1. Mini Conversation ミニ会話 J → E

1. Polite conversation between friends from different cities

A: 田中さんの家に、ごみ箱はいくつありますか。

B: ５つ、ありますよ。プラスチック用や燃えるごみ用やペットボトル用のごみ箱です。

A: ペットボトルはプラスチックですよね？

B: はい。でも、リサイクルの日が違うから、別々に捨てなければなりません。

A: How many trash cans do you have in your house? (Tanaka-san = You)

B: I have 5. One for plastics, one for burnable trash, and one for PET bottles.

A: PET bottles are plastic right?

B: Yes, but the day for recycling is different, so they need to be thrown out separately.

2. Casual conversation between friends

A: 何を考えてるの？

B: 食べ物の事。今、ダイエット中だから。

A: 食べる量を減らしてるの？

B: うん、野菜しか食べてない。辛いよ〜。

A: What are you thinking about?

B: About food. Because I am on a diet now.

A: Have you lowered the amount you eat?

B: Yeah, I'm only eating vegetables. It's rough~.

3. Polite conversation between neighbors

A: 明日は粗大ごみの日ですね。

B: はい。うちは古い家具をたくさん捨てますよ。

A: それはもったいないです。きっと、ほしがっている人がいます。

B: そうですか。じゃあ、誰か近所の人に聞いてみましょう。

A: Tomorrow is bulk trash day right?

B: Yes. I will be throwing out a lot of our old furniture.

A: That's such a waste. Certainly, there are people who want it.

B: Is that so? Well then, I will ask people in the neighborhood.

● 2. Mini Conversation ミニ会話 E → J

1. Polite conversation between a boss and an employee

A: I made a mistake when making copies. Sorry.

B: Please do not throw away the paper since it is going to be a waste.

A: Well then, where shall I put it?

B: Put it in the box on the side of the copy machine. Because this is for recycling.

- -

A: コピーをとる時、間違えてしまいました。すみません。

B: 紙がもったいないから、捨てないで下さい。

A: じゃあ、どこに置きましょうか。

B: コピー機の横の箱に置いて下さい。ここはリサイクル用ですから。

2. Casual conversation between friends

A: I have to do my homework by the end of today. I don't have time.

B: What kind of homework is it? I will help you out.

A: Because it's an essay, I have to do it by myself. I will keep going without a break.

- -

A: 今日中に、この宿題をしないといけない。でも、時間がないよ。

B: どんな宿題？手伝うよ。

A: 作文だから、一人でしないと。休みなしで頑張るよ。

3. Polite conversation between two strangers

A: Excuse me, how do I buy a train ticket?

B: You have to put money in here. How far do you want to go?

A: To Tokyo station.

B: Ok then, put 270 yen in here.

- -

A: すみません。電車の切符をどうやって買いますか。

B: ここにお金を入れなければなりません。どこまで行くんですか。

A: 東京駅までです。

B: じゃあ、ここに 270円、入れて下さい。

● 3. Short Dialogue

A pushy wife is complaining about her husband's collections.

奥さん   「ねえ、パパ。この家、狭くなったと思わない？」

旦那さん   「え？そうかな。僕は平気だよ。」

奥さん   「あなたのゴルフクラブや本がたくさんあるでしょう。何とかしない？」

旦那さん   「貯金して買って集めた物だよ。全部、大事だよ。」

奥さん   「でも、全然使ってないでしょう。少し、捨てないといけないよ。」

旦那さん   「えっ！捨てる？！バカなこと言わないでよ。」

奥さん   「私達のスペースがないでしょう！リサイクル・ショップで売ってよ。」

旦那さん   「だめ。絶対、売らない、捨てない、減らさない！」

奥さん   「じゃあ、もっと大きい家を買ってもらわないといけないね。」

旦那さん   「もっと大きい家が買いたいなら、良子も働かないといけないよ！」

奥さん   「あなたがゴルフクラブを捨てたら、働きます。」

7 Kanji Lesson 7:
国市京公内外

7 | New Kanji　新しい漢字

From the teacher...

This kanji in this lesson are grouped into large locations such as cities and countries.

197	口	8画	country; nation

くんよみ	くに
おんよみ	コク

国 (くに) country	雪国 (ゆき・ぐに) snow country
国際 (こく・さい) international	国内 (こく・ない) domestic
帰国 (き・こく) return to country	外国 (がい・こく) foreign country

国										

198	巾	5画	market; city; municipal

くんよみ	いち
おんよみ	シ

市場 (いち・ば) marketplace	朝市 (あさ・いち) morning market
市役所 (し・やく・しょ) city hall	市立 (し・りつ) municipal
市民 (し・みん) citizen	市長 (し・ちょう) mayor

市										

199	亠	8画	capital; ten quadrillion

くんよみ	none
おんよみ	キョウ、ケイ

京都 (きょう・と) Kyoto	上京 (じょう・きょう) proceeding to the capital
東京 (とう・きょう) Tokyo	京阪 (けい・はん) Keihan (Kyoto-Osaka area)
帰京 (き・きょう) returning to Tokyo	東京都 (と・きょう・と) Tokyo metropolitan area

京										

200	八	4画	public; official; governmental			
			くんよみ	おおやけ		
			おんよみ	コウ		
			公 (おおやけ) official, public		公民館 (こう・みん・かん) community center	
			公園 (こう・えん) park		公務員 (こう・む・いん) civil servant	
			公平 (こう・へい) fair		不公平 (ふ・こう・へい) unfair	

公 | | | | | | | | | | |

201	入	4画	inside; within			
			くんよみ	うち		
			おんよみ	ナイ、ダイ		
			以内 (い・ない) within		家内 (か・ない) own wife	
			内側 (うち・がわ) inside; interior		内容 (ない・よう) contents; detail	
			内緒 (ない・しょ) secret		社内 (しゃ・ない) within the company	

内 | | | | | | | | | | |

202	夕	5画	outside			
			くんよみ	そと、ほか、はず(す)		
			おんよみ	ゲ、ガイ		
			外 (そと) outside		外見 (がい・けん) outward appearance	
			外す (はず・す) to remove		外国人 (がい・こく・じん) foreigner	
			外貨 (がい・か) foreign currency		海外 (かい・がい) abroad; overseas	

外 | | | | | | | | | | |

7 | Kanji Culture 漢字の文化

● Demons on the outside, fortune on the inside!

節分 is a traditional event performed on the day before the first day of spring. Although the tradition has evolved over many years, it currently is the tradition of keeping demons out of Japanese homes and keeping fortune inside. The entire family takes part in spreading of soybeans. Facing the doors and windows of the house they proclaim「鬼は外！」(demons outside) while spreading beans. Then facing toward the rooms of the house they proclaim「福は内！」(fortune inside) while spreading more beans. The tradition can vary a bit from region to region. After the beans are spread, they ward off evil spirits by eating an amount of beans equal to the age of the children plus one.

鬼は外！

副は内！

7 | Words You Can Write　書ける言葉

帰国 (きこく) to return to one's own country

帰	国								

雪国 (ゆきぐに) snow country

雪	国								

市場 (いちば) market; marketplace

市	場								

上京 (じょうきょう) proceeding to the capital

上	京								

東京 (とうきょう) Tokyo

東	京								

公園 (こうえん) park

公	園										

公立 (こうりつ) institution

公	立										

家内 (かない) speaker's wife

家	内										

内心 (ないしん) back of one's mind; real intention

内	心										

外す (はずす) to remove

外	す										

外見 (がいけん) outward appearance

外	見										

外国 (がいこく) foreign country

外	国										

市内 (しない) (within a) city; local

市	内										

国内 (こくない) domestic

国	内										

7 Workbook 7: Workbook Activities

7 | Kanji Drills 漢字ドリル

● **1. Prefectures in Japan**
Write the following prefectures in kanji.

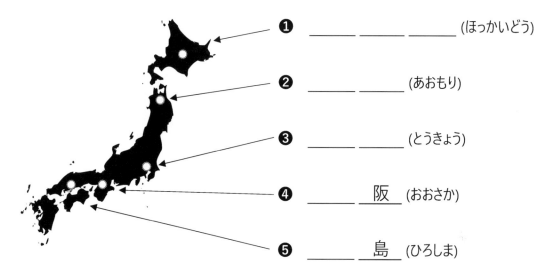

❶ _____ _____ _____ (ほっかいどう)

❷ _____ _____ (あおもり)

❸ _____ _____ (とうきょう)

❹ _____ 阪 (おおさか)

❺ _____ 島 (ひろしま)

● **2. Fill in the kanji**
Fill in the appropriate kanji in the blanks for each sentence.

1. きのう、___ ___<small>に ほん</small>に ___ ___<small>き こく</small>しました。

    Yesterday, I returned to Japan.

2. わたしは よく ___ ___<small>いち ば</small>で ___<small>さかな</small>を ___<small>か</small>います。

    I often buy fish at the marketplace.

3. ___ ___<small>とう きょう</small>に ___ ___<small>ひ がえ</small>りりょ___<small>こう</small>を しましょう。

    Let's take a day trip to Tokyo.

4. ＿＿ は ＿＿ ＿＿の＿＿ ＿＿ ＿＿で ＿＿えています。
<ruby>ちち</ruby> <ruby>こう</ruby> <ruby>りつ</ruby> <ruby>しょう</ruby> <ruby>がっ</ruby> <ruby>こう</ruby> <ruby>おし</ruby>

My father teaches at a public elementary school.

5. ＿＿ だちが いないと、＿＿ ＿＿ いです。
<ruby>とも</ruby> <ruby>こころ</ruby> <ruby>ぼそ</ruby>

If you don't have friends, it's lonely.

6. ＿＿ は ＿＿ ＿＿だけでは、はんだんできません。
<ruby>ひと</ruby> <ruby>がい</ruby> <ruby>けん</ruby>

You can't decide on a human just by outer appearance.

7. ＿＿ さんは＿＿ ＿＿、みんなと＿＿きたかったんですよ。
<ruby>はら</ruby> <ruby>ない</ruby> <ruby>しん</ruby> <ruby>い</ruby>

Hara-san's real intention was to go with everyone.

7 | Usage Activities 文法アクティビティー

● 3. Reading comprehension

Translate the following on a separate piece of paper or type in an electronic device.

リサイクルの決まり	*Different cities and countries have varying rules on recycling. Japan's rules for recycling are strict.*

❶ 皆さんは環境問題をどう考えていますか。

❷ 皆さんが住んでいる所では、ちゃんとごみがリサイクルされていますか。

❸ 紙やプラスチックをリサイクルすると、エネルギーや資源の節約になります。

❹ リサイクル用のごみ箱は、ほとんどの日本のスーパーに置いています。

❺ でも、そのごみ箱に何でも捨ててはいけません。

❻ 例えば、空き缶は空き缶用のごみ箱に、ビンはビン用のごみ箱に、ペットボトルはペットボトル用のごみ箱に捨てなければなりません。

❼ 家にリサイクル用のごみがたまったら、買い物をする時に、スーパーへ持って行って捨てられます。

❽ レジ袋をリサイクルすることも大切です。

❾ 日本のスーパーでは、レジ袋をもらう時にお金を払わなければならない所があります。

❿ 自分の買い物袋をいつも持っていると、お金もかからなくて、エネルギーの節約にもなります。

⓫ それから、日本には、ごみの日の細かい決まりがあります。

⓬ 例えば、月曜日は燃えるごみ、水曜日は紙のごみ、金曜日はプラスチックのごみを決められた場所に捨てなければなりません。

⓭ 粗大ごみは、毎週捨てられません。

⓮ 二か月に一度ぐらい、家の近くまで取りに来てくれますが、リサイクルセンターに持っていってもいいです。

⓯ 日本は、リサイクルの決まりがとても厳しいです。

● 4. Reading comprehension questions

Translate the questions about the reading comprehension then answer in Japanese.

1. あなたが住んでいる所では、どんな物をリサイクルしていますか。

Translation: _____

Answer: _____

2. リサイクルすると、どうなりますか。

Translation: _____

Answer: _____

3. 日本のスーパーのリサイクル用のごみ箱は、数が少ないですか。

Translation: _____

Answer: _____

4. 日本では、リサイクル用のごみの日は、一週間に一回ぐらいですか。

Translation: _____

Answer: _____

5. 日本では毎週、粗大ごみが捨てられますか。

Translation: _____

Answer: _____

6. あなたの国と日本と、どちらのほうがリサイクルの決まりが厳しいですか。

Translation: _____

Answer: _____

● 5. Fill in the blanks
Fill in the missing part based on the English sentence.

1. 最近、食べる量を_____。

    I have started reducing the amount of food that I eat.

2. 私はリサイクル用に_____。

    I am collecting plastic bottles for recycling.

3. 明日することを_____。

    I have to think about what to do tomorrow.

4. 地震の_____、学校まで_____。

    I had to walk to school due to the earthquake.

5. ひろしさんと前に_____。

    I think I have met Hiroshi somewhere before.

● 6.Translation
Translate the following sentences into Japanese.

1. I have to lose weight (lower my weight) by the end of this month.

    _____

2. I have to throw away oversized trash before morning ends.

_____

3. I have to become able to eat more vegetables. (lesson 4 "to become able to")

_____

4. I have to take (get on) a bus because my car is broken.

_____

5. My mother has to do things like going to a hospital and paying rent today.

_____

● 7. Practice
Select an appropriate word from the box below and complete each sentence.

いつでも	なにも	だれでも	いくつか
なんでも	だれか	どれも	いくつでも
どこでも	いつか	どこも	どれでも

1. 質問(しつもん)があったら、_____ 聞(き)いて下(くだ)さい。
    If you have questions, please ask me anytime.

2. _____ 日本(にほん)に行(い)きたいですね。
    I want to go to Japan someday.

3. 私(わたし)は日本食(にほんしょく)なら、_____ 食(た)べられます。
    I can eat anything if it's Japanese food.

4. 昨日(きのう)は病気(びょうき)だったから、_____ 食(た)べませんでした。
    I was sick yesterday, so I didn't eat anything.

5. 「七人(しちにん)の侍(さむらい)」という映画(えいが)は _____ 知(し)っていますよ。
    Everyone knows the movie called "Seven Samurai".

6. 冷蔵庫(れいぞうこ)に _____ ケーキがあるから、食(た)べて下(くだ)さい。
    There are some cakes in the fridge, so please eat them.

● **8. Question and Answer**

Answer the following questions.

1. 何を節約していますか。

_____

2. 食事中に、どんなことをしますか。

_____

3. どんなことをよく考えますか。

_____

4. 子供は何をしなければなりませんか。

_____

5. 日本ではどんなことをしないといけませんか。

_____

6. 自分は何をしないといけないと思いますか。

_____

---

7 | Answer Key 答え合わせ

Short Dialogue (translation)

Wife	Hey, Papa. Don't you think this house has gotten smaller/narrower?
Husband	What? I wonder if that's so. I'm okay with it.
Wife	You have a lot of books and golf clubs, don't you?
	Can't you do something about it?
Husband	Those are the things I collected by saving up to buy them. They are all important.
Wife	But you don't use them at all. We have to throw a bit of them away.
Husband	What?! Throw away?! Don't say ridiculous things.
Wife	We don't have space! Sell them at a recycle shop!
Husband	No way. I definitely won't sell, throw away, or lessen them!
Wife	Well then, I will have to have you buy a bigger house.
Husband	If you want to buy a bigger house, you also have to work!
Wife	I will work if you throw away your golf clubs.

1. Prefectures in Japan

1. 北海道　2. 青森　3. 東京　4. 大阪　5. 広島

2. Fill in the kanji

1. きのう、日本に帰国しました。
2. わたしはよく市場で魚を買います。
3. 東京に日帰りりょ行をしましょう。
4. 父は公立の小学校で教えています。
5. 友だちがいないと、心細いです。
6. 人は外見だけでは、はんだんできません。
7. 原さんは内心、みんなと行きたかったんですよ。

3. Reading comprehension (translation)

❶ What do you all think about environmental problems?
❷ Is trash being recycled properly where you all live?
❸ We can save resources by recycling things such as paper or plastic.
❹ There are trash cans for recycling placed in most Japanese supermarkets.
❺ But you can't dump just anything into those trash cans.
❻ For example, you have to dump empty cans into a trash can for empty cans, bottles into a trash can for bottles and plastic bottles into a trash can for plastic bottles.
❼ Once recyclable trash has built up at your house, you can bring it to the supermarket when you shop and throw it away.
❽ Recycling plastic shopping bags is also important.
❾ There are some Japanese supermarkets where you have to pay money when you receive a plastic shopping bag. (NOTE: There is a new law proposed to make this countrywide for all supermarkets.)
❿ If you always bring your own shopping bag, it won't cost money and you will save energy.
⓫ Also, there are detailed rules about trash day in Japan.
⓬ For example, you must throw away burnable trash on Mondays, paper on Wednesdays, and plastics on Fridays in designated places.
⓭ You can't throw away bulk trash every week.
⓮ About once every two months they will come to pick it up near your house, but you can bring it to a recycling center.
⓯ The recycling rules in Japan are very strict.

4. Reading comprehension questions (answers)

1. Translation: What type of things are recycled where you live?
   Answer(s): 日本と同じです。／紙とプラスチックとビンです。

2. Translation: What happens when you recycle?
   Answer(s): エネルギーや資源の節約になります。

3. Translation: Are trash cans for recycling scarce in Japanese supermarkets?
   Answer(s): いいえ、たくさんあります。
   いいえ、多いです。空き缶用、ビン用、ペットボトル用などがあります。

4. Translation: Are days for recyclable trash about once a week in Japan?
   Answer(s): いいえ、たくさんあります。／いいえ、一回以上あります。

5. Translation: Can you throw away bulk trash every week in Japan?

   Answer(s):   いいえ、捨てられません。／いいえ、二か月に一回ぐらいです。

   はい、リサイクルセンターなら捨てられます。

6. Translation: Which country has stricter recycling rules, your country or Japan?

   Answer(s):   日本のほうが厳しいです。

   自分の国のほうが厳しいと思います。

5. Fill in the blanks (answers)

1. 最近、食べる量を減らし始めました。

2. 私はリサイクル用にペットボトルを集めています。

3. 明日することを考えなければなりません。／明日することを考えないといけません。

4. 地震のせいで、学校まで歩かなければなりませんでした。／地震のせいで、学校まで歩かないといけませんでした。

5. ひろしさんと前にどこかで会ったと思います。／ひろしさんと前にどこかで会ったことがあると思います。

6. Translation (sample answers)

1. 今月中に体重を減らさないといけません。／　今月中に体重を減らさなければなりません。

2. 午前中に粗大ごみを捨てないといけません。／　午前中に粗大ごみを捨てなければなりません。

3. もっと野菜を食べられるように ならないといけません。

   もっと野菜を食べられるように ならなければなりません。

4. 車が壊れているので、バスに乗らないといけません。

   車が壊れているので、バスに乗らなければなりません。

5. 母は今日、病院に行ったり 家賃を払ったりしないといけません。

   母は今日、病院に行ったり 家賃を払ったりしなければなりません。

7. Practice (answers)

1. 質問があったら、いつでも聞いて下さい。

2. いつか日本に行きたいですね。

3. 私は日本食なら、何でも食べられます。

4. 昨日は病気だったから、何も食べませんでした。

5. 「七人の侍」という映画は誰でも知っていますよ。

6. 冷蔵庫にいくつかケーキがあるから、食べて下さい。

8. Question and Answer (answers may vary)

1. What are you economizing?
   <ruby>水<rt>みず</rt></ruby>を<ruby>節約<rt>せつやく</rt></ruby>しています。/ <ruby>家<rt>うち</rt></ruby>のものは<ruby>全部<rt>ぜんぶ</rt></ruby>しています。

2. What do you do when you are having dinner?
   <ruby>家族<rt>かぞく</rt></ruby>と<ruby>話<rt>はなし</rt></ruby>をします。/ テレビを<ruby>観<rt>み</rt></ruby>ます。

3. What do you often think about?
   <ruby>仕事<rt>しごと</rt></ruby>のことです。/ <ruby>家族<rt>かぞく</rt></ruby>のことをよく<ruby>考<rt>かんが</rt></ruby>えます。

4. What do children need to do?
   <ruby>勉強<rt>べんきょう</rt></ruby>をしなければなりません。/ たくさん<ruby>遊<rt>あそ</rt></ruby>んで、<ruby>宿題<rt>しゅくだい</rt></ruby>をしなければなりません。

5. In Japan, what type of things must be done?
   <ruby>玄関<rt>げんかん</rt></ruby>で<ruby>靴<rt>くつ</rt></ruby>を<ruby>脱<rt>ぬ</rt></ruby>がないといけません。/ <ruby>他<rt>ほか</rt></ruby>の<ruby>人<rt>ひと</rt></ruby>のことを<ruby>考<rt>かんが</rt></ruby>えないといけません。

6. What do you think you need to do?
   もっと<ruby>日本語<rt>にほんご</rt></ruby>を<ruby>勉強<rt>べんきょう</rt></ruby>しないといけません。/ <ruby>自分<rt>じぶん</rt></ruby>がしたいことを<ruby>探<rt>さが</rt></ruby>さないといけません。

8

| 15 PAGES | 5 USAGE SECTIONS | 21 NEW WORDS |

Lesson 8:
Trying to Do Something

8 | New Words 新しい言葉

Nouns etc.

しょうらい 将来	future; in the years to come	ゆめ 夢	dream
ゆうびん ぶつ 郵便(物)	postal mail	ぜん いん 全員	all of the members; everybody
がん 癌	cancer	じょうきゃく 乗客	passengers
ま さお 真っ青	pale	ふた ご 双子	twins

Adjectives

そっくり（な）spitting image; be just like

Verbs

とど 届ける	to deliver; to send	とど 届く	to reach; to get to
み 見かける	to notice; to happen to see	に 似る	to look like
お 追いかける	to pursue; to chase down	な 亡くなる	to die; to pass away
たず 尋ねる	to ask; to inquire	たす 助ける	to help; to save
の おく 乗り遅れる	to miss getting on train etc.	き 消える	to disappear; to go out

Adverbs

か 代わりに	instead of; in exchange for; in return	じつ 実は	as a matter of fact; actually

8 | Word Usage 言葉の使い方

| W-1 | ま
真~ | pure~; bright~ |

「真」 is sometimes attached to a noun or adjective to strengthen the meaning of the word. It can't be used for everything, but it is commonly used with these colors.

ま しろ 真っ白	pure white; feel numb; blank	ま か 真っ赤	bright red; clear red
ま くろ 真っ黒	coal-black; as black as an ink	ま さお 真っ青	bright blue; pale

The meaning of 真っ青 changes based on context. For example, if we were talking about the sky, it would mean "bright blue". However, a person's face can also be 真っ青 (pale) when they are sick or scared. 真っ白 can also mean "head is blank" when you can't remember or also to "feel numb" due to a shock and are unable to think.

EXAMPLE SENTENCES

> "真 + color word" is often used with a body part.

1. 私はお酒を飲むと、顔が<u>真っ赤</u>になります。
   When I drink, my face turns bright red.

> You can also say あたまのなかが instead of あたま.

2. テスト中に頭が<u>真っ白</u>になって、答えが書けませんでした。
   During the test my head went blank and I couldn't write the answers.

3. ゆきこさん、顔が<u>真っ青</u>ですよ。大丈夫ですか。
   Your face (Yukiko san) is pale. Are you okay?

RELATED WORD

Japanese From Zero! ⑤ Lesson 4 Word Usage (W-2) 真~ (directly~; right~)

W-2

しょうらい 将来	future; in the years to come

将来 is used when talking about the "future prospects" of a specific person or company etc. When saying "your future" or "my future" 将来 is used.

EXAMPLE SENTENCES

1. 私は将来、お医者さんになりたいです。
   I want to be a doctor in (my) future.

2. もう18歳だから、将来のことを考えたほうがいいよ。
   You should think about your future since you are already 18 years old.

3. 近い将来、自分でビジネスを始めようと思っています。
   In the near future, I'm thinking of starting my own business.

📖 もっと詳しく… More Details ℹ️

Your future VS the future

未来 (みらい) also means "future", however it's not about any single person's future, but instead about the future in general. It's just the opposite of the "past". When you say "the future", then 未来 (みらい) should be used.

EXAMPLE SENTENCES

1. 150年後 (ねんご) の未来 (みらい) のことは、誰 (だれ) も分 (わ) からない。
   Nobody knows (what will happen) 150 years in the future.

> しょうらい can't be used here since we are talking about a general future.

2. 「ドラえもん」は、タイムマシンで未来 (みらい) から来 (き) ました。
   Doraemon came from the future with a time machine.

> ドラえもん is a robot cat and the main character of a Japanese anime.

---

8 | Verb Usage 動詞の使い方

V-1	助 (たす) ける	to help; to save	いる/える
	1. (person) を助ける	to save a (person)	

This "help" is used when helping someone out of a perilous situation. In normal "lending a hand" type situations, 手伝 (てつだ) う is more appropriate.

EXAMPLE SENTENCES

1. 寺田 (てらだ) さんは私 (わたし) に何 (なに) かあったら、いつも助 (たす) けてくれます。
   When something happens to me, Mr. Terada always helps me.

2. 私 (わたし) は事故 (じこ) に遭 (あ) った人を助 (たす) けたことがあります。
   I have saved a person who had an accident before.

> 事故に遭う means "to have an accident."

たすけて！

NOTE: When you need to be saved, you should yell たすけて and not てつだって。

RELATED VERB(S)

Japanese From Zero! ④ Lesson 13 V-5. 手伝う (to help out)

V-2	亡くなる （な）	to die; to pass away	regular
	1. (person etc.) が亡くなる	a (person etc.) passes away	
	2. (cause) で亡くなる	to pass away due to (cause)	

This verb is similar to 死ぬ (し) (to die), but is less direct and more sensitive.

EXAMPLE SENTENCES

1. 私の叔父は去年、癌で亡くなりました。
   My uncle died of cancer last year.

2. あの事故でたくさんの人が亡くなりました。
   Many people passed away due to that accident.

もっと詳しく… More Details ⓘ

All about death

There are a few ways to say "die". The most basic is 死ぬ and very commonly 亡くなる is used to be less direct. 亡くなる doesn't sound natural to use for animals. On TV and news, it's common to hear 死亡する (しぼう) in a very dry, matter-of-fact way. A more poetic way, to die is 他界する (たかい), meaning "to go to another world".

RELATED VERB(S)

Japanese From Zero! ④ Lesson 7 V-6. しぬ (to die)

V-3	届ける （とど）	to deliver; to send (ACTION)	いる/える
	1. (something) を届ける	to deliver (something)	

EXAMPLE SENTENCES

1. 先生にこの手紙を届けてください。
   Please deliver this letter to the teacher.

2. この住所に花を届けたいんですが、何日ぐらいかかりますか。
   I want to send the flowers to this address, but about how many days does it take?

V-4	届<ruby>届<rt>とど</rt></ruby>く	to reach; to get to (DESCRIPTIVE)	regular
1. (something) が届く		(something) has reached	

This verb is used when talking about the arrival of something that was sent (届<ruby><rt>とど</rt></ruby>ける).

EXAMPLE SENTENCES

1. 今日<ruby><rt>きょう</rt></ruby>、多田<ruby><rt>た だ</rt></ruby>さんからの手紙<ruby><rt>て がみ</rt></ruby>が届<ruby><rt>とど</rt></ruby>きました。
   The letter from Mr. Tada arrived (got here) today.

   > The の modifies the "letter" to be "the letter from Mr. Tada." Without the の, the sentence is "A letter came from Mr. Tada."

2. いつも要<ruby><rt>い</rt></ruby>らない郵便物<ruby><rt>ゆう びん ぶつ</rt></ruby>が届<ruby><rt>とど</rt></ruby>きます。
   Unwanted mail always gets delivered.

V-5	乗<ruby><rt>の</rt></ruby>り遅<ruby><rt>おく</rt></ruby>れる	to miss getting on	いる/える
1. (thing)に乗り遅れる		to miss getting on (thing)	

This verb is made up by combining 乗<ruby><rt>の</rt></ruby>る (to ride) and 遅<ruby><rt>おく</rt></ruby>れる (to be late).

EXAMPLE SENTENCES

1. 今日<ruby><rt>きょう</rt></ruby>はバスに乗<ruby><rt>の</rt></ruby>り遅<ruby><rt>おく</rt></ruby>れてしまいました。
   Today I ended up missing the bus.

2. ジェニーさんはいつも電車<ruby><rt>でん しゃ</rt></ruby>に乗<ruby><rt>の</rt></ruby>り遅<ruby><rt>おく</rt></ruby>れて、先生<ruby><rt>せん せい</rt></ruby>に怒<ruby><rt>おこ</rt></ruby>られます。
   Jenny always misses the train and the teacher gets mad at her.

V-6	見<ruby><rt>み</rt></ruby>かける	to happen to see; to notice	いる/える
1. (thing, person) を見かける		to happen to see a (thing, person)	

EXAMPLE SENTENCES

1. 今朝<ruby><rt>けさ</rt></ruby>、デパートの近<ruby><rt>ちか</rt></ruby>くでフェラーリを見<ruby><rt>み</rt></ruby>かけました。
   This morning, I saw a Ferrari near the department store.

2. ここで五才<ruby><rt>ご さい</rt></ruby>の女<ruby><rt>おんな</rt></ruby>の子<ruby><rt>こ</rt></ruby>を見<ruby><rt>み</rt></ruby>かけませんでしたか。
   Did you happen to see a 5-year-old girl here?

V-7	消<ruby>き</ruby>える	to disappear; to vanish; to go out	いる/える
1. (thing) が消える		(thing) disappears	

EXAMPLE SENTENCES

1. ろうそくの火<ruby>ひ</ruby>が消<ruby>き</ruby>えましたよ。
   The candle flame went out.

2. どこかな・・・。財布<ruby>さいふ</ruby>が消<ruby>き</ruby>えた。
   I wonder where it is... my wallet disappeared.

3. あああ！コンピューターからデータが全部<ruby>ぜんぶ</ruby>、消<ruby>き</ruby>えてしまいました。
   AAH! All of the data from this computer disappeared.

RELATED VERB(S)

Japanese From Zero! ④ Lesson 11 V-6. 消す (to erase; to turn off)

V-8	似<ruby>に</ruby>る	to look like	いる/える
1. (person A)と(person B)は似ている		(person A) and (person B) look alike	
2. (person A)は(person B)に似ている		(person A) looks like (person B)	

This verb is almost always in the ています form because looking like someone is constant. This verb can be used in two ways to say that two people look alike.

EXAMPLE SENTENCES

1. 妹<ruby>いもうと</ruby>と私<ruby>わたし</ruby>は似<ruby>に</ruby>ています。
   My younger sister and I look alike.

2. 私<ruby>わたし</ruby>は誰<ruby>だれ</ruby>に似<ruby>に</ruby>ていると思<ruby>おも</ruby>いますか。
   Who do you think I look like?

3. 姉<ruby>あね</ruby>は昔<ruby>むかし</ruby>の母<ruby>はは</ruby>にとてもよく似<ruby>に</ruby>ています。
   My older sister really looks like my mother from long ago.

V-9	追^おいかける	to pursue; to chase down	いる/える

1. (thing, person) を追いかける	to chase (something)

EXAMPLE SENTENCES

1. バスを追^おいかけたけど、だめだった。
   I chased after the bus, but I didn't make it.

2. 僕^{ぼく}はシャイなので、女性^{じょせい}を追^おいかけるのが苦手^{にがて}です。
   Since I'm shy, I'm bad at pursuing women.

3. 夢^{ゆめ}を追^おいかけている人^{ひと}は、かっこいいですね。
   People who are pursuing their dreams are cool.

V-10	尋^{たず}ねる	to ask; to inquire	いる/える

1. (something) を尋ねる	to ask (something)

尋^{たず}ねる is more formal than 聞^きく.

EXAMPLE SENTENCES

1. 迷^{まよ}ったので、道^{みち}を尋^{たず}ねました。
   I got lost, so I asked for directions.

2. 警察^{けいさつ}に、近所^{きんじょ}であった火事^{かじ}のことを尋^{たず}ねられました。
   I was asked about the fire in the neighborhood by the police.

RELATED VERB(S)

Japanese From Zero! ② Lesson 10 V-2. 聞く (to ask)

8 | Grammar and Usage 文法と使い方

頭痛しゃしない ~しようと思う is used when the speaker expresses a decision to do a certain action. At the point that the speaker says this statement, it's very certain that they are planning to do the action. To make it, you add と思う to ANY informal "let's do" verb.

> (informal let's verb form) + と思う

EXAMPLES

しようと思う (to think to do)
しようと思った (was going to do; thought to do)
しようと思っている (thinking of doing)
しようと思っていた (was thinking of doing)

しようと思わない (to not think to do)
しようと思わなかった (didn't think to do)
しようと思っていない (not thinking of doing)
しようと思ったら (When ~ thought to do)

EXAMPLE SENTENCES

1. 今日、早く家に帰ろうと思っています。
   I am thinking about going home early today.

2. 図書館に行こうと思ったら、雨が降り始めました。
   When I thought to go to the library, it began raining.

3. 私は寒がりなので、寒い所に住もうと思わないです。
   Since I'm weak to cold, I don't think to live in a cold place.

EXAMPLE CONVERSATION

1. **Conversation between boyfriend and girlfriend**

   A: じゅん君。昨日、電話をくれなかったね。
   B: 電話しようと思ってたよ。でも、忙しかったんだ。ごめん。
   A: いいよ。今日はピザを注文しようと思ってるから、一緒に食べよう。

   A: Jun. You didn't call me yesterday...
   B: I was going to call you. But I was busy. Sorry.
   A: It's okay. I'm thinking of ordering pizza today, let's eat together.

RELATED GRAMMAR

Japanese From Zero! ③ Section 8-2. Informal let's form verbs

● **8-2. 〜しようとする (trying to do)**

〜しようと思<ruby>思<rt>おも</rt></ruby>う is just the thought to do something, however, 〜しようとする is an actual attempt to do. The verb must always be in the informal "let's do" form.

> **(informal let's verb form) + とする**

EXAMPLES

しようとする (to try to do)   しようとしない (to not try to do)

しようとした (tried to do)   しようとしなかった (didn't try to do)

しようとしている (trying to do)   しようとしていない (isn't trying to do)

しようとしていた (was trying to do)   しようとしたら (when ~ tried to do)

EXAMPLE SENTENCES

1. 8時<ruby>時<rt>じ</rt></ruby>まで寝<ruby>寝<rt>ね</rt></ruby>ようとしたんだけど、地震<ruby>地震<rt>じしん</rt></ruby>のせいで早<ruby>早<rt>はや</rt></ruby>く起<ruby>起<rt>お</rt></ruby>きてしまいました。
   I tried to sleep until 8 o'clock, but due to an earthquake, I ended up waking up early.

2. 彼女<ruby>彼女<rt>かのじょ</rt></ruby>のことを忘<ruby>忘<rt>わす</rt></ruby>れようとしているのに、忘<ruby>忘<rt>わす</rt></ruby>れられないです。
   Although I'm trying to forget about my girlfriend, I can't.

   > のに (even though) is taught in lesson 1.

3. 漢字<ruby>漢字<rt>かんじ</rt></ruby>の練習<ruby>練習<rt>れんしゅう</rt></ruby>をしようとするけど、いつも10分<ruby>分<rt>ふん</rt></ruby>で嫌<ruby>嫌<rt>いや</rt></ruby>になる。
   I try to practice kanji, but I always hate it after 10 minutes.

   > いわれる is the passive form of いう.

4. 二<ruby>二<rt>ふた</rt></ruby>つ目<ruby>目<rt>め</rt></ruby>のマフィンを食<ruby>食<rt>た</rt></ruby>べようとしたら、彼<ruby>彼<rt>かれ</rt></ruby>に「太<ruby>太<rt>ふと</rt></ruby>るからだめだ」と言<ruby>言<rt>い</rt></ruby>われました。
   When I tried to eat a second muffin, my boyfriend told me not to because I would gain weight.

5. 私<ruby>私<rt>わたし</rt></ruby>のいとこは、なんでダイエットをしようとしないかな。
   I wonder why my cousin won't try to diet.

EXAMPLE CONVERSATION

1. **Conversation between two people in a car**

   A: さっき、あの道<ruby>道<rt>みち</rt></ruby>を通<ruby>通<rt>とお</rt></ruby>ろうとしたら、工事中<ruby>工事中<rt>こうじちゅう</rt></ruby>で通<ruby>通<rt>とお</rt></ruby>れませんでした。

   B: そうですか。じゃあ、どうやって行<ruby>行<rt>い</rt></ruby>きましょうか。

   A: 少<ruby>少<rt>すこ</rt></ruby>し遠<ruby>遠<rt>とお</rt></ruby>くなりますが、あの細<ruby>細<rt>ほそ</rt></ruby>い道<ruby>道<rt>みち</rt></ruby>を行<ruby>行<rt>い</rt></ruby>こうと思<ruby>思<rt>おも</rt></ruby>っています。

   A: When I tried to go down that road just before, I couldn't due to it being under construction.
   B: Is that so? Well then, which way should we take? (how should we go)
   A: It will be a bit far, but I am thinking of going down that narrow road over there.

● 8-3. The moment I ... (とたんに)

When saying that something happened at the instant or moment that something else happened, とたん is added after the た form of the verb. Since a moment in time is being described, the time marker に usually follows とたん.

> ### (action 1 / た form) + とたんに、(action 2)
> ### The moment I (action 1), (action 2) happens

ACTION 2 (after とたん) occurs immediately after ACTION 1, and is usually uncontrollable or occurs without much thought.

EXAMPLE SENTENCES

1. 黒田さんに会った途端に、好きになりました。
   The moment I met Mr. Kuroda, I liked him.

2. 飛行機に乗った途端に、気分が悪くなりました。
   The moment I got on the plane, I felt sick.

3. あのピザを食べた途端に、お腹が痛くなりました。
   The moment I ate that pizza, my stomach began to hurt.

4. 家族を見た途端に、嬉しくて泣いてしまいました。
   The moment I saw my family, I was so happy I cried.

● 8-4. Using ため with nouns

ため can mean "for", "for the benefit of" and similar expressions. ため is used to mark the cause or reason for an action. ため must be connected to the noun with の.

EXAMPLE SENTENCES

1. 旅行のために、お金を貯めています。
   I am saving money <u>for</u> a trip.

2. 家族のために、頑張らなければなりません。
   I have to do my best <u>for</u> my family.

3. 将来のために、いい大学に入りたいです。
   <u>For</u> my future, I want to enter a good college.

EXAMPLE Q&A

1. なんでこんなにアイスクリームを買うんですか。

   娘の誕生日パーティーのためです。

   あさって遊びに来る友達のためです。

   風邪を引いてるから、喉のために買いました。

   > に is not needed when ため is used at the end of a sentence.

   How come you are buying so much ice cream?
   It's for my daughter's birthday party.
   It's for friends who are coming to hang out the day after tomorrow.
   I bought it for my throat because I have a cold.

● 8-5. Using ため with verbs

When ため is used with verbs, it means something close to, "so that I can", "in order to". It's used much like から, but is more formal.

> **(informal verb phrase) ために**
> **so that I can (verb phrase)**

Since literal translations can sound stiff, you may need to add or remove words to make the Japanese or English sentence sound natural.

EXAMPLE SENTENCES

1. リサイクルするために、家でプラスチックを集めています。
   In order to recycle, I'm collecting plastic at my house.

2. 日本語を話すために、ネットで日本人の友達を作ろうと思っています。
   I'm thinking to make Japanese friends on the net, so that I can speak Japanese.

3. 会社でいい成績を残すために、残業しないといけません。
   In order to maintain good results at my company, I have to work overtime.

RELATED VERB(S)

Japanese From Zero! ⑤ Lesson 4 V-4. のこす (to leave behind; to save) ACTION
Japanese From Zero! ⑤ Lesson 4 V-5. ざんぎょうをする (to work overtime)

もっと詳_{くわ}しく… More Details ⓘ

Differences between ために and ように (in order to, so that)
Both ために and ように can be translated into "in order to", however, to correctly use ために and ように, you need to know which type of verb is being used. The following verb types are used differently with ために and ように.

Action verbs (also called *volitional verbs*)
The subject has control or ability to make something happen.

Examples: 行_いく、食_たべる、書_かく、話_{はな}す、する、作_{つく}る、休_{やす}む、走_{はし}る、聞_きく、歩_{ある}く

Descriptive Verbs (also called *non-volitional verbs*)
The subject cannot control the situation. The situation is just being described.

Examples: ある、なる、できる、降_ふる、壊_{こわ}れる、分_わかる、ぶつかる、転_{ころ}ぶ

ために Rules	**ように Rules**
- Use with Action verbs (plain form)	- Use with Descriptive verbs (plain form)
- Potential (can do) form is NEVER used	- Verbs are often potential (can do) form

Remember, with ために, action verbs are used in their plain form. However, with ように the verb changes to potential form.

ために Action (plain form)

1. 日本_{にほん}に|行_いく|ために、頑張_{がんば}ります。
   I'll work hard in order to go to Japan.

ように Action (potential form)

2. 日本_{にほん}に|行_いける|ように、頑張_{がんば}ります。
   I'll work hard in order to be able to go to Japan.

3. 仕事_{しごと}を|休_{やす}む|ために、電話_{でんわ}します。
   I'll call in order to take a day off from work.

4. 仕事_{しごと}を|休_{やす}める|ように、電話_{でんわ}します。
   I'll call so I can take a day off from work.

The only time you can use plain form with ように is when the verbs are Descriptive. Action verbs are always potential form.

ように Descriptive (plain form)

> ない form can also be used with ように.

5. |分_わかる|ように、ゆっくり話_{はな}して下_{くだ}さい。
   Speak slow, so that I can understand.

6. |転_{ころ}ばない|ように、気_きを付_つけて下_{くだ}さい。
   Be careful so you don't trip.

Put this in your head summary!
- Descriptive verbs ONLY use ように
- Action verbs use BOTH ために and ように, but MUST be potential form for ように.

RELATED GRAMMAR
Japanese From Zero!⑤ Section 4-1. In order to, so that 〜ように

8 | Practice and Review　練習と復習

● 1. Mini Conversation ミニ会話 J → E

1. Informal conversation between friends

A: 今朝はびっくりしたよ。

B: どうしたの？

> Remember, Japanese people say あお for the green light.

A: 信号が青になって、行こうとしたら、大きいトラックが横から突然出てきた。

B: それは怖いね。

A: I was surprised this morning.

B: What happened?

A: The light turned green and when I tried to go, a big truck suddenly appeared from the side.

B: That sure is scary.

2. Polite conversation between two housewives

A: 田中さんはかわいそうな人ですね。

B: どうしてですか。

A: 奥さんが亡くなった途端に、病気になったんです。

B: そうですか・・・まだ奥さんが亡くなってから半年ですよね。

A: はい。息子さんのために、早くよくなってほしいですね。

B: 私もそう思います。

A: Mr. Tanaka is a poor person, isn't he? (I feel sorry for Mr. Tanaka.)

B: Why?

A: The moment his wife passed away, he got sick.

B: I see... It's only been half a year since his wife passed away.

A: Yes. I want him to get better soon for his son.

B: I hope (think) so, too.

3. Polite conversation between friends

A: 西田さんの二人のお子さんは似ていますね。

B: はい。でも、上の子は高校に行った途端に、髪を茶色に変えてしまいました。

A: 下の子の髪の色は何ですか。

B: 黒です。でも、赤に変えたいと言っていて、困っています。

A: Your two children look alike, don't they, Mrs. Nishida?

B: Yes. But the moment my older child went to high school, she changed her hair color to brown. (shows some regret)

A: What color is your younger child's hair?

B: It's black. But she is saying she wants to change it to red, so I am troubled.

● 2. Mini Conversation ミニ会話 E → J

1. Mixed conversation between friends

A: When I try to watch TV, my dog always comes close to me.

B: Because he likes you, Hiroko.

A: No, it is not that. It is not because of me, because he likes TV.

A: 私がテレビを見ようとすると、いつも犬が近くに来るんだ。

B: ひろこさんが好きだからですよ。

A: ううん、違うよ。私じゃなくて、テレビが好きだから。

2. Polite conversation between friends

A: How was yesterday's movie?

B: Actually, I couldn't watch it until the end.

A: Was it not interesting?

B: No. The moment the movie started, I got a stomachache, so I went home.

A: That was too bad.

A: 昨日の映画はどうでしたか。

B: 実は、最後まで見られませんでした。

A: 面白くなかったんですか。

B: いいえ。映画が始まった途端に、お腹が痛くなったから、家に帰ったんです。

A: それは残念でしたね。

3. Informal conversation between friends

A: I heard Yoshida from the neighborhood passed away due to cancer.

B: Yeah. I hadn't seen him recently.

A: I wonder if there is anything we can do for his wife.

B: I'm thinking about getting some flowers and going to see him. Won't you go with me?

A: 近所の吉田さんが癌で亡くなったと聞いたよ。

B: うん。最近、見かけなかったね。

A: 奥さんのために、できることはないかな。

B: 私はお花を持って、会いに行こうと思ってる。一緒に行かない？

● 3. Short Dialogue

Kaori is talking about her mysterious dream to Hiroshi.

かおり:　「ねえ、ひろしくん。昨日、不思議な夢を見たよ。」

ひろし:　「どんな夢？」

かおり:　「私のおばあちゃんが先週、亡くなったでしょう。そのおばあちゃんが夢に出てきたの！」

ひろし:　「へえ〜。何か忘れ物をしたのかな。」

かおり:　「してないよ。でも、おばあちゃんが『車の運転に気をつけて』って言ってくれた。」

ひろし:　「かおりちゃんの運転は危ないからね。かおりちゃんのために出てきたんだよ。」

かおり:　「多分ね・・・。それで、私が何か聞こうとしたら、消えてしまったの！」

ひろし:　「亡くなった人に質問しない方がいいよ。」

かおり:　「そうだね。でも、今度出てきたら、私が将来、誰と結婚するか聞きたいな！」

な at the end of a sentence relays the envy or desire of the speaker.

8 Kanji Lesson 8:
色黄黒茶紙絵線

From the teacher...

We have gathered kanji relating to color and drawing/painting in this lesson.

8 | New Kanji 新しい漢字

203	色	6画	color

くんよみ	いろ
おんよみ	ショク、シキ

色々 (いろ・いろ) various	顔色 (かお・いろ) complexion
三色 (さん・しょく) three-color	色っぽい (いろ・っぽい) sexy
色紙 (しき・し) cardboard placard	景色 (け・しき) scenery; landscape

204	黄	11画	yellow

くんよみ	き、こ
おんよみ	コウ、オウ

黄河 (こう・が) Yellow River	黄金 (おう・ごん) gold
黄色 (き・いろ) yellow	黄海 (こう・かい) Yellow Sea
黄身 (き・み) egg yolk	黄緑 (き・みどり) yellow-green

205	黒	11画	black

くんよみ	くろ、くろ(い)
おんよみ	コク

真っ黒 (ま・っ・くろ) pitch black	黒髪 (くろ・かみ) black hair
黒い (くろ・い) black	黒点 (こく・てん) black spot; sunspot
黒板 (こく・ばん) blackboard	黒人 (こく・じん) black person

206	⺾	9画	tea		
			くんよみ	none	
			おんよみ	チャ、サ	

お茶 (お・ちゃ) tea
茶色 (ちゃ・いろ) brown
茶道 (さ・どう) tea ceremony

喫茶店 (きっ・さ・てん) coffee shop; teahouse
茶髪 (ちゃ・ぱつ) brown dyed hair
茶碗 (ちゃ・わん) rice bowl

茶

207	糸	10画	paper		
			くんよみ	かみ	
			おんよみ	シ	

手紙 (て・がみ) letter
折り紙 (お・り・がみ) origami
紙 (かみ) paper

紙幣 (し・へい) paper money
紙飛行機 (かみ・ひ・こう・き) paper airplane
紙袋 (かみ・ぶくろ) paper bag

紙

208	糸	12画	picture		
			くんよみ	none	
			おんよみ	カイ、エ	

絵の具 (え・の・ぐ) paints
絵文字 (え・も・じ) emoji
絵本 (え・ほん) picture book

絵画 (かい・が) picture, painting
塗り絵 (ぬ・り・え) coloring book
絵日記 (え・にっ・き) picture diary

絵

209	糸	15画	line		
			くんよみ	none	
			おんよみ	セン	

直線 (ちょく・せん) straight line
線 (せん) line
線路 (せん・ろ) railway track

新幹線 (しん・かん・せん) bullet train
線香 (せん・こう) incense
線香花火 (せん・こう・はな・び) sparkler (firework)

線

8 | Kanji Culture 漢字の文化

● **What is "yellow voice" like?**

Despite its literal meaning of "yellow voice", 「黄色い声」 means "high-pitched voice".
This is the type of voice a child or woman might make when screaming.

● **What does "to become a picture" mean?**

「絵になる」, literally "to become a picture" is an expression used to describe people
or scenery that make an impression due to their beauty. A beauty so significant that
it could be used as the subject of a painting. It's similar to the English saying,
"picture-perfect".

EXAMPLE SENTENCES

1. アイドルがステージに出ると、会場はファンの黄色い声でいっぱいになりました。
   When the idols appeared on stage, the screams of the fans filled the concert hall.

2. 幸奈さんと彼は、本当に絵になるカップルです。
   Yukina and her boyfriend are a picture-perfect couple.

絵になる
カップル

8 | **Words You Can Write** 書ける言葉

三色 (さんしょく) three-color

三	色								

黄色 (きいろ) yellow

黄	色								

黄金 (おうごん) gold

黄	金								

白黒 (しろくろ) black and white

白	黒								

黒い (くろい) black

黒	い								

お茶 (おちゃ) tea

お	茶								

茶色 (ちゃいろ) brown

茶	色								

手紙 (てがみ) letter

手	紙								

絵本 (えほん) picture book

絵	本								

黒人 (こくじん) black person

黒	人								

絵画 (かいが) picture; painting

絵	画								

下線 (かせん) underline; underscore

下	線								

直線 (ちょくせん) straight line

直	線								

色紙 (いろがみ) colored paper

色	紙								

中国人 (ちゅうごくじん) Chinese person

中	国	人							

絵日記 (えにっき) picture diary

絵	日	記							

外国人 (がいこくじん) foreigner

外	国	人							

8 Workbook 8: Workbook Activities

8 | Kanji Drills 漢字ドリル

● 1. Pick the correct kanji
Circle the correct/appropriate kanji and write FURIGANA above it.

1. <ruby>友<rt>とも</rt></ruby><ruby>達<rt>だち</rt></ruby>に<ruby>手<rt>て</rt></ruby>（ 線 ・ 紙<rt>だ</rt> ）を<ruby>出<rt></rt></ruby>したいんですが、<ruby>住所<rt>じゅうしょ</rt></ruby>が<ruby>分<rt>わ</rt></ruby>かりません。

2. <ruby>日本<rt>にほん</rt></ruby>の<ruby>信号<rt>しんごう</rt></ruby>は、<ruby>赤<rt>あか</rt></ruby>と（ <ruby>青<rt>あお</rt></ruby> ・ <ruby>緑<rt>みどり</rt></ruby> ）と（ オレンジ ・ <ruby>黄色<rt></rt></ruby> ）です。

3. うちの<ruby>犬<rt>いぬ</rt></ruby>は<ruby>目<rt>め</rt></ruby>が（ 茶 ・ 黄 ）<ruby>色<rt></rt></ruby>で、とてもかわいいです。

4. この<ruby>辺<rt>へん</rt></ruby>はよく<ruby>分<rt>わ</rt></ruby>からないので、（ 地 ・ 池 ）<ruby>図<rt>ず</rt></ruby>を<ruby>見<rt>み</rt></ruby>てみましょう。

5. <ruby>今度<rt>こんど</rt></ruby>、（ 線 ・ 絵<rt>が</rt> ）<ruby>画<rt>み</rt></ruby>を<ruby>見<rt>い</rt></ruby>に行きませんか。

● 2. Fill in the kanji
Fill in the appropriate kanji in the blanks for each sentence.

1. わたしのすきな___<rt>いろ</rt> は ___<rt>あか</rt>と___<rt>しろ</rt>です。
   My favorite colors are red and white.

2. ___<rt>あお</rt> がすきだけど、___ ___<rt>き いろ</rt>は すきじゃないです。
   I like blue, but I don't like yellow.

3. さい___<rt>きん</rt>、___い<rt>くろ</rt>___<rt>くるま</rt>を ___<rt>に</rt> ___<rt>だい</rt>、___<rt>う</rt>りました。
   Recently, I sold two black cars.

4. ひる ___みに きっ___ ___で お___をしませんか。
<small>やす　　　　　さ　てん　　　ちゃ</small>

At the lunch break, won't you have tea (with me) at the coffee shop?

5. ___しつで___ ___を ___きました。
<small>きょう　　　て　がみ　　　か</small>

I wrote a letter in the classroom.

6. ヨーロッパで ___が___たいです。
<small>え　み</small>

I want to see paintings in Europe.

7. ___ ___は、___かん___ に のるのが すきです。
<small>か　ない　　　しん　　せん</small>

My wife likes riding the bullet train.

8   Usage Activities 文法アクティビティー

● **3. Reading comprehension**

Translate the following on a separate piece of paper or type in an electronic device.

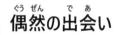

偶然の出会い
<small>ぐう　ぜん　　で　あ</small>

You never know who you might randomly meet on a bus or train, but you also never know how that meeting might change your life forever.

❶ これは、三年前に友達から聞いた話です。

❷ ティムという男の人がいました。

❸ ティムはお母さんの家に、誕生日のプレゼントとカードを届けに行きました。

❹ お母さんの家に行くために、12時の電車に乗ろうとしたら、駅で自分にそっくりな男の人を見かけました。

❺ ティムはとても驚きました。

❻ ティムは追いかけて、その人と同じ電車に乗りましたが、乗った途端にその人は消えてしまいました。

❼ ティムは自分の電車に乗り遅れてしまいました。

❽ そのせいで、代わりにバスでお母さんの家に行くことにしました。

❾ その日の夜、電車事故のニュースを見ました。

⑩ 自分が乗ろうとしていた 12時の電車の乗客が全員、事故で亡くなったんです。

⑪ 自分にそっくりな人に会ったことと、電車事故のことをお母さんに話したら、お母さんは真っ青になりました。

⑫ 「それはきっとティムの弟だよ」と、お母さんは言いました。

⑬ ティムは知らなかったけど、実は生まれた時に双子の弟がいたんです。

⑭ その双子は生まれてすぐ、亡くなりました。

⑮ ティムは亡くなった弟に助けられて、不思議な気持ちになりました。

● 4. Reading comprehension questions

Translate the questions about the reading comprehension then answer in Japanese.

1. これは、いつ聞いた話ですか。

Translation: _____

Answer: _____

2. ティムさんは最初、何に乗ろうとしましたか。

Translation: _____

Answer: _____

3. ティムさんはどんな人を見かけましたか。

Translation: _____

Answer: _____

4. ティムさんが 12時の電車に乗っていたら、どうなったでしょうか。

Translation: _____

Answer: _____

5. 誰^{だれ}が助^{たす}けてくれましたか。

Translation: _____

Answer: _____

6. あなたがティムさんなら、どんな気持^{き も}ちになりますか。

Translation: _____

Answer: _____

● 5. Fill in the blanks
Fill in the missing part based on the English sentence.

1. _____、がんばっているんです。

   I am trying my best to help people who are in need.

2. _____、毎日家^{まい にち うち}でごはんを作^{つく}っています。

   I cook at home every day to cut down on spending.

3. ごみを_____、電話^{でん わ}が鳴^なりました。

   When I thought to throw away trash, the phone rang.

4. _____、ドアが閉^しまってしまいました。

   When I tried to get on the train, the door closed.

5. 田中^{た なか}さんに_____、好^すきになりました。

   The moment I met Mr. Tanaka, I liked him.

● 6. Verb Conjugation Chart
Complete the following chart.

A) Regular Verbs	Plain Form	Polite let's form	Informal let's form
to hand over	わたす	わたしましょう	わたそう
to lower (active)			
to put away			
to ask; to inquire			

B) いる・える Verbs	Plain Form	Polite let's form	Informal let's form
to deliver	とどける	とどけましょう	とどけよう
to chase down			
to save, help			
to collect (active)			

C) Irregular Verbs	Plain Form	Polite let's form	Informal let's form
to do			
to come			

● 7. Question and Answer
Answer the following questions as if they are being asked to you.

1. よく何がポストに届きますか。

_____

2. 道路で何を見かけますか。

_____

3. あなたはお母さんに似ていますか。

_____

4. 電車やバスに乗り遅れたことがありますか。

_____

5. 時々、人に道を尋ねられますか。

_____

6. 誰のために、働いていますか。(This doesn't mean "where do you work".)

_____

7. 健康のために、何をしていますか。

_____

8. いつ、日本語を勉強しようと思いましたか。

_____

● 8. Translation

Translate the following sentences into Japanese.

1. When I thought to talk to Mr. Smith, he went somewhere (before I knew it.)

_____

2. When I thought to call my friend, he came to my house.

_____

3. When I tried to watch a movie, my baby started crying.

_____

4. When I tried to open the window, it started raining.

_____

5. When I tried to study Japanese, my roommate started listening to music.

_____

6. The moment I left home it began raining.

_____

7. The moment I saw my test results, my face turned pale.

---

8 | Answer Key 答え合わせ

Short Dialogue (translation)

Kaori	Hey, Hiroshi. Yesterday I had a weird (mysterious) dream.
Hiroshi	What kind of dream?
Kaori	You know my grandmother passed away last week. That grandmother appeared in my dream.
Hiroshi	Hmmm. I wonder if she forgot something.
Kaori	She didn't. But she told me to "be careful driving".
Hiroshi	Well your driving is dangerous. She appeared for your sake.
Kaori	Maybe... And, when I tried to ask her something, she disappeared!
Hiroshi	You shouldn't ask questions to people that have passed away.
Kaori	Yeah. But next time she appears, I want to ask who I will marry in my future.

1. Pick the correct kanji (answers)

1. 友達に手紙を出したいんですが、住所が分かりません。
2. 日本の信号は、赤と青と黄色です。
3. うちの犬は目が茶色で、とてもかわいいです。
4. この辺はよく分からないので、地図を見てみましょう。
5. 今度、絵画を見に行きませんか。

2. Fill in the kanji (answers)

1. わたしのすきな色は赤と白です。
2. 青がすきだけど、黄色はすきじゃないです。
3. さい近、黒い車を二台、売りました。
4. ひる休みにきっ茶店でお茶をしませんか。
5. 教しつで手紙を書きました。
6. ヨーロッパで絵が見たいです。
7. 家内は、新かん線にのるのがすきです。

3. Reading comprehension (translation)

❶ This is a story that I heard from a friend three years ago.

❷ There was a man called Tim.

❸ Tim went to deliver a birthday gift and a card to his mother's house.

❹ When he tried to get on the 12 o'clock train to go to his mother's house, he happened to see a person who looked exactly like himself.

❺ Tim was very surprised.

❻ Tim chased the person and got on the same train, but the moment he got on it, the man disappeared.

❼ Tim ended up missing his train.

❽ Due to that, he decided to go to his mother's house by bus instead.

❾ That night, he saw news of a train accident.

❿ All of the passengers from the 12 o'clock train that he tried to get on died in the accident.

⓫ When he told his mother about meeting the person that looked exactly like him and the train accident, her face turned pale.

⓬ His mother said, "That was certainly your younger brother."

⓭ Tim didn't know it, but actually he had a twin younger brother when he was born.

⓮ That twin died immediately after birth.

⓯ Tim got a mysterious feeling from being saved by his younger brother who passed away.

4. Reading comprehension questions (answers)

1. Translation: When was this story heard?
   Answer(s): 三年前に聞いた話です。

2. Translation: What did Tim try to ride at first?
   Answer(s): 12時の電車に乗ろうとしました。

3. Translation: What type of person did Tim happen to see?
   Answer(s): 自分にそっくりな人を見かけました。

4. Translation: If Tim had taken the 12 o'clock train, what would have happened?
   Answer(s): 亡くなっていたでしょう。
   事故にあって、死んでいたと思います。

5. Translation: Who saved him?
   Answer(s): 生まれた時に亡くなった双子の弟が助けてくれました。
   天国にいる双子の弟が助けてくれました。

6. Translation: If you were Tim, how would you feel?
   Answer(s): とてもうれしいと思います。
   複雑な気持になります。

5. Fill in the blanks (answers)

1. 困っている人を助けるために、がんばっているんです。
2. 節約するために、毎日家でごはんを作っています。
3. ごみを捨てようと思ったら、電話が鳴りました。
4. 電車に乗ろうとしたら、ドアが閉まってしまいました。
5. 田中さんに会ったとたんに、好きになりました。

6. Verb Conjugation Chart (answers)

A) Regular Verbs	Plain Form	Polite let's form	Informal let's form
to hand over	わたす	わたしましょう	わたそう
to lower (active)	へらす	へらしましょう	へらそう
to put away	しまう	しまいましょう	しまおう
to ask; to inquire	たずねる	たずねましょう	たずねよう

B) いる・える Verbs	Plain Form	Polite let's form	Informal let's form
to deliver	とどける	とどけましょう	とどけよう
to chase down	おいかける	おいかけましょう	おいかけよう
to save, help	たすける	たすけましょう	たすけよう
to collect (active)	あつめる	あつめましょう	あつめよう

C) Irregular Verbs	Plain Form	Polite let's form	Informal let's form
to do	する	しましょう	しよう
to come	くる	きましょう	こよう

7. Question and Answer (sample answers)

1. What often arrives in your mail?
   いらない郵便物が届きます。 / 請求書 (bills) が届きます。

2. What do you happen upon on a road?
   人を見かけます。 / 車を見かけます。

3. Do you look like your mother?
   はい、似ています。 / いいえ、あまり似ていません。

4. Have you ever missed a train or bus?
   はい、あります。 / いいえ、ありません。

5. Are you asked for directions by someone sometimes?
   はい、尋ねられます。 / いいえ、あまりないです。

6. On whose behalf do you work?
   家族のために働いています。 / 今は自分のために働いています。

7. What do you do for your health?
   ジムに行っています。 / 野菜をたくさん食べています。

8. When did you decide (think) to study Japanese?
　2、3年前に思いました。 / 高校の時、勉強しようと思いました。

8. Translation (answers)

1. スミスさんに話そうと思ったら、どこかに行ってしまいました。
2. 友達に電話しようと思ったら、彼が家に来ました。
3. 映画を観ようとしたら、赤ちゃんが泣き始めました。
4. 窓を開けようとしたら、雨が降り始めました。
5. 日本語を勉強しようとしたら、ルームメートが音楽を聴き始めました。
6. 家を出たとたんに、雨が降り始めました。
7. テストの成績(結果)を見たとたんに、(顔が)真っ青になりました。

| 16 PAGES | 6 USAGE SECTIONS | 26 NEW WORDS |

9

Lesson 9:
Making Assumptions

From the teacher...

This lesson has 4 new verbs that all share the same sound つく. Context should make it easy to know which one is being used.

9 | New Words 新しい言葉

Nouns etc.

泥棒 (どろぼう)	thief	年下 (としした)	younger in age
犯人 (はんにん)	perpetrator; criminal	年上 (としうえ)	older in age
結果 (けっか)	results	浮気相手 (うわきあいて)	adulterous lover
殺人事件 (さつじんじけん)	murder case	死体 (したい)	dead body
死亡時刻 (しぼうじこく)	time of death	借用書 (しゃくようしょ)	proof of debt document
借金 (しゃっきん)	debt	殺人犯 (さつじんはん)	murderer
銃 (じゅう)	gun; pistol	誰よりも (だれ)	more than anyone
嘘つき (うそ)	a liar	結婚記念日 (けっこんきねんび)	wedding anniversary
～みたい	similar to; like; seems like		

Verbs

殺す (ころ)	to kill	調べる (しら)	to investigate; check out
殴る (なぐ)	to strike; to hit (active)	信じる (しん)	to believe; to trust
塗る (ぬ)	to apply; to paint		
付く (つ)	to be included; to be attached	つく	to be on (electrically)
着く (つ)	to arrive; to reach	嘘をつく (うそ)	to tell a lie

9 | Word Usage 言葉の使い方

| W-1 | ～みたい | similar to; -like; seems like |

You can add みたい to any noun to say "similar to" that noun.

EXAMPLE SENTENCES

1. この絵はピカソみたいです。
   This painting is similar to a Picasso.

2. このサウナは日本の夏みたいです。
   This sauna is similar to a Japanese summer.

> Seriously... Japanese summers are really humid!

NOUN + みたい can be used as an adjective by adding な.

3. ピカソみたいな絵を描きたいです。
   I want to paint a Picasso-like painting.

> 書く (かく) means "to write"
> 描く (かく) means "to draw; to paint"

4. 日本の夏みたいな蒸し暑い天気が嫌いです。
   I dislike humid weather like Japan's summer.

> Did I mention Japanese summers are humid?

NOUN + みたい can be used as an adverb by adding に.

5. ピカソみたいに絵を描けるようになりたいです。
   I want to become able to paint like Picasso.

> Las Vegas' summers are VERY dry unlike the jungle summers of Japan!

6. ラスベガスが日本の夏みたいに蒸し暑かったら、嫌です。
   If Las Vegas' summers were humid like Japan's, I wouldn't like it.

9 | Verb Usage 動詞の使い方

V-1	殺す	to kill	regular
1. (someone) を殺す		to kill (someone)	
2. (weapon) で殺す		to kill with (weapon)	
3. (someone) に殺される		to be killed by (someone)	

EXAMPLE SENTENCES

1. あの犯人は、たくさんの人を殺しました。
   That criminal killed a lot of people.

2. 娘は優しい子で、虫も殺せないんです。
   My daughter, being kind, can't even kill a bug.

3. スミスさんは殺人犯に銃で殺されました。
   Mr. Smith was killed by the murderer with a gun.

4. 有名な歌手が殺されて、大ニュースになりました。
   A famous singer was killed, and it became big news.

V-2	殴る	to hit; to strike	regular
	1. (a thing; person) を殴る	to hit a (thing; person)	
	2. (a person) に殴られる	to be hit by (a person)	

EXAMPLE SENTENCES

1. 子供を殴ってはいけません。
   You shouldn't hit children.

2. 僕は友達と喧嘩をして、殴ってしまいました。
   I had a fight with my friend and hit him before I knew it.

3. 私は昨日の夜、後ろから誰かに殴られました。
   I was hit from behind by somebody last night.

V-3	調べる	to investigate; to check out	いる/える
	1. (person etc.) を調べる	to investigate a (person etc.)	

EXAMPLE SENTENCES

1. この単語を辞書で調べて下さい。
   Please look this word up in your dictionary.

2. 家は買う前に、よく調べた方がいいですよ。
   It's better to investigate well before you buy a house.

V-4	信じる しん	to trust; to believe; to have faith in	いる/える
	1. (person etc.) を信じる	to trust a (person etc.)	

EXAMPLE SENTENCES

1. 神様を信じますか。
   かみ さま　 しん
   Do you believe in God?

2. あなたを信じてもいいですか。
   しん
   Is it okay to trust you?

3. それは、信じられない話ですね。
   しん　　　　 はなし
   That is an unbelievable story.

4. 僕は彼女を信じてるから、彼女の携帯を見たりしません。
   ぼく　かの じょ　しん　　　　　 かの じょ　けい たい　み
   Because I trust my girlfriend, I don't do things like look at her cell phone.

もっと詳しく… More Details ⓘ
くわ

Other ways to trust (信用する VS 信頼する)
しん よう　　　　しん らい

There are two other ways to say "to trust" in Japanese.

信用する is trust based on evaluation of <u>past performance</u> and results.
信頼する is trust of an expectation of <u>future performance</u> based on past results, but past results aren't always required. The trust can be based on feelings alone.

EXAMPLE SENTENCES

1. あなたのことは信用してるけど、簡単にお金は貸せません。
   しん よう　　　　　　　 かん たん　　かね　か
   I trust you, but I can't easily lend you money.

   > This is a sense of expectation.

2. 橋本さんは信頼できる人だから、うちの娘のベビーシッターになってほしいです。
   はし もと　　　しん らい　　　ひと　　　　　　　 むすめ
   Because Hashimoto-san can be trusted, I want her to become our daughter's babysitter.

NOTE: 信用する and 信頼する, although having different nuances as explained above, are often used in the same way by Japanese people without regard for the nuance of the verb.

RELATED PHRASE

Japanese From Zero! ② Lesson 11 New Expressions 1. しんじられない (I can't believe it!)

V-5	つく	to be on (electrically)	regular
	1. (device/light) がつく	(device/light) turns on / is on	

つける is used for the action of "turning on" an electrical device such as a light or a TV. つく is used to describe when the item is "on" or "off".

Let's take a quick moment to cover some important notes about electricity.

1. 電気 means "electricity," but in Japan it's often used just to mean "a / the light".

2. The kanji, 点く can be used, but normally just the hiragana つく is used.

3. If something is ON or OFF, since the state is constant, you must use ています form.

EXAMPLES

1. ついている。/ ついています。   It's on.

2. ついていない。/ ついていません。   It's off.

EXAMPLE SENTENCES

1. あの部屋に誰もいないのに、電気がついていますよ。
   The light is on even though nobody's in that room.

   > 停電する means "to be in a blackout".

2. 停電してたけど、やっと電気がつきました。
   There was a blackout, but finally the electricity came back on.

3. 私の車のステレオがつかないです。
   The stereo in my car won't turn on.

RELATED VERB(S)

Japanese From Zero! ④ Lesson 11 V-5. つける (to turn on)

V-6	付(つ)く	to be attached; to stick; to be included	regular
	1. (something) が付く	(something) is attached/stuck	
	2. (something) に付く	to be attached/stuck on (something)	

The action of attaching is 付(つ)ける (to attach) and the descriptive verb is 付(つ)く.
付(つ)く is commonly used when describing things that are included with products.

EXAMPLE SENTENCES

1. マクドナルドのハッピーセットには、おもちゃが付(つ)いています。
   There is a toy included in McDonald's Happy Meals.

   > What is called "Happy Meals" in America are called "happy sets" in Japan.

2. お母(かあ)さんの歯(は)に、いつも口紅(くちべに)が付(つ)いています。
   My mother's teeth always have lipstick on them.

   > 付(つ)く is best translated to "on" here as it would sound weird to say lipstick is "attached" or "stuck".

3. ペンキを塗(ぬ)る時(とき)、服(ふく)に付(つ)かないようにしてね。
   When you paint, be careful to not get any on your clothes.

4. 赤(あか)いシールが付(つ)いていない物(もの)は、セールじゃないです。
   Things without a red sticker stuck on them aren't on sale.

V-7	着(つ)く	to arrive; to reach	regular
	1. (place) に着く	to arrive at (place)	

EXAMPLE SENTENCES

1. ホテルに着(つ)いたら、電話(でんわ)して下(くだ)さいね。
   Please call me when you reach the hotel.

2. 私(わたし)が乗(の)っている新幹線(しんかんせん)は、4時(じ)に東京駅(とうきょうえき)に着(つ)きます。
   The bullet train we're taking will arrive at Tokyo station at 4 o'clock.

3. 飛行機(ひこうき)が遅(おく)れているので、何時(なんじ)に着(つ)くか分(わ)かりません。
   Since the plane is late, I don't know when we will arrive.

   > 〜か is taught in Book 4 Lesson 7.

V-8	<ruby>嘘<rt>うそ</rt></ruby>をつく	to tell a lie; to lie	regular
	1. (someone) に嘘をつく	to tell (someone) a lie	

つく alone doesn't mean "to lie". 嘘をつく is a set verb phrase.

EXAMPLE SENTENCES

1. もう<ruby>嘘<rt>うそ</rt></ruby>をつかないでください。
   Please don't lie anymore.

2. お<ruby>母<rt>かあ</rt></ruby>さんに<ruby>嘘<rt>うそ</rt></ruby>をついてしまいました。
   I told my mother a lie.

3. <ruby>嘘<rt>うそ</rt></ruby>をつく<ruby>人<rt>ひと</rt></ruby>は<ruby>信用<rt>しん よう</rt></ruby>できないです。
   You can't trust people that lie.

V-9	<ruby>塗<rt>ぬ</rt></ruby>る	to apply; to paint; to spread on	regular
	1. (thing) を塗る	to apply a (thing)	
	2. (thing) に塗る	to apply to (thing)	

This can be used for spreading on butter, painting, putting on lipstick etc.

EXAMPLE SENTENCES

1. <ruby>私<rt>わたし</rt></ruby>はいつもご<ruby>飯<rt>はん</rt></ruby>を<ruby>食<rt>た</rt></ruby>べた<ruby>後<rt>あと</rt></ruby>に、<ruby>口紅<rt>くち べに</rt></ruby>を<ruby>塗<rt>ぬ</rt></ruby>ります。
   I always put on lipstick after eating a meal.

2. <ruby>痛<rt>いた</rt></ruby>いところに、この<ruby>薬<rt>くすり</rt></ruby>を<ruby>塗<rt>ぬ</rt></ruby>ってください。
   Apply this medicine where it hurts.

3. 10<ruby>分<rt>ぶん</rt></ruby><ruby>前<rt>まえ</rt></ruby>にその<ruby>壁<rt>かべ</rt></ruby>にペンキを<ruby>塗<rt>ぬ</rt></ruby>ったから、<ruby>気<rt>き</rt></ruby>をつけてください。
   I painted that wall 10 minutes ago so be careful.

9 | Grammar and Usage 文法と使い方

● 9-1. Making assumptions (VERB + そうです)

You have learned how to use 〜そうです using adjectives in Book 4 Lesson 3. Now we will use VERBS with そうです. 〜そうです is used when stating how something appears to you. It doesn't need to be true and can be based on your observations.

Depending on the sentence, you can translate そう to "seems like", "looks like", "feels like", "I think", "it appears", "I bet" etc.

> ます form (drop the ます) + そうです。
> It looks like/It appears/I think (verb).

* We use "they" and "I" as generic pronoun placeholders for the subject of the conversation.

Verb Form	Polite Form		〜そうです	
Present / future	かえります ねます します	(will) return (will) sleep (will) do	かえりそうです ねそうです しそうです	looks like (they) will return looks like (they) will sleep looks like (they) will do
Ongoing present	かえっています ねています しています	is returning is sleeping is doing	かえっていそうです ねていそうです していそうです	seems like (they) are home seems like (they) are sleeping seems like (they) are doing
Potential form	かえれます ねられます できます	can return can sleep can do	かえれそうです ねられそうです できそうです	(I) think (I) can go home (I) think (I) can sleep (I) think (I) can do it

RELATED GRAMMAR

Japanese From Zero! ④ Section 3-2. It appears to be 〜そう adjective ending

---

EXAMPLE SENTENCES (FUTURE TENSE)

1. 授業が始まりそうです。
   It looks like class is going to start.

2. あの殺人犯は、すぐ見つかりそうですね。
   I think the murderer will be found right away.

3. 日本は来年、観光客がもっと増えそうですね。
   It seems like there will be an increase in tourists next year in Japan.

EXAMPLE SENTENCES (ONGOING PRESENT)

1. あの人は道に迷ってそうです。
That person over there appears to be lost.

> The い in まよっています (to be lost) can be omitted.

2. お隣さんは何でもよく知っていそうです。
It seems my neighbor knows everything well.

> When you are just assuming something, not viewing it, "I bet" is a better translation.

3. 隆二君はまだ大学生だから、狭いアパートに住んでそうですね。
I bet Ryuuji lives in a small apartment since he is still a college student.

EXAMPLE SENTENCES (POTENTIAL FORM)

1. 息子は去年の服がまだ着られそうです。
It seems my son can still wear last year's clothing.

2. このお店は、待たないで入れそう。
It seems we can go in without waiting at this restaurant.

> お店 (store) can also be used to refer to restaurants, bars, clubs etc.

3. 今日は日曜日だから、電車で座れそうだ。
I bet I can sit on the train because it's Sunday today.

● 9-2. Using そうです when talking about yourself

You can also use 〜そうです to refer to yourself. In this case, the meaning changes to "I feel like~" or "I almost~." It's commonly used when you are at your limit in bearing a situation, or on the verge of a dangerous or disadvantageous situation.

EXAMPLE SENTENCES

1. 気持ちが悪くて、吐きそうです。。。
I'm not feeling good, I feel like I'm going to throw up.

> The そう＋になる pattern is often used.

2. あの映画のラストシーンを観ると、いつも泣きそうになります。
When I watch the last scene in that movie, I always feel like I'm going to cry.

3. 校長先生の長い話を聞いていて、寝そうでした。
I almost fell asleep listening to the principal's long story.

> To make the past tense, simply change そうです into そうでした.

● 9-3. Two ways to make negative assumptions そうにない, なさそう

There are two negative assumption そう patterns. They have the same meaning.

Negative Assumption Pattern 1:	ます form (drop the ます) +そうにない	
ます form	**〜そうにない**	**English**
帰_{かえ}ります	帰_{かえ}りそうにない	doesn't seem like (they) will return
食_たべられます	食_たべられそうにない	doesn't seem like (they) will be able to eat
節約_{せつやく}します	節約_{せつやく}しそうにない	doesn't seem like (they) will conserve
来_きます	来_きそうにない	doesn't seem like (they) are coming
NOTE: 〜そうにない can be rephrased as 〜そうもない.		

Negative Assumption Pattern 2:	ない form (drop the い) +さそう	
ない form	**〜なさそう**	**English**
帰_{かえ}らない	帰_{かえ}らなさそう	doesn't seem like (they) will return
食_たべられない	食_たべられなさそう	doesn't seem like (they) will be able to eat
節約_{せつやく}しない	節約_{せつやく}しなさそう	doesn't seem like (they) will conserve
来_こない	来_こなさそう	doesn't seem like (they) are coming

EXAMPLE SENTENCES

1. この映画_{えいが}は長_{なが}いね。まだ終_おわりそうにないよ。
   This movie sure is long. It doesn't seem like it's going to end yet.

2. 松田_{まつだ}さんは来_きそうにないから、もう行_いきましょう。
   It doesn't seem like Matsuda-san is coming, let's go already.

3. 息子_{むすこ}は熱_{ねつ}があるから、学校_{がっこう}に行_いけなさそうです。
   Since my son has a fever, it doesn't seem that he will be able to go to school.

> Notice this is the negative potential form 行けない (unable to go).

RELATED GRAMMAR

Japanese From Zero! ④ Section 3-3. It DOESN'T appear to be 〜なさそう adjective ending
Japanese From Zero! ④ Section 3-4. な adjectives with そう and 〜なさそう ending

● 9-4. Using VERB + そう to modify

Even though we are making the ~そう phrases using verbs, they can be used just like な adjectives. This means they can be used to modify nouns by adding な after そう.

EXAMPLES (POSITIVE)

1. 雪が降りそうな日   a day that looks like it's going to snow
2. 英語が話せそうな人   one who looks like they can speak English
3. 腐ってそうなミルク   milk that looks like it's spoiled

EXAMPLES (NEGATIVE)

4. 雪が降りなさそうな日   a day that looks like it isn't going to snow
5. 英語が話せなさそうな人   a person who looks like they can't speak English
6. 腐ってなさそうなミルク   milk that looks like it isn't spoiled

When ～そうにない or ～そうもない is used to modify a noun, な isn't needed.

7. 英語が話せそうにない人   a person who looks like they can't speak English
8. 雪が降りそうもない日   a day that looks like it isn't going to snow

EXAMPLE SENTENCES

1. 新しい社員の宮田さんは、仕事ができそうな人ですね。
   The new employee Miyata-san appears to be a person who can do the work.

2. ディズニーランドに行くなら、雨が降らなさそうな日に行ったほうがいいですよ。
   If you are going to Disneyland, you should go on a day that doesn't look like rain.

3. 翔太君は、悪い事をしそうにない子ですが、実は大変な子なんです。
   Shouta doesn't seem like a kid that would do bad things, but he is really terrible.

EXAMPLE CONVERSATION

1. **Informal conversation between friends.**

   A: いつも忙しそうだね。今週、出かけられそうな日はある？
   B: う～ん... ないね。でも、来週は大丈夫。

   > We use "think" here because it's the ONLY English that makes sense. See 9-6.

   A: You always seem busy. Is there a day you think you can go out this week?
   B: Let's see... there isn't one. But next week is okay.

● 9-5. Expressing hearsay 〜そうです

〜そうです is also used when giving information you heard or read. Any of the informal verb forms can be used.

EXAMPLES

1. 食<ruby>た</ruby>べるそうです。
   I heard they do/will eat.

5. 食<ruby>た</ruby>べないそうです。
   I heard they don't/won't eat.

2. 食<ruby>た</ruby>べたそうです。
   I heard they ate.

6. 食<ruby>た</ruby>べなかったそうです。
   I heard they didn't eat.

3. 食<ruby>た</ruby>べたいそうです。
   I heard they want to eat.

7. 食<ruby>た</ruby>べたくないそうです。
   I heard they don't want to eat.

4. 食<ruby>た</ruby>べているそうです。
   I heard they are eating.

8. 食<ruby>た</ruby>べていないそうです。
   I heard they aren't eating/haven't eaten.

EXAMPLE SENTENCES

1. このレストランは週末<ruby>しゅうまつ</ruby>、24時間営業<ruby>じかんえいぎょう</ruby>しているそうです。
   I heard that this restaurant is open 24 hours on the weekend.

> 食べていない can mean, "haven't eaten" since it's a state of not eating until this point.

2. 昨日<ruby>きのう</ruby>、サンフランシスコで山火事<ruby>やまかじ</ruby>があったそうです。
   I heard that there was a forest fire in San Francisco yesterday.

3. 山田<ruby>やまだ</ruby>さんが電車<ruby>でんしゃ</ruby>に乗<ruby>の</ruby>り遅<ruby>おく</ruby>れたので、仕事<ruby>しごと</ruby>に遅<ruby>おく</ruby>れるそうです。
   I heard that Mr. Yamada will be late for work because he missed the train.

You can also use this pattern with nouns, but informal / plain forms (だ、だった) must be used before そう.

EXAMPLE SENTENCES

1. 結婚記念日<ruby>けっこんきねんび</ruby>だそうです。   I heard that it's (their) anniversary.
2. 結婚記念日<ruby>けっこんきねんび</ruby>だったそうです。   I heard that it was (their) anniversary.
3. 結婚記念日<ruby>けっこんきねんび</ruby>じゃないそうです。   I heard that it's not (their) anniversary.
4. 結婚記念日<ruby>けっこんきねんび</ruby>じゃなかったそうです。   I heard that it wasn't (their) anniversary.

* REMINDER: Informal form and plain form are the same thing. All plain forms act as informal but also are commonly in grammar constructions that aren't informal.

📖 もっと詳^{くわ}しく… More Details ⓘ

〜そうです (appears to be) vs. 〜そうです (hearsay)
Make sure not to confuse the similar sounding patterns.

> い is optional.

Directly observed by speaker: (い form + そうです)

雨^{あめ}が降^ふりそうです。(い form)   It looks like it will rain.

雨^{あめ}が降^ふっていそうです。(ongoing form drop る)   It looks like it's raining.

Told to or heard by speaker: (* Informal/plain form + そうです)

雨^{あめ}が降^ふるそうです。(う form)   Apparently, it's going to rain.

雨^{あめ}が降^ふらないそうです。(ない form)   Apparently, it isn't going to rain.

雨^{あめ}が降^ふったそうです。(た form)   Apparently, it rained.

雨^{あめ}が降^ふっているそうです。(ongoing form)   Apparently, it's raining.

● **9-6. によると (according to; depending on)**

によると is added after an information source to say "according to this source".
〜によると and 〜そうです are often used together in a sentence when you say how and what you have heard. Only the "hearsay" versions of そうです can be used as you don't need a source when you have made a direct observation.

> **(person; thing) によると、**
> **according to / depending on (person, thing)**

EXAMPLE SENTENCES

1. 村田^{むらた}さんの話^{はなし}によると、あそこはすごくいい学校^{がっこう}だそうです。
   According to Mr. Murata's story, that (place) is a very good school.

2. 天気予報^{てんきよほう}によると、明日^{あした}は雪^{ゆき}だそうです。
   According to the weather report, it is going to snow tomorrow.

3. 昨日^{きのう}のニュースによると、ここで交通事故^{こうつうじこ}があったそうです。
   According to yesterday's news, there was a traffic accident here.

9 Practice and Review 練習と復習

● 1. Mini Conversation ミニ会話 J → E

1. Polite conversation between a student and a teacher

A: 今日の宿題は何ですか。

B: 43 ページから 50 ページまでの単語の意味を調べて下さい。

A: ええっ。たくさん、ありますね。死んでしまいます。

A: What is today's homework?

B: Please find out the meanings of the words on pages 43 through 50.

A: What? It is a lot. I am going to die...

2. Polite conversation between neighbors

A: 林さんは旦那さんに殴られるそうですね。

B: ええ？本当ですか。

A: はい。「殺されたら、どうしよう」と言っていました。

B: 警察に電話した方がいいですね。

A: I heard that Mrs. Hayashi gets hit by her husband.

B: What? Really?

A: Yes. She was saying "I don't know what to do...if he tries to kill me".

B: We should call the police.

3. Polite conversation between friends

A: この前、家を探しに行って、いいのを見つけました。

B: そうですか。よかったですね。いくらですか。

A: ダウンタウンでは 30万ドルだそうです。

B: そこで、30万ドルなら、他の場所も調べた方がいいですよ。もっといい家がありますから。

A: I went to look for a house and found a good one the other day.

B: Is that right? That's good. How much is it?

A: I heard that it's $300,000 downtown.

B: If it's $300,000 there, you should check out other places too. Because there are more good houses.

● 2. Mini Conversation ミニ会話 E → J

1. Polite conversation between neighbors

A: Did you see yesterday's news?

B: No, I didn't.

A: What? There was a murder case in the next town and apparently the perpetrator is near here now.

B: That sure is frightening. We should stay in our houses.

A: 昨日のニュースを見ましたか。

B: いいえ、見ませんでした。

A: ええっ！隣の町で殺人事件があって、今、犯人がこの近くにいるそうです。

B: 怖いですね。家にいた方がいいですね。

2. Polite conversation between housewives

A: Today is my wedding anniversary.

B: Congratulations. How many years have you been married?

A: Three years.

B: I heard that your husband does housework often.

A: Yes. He always helps me out.

A: 今日は結婚記念日です。

B: おめでとうございます。結婚して、何年ですか？

A: 三年です。

B: ご主人は、よく家事をするそうですね。

A: はい。いつも手伝ってくれます。

3. Polite conversation between two strangers on the train

A: Yesterday was cold, but today is hot, isn't it?

B: Yes, the weather always changes here.

A: According to Mr. Akita, it appeared to be colder a long time ago.

A: 昨日は寒かったけど、今日は暑いですね。

B: ええ、ここの天気はいつも変わります。

A: 秋田さんによると、昔はもっと寒かったそうですよ。

● 3. Short Dialogue

Ms. Iwata and her neighbor are talking about a murder case in their neighborhood.

近所の人	「ちょっと、岩田さん！昨日の殺人事件のこと、聞いた？」
岩田さん	「うん、聞いたよ。あの一人暮らしのおばあさんが殺されたでしょう。」
近所の人	「そう。犯人はまだわからないそうよ。」
岩田さん	「怖いね・・・。でも、どうやって家の中に入ったのかな。」
近所の人	「おばあさんの家はマンションの5階だから、玄関からだと思うよ。」
岩田さん	「ニュースによると、鍵は壊されていないそうだね。」
近所の人	「うん。だから多分、知り合いじゃないかな。」
岩田さん	「そうかあ・・・。知っている人が急に亡くなると、ショックだね。」
近所の人	「うん、ショックだね。早く犯人を見つけてほしいね。」
岩田さん	「そうじゃないと、私たちも怖いね。」

9 Kanji Lesson 9:
春夏秋冬時間

From the teacher...

In this lesson we have gathered kanji related to the seasons and time.

9 | New Kanji 新しい漢字

210	日	9画	spring										

	くんよみ	はる
	おんよみ	シュン

思春期 (し・しゅん・き) puberty　　　　春一番 (はる・いち・ばん) first storm of spring
春の日 (はる・の・ひ) a spring day　　　売春 (ばい・しゅん) prostitution
青春 (せい・しゅん) youth　　　　　　　春休み (はる・やす・み) spring break

春											

211	夂	10画	summer										

	くんよみ	なつ
	おんよみ	カ、ゲ

初夏 (しょ・か) early summer　　　　夏休み (なつ・やす・み) summer vacation
真夏 (ま・なつ) mid-summer　　　　　夏祭り (なつ・まつ・り) summer festival
夏至 (げ・し) summer solstice　　　　夏時間 (なつ・じ・かん) daylight savings time

夏											

212	禾	9画	fall; autumn										

	くんよみ	あき
	おんよみ	シュウ

秋 (あき) fall, autumn　　　　　　　　秋分 (しゅう・ぶん) autumnal equinox
秋田犬 (あき・た・けん) Akita (dog)　　秋田県 (あき・た・けん) Akita Prefecture
秋季 (しゅう・き) fall season　　　　　立秋 (りっ・しゅう) first day of autumn

秋											

213	冫	5 画	winter		
冬		くんよみ	ふゆ		
		おんよみ	トウ		

冬 (ふゆ) winter   冬休み (ふゆ・やす・み) winter vacation
冬眠 (とう・みん) hibernation   春夏秋冬 (しゅん・か・しゅう・とう) the four seasons
真冬 (ま・ふゆ) mid-winter   冬物 (ふゆ・もの) winter clothing

冬

214	日	10 画	time; hour; occasion		
時		くんよみ	とき		
		おんよみ	ジ		

時々 (とき・どき) sometimes   若い時 (わか・い・とき) when (I) was young
時差 (じ・さ) time difference   五時 (ご・じ) 5 o'clock
時計 (と・けい) watch, clock   今時 (いま・どき) modern times; these days

時

215	門	12 画	space; interval		
間		くんよみ	あいだ、ま		
		おんよみ	カン、ケン		

人間 (にん・げん) human being   時間 (じ・かん) time, hour
昼間 (ひる・ま) during the day   間もなく (ま・もなく) soon; before long
間 (あいだ) between   この間 (この・あいだ) the other day

間

9 | Kanji Culture 漢字の文化

● What does "a space of a hair" mean?

かん　いっ　ぱつ
間一髪
space   one strand of hair

The expression 「間一髪」 literally means, "the space that one strand of hair can fit into". It's similar to the English expression, "by the skin of our teeth", meaning it was a close call or a narrow escape.

EXAMPLE SENTENCES

1. 危なかった！間一髪だったね。
   That was dangerous! We barely escaped!

2. 私は間一髪で助かりました。
   I was saved in the nick of time.

9 | Words You Can Write かける ことば

青春 (せいしゅん) youth

青	春								

立秋 (りっしゅう) the first day of autumn

立	秋								

今時 (いまどき) nowadays; present day

今	時								

秋分 (しゅうぶん) autumnal equinox

秋	分								

時間 (じかん) time

時	間								

時計 (とけい) watch; clock

時	計								

人間 (にんげん) human being

人	間								

冬場 (ふゆば) the winter season

冬	場								

時点 (じてん) point in time

時	点								

春休み (はるやすみ) spring vacation

春	休	み						

秋晴れ (あきばれ) fine autumn day

秋	晴	れ						

この間 (このあいだ) the other day

こ	の	間						

夏休み (なつやすみ) summer vacation

夏	休	み						

冬休み (ふゆやすみ) winter vacation

冬	休	み						

春夏秋冬 (しゅんかしゅうとう) the four seasons

春	夏	秋	冬					

9 Workbook 9:
Workbook Activities

9 | Kanji Drills 漢字ドリル

● 1. Reading practice
Write FURIGANA above the underlined kanji words.

1.   <u>日本</u>の<u>春</u>は、<u>三月</u>から<u>五月</u>の<u>三</u>か<u>月間</u>です。

2.   <u>六月</u>から<u>七月</u>ごろまで<u>雨</u>が<ruby>続<rt>つづ</rt></ruby>いたあと、<ruby>暑<rt>あつ</rt></ruby>い<u>夏</u>がはじまります。

3.   <u>日本</u>の<u>秋</u>は、<u>九月</u>から<u>十一月</u>で、<u>食</u>べ<ruby>物<rt>もの</rt></ruby>のおいしい<ruby>季節<rt>き せつ</rt></ruby>です。

4.   <u>日本</u>の<u>冬</u>は、<u>十二月</u>から<u>二月</u>で、お<u>正月</u>には、<ruby>神社<rt>じん じゃ</rt></ruby>やお<u>寺</u>に<u>行</u>きます。

5.   <u>日本</u>は<u>南北</u>に<u>長</u>いので、<u>冬</u>でも<u>南</u>はあたたかくて、<u>北</u>は<u>大雪</u>が<ruby>降<rt>ふ</rt></ruby>ったりします。

● 2. Fill in the Kanji
Fill in the appropriate kanji in the blanks for each sentence.

1.   ＿＿ ＿＿みに ＿＿ ＿＿を ＿＿きました。
（はる やす　　さく ぶん　　か）
I wrote an essay on spring vacation.

2.   ＿＿ ＿＿みに ＿＿ ＿＿に ＿＿ ＿＿りしました。
（なつ やす　　に ほん　　さと がえ）
Over summer vacation I went to Japan to visit my parents.

3.   ＿＿には、＿＿ ＿＿や＿＿に ＿＿きたいです。
（あき　　こう えん　うみ　い）
In Autumn, I want to go to the park and to the ocean.

4. ___ ___みに___ ___に べん___しに___きます。
<ruby>冬<rt>ふゆ</rt></ruby> <ruby>休<rt>やす</rt></ruby> <ruby>中<rt>ちゅう</rt></ruby> <ruby>国<rt>ごく</rt></ruby> <ruby>強<rt>きょう</rt></ruby> <ruby>行<rt>い</rt></ruby>

Over winter vacation I am going to China to study.

5. ___ ___がない___は、ごはんを___べるのを わすれます。
<ruby>時<rt>じ</rt></ruby> <ruby>間<rt>かん</rt></ruby> <ruby>時<rt>とき</rt></ruby> <ruby>食<rt>た</rt></ruby>

When I don't have time, I forget to eat dinner.

6. この___ 、___が ___しい ___ ___を___ってくれた。
<ruby>間<rt>あいだ</rt></ruby> <ruby>母<rt>はは</rt></ruby> <ruby>新<rt>あたら</rt></ruby> <ruby>時<rt>と</rt></ruby> <ruby>計<rt>けい</rt></ruby> <ruby>買<rt>か</rt></ruby>

The other day, my mother bought me a new watch.

7. ___ ___ ___ ___とは、えい___で「four seasons」と___います。
<ruby>春<rt>しゅん</rt></ruby> <ruby>夏<rt>か</rt></ruby> <ruby>秋<rt>しゅう</rt></ruby> <ruby>冬<rt>とう</rt></ruby> <ruby>語<rt>ご</rt></ruby> <ruby>言<rt>い</rt></ruby>

Shun-Ka-Shuu-Tou is "four seasons" in English,

---

9 | Usage Activities 文法アクティビティー

● 3. Reading comprehension

Translate the following reading comprehension. Write on a separate piece of paper or type in an electronic device if needed. Answer the questions in the next section.

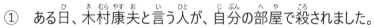

殺人事件
<ruby>殺<rt>さつ</rt></ruby><ruby>人<rt>じん</rt></ruby><ruby>事<rt>じ</rt></ruby><ruby>件<rt>けん</rt></ruby>

Oh No! Something has happened! Can you solve a crime with your Japanese skills alone? It's a real who-dun-it!

① ある<ruby>日<rt>ひ</rt></ruby>、<ruby>木村康夫<rt>きむらやすお</rt></ruby>と<ruby>言<rt>い</rt></ruby>う<ruby>人<rt>ひと</rt></ruby>が、<ruby>自分<rt>じぶん</rt></ruby>の<ruby>部屋<rt>へや</rt></ruby>で<ruby>殺<rt>ころ</rt></ruby>されました。

② <ruby>彼<rt>かれ</rt></ruby>は<ruby>後<rt>うし</rt></ruby>ろからハンマーみたいな<ruby>物<rt>もの</rt></ruby>で<ruby>頭<rt>あたま</rt></ruby>を<ruby>殴<rt>なぐ</rt></ruby>られて、<ruby>死<rt>し</rt></ruby>んでいました。

③ <ruby>死亡時刻<rt>しぼうじこく</rt></ruby>は、<ruby>午後<rt>ごご</rt></ruby>8<ruby>時<rt>じ</rt></ruby>から <ruby>午後<rt>ごご</rt></ruby>10<ruby>時<rt>じ</rt></ruby>の<ruby>間<rt>あいだ</rt></ruby>でした。

④ その<ruby>日<rt>ひ</rt></ruby>は<ruby>大雨<rt>おおあめ</rt></ruby>で、<ruby>家<rt>うち</rt></ruby>の<ruby>外<rt>そと</rt></ruby>の<ruby>電気<rt>でんき</rt></ruby>はついていませんでした。

⑤ <ruby>犯人<rt>はんにん</rt></ruby>は<ruby>靴<rt>くつ</rt></ruby>を<ruby>履<rt>は</rt></ruby>かないで、やすおさんの<ruby>部屋<rt>へや</rt></ruby>に<ruby>入<rt>はい</rt></ruby>ったそうです。

⑥ <ruby>最初<rt>さいしょ</rt></ruby>に<ruby>死体<rt>したい</rt></ruby>を<ruby>見<rt>み</rt></ruby>つけた<ruby>人<rt>ひと</rt></ruby>は、<ruby>奥<rt>おく</rt></ruby>さんでした。

⑦ <ruby>奥<rt>おく</rt></ruby>さんが<ruby>家<rt>うち</rt></ruby>に<ruby>帰<rt>かえ</rt></ruby>った<ruby>時<rt>とき</rt></ruby>、<ruby>家<rt>うち</rt></ruby>のドアは<ruby>開<rt>あ</rt></ruby>けっぱなしだったそうです。

⑧ <ruby>警察<rt>けいさつ</rt></ruby>は、<ruby>次<rt>つぎ</rt></ruby>の<ruby>三人<rt>さんにん</rt></ruby>から<ruby>話<rt>はなし</rt></ruby>を<ruby>聞<rt>き</rt></ruby>くことにしました。

木村よしみ（奥さん）31歳

⑨　奥さんが警察に電話したのは、午後10時半頃でした。

⑩　奥さんは、旦那さんの死体を見てパニックになったので、警察にすぐ電話

できなかったそうです。

⑪　奥さんには、3才年下の浮気相手がいました。

⑫　奥さんと浮気相手は、その日の午後8時頃、喫茶店で会っていました。

⑬　奥さんによると、隣の佐々木さんに貸したお金の借用書がなくなったそうです。

佐々木 まこと (お隣さん) 43歳

⑭　隣の佐々木さんと木村さんは、高校からの友達でした。

⑮　佐々木さんは去年、会社を始めて、お金に困っていました。

⑯　木村さんは佐々木さんを信用して、五百万円、貸したそうです。

⑰　それからは佐々木さんが借金を返さないせいで、二人は会わなくなりました。

⑱　その日は、遅くまで家で仕事をしていたと言っています。

⑲　佐々木さんによると、午後9時15分頃、青い服を着た若い男性が、木村さんの家に入るのを
二階の窓から見たそうです。

永井 翔太 (浮気相手) 28歳

⑳　永井さんと木村さんは、2年前から会っていました。

㉑　木村さんが旦那さんと別れそうにないので、二人はよく喧嘩していました。

㉒　その日は午後9時半頃、木村さんと喫茶店を出て、別々に帰ったと言って
います。

㉓　奥さんによると、永井さんと殺された木村さんは、会ったことがないそうです。

㉔　犯人は誰だと思いますか。

● 4. Reading comprehension questions

After translating the following questions about the reading comprehension into English, answer in Japanese below.

1. 誰が犯人だと思いますか。それは、どうしてですか。

Translation: _____

Answer: _____

2. 「死亡時刻」という言葉の意味を、日本語で説明してください。

Translation: _____

Answer: _____

3. 奥さんはいつ、警察に電話をしましたか。

Translation: _____

Answer: _____

4. どうして、すぐ電話しませんでしたか。

Translation: _____

Answer: _____

5. 木村さんと佐々木さんは、ずっといい友達でしたか。それは、どうしてですか。

Translation: _____

Answer: _____

6. 木村さんの結婚生活はよかったですか。それはなぜですか。

Translation: _____

Answer: _____

7. 木村さんが殺された時、奥さんは誰とどこにいましたか。

Translation: _____

Answer: _____

● 5. Reading comprehension case solved!
Translate the following continuation of the reading comprehension to know who killed Mr. Kimura.

❶ 警察によると、犯人は佐々木さんでした。

❷ その日の夜は大雨で外の電気がついていなかったのに、「青い服を着た若い男性を見た」と言っていたからです。

❸ 夜の大雨の中では、シャツの色は見えません。

❹ それに、若いかどうかも分かりません。

❺ 佐々木さんは嘘をついているので、犯人です。

Translation:

_____

_____

_____

_____

● 6. Practice (I almost...)

Match the left sentence with an appropriate choice from the box.

Ex. 昨日は、寝られなかったから、(e)

1. テーブルにおいしそうなケーキがあったから、(   )

2. お母さんにうそをついたから、(   )

3. 悪い人にだまされて、(   )

4. お店でいいスーツを見つけて、(   )

5. 仕事は六時に終わるから、   (   )

6. 今朝、寝坊をしたから、(   )

---

a. 泣きそうでした。

b. 食べそうでした。

c. 買いそうだったけど、止めました。

d. そこに七時ごろ行けそうです。

e. 今、ここで寝そうです。

f. 会社に遅れそうでした。

g. 怒られそうです。

● 7. Fill in the blanks

Fill in the missing part based on the English sentence.

1. 男の人が_____ので、警察が_____。

   Since a man was murdered, the police are investigating.

2. ボクシングの試合で顔を強く_____。

   My face got hit hard in a boxing match.

3. 私の高校の_____。

   I heard that my high school teacher passed away.

4. 今朝、バスに_____。

   I almost missed the bus this morning!

5. _____、明日は雪が_____。

   According to the weather report, it is going to snow tomorrow.

● 8. Question and Answer

Answer the following questions as if they are being asked to you.

1. 誰かにうそをついたことがありますか。

   _____

2. 明日はどんな天気になりますか。（use ～そうです）

   _____

3. 辞書を使って、言葉の意味を調べたりしますか。

   _____

4. 殴ったり、殴られたりするスポーツは何ですか。

   _____

5. ゴキブリが部屋の中にいたら、殺せますか。

   _____

● 9. Verb Conjugation Chart (Negative assumptions)

Complete the following chart.

English meaning	ます Form	～そうにない	～なさそう
to sleep	ねます	ねそうにない	ねなさそう
to turn rotten			
to tell a lie			
to collect (active)			
to get mad			
to forget			

● 10. Translation

Translate the following sentences into Japanese using そうです.

1. According to the news, a high school teacher was killed by a thief.

    _____

2. According to the weather forecast, it will rain heavily tomorrow.

    _____

3. According to Mrs. Toda, the new coffee shop near the station is really nice.

    _____

4. It looks like I might be able to make dinner for my family tonight.

    _____

5. I heard that Kimiko's boyfriend looks younger than her.

    _____

9 | Answer Key 答え合わせ

Short Dialogue (translation)

Neighbor	Hey Iwata-san! Did you hear about the murder (case) yesterday?
Iwata	Yeah, I did. The old lady that lived alone got killed, right?
Neighbor	Right. Apparently, they don't know who did it (the criminal) yet.
Iwata	So scary... But I wonder how they got into the house.
Neighbor	Since her apartment was on the 5th floor, I think it was from the main entrance.
Iwata	According to the news, apparently the lock wasn't broken.
Neighbor	Right. So, I wonder if it wasn't maybe an acquaintance.
Iwata	I see... It's a shock when someone you know suddenly dies.
Neighbor	Yeah, it's a shock. I want them to find who did it (the criminal) soon.
Iwata	If not, it's scary for us too.

1. Reading practice (answers)

1. 日本の春は、三月から五月の三か月間です。
2. 六月から七月ごろまで雨が続いたあと、暑い夏がはじまります。
3. 日本の秋は、九月から十一月で、食べ物のおいしい季節です。
4. 日本の冬は、十二月から二月で、お正月には、神社やお寺に行きます。
5. 日本は南北に長いので、冬でも南はあたたかくて、北は大雪が降ったりします。

2. Fill in the kanji (answers)

1. 春休みに作文を書きました。

2. 夏休みに日本に里帰りしました。

3. 秋には、公園や海に行きたいです。

4. 冬休みに中国にべん強しに行きます。

5. 時間がない時は、ごはんを食べるのをわすれます。

6. この間、母が新しい時計を買ってくれた。

7. 春夏秋冬とは、えい語で「four seasons」と言います。

3. Reading comprehension (translation)

① One day a person named Yasuo Kimura was killed in his own room.
② He was dead having been hit in the head with a hammer-like item from behind.
③ The time of death was between 8PM and 10PM.
④ That day it was raining heavily and the outside lights of the house weren't on.
⑤ Apparently the criminal entered Yasuo's room without wearing any shoes.
⑥ The first one to find the body was his wife.
⑦ Apparently, the door was (left) open when the wife returned home.
⑧ The police decided to talk with the following three people.

YOSHIMI KIMURA (WIFE) 31 YEARS OLD
⑨ The wife called the police around 10:30PM.
⑩ Apparently the wife didn't call the police right away since she panicked seeing her husband's body.
⑪ The wife had a lover three years younger than herself.
⑫ On that day, the wife and her lover met at a coffee shop from around 8PM.
⑬ According to the wife, the proof of debt document proving that the neighbor, Sasaki, borrowed money is missing.

MAKOTO SASAKI (NEIGHBOR) 43 YEARS OLD
⑭ The neighbor Sasaki-san was friends with Kimura-san since high school.
⑮ Sasaki-san started a company last year and was troubled over money.
⑯ Kimura-san trusted Sasaki-san and apparently loaned him 5 million yen.
⑰ From then, due to Sasaki-san not having returned his debt, they stopped meeting.
⑱ He says that on that day he was working at home until late.
⑲ According to Sasaki-san, from his 2nd story window around 9:15PM, he saw a young man wearing blue clothes enter Kimura's house.

SHOUTA NAGAI (LOVER) 28 YEARS OLD
⑳ Nagai-san and Mrs. Kimura had been seeing each other for 2 years.
㉑ Since it seemed that Mrs. Kimura wouldn't split with her husband, the two often fought.
㉒ He says that on that day around 9:30PM he left the coffee shop with Mrs. Kimura and they went home separately.
㉓ According to the wife, Nagai-san and her murdered husband hadn't met.
㉔ Who do you think the killer is?

4. Reading comprehension questions (answers)

1. Translation: Who do you think the perpetrator is? Why?
   Answer(s):
   1. 佐々木さんがうそをついていると思います。借金を返したくないからです。

   2. 奥さんがうそをついていると思います。
   旦那さんと別れたいからです。／浮気相手と一緒にいたいからです。

   3. 永井さんがうそをついていると思います。
   奥さんと結婚したいからです。／奥さんが旦那さんと別れそうにないからです。

2. Translation: Explain the meaning of the words 「死亡時刻」 in Japanese.
   Answer(s): 「死んだ時間」という意味です。／「誰かが亡くなった時間」という意味です。

3. Translation: When did the wife call the police?
   Answer(s): 午後10時半ごろ、しました。

4. Translation: How come she didn't call right away?
   Answer(s): だんなさんの死体を見て、パニックになったからです。

5. Translation: Were Mr. Suzuki and Mr. Kimura always good friends? Why?
   Answer(s): いいえ。佐々木さんが借りたお金を返さないからです。

6. Translation: Was Mr. Kimura's married life good? Why?

    Answer(s):   よくなかったです。／全然よくなかったです。

    奥さんが浮気をしていたからです。

7. Translation: Where and who was the wife with when Mr. Kimura was murdered?

    Answer(s):   奥さんは浮気相手の永井さんと喫茶店にいました。

5. Reading comprehension case solved! (translation)

❶ According to the police, the perpetrator was Mr. Sasaki.
❷ It's because despite that night raining heavily and the lights being out, he said that he saw a young man wearing blue clothes.
❸ In heavy rain at night, you can't see the color of a shirt.
❹ And also you wouldn't know if they are young or not.
❺ Since Sasaki-san is lying, he is the perpetrator.

6. Practice (I almost...) (answers)

1. (b) テーブルにおいしそうなケーキがあったから、食べそうでした。

2. (g) お母さんにうそをついたから、怒られそうです。

3. (a) 悪い人にだまされて、泣きそうでした。

4. (c) お店でいいスーツを見つけて、買いそうだったけど、止めました。

5. (d) 仕事は六時に終わるから、そこに七時ごろ行けそうです。

6. (f) 今朝、寝坊をしたから、会社に遅れそうでした。

7. Fill in the blanks (answers)

1. 男の人が殺されたので、警察が調べています。

2. ボクシングの試合で顔を強く殴られました。

3. 私の高校の先生が亡くなったそうです。

4. 今朝、バスに乗り遅れそうでした。

5. 天気予報によると、明日は雪が降るそうです。

8. Question and Answer (sample answers)

1. Have you ever lied to someone?

    いいえ、ありません。/ はい、2、3回あります。

2. What type of weather will it be tomorrow?

明日は晴れるそうです。 / 明日の午前中はくもりで、午後は雨が降るそうです。

3. Do you use the dictionary to look up the meanings of words?

はい、時々します。 / いいえ、携帯を使って調べます。

4. What is a sport where you hit and get hit?

ボクシングです。 / 格闘技 (martial arts)だと思います。

5. If there was a cockroach in the room, could you kill it?

いいえ、無理です。 / はい、殺せます。

9. Verb Conjugation Chart (answers)

English meaning	ます form	〜そうにない	〜なさそう
to sleep	ねます	ねそうにない	ねなさそう
to turn rotten	くさります	くさりそうにない	くさらなさそう
to tell a lie	うそをつきます	うそをつきそうにない	うそをつかなさそう
to collect (active)	あつめます	あつめそうにない	あつめなさそう
to get mad	おこります	おこりそうにない	おこらなさそう
to forget	わすれます	わすれそうにない	わすれなさそう

10. Translation (answers)

1. ニュースによると、高校の先生が泥棒に殺されたそうです。

2. 天気予報によると、明日は大雨が降るそうです。/明日はどしゃぶりだそうです。/明日は大雨だそうです。

3. 戸田さんによると、駅の近くの新しい喫茶店がとてもいいそうです。

4. 今晩、家族のために晩ご飯が作れそうです。

5. きみこさんの彼氏は彼女より年下に見えるそうです。

10

| 11 PAGES | 7 USAGE SECTIONS | 14 NEW WORDS |

Lesson 10:
ばかり and かもしれない

10 | New Words 新しい言葉

Nouns etc.

おう えん 応援	cheering; backup; boost; rooting	うわさばなし 噂話	gossip
に ほんしょく 日本食	Japanese food; cuisine		

Adverbs

だい ぶ 大分	fairly; quite; pretty	たし 確かに	surely; certainly; for sure
さっ そく 早速	immediately; right away; at once		

Verbs

つか 疲れる	to get tired; to tire	った 伝える	to convey
つづ 続ける	to continue	はまる	to be addicted
かん ちが 勘違いする	to be mistaken	こう かい 後悔する	to regret
ま あ 間に合う	to make it in time	こく はく 告白する	to confess one's love

10 | Word Usage 言葉の使い方

| W-1 | ～食 しょく | food |

しょく
食 is also part of other words.

EXAMPLES

わ しょく
和食 (Japanese food)

よう しょく
洋食 (western food)

てい しょく
定食 (set meal)

や しょく
夜食 (late night snack)

しょうしょく
少食 (light eater; light eating)

かん しょく
間食 (eating between meals; snacking)

10 | Verb Usage 動詞の使い方

V-1	疲れる (つか)	to get tired; to tire	いる/える

This verb is used to describe a person's state after working a hard day. It's NOT used to say you are tired as in being sleepy. Instead the adjective ねむい would be used.

> **EXAMPLE SENTENCES**
>
> 1. 夏は暑くて、疲れます。
>   I get tired because summer is hot.
>
> 2. 朝 九時から 夜 十時まで仕事をしたので、疲れました。
>   I was tired because I worked from 9 o'clock in the morning until 10 o'clock at night.

V-2	続ける (つづ)	to continue the (item/action) (ACTION)	いる/える
1. (item/action) を続ける		to continue an (item/action)	

> **EXAMPLE SENTENCES**
>
> 1. 勉強はずっと続けた方がいいです。
>   You should continue to study all the time.
>
> 2. 先週、三日続けて残業しました。
>   Last week I worked overtime 3 days in a row.
>
> 3. もうこの仕事を続けたくないです。
>   I don't want to continue this job anymore.
>
> > When 続けて is used after a time or counter, it can translate to "in a row".

V-3	後悔する (こうかい)	to regret	する
1. (something) に／を後悔する		to regret (something)	

Depending on the sentence, the item that you regret is marked with に or を.

> **EXAMPLE SENTENCES**
>
> 1. 学生の時、よく勉強しなかったことを今、後悔しています。
>   Now I regret that I didn't study well when I was a student.
>
> 2. 私は自分の選択に後悔したことがありません。
>   I have never regretted any of my choices.

V-4	伝える（つた）	to convey; to relay information; to tell	いる/える
	1. (statement) と伝える	to relay a (statement)	
	2. (person) に伝える	to relay to a (person)	
	3. (something) を伝える	to relay (something)	

The verb 伝える（つた） is used almost in place of "tell", as in "tell someone this". It always uses the quotation/idea marker と when relaying a statement.

伝える（つた） uses all the same grammar as the verb 言う（い） (to say).

EXAMPLE SENTENCES

1. 東さんに明日会いに行くと伝えて下さい。
   Please tell Mr. Higashi that I am going to see him tomorrow.

2. すみませんが、ジェフさんに伝えてほしいことがあります。
   Excuse me, but I have something I want you to tell Jeff about.

3. 飛行機が3時間遅れていることをお母さんに伝えてくれる？
   Can you please tell mom that the flight is 3 hours late?

V-5	勘違いする（かんちが）	to be mistaken; to be misunderstood	する
	1. (situation) と勘違いする	to misunderstand (situation)	
	2. (person) に勘違いされる	to be mistaken by (person)	

This is a good word to use when you confused one thing for another. It's similar to saying "I thought it was XXX, but I was wrong." The XXX is followed by と.

EXAMPLE SENTENCES

1. ああ、すみません。勘違いしていました。
   Oh, I am sorry. I have misunderstood.

2. 私は田中さんが日本に帰ったと勘違いしていました。
   I have misunderstood that Mr. Tanaka went back to Japan.

3. 私は背が高いから、よくバスケットボール選手だと日本人に勘違いされます。
   Because I'm tall, I'm often mistaken as a basketball player by Japanese people.

V-6	はまる	to be addicted; to be into something	regular
	1. (thing) に はまる	to be addicted to (thing)	

はまる is used when you are into a game, food, or fun activity etc. so much that it's hard to stop. Remember that if you are currently addicted, you need to use the ています form because it's an ongoing event.

EXAMPLE SENTENCES

1. 私は今、日本映画に はまっています。
   I am addicted to (love) Japanese movies now.

2. 私の息子は音楽に はまっているので、ギターを買ってあげました。
   My son is addicted to music, so I bought him a guitar.

V-7	間に合う	to make it in time	regular
	1. (event, etc.) に間に合う	to make it on time for an (event, etc.)	

EXAMPLE SENTENCES

1. 今朝8時13分の電車に間に合いませんでした。
   I didn't make the 8:13 train this morning.

2. 朝ご飯を食べると、仕事に間に合わない。
   If I eat breakfast, I won't make it to work on time.

V-8	告白する	to confess one's love	する
	1. (someone) に告白する	to confess your love to (someone)	
	2. (someone) に／から告白される	to have (someone) confess their love to/for you	

EXAMPLE SENTENCES

1. 唯ちゃんに告白したけど、もう後悔しています。
   I confessed my love to Yui, but I am already regretting it.

2. この間、クラスメートに告白されました。
   The other day a classmate confessed their love to me.

10 | Grammar and Usage 文法と使い方

● 10-1. Using ばかり with a noun

When following a noun, ばかり means "just this thing" or "only this thing".

EXAMPLE SENTENCES

1. 近所のおばさんは、噂話ばかりします。
   The neighborhood ladies just gossip.

2. 仕事ばかりしないで、遊びに行きましょう。
   Don't just work (all the time), let's go hang out.

3. コーヒーばかり飲んでいたら、夜、寝られませんよ。
   If I only drink coffee, I can't sleep at night.

● 10-2. Using ばかり with a number

When ばかり is used with a number and counter word, it means "about" or "around" which is very similar to what ぐらい does.

```
(number + counter) + ばかり
about (number)
```

EXAMPLE SENTENCES

1. 毎日5キロばかり、走ります。
   I run around 5 kilometers every day.

2. 今日は髪の毛を10センチばかり、切りました。
   Today I cut my hair about 10 centimeters.

3. 娘の誕生日パーティーに20人ばかり来ると思います。
   I think around 20 people will come to my daughter's birthday party.

● 10-3. Using ばかり with an う form verb

When attaching ばかり after an う form verb, it means "all that can be done is~" or "all that is done is~".

```
(う form of verb) + ばかり
only, all can do is~ (verb)
```

EXAMPLE SENTENCES

1. 父が入院しているので、私たちは心配するばかりです。
   All I can do is worry since my father is hospitalized.

2. 週末は家にいるばかりで、出かけたりしません。
   On weekends, I only stay at home and don't go out.

3. 毎日スイーツを食べているから、太るばかりです。
   Because I eat sweets every day, all I do is gain weight.

> You can use で to string nouns and な adjectives. This is introduced in book 3 Lesson 6.

● **10-4. てばかり constantly or always doing something**

In this lesson, there are two very similarly looking grammar, てばかり and たばかり. They are NOT the same or even close to be the same. One hiragana slip and the meaning completely changes. てばかり means "constantly does this thing."

> **(て form verb) + ばかり**
> **constantly doing (verb)**

EXAMPLE SENTENCES

1. 6月は雨が降ってばかりで、嫌ですね。
   It is always raining in June, so it is unpleasant (I don't like that).

2. あの人は食べてばかりですね。
   That person is constantly eating.

3. 高田さんは仕事をしてばかりです。
   Mr. Takada is always working.

● **10-5. たばかり just now completed an action**

たばかり is deceptively similar looking and sounding to てばかり, so let's be careful! It is even made almost the same way. Except you just add ばかり to the た form of the verb. It means, "I just did it now."

> **(た form verb) + ばかり**
> **just did (verb)**

EXAMPLE SENTENCES

1. 今日、掃除したばかりだから、部屋はきれいですよ。
   I just cleaned the room today, so it is clean.

2. 日本から帰ってきたばかりだから、ちょっと疲れています。
   I just came back from Japan, so I am a little tired.

3. お給料が出たばかりです。
   I just got paid.

● 10-6. Indicating degree of certainty (〜かも知れない)

かもしれない is always added to the end of sentence. It's a bit different from たぶん, which is used in front of a sentence. たぶん is a much more certain way to say "maybe". But かもしれない gives a lesser degree of certainty in the statement.

NOUN EXAMPLES

1. 一番いい季節は春かも知れないです。
   The best season might be spring.

2. 私の娘は今、家かも知れないです。
   My daughter might be at home now.

ADJECTIVE EXAMPLES

3. 私は大阪が一番好きかも知れないです。
   I might like Osaka the most.

4. このパンは甘いかも知れないです。
   This bread might be sweet.

VERB EXAMPLES

5. 明日は雨が降るかも知れません。
   It might rain tomorrow.

6. 中山さんは転勤になるかも知れない。
   Nakayama-san might get transferred.

1. **Informal conversation between friends trying to get to the airport**

   A: だめだ！もう間に合わない！
   B: 急いだら、間に合うかも知れない！

   A: It's no good! We won't make it now!
   B: If we rush, we might make it.

2. **Conversation between two high school girls**

   A: 田中君にもう告白したの？
   B: ううん、まだ。でも、田中君は私の気持ちに気が付いたかも知れない。

   A: Did you already tell Tanaka-kun you like him?
   B: Not yet, but Tanaka-kun might have realized my feelings.

3. **Conversation between friends living in Osaka**

A: 金曜日に京都へ行ったけど、交通渋滞のせいで 3 時間かかってしまった。

B: 京都へは、車より電車のほうが便利かも知れないですね。

A: On Friday I went to Kyoto, but due to traffic jams, it ended up taking 3 hours.

B: A train might be more convenient than a car for Kyoto.

4. **Conversation between a father and mother about their son**

A: なんで最近、成績が良くないかな。

B: ビデオゲームにはまってるからかも知れないね。

A: うん、そうかも知れない。

A: I wonder why his grades aren't good recently.

B: Maybe he's hooked on video games.

A: Yeah, that might be so.

● 10-7. I wish I could... たら いい

You can say "I wish..." or "I hope..." using たら **form** of verbs and adjectives followed by いい. We are essentially using たら **form** to say "If it was this, it would be good."

> **(たら form) + いい**
> **I hope I / I wish I / It would be good if ～**

EXAMPLE SENTENCES

1. 月曜日も休みだったらいいな。
   I wish Monday was also a day off.

   > な、なあ、なぁ shows desire or envy.

2. 日本語がスペイン語みたいに簡単だったらいいのに。
   I wish Japanese was easy like Spanish.

   > のに at the end shows a bit of frustration.

3. アイフォンがもっと安かったらいいのに。
   I wish the iPhone was cheaper.

4. 来年、卒業出来たらいいなぁ。
   I wish I could graduate next year.

   > Sentence endings are important to relay emotion. な、なあ、なぁ sounds more positive, while のに sounds a bit negative or more like a complaint.

5. 明日、雨が降らなかったらいいですね。
   I hope it doesn't rain tomorrow.

10 | Practice and Review 練習と復習

● 1. Mini Conversation ミニ会話 J → E

1. Polite conversation between friends

A: ああ、どうしよう。。。

B: どうしましたか。

A: テストの日を勘違いしていました。明日だと思っていました。

B: ええ？ 今日の 2時からでしょう？ 後、30分しかないですよ！

A: Oh, no. What should I do...?

B: What happened?

A: I misunderstood the test date. I thought it was tomorrow.

B: What? It's from 2 o'clock today, right? You only have 30 minutes left!

2. Casual conversation between girls

> Japanese people tend to use 好き rather than 愛してる.

A: 彼と結婚するかしないか、迷ってるの。

B: どうして？ 彼が好きなんでしょう？

A: うん。でも、仕事を辞めてばかりだから、心配なの。

B: そうか・・・。確かに、心配だね。

A: I don't know if I should marry my boyfriend or not.

B: Why? You like (love) him, right?

A: Yeah. But he keeps quitting his job, so I am worried.

B: I see... certainly, that is worrying.

3. Casual conversation between friends

A: 日本に行って、日本語を 2年ぐらい勉強したい！

B: 2年は長いね。私も行けたら、いいなあ。でも、仕事があるでしょう？

A: うん、だから後悔しないように、会社を辞めて、行くよ。

B: 日本に行ったら、絶対日本食にはまるよ。

A: I want to go to Japan and study Japanese for about 2 years.

B: 2 years is long. I wish I could go, too. But you have work, right?

A: Yeah, that's why I'm going to quit my job and go, so I won't have any regrets.

B: When you go to Japan, you'll definitely get hooked on Japanese food.

● 2. Mini Conversation ミニ会話 E → J

1. Casual conversation between roommates

A: It's not good for your body if you constantly drink coffee.

B: I need caffeine since I have to write 10 reports tonight.

A: I see. But when you're tired, you should rest.

B: I know. I'm going to work hard for a bit since I just started.

A: コーヒーを飲んでばかりだと、体によくないよ。

B: 今晩はレポートを 10枚書かないといけないから、カフェインが要るんだ。

A: そうか。でも、疲れたら休んだほうがいいよ。

B: 分かってる。今、始めたばかりだから、しばらく頑張るよ。

2. Polite conversation between anime fans

A: I am addicted to anime now.

B: I see. What kind of anime do you like?

A: I like "Yo-kai watch". Yesterday I watched it for three hours in a row.

B: Ha, ha, ha. You are addicted, aren't you?

A: 今、アニメに はまっています。

B: そうですか。どんなアニメが好きですか。

A: 「妖怪ウォッチ」がいいですね。昨日は 3時間続けて、見ました。

B: ははは。はまっていますね。

> 妖怪ウォッチ is a popular animation.

3. Casual conversation between friends

A: I'm not sure if I should or shouldn't relay my feelings to Hanako.

B: You've always liked her right? Just tell her!

A: But what would I do if she says she doesn't like me.

B: If that's the case, it can't be helped. But if you don't say it, you will regret it later.

A: 花子ちゃんに自分の気持ちを伝えるか伝えないか、迷ってる。

B: ずっと好きだったんでしょう？言ってしまおうよ！

A: でも、好きじゃないと言われたら、どうしよう。

B: それなら、しょうがない。でも、言わないと、後で後悔するよ。

● **2. Short Dialogue**

Hisashi is talking about his current job and his future plans.

友達	「ひさし、新しい仕事はどう？」
ひさし	「う〜ん・・・。多分、来月辞めると思う。面白くないから。」
友達	「でも、先月始めたばかりだから、もう少し続けた方がいいよ。」
ひさし	「毎日、同じことをしてばかりだから、嫌だよ。会社ではずっと時計を見てるんだ。」
友達	「辞めて、後悔しないと思う？」
ひさし	「しないよ。今、ギターに はまってるから、ミュージシャンになろうかな。」
友達	「えっ？ミュージシャン？！それは無理だよ。」
ひさし	「なれるかどうか分からないけど、応援するのが友達でしょう！」

10 Kanji Lesson 10:
朝昼夜前後午今

In this lesson we have gathered time-related kanji.

10 | New Kanji 新しい漢字

216	月	12 画	morning	
	くんよみ	あさ		
	おんよみ	チョウ		
	早朝 (そう・ちょう) early morning		毎朝 (まい・あさ) every morning	
	朝日 (あさ・ひ) morning sun		北朝鮮 (きた・ちょう・せん) North Korea	
	朝食 (ちょう・しょく) breakfast		今朝 (けさ) this morning	

217	日	9 画	noon; midday	
	くんよみ	ひる		
	おんよみ	チュウ		
	昼食 (ちゅう・しょく) lunch		昼休み (ひる・やす・み) lunch break	
	昼寝 (ひる・ね) nap		昼前 (ひる・まえ) just before noon	
	昼間 (ひる・ま) daytime		昼過ぎ (ひる・す・ぎ) just past noon	

218	夕	8 画	night	
	くんよみ	よ、よる		
	おんよみ	ヤ		
	夜 (よる) night		夜中 (よ・なか) midnight, dead of night	
	夜勤 (や・きん) night shift		夜明け (よ・あ・け) dawn; daybreak	
	夜景 (や・けい) night view		一夜 (いち・や) one night; all night	

219	リ	9画	front; before								

くんよみ まえ
おんよみ ゼン

前 (まえ) in front　　　　　駅前 (えき・まえ) in front of station
人前 (ひと・まえ) the public　前回 (ぜん・かい) last time
名前 (な・まえ) name　　　　前日 (ぜん・じつ) previous day; day before

前

220	彳	9画	after; behind; later								

くんよみ のち、うし(ろ)、あと、おく(れる)
おんよみ ゴ、コウ

後ろ (うし・ろ) behind　　　　後ほど (のち・ほど) later on, afterwards
後半 (こう・はん) second half　後回し (あと・まわ・し) to postpone
最後 (さい・ご) last　　　　　後れる (おく・れる) to fall behind; to fall back

後

221	十	4画	noon								

くんよみ none
おんよみ ゴ

午前 (ご・ぜん) morning, A.M.　　午前中 (ご・ぜん・ちゅう) in the morning
午後 (ご ご) afternoon, P.M.　　子午線 (し・ご・せん) meridian
正午 (しょう・ご) noon　　　　端午の節句 (たん・ご・の・せっ・く) Boy's Day

午

222	亻	4画	now; immediately								

くんよみ いま
おんよみ コン、キン

今 (いま) now　　　　　　　今週 (こん・しゅう) this week
今回 (こん・かい) this time　今日 (きょう) today
今後 (こん・ご) from now on　今年 (ことし) this year

今

10 | Kanji Culture 漢字の文化

● **What does "before breakfast" really mean?**

あ さ　　め し　　ま え
朝飯前

breakfast　　　before
(this rough version
is only used by men)

The Japanese expression 「朝飯前」, literally means "before breakfast", but its actual meaning is that something is so simple it can be done before breakfast. This expression is similar to the English expression, "a piece of cake" or "as easy as pie".

EXAMPLE SENTENCES

1. 今日の仕事は、朝飯前ですよ。
   Today's work was a piece of cake.

2. 学生の時は、10キロ走るのは朝飯前だったけど、今は無理です。
   When I was a student, it was easy as pie to run 10 kilometers, but now it's impossible.

10 | Words You Can Write かける言葉

朝日 (あさひ) morning sun

朝	日								

早朝 (そうちょう) early morning

早	朝								

昼間 (ひるま) daytime

昼	間								

昼食 (ちゅうしょく) lunch

昼	食										

夜中 (よなか) midnight

夜	中										

夜間 (やかん) night time

夜	間										

前後 (ぜんご) before and after

前	後										

前回 (ぜんかい) last time

前	回										

後ろ (うしろ) behind; back

後	ろ										

正午 (しょうご) noon

正	午										

午後 (ごご) afternoon; PM

午	後										

今年 (ことし) this year

今	年										

今日 (きょう) today

今	日										

昼休み (ひるやすみ) lunch break

昼	休	み									

10 Workbook 10: Workbook Activities

10 Kanji Drills 漢字ドリル

● 1. Writing the time in kanji
Write the following times using only kanji.

1. 5:00 p.m.

   _____

2. 7:30 a.m.

   _____

3. 12:00 p.m. (there are two ways.)

   _____

4. 9:45 a.m.

   _____

● 2. Fill in the kanji
Fill in the appropriate kanji in the blanks for each sentence.

1. ___は ___ ___、お___ で ___ ___を ___いました。
   <small>はは　　け　さ　　　みせ　　と　けい　　か</small>

   My mother bought a watch at the store this morning.

2. ___ ___ みに きっさ___で お___を しませんか。
   <small>ひる やす　　　　てん　　ちゃ</small>
   Won't you have tea at the coffee shop with me during the lunch break?

3. ___ ___ に ___きな___がして、びっくりしました。
   <small>よ　なか　　　　おお　　おと</small>
   In the middle of the night, I was surprised by a big (loud) sound.

4. ___ ___ と___ ___と どっちが いいですか。
   <small>ご　ぜん　　　　ご　ご</small>
   Which is better, morning or afternoon?

5. ___ろに ___ ___が いますよ。
   <small>うし　　　　せん　せい</small>
   The teacher is behind you.

6. ___ ___、お___ ___に ___いましょう。
   <small>きょ　う　　　　ひる　まえ　　あ</small>
   Let's meet today before noon.

7. わたしは ___ ___、___ ___ ___ ___に なります。
   <small>こと　し　　　　に　じゅう　ろく　さい</small>
   I will turn 26 years old this year.

10 | Usage Activities 文法アクティビティー

● 3. Reading comprehension
Translate the following on a separate piece of paper or type in an electronic device.

大学に入った時 <small>だい がく　はい　とき</small>	*They say you don't know the value of something until you lose it. You also often lose the thing you don't value.*

❶ 私は、大学に入ったばかりの 19歳です。
<small>わたし　　だい がく　はい　　　　　　　さい</small>

❷ 家から近い大学に入れて、とても嬉しいです。
<small>いえ　　ちか　だい がく　はい　　　　　　　　うれ</small>

❸ だけど、大学生になったとたん、両親がとても厳しくなりました。
<small>だい がく せい　　　　　　　　　りょう しん　　　　　　きび</small>

❹ 「高校を卒業したから、お小遣いはもうあげない。自分でアルバイトをしてね。」と言うんです。
<small>こう こう　そつ ぎょう　　　　　　こ づか　　　　　　　　　　じ ぶん　　　　　　　　　　　　　　　い</small>

❺ 「これから、お昼ご飯は自分で何とかしてね。」とも言われました。
<small>ひる　はん　じ ぶん　なん　　　　　　　　　　い</small>

❻ まだお金も貯めていないのに、どうしようと思いました。
<small>かね　た　　　　　　　　　　　　　　　　おも</small>

❼ でも、考えてみたら、この 19年間、両親に全部してもらっていた気がします。

❽ 学校が終わったら、友達と遊んでばかりで、家の手伝いをしませんでした。

❾ ビデオゲームに はまっていた時は、自分の部屋で一日中遊んでいました。

❿ 家から近い大学に行くか、遠い大学に行くかを決める時は、迷いませんでした。

⓫ 家にいたら、両親が何でもしてくれると思ったからです。

⓬ 今になって、その考えが甘いのが分かりました。

⓭ でも、自立する話を突然してほしくなかったのが、私の正直な気持ちです。

● 4. Reading comprehension questions

Translate the questions about the reading comprehension then answer in Japanese.

1. 「お小遣い」とは何ですか。(Not the English meaning, but a short explanation.)

   Translation: _____

   Answer: _____

2. この人はどうしてアルバイトをしなければなりませんか。

   Translation: _____

   Answer: _____

3. この人は高校生の時、よく勉強しましたか。

   Translation: _____

   Answer: _____

4. この人はどうして家から近い大学に決めたんですか。

   Translation: _____

   Answer: _____

5. 「考えが甘い」とは、どういう意味ですか。(Not the English meaning, but an explanation.)

Translation: _____

Answer: _____

● 5. Fill in the blanks
Fill in the missing part based on the English sentence.

1. どうしたんですか。_____ですね。

   What happened to you? You keep yawning.

2. おじいちゃんが_____ので、元気が出ません。

   Because my grandfather has just passed away, I don't have energy.

3. キムさんが日本料理に_____ですよ。

   I heard that Kim is addicted to Japanese cuisine.

4. 吉田さんは英語が_____。

   I have misunderstood that Mr. Yoshida was able to speak English.

5. 私は_____、まだ分かりません。

   I still don't know if I will succeed or fail.

● 6. Question and Answer
Answer the following questions.

1. 今、何に はまっていますか。

   _____

2. 今まで、何かに後悔したことがありますか。

_____

3. どれぐらい、日本語の勉強を続けていますか。

_____

4. 明日、何をしますか。(use 〜かもしれない)

_____

5. あなたは仕事から帰ったばかりです。最初に何がしたいですか。

_____

● 7. Translation

Translate the following sentences into Japanese.

1. All I do is think about my mother who is in the hospital. (use う form + ばかり)

_____

2. Mr. Yoshida's class is boring because all I do is listen. (use う form + ばかり)

_____

3. My husband may be tired today.

_____

4. You may regret it, so please continue your Japanese studies.

_____

5. It may be gossip, so don't believe it.

_____

● 8. Practice 1

Look at the pictures below and make sentences using 〜てばかり.

1. My mother is always working.

_____

2. My older brother is always smoking.

_____

3. My friend is always sleeping.

_____

4. My teacher is always upset.

_____

4. My baby is always crying.

_____

● **9. Practice 2**

Read each sentence on the left and select an appropriate sentence that matches up from those in the box.

1. 掃除したばかりだから、 （　　）

2. 今、バスが出たばかりだから、（　　）

3. お給料が出たばかりだから、（　　）

4. 火山が噴火したばかりだから、（　　）

5. 親とけんかしたばかりだから、（　　）

a. 気をつけて下さい。

b. 家にいたくないです。

c. きれいでしょう。

d. 何も期待していません。

e. しばらく来ませんよ。

f. 何か食べに行きませんか。

10 | Answer Key 答え合わせ

Short Dialogue (translation)

Friend	Hisashi, how is your new job?
Hisashi	Umm. I think maybe I'm going to quit next month. Because it isn't interesting.
Friend	But you should continue for a bit more since you just started last month.
Hisashi	It bothers me since I only do the same things every day. I'm always looking at the clock at work.
Friend	Do you think you won't regret quitting?
Hisashi	I won't. I'm into guitar, so I wonder if I should try to be a musician.
Friend	What? A musician?! That's impossible.
Hisashi	I don't know if I can be one or not, but friends are supportive, right?

1. Writing the time in kanji (answers)

1. 午後五時　　2. 午前七時三十分　　3. 午後十二時 or 正午　　4. 午前九時四十五分

2. Fill in the kanji (answers)

1. 母は今朝、お店で時計を買いました。
2. 昼休みにきっさ店でお茶をしませんか。
3. 夜中に大きな音がして、びっくりしました。
4. 午前と午後とどっちがいいですか。
5. 後ろに先生がいますよ。
6. 今日、お昼前に会いましょう。
7. わたしは今年、二十六才になります。

3. Reading comprehension (translation)

❶ I'm a 19 year-old that just got into college.

❷ I am very happy being able to get into a college close to home.

❸ But the moment I became a college student, my parents got very strict.

❹ They say, "Because you have graduated high school, we won't be giving you allowance anymore. Do a part-time job, okay?"

❺ I was also told, "From now on, take care of lunch by yourself."

❻ I thought "what should I do even though I haven't saved money yet?"

❼ But upon thinking about it, I feel like for these 19 years, I've had my parents do everything.

❽ After school, I would always hang out with friends and not help out around the house.

❾ When I was hooked on video games, I was playing in my room the entire day.

❿ I didn't waver when it was time to decide whether to go to a college close to home or a college far from home.

⓫ It's because I thought my parents would do anything for me if I was at home.

⓬ Only now have I understood that this thought was naive.

⓭ But my honest feelings are that I didn't want to suddenly talk of self-reliance.

4. Reading comprehension questions (answers)

1. Translation: What is 「おこづかい」?

   Answer(s): 親からもらうお金です。

2. Translation: Why does this person need to do part-time work?

   Answer(s): 親からお小遣いをもうもらえないからです。

   お昼ご飯を自分で買わないといけないからです。

3. Translation: Did this person study often when he was a high school student?

   Answer(s): いいえ、しなかったと思います。

   いいえ、友達と遊んだり、ビデオゲームで遊んだりしていました。

4. Translation: Why did this person decide on a college close to home?

   Answer(s): 家にいたら、両親が何でもしてくれると思ったからです。

   お金や食べ物の心配がないからです。

5. Translation: What does 「かんがえが あまい」 mean?

   Answer(s): 「よく考えていない」という意味です。

   「考えが足りない」という意味です。

5. Fill in the blank (answers)

1. どうしたんですか。あくびをしてばかりですね。

2. おじいちゃんが亡くなったばかりなので、元気が出ません。

3. キムさんが日本料理にはまっているそうですよ。

4. 吉田さんは英語が話せると勘違いしていました。

5. 私は成功するか失敗するか、まだ分かりません。

6. Question and Answer (sample answers) (answers may vary)

1. What are you hooked on right now?

ビデオゲームにはまっています。／特に何もありません。

2. Until now, do you have any regrets?
はい、あります。／ いいえ、ありません。

3. For how long have you continued your Japanese studies?

２、３年、続けています。／ 高校の時から続けていますが、何度か止めたりしました。

4. What will you do tomorrow?

買い物に行くかも知れないです。／ 仕事が終わったら、友達と飲みに行くかも知れない。

5. You just got home from work. What do you want to do first?

すぐに寝たいです。／ 晩ご飯を食べて、ゆっくりしたいです。

7. Translation (answers)

1. 病院にいる母のことを考えるばかりです。

2. 吉田先生の授業は、聞くばかりで面白くないです。／聞くだけだから面白くないです。

3. 主人は今日、疲れているかも知れません。

4. 後悔するかも知れないから、日本語の勉強を続けて下さい。

5. 噂話かも知れないから、信じないで。

8. Practice 1 (answers)

1. 母は働いてばかりです。／お母さんは仕事をしてばかりです。

2. 兄はたばこを吸ってばかりです。

3. 友達は寝てばかりです。

4. 先生は怒ってばかりです。

5. 私の赤ちゃんは泣いてばかりです。

9. Practice 2 (answers)

1. (c) 掃除したばかりだから、きれいでしょう。

2. (e) 今、バスが出たばかりだから、しばらく来ませんよ。

3. (f) お給料が出たばかりだから、何か食べに行きませんか。

4. (a) 火山が噴火したばかりだから、気をつけて下さい。

5. (b) 親とけんかしたばかりだから、家にいたくないです。

11 | Lesson 11: Intentions and Beliefs

15 PAGES	8 USAGE SECTIONS	21 NEW WORDS

11 | New Words 新しい言葉

Nouns etc.

てんすう 点数	score; number	ひみつ 秘密	a secret
ごうかく 合格	pass	れんあい 恋愛	love; romance
てんちょう 店長	shop manager	そば	near; close; beside
いまふう 今風	fashionable; modern	かんぺき 完璧	perfect; complete
としよ お年寄り	old person; senior citizen	いま 今のうち	while you can
がらくた	junk; rubbish; garbage		

> がらくた is not used for "junk food." Use ジャンクフード instead.

Verbs

かく 隠す	to hide something; to conceal	かく 隠れる	to conceal oneself
ばらす	to leak out information	ばれる	to be found out
よ 酔う	to become intoxicated; become sick	もんくい 文句を言う	to complain
よ 呼ぶ	to call; to refer to as; to invite		

Adjectives

ふか 深い	deep (water); profound	ひく 低い	low; deep (voice)

Adverbs

やっぱり	as was expected; all in all; as suspected

11 | Word Usage 言葉の使い方

W-1	〜風 (ふう)	style of ~; in the way of

風 (ふう) can be added to a word to say "in the style of~" that thing. There are also set words with 風 (ふう) in them, such as 今風 (いまふう) introduced in this lesson.

> **EXAMPLES**
>
> Some words contain 風 (ふう) in them.
>
> 和風 (わふう) (Japanese style)   古風 (こふう) (old-fashioned)
>
> 洋風 (ようふう) (western style)   新風 (しんぷう) (new style)
>
> Other words can have 風 (ふう) attached.
>
> 日本風 (にほんふう) (Japanese style)   アラビア風 (ふう) (Arabic style)
>
> A powerful usage of 風 (ふう) is the "how" and "in this way" combination.
>
> どんな風 (ふう) に (in which way?)   こんな風 (ふう) に (in this way)
>
> **EXAMPLE SENTENCES**
>
> 1. 猫 (ねこ) をこんな風 (ふう) にも描 (か) けます。
>   You can also draw a cat in this way.
>
> 2. 私 (わたし) は和風 (わふう) の生地 (きじ) が美 (うつく) しいと思 (おも) います。
>   I think Japanese style fabrics are beautiful.

W-2	低い (ひく)	low; short; deep

低い (ひくい) has more than one meaning. The usage determines its English translation.

> **EXAMPLE SENTENCES**
>
> 1. 私 (わたし) のお兄 (にい) さんの声 (こえ) は低 (ひく) いです。
>   My older brother's voice is deep.
>
>   > This "deep" can NEVER be 深い (ふかい).
>
> 2. 小 (ちい) さい時 (とき) は背 (せ) が低 (ひく) かったけど、今 (いま) は背 (せ) が高 (たか) いです。
>   When I was small I was short, but now I am tall.
>
>   > 背が低い = short
>   > 背が高い = tall

11 | Verb Usage 動詞の使い方

V-1	酔う（よ）	to become intoxicated; to become sick	regular
	1. (thing) に酔う	to be sick / intoxicated by (thing);	

よう can be used when someone has become intoxicated or sick. The item that causes the intoxication is marked with に.

> **EXAMPLE SENTENCES**
>
> 1. お酒に酔ったことがありません。
>   I have never been intoxicated (by alcohol).
>
> 2. ビールをたくさん飲んで、酔ってしまいました。
>   I drank a lot of beer and ended up getting drunk.
>
> 3. うちの子は、車によく酔うんです。
>   My child often gets sick in cars.

V-2	呼ぶ（よ）	to call (a name); to call out; to invite	regular
	1. (a person) を呼ぶ	to call (a person)	
	2. (a person, thing) を (name) と呼ぶ	to call a (person, thing) (name)	

> **EXAMPLE SENTENCES**
>
> 1. 旦那さんを何と呼んでいますか。
>   What do you call your husband?
>
> 2. 何か必要だったら、いつでも呼んで下さい。
>   If you need something, call me anytime.
>
> 3. 友達に「けんちゃん」と呼ばれています。
>   My friends call me "Ken-chan".
>
> 4. あなたの名前を大き声で３回呼んだけど、返事がなかった。
>   I called out your name with a loud voice 3 times, but there wasn't a response.

V-3	ばらす	to leak out information; to let out purposely a secret (ACTION)	regular
	1. (a secret) をばらす	to tell/leak (a secret)	
	2. (a person) がばらす	(a person) tells secret	
	3. (somebody) にばらす	to tell a secret (somebody)	

ばらす is used when a secret is let out by someone.

EXAMPLE SENTENCES

1. これは秘密（ひみつ）だから、誰（だれ）にもばらさないで下（くだ）さい。
   This is a secret, so please don't tell anyone.

2. だめだと分（わ）かっていたけど、ばらしてしまいました。
   I knew that it was bad, but I couldn't help telling.

3. 十万円（じゅうまんえん）をくれないと、あなたの秘密（ひみつ）を皆（みんな）にばらすちゃうよ！
   If you don't give me 100,000 yen, I am going to tell everyone your secret!

V-4	ばれる	to be found out (DESCRIPTIVE)	いる/える
	1. (a secret) がばれる	to have (a secret) found out	
	2. (a person) にばれる	to be found out by (a person)	

ばれる is used when something that has been hiding was found out.

EXAMPLE SENTENCES

1. 有名（ゆうめい）なスターの浮気（うわき）がばれました。
   A famous star's cheating was found out.

2. お父（とう）さんにタバコを吸（す）っていることが、ばれました。
   My father found out that I am smoking.

3. 友達（ともだち）に嘘（うそ）がばれてから、話（はな）してくれないです。
   After my lie got found out by my friend, she won't speak with me.

V-5	隠<ruby>す<rt>かく</rt></ruby>	to hide something, to conceal (ACTION)	regular

1. (thing, someone) を隠す	to hide (thing, someone)
2. (place) に隠す	to hide in a (place)
3. (person, animal) から隠す	to hide from (person, animal)

かくす is NOT used in a sentence like "I am going to hide." It's ALWAYS used as the action of hiding something besides the speaker.

EXAMPLE SENTENCES

1. クリスマスまでプレゼントを押し入れに隠しましょう。
   Let's hide the presents in the closet until Christmas.

   > 押し入れ literally means "push and put in". It's a Japanese closet designed to hold folded blankets and futons more than clothing.

2. お母さんには、すぐばれるから、何も隠せないんです。
   I can't hide anything since my mother finds out right away.

3. 喧嘩した時、妹 から好きなぬいぐるみを隠しました。
   When we fought, I hid her favorite stuffed animal from my little sister.

V-6	隠<ruby>れる<rt>かく</rt></ruby>	to conceal; to hide (oneself)	いる/える

1. (a person, an animal) が隠れる	(a person, an animal) hides themselves
2. (thing) が隠れる	to hide/conceal (thing)
3. (place) に隠れる	to hide oneself in a (place)
4. (a thing, a person) から隠れる	to hide oneself from (a thing, a person)

隠れる is used when the action of hiding or concealing is carried out by the speaker (or animal) of its own will, as in "I am going to hide" or "They hid over there."

EXAMPLE SENTENCES

1. 友達が来ると、私の猫はいつも他の部屋に隠れます。
   My cat always hides in the other room when my friends come.

   > Here, 隠れる is an "action" and means the hiding of oneself (the cat)

2. 眼鏡がないと思ったけど、かばんの下に隠れていました。
   I thought my glasses were gone, but they were hiding under the bag.

3. 膝が隠れるスカートを履いてきてください。
   Please come wearing a skirt that hides your knees.

   > Here, 隠れる isn't an "action" but is "descriptive".

| V-7 | 文句を言う
もん く い | to voice or say complaints | regular |

EXAMPLE SENTENCES

1. 私はつまらないことに文句を言ってしまいます。
   I can't help complaining about something unimportant.

2. 中学生の娘は、今風の洋服を買ってあげないと、文句を言います。
   My junior high school student daughter complains if I don't buy her modern style clothing.

3. 東さんはいつもよくしてくれるから、何も文句が言えません。
   I can't complain to Higashi-san because he does a lot of things for me.

11 Grammar and Usage 文法と使い方

● 11-1. Using つもり to show intentions with verbs

つもり can be thought of to mean "intend" or "plan".

> ### (positive plain verb phrase) + つもりです
> I intend to (verb)/I plan on ~*ing*

> ### (positive plain verb phrase) + つもりでした
> I had intended to (verb)

By just changing です to でした, while keeping the same verb phrase, we can convey our intentions in past tense.

> **PRESENT INTENTION**
> 1. 六時に起きるつもり<u>です</u>。
>   I plan to get up at six.

> **PAST INTENTION**
> 2. 六時に起きるつもり<u>でした</u>。
>   I had planned to get up at six.

> **EXAMPLE SENTENCES**
>
> 1. ずっと東京に住むつもりです。
>   I plan on always living in Tokyo.
>
> 2. パーティーに弟家族を呼ぶつもり<u>だよ</u>。
>   I plan on inviting my younger brother's family to my party.
>
> 3. 今日、新車を買うつもり<u>でした</u>。
>   I had planned on buying a new car today.
>
> 4. 電話をするつもり<u>だった</u>けど、忘れてしまいました。
>   I had intended to call, but I forgot.

> The sentence politeness level can be made informal by using だ or だった.

There are 3 ways to say "I don't intend to..."

> ### (negative informal verb phrase) + つもりです
> ### (positive informal verb phrase) + つもりはないです
> ### (positive informal verb phrase) + つもりはありません
> I don't intend to (verb)

PRESENT NEGATIVE INTENTION

1. 六時に起きないつもりです。   I plan on not getting up at six.
2. 六時に起きるつもりはないです。   I don't plan on getting up at six.
3. 六時に起きるつもりはありません。   I don't plan on getting up at six.

EXAMPLE SENTENCES

1. 冬休みは何もしないつもりです。
   I intend to do nothing on my winter break.

2. 明日は仕事が早いので、夜ふかしするつもりはないです。
   Since I work early tomorrow, I don't plan on staying up late.

3. 小林さんはすぐ結婚するつもりはなさそうです。
   It doesn't seem that Kobayashi-san has any intention of getting married right away.

We can also make the negative intentions past tense by modifying the tense of either です or the tense of ない.

EXAMPLE SENTENCES

1. 最初から大学院に行かないつもりでした。
   From the beginning, I didn't intend on going to graduate school.

2. 借金があることを隠すつもりはなかったです。
   I didn't intend to hide my debt.

3. バレンタインデーに彼に告白するつもりはなかったけど、してしまいました。
   I hadn't planned on confessing to him on Valentine's day, but I ended up doing it.

EXAMPLE CONVERSATION

1. **Conversation between two high school students on a Monday at school.**

   A: なんでパーティーに来なかったの？皆が待ってたんだよ。
   B: 行くつもりだったけど、お母さんに怒られて外出禁止になった。
   A: ラインしたのに、全然返事をくれなかったね。
   B: ごめん。電話まで取られてた。

   > ラインする = to send mobile text using the popular texting app, "LINE"

   A: Why didn't you come to the party? Everyone was waiting.
   B: I had intended on going, but I got in trouble with my mother and got grounded.
   A: You didn't respond at all even though I did LINE you.
   B: Sorry, even my phone got taken away.

● 11-2. Using つもり to show belief in something false

つもり is also used to indicate a person's belief in something that is not true. It's equivalent to saying "think" as in "he thinks he's a star" when in reality he is not.

> **(plain form verb phrase) + つもりです。**
> **They think (verb phrase) / Imagine (verb phrase)**

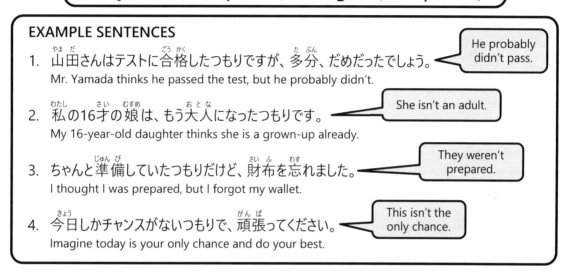

EXAMPLE SENTENCES

1. 山田さんはテストに合格したつもりですが、多分、だめだったでしょう。

   He probably didn't pass.

   Mr. Yamada thinks he passed the test, but he probably didn't.

2. 私の16才の娘は、もう大人になったつもりです。

   She isn't an adult.

   My 16-year-old daughter thinks she is a grown-up already.

3. ちゃんと準備していたつもりだけど、財布を忘れました。

   They weren't prepared.

   I thought I was prepared, but I forgot my wallet.

4. 今日しかチャンスがないつもりで、頑張ってください。

   This isn't the only chance.

   Imagine today is your only chance and do your best.

● 11-3. Beginning an explanation of "why"

Sometimes you need to explain "why" or "how" you did something.
You can use either of the three "why" words in the phrase depending on the politeness level. Here is what you say just before you start your explanation.

> **(どうして / なんで / なぜ) かと言うと、(explanation)**
> If you ask me why... (it's because...)

To use this phrase, you MUST have already said what you did OR have been asked WHY you did the action. Look at the following example Q&A.

1. なんで私のピザを食べたの？

   なんでかと言うと、お腹が空いていたから。

   どうしてかと言うと、お腹が空いていたから。

   Why did you eat my pizza?
   If you ask me why, it's because I was hungry.
   If you ask me why, it's because I was hungry.

You can also combine the entire thing into one phrase by squeezing the question asked in between the question word and というと. Let's look at the same example:

2. なんで私のピザを食べたの？

なんであなたのピザを食べたかと言うと、お腹が空いていたから。

どうしてあなたのピザを食べたかと言うと、お腹が空いていたから。

These sentences combine both action and reason.

Why did you eat my pizza?
If you ask me why I ate your pizza, it's because I was hungry.
If you ask me why I ate your pizza, it's because I was hungry.

● 11-4. Using different question words with かと言うと

"Why" words aren't the only question words that are used before かと言うと.

EXAMPLES (QUESTION WORD + かと言うと)

1. どっちかと言うと
   If you ask me which one

2. どこかと言うと
   If you ask me where

3. いくらかと言うと
   If you ask me how much

4. なにかと言うと
   If you ask me what it is

● 11-5. Using different tenses with かと言うと

The verb phrase can be any informal (also called plain) form (た, ない, ている etc.).
To sound less weird, the English can be flexibly translated to something like, "if you ask me how, why, when etc." or "if you want to know how, why, when etc."

EXAMPLE SENTENCES

1. 毎朝何を食べるかと言うと、ご飯と納豆ですね。
   If you want to know what I eat every morning, it's rice and natto (fermented beans).

2. いつ日本に行ったかと言うと、去年の九月でした。
   If you ask when I went to Japan, it was last September.

   の is optional.

3. 今、何をしてるのかと言うと、スマホでゲームをしてます。
   If you ask what I'm doing now, it's playing a game on my smartphone.

4. 犯人がどこに隠れていたのかと言うと、森の中だそうです。
   If you ask where the perpetrator was hiding, apparently, it was in the forest.

● 11-6. Within a time span or amount (うち)

When saying expressions such as "3 out of the 10 days", or "2 out of 10 people", the following pattern is used. うち (内) basically means "within", "among", or "out of..."

> **(total amount) のうち、(number of items)**
> **out of (total amount), (number of items)**

EXAMPLE SENTENCES (USING AMOUNTS AND DURATION)

1. 私のクラスメートは、30人のうち、10人が女の子です。

   Out of my 30 classmates, 10 are girls.

2. 一か月のうち、半月ぐらい出張をしています。

   Out of a month, I'm away on business trips about half the month.

～のうち can also be used to say "while it's still this time" or "before this time ends".

EXAMPLE SENTENCES (USING TIME RELATED WORDS)

1. 午前中のうちに、運動するようにしています。

   I make it a rule to exercise while it's still morning.

   > This is the same as ~ことにしています (make it a rule to~)

2. 今のうちにテレビを買ったほうがいいよ。なぜかというと、もうすぐ消費税が上がるからです。

   You should buy a TV while you can. The reason why is that soon the consumption tax will go up.

3. 洗濯物がたまっているから、今晩のうちに、洗濯してしまいましょう。

   Because the laundry is piling up, before tonight ends, let's do laundry.

うち is also used with verbs in plain form and adjectives to say "during" or "while".

EXAMPLE SENTENCES (USING VERBS AND ADJECTIVES)

1. 若いうちに、いろんな国に旅行したほうがいいです。
   You should travel to various countries while you're still young.

   > の is NOT required for verbs and い adjectives.

2. 日本にいるうちに、一度相撲の試合が見たいです。

   While I'm in Japan, I want to see a sumo match once.

   > な is required for な adjectives. Also forgive this grandmother's old way of thinking!

3. おばあさんに「女性はきれいなうちに結婚したほうがいい」と言われた。

   I was told by my grandmother that women should get married while they are still pretty.

● 11-7. Being full of something

This expression can be used in everyday phrases such as "The bathtub is full of hot water"「お風呂(ふろ)がお湯(ゆ)でいっぱいです」or a more poetic phrase can be made as in "my heart is filled with my daughter"「私(わたし)の心(こころ)は娘(むすめ)でいっぱいです」.

> (item/person) でいっぱい
> be full of OR overflowing with (item)

EXAMPLE SENTENCES

1. 頭(あたま)の中(なか)は、家族(かぞく)のことでいっぱいです。
   The inside of my head is filled with my <u>thoughts of my family</u>.

2. 交通事故(こうつうじこ)があって、周(まわ)りは人(ひと)でいっぱいになりました。
   There was an accident, and the area (around) became full of <u>people</u>.

3. 車(くるま)のトランクは、がらくたでいっぱいです。
   The trunk of my car is filled with <u>junk</u>.

● 11-8. More nouns made from verbs

As we covered in lesson 4, there are quite a few nouns that are derived using the い form of verbs. So many in fact that we wanted to do some more of them here. Some of these nouns made from verbs aren't easily translated into English, so make sure you remember the difference between a "direct" translation versus a "natural" translation as discussed in Lesson B of this book.

Verb	English	Noun	English
疲(つか)れます	to be tired	疲(つか)れ	tiredness; fatigue
驚(おどろ)きます	to be surprised	驚(おどろ)き	surprise; amazement
別(わか)れます	to separate	別(わか)れ	separation; farewell
始(はじ)まります	to begin	始(はじ)まり	beginning; origin
終(お)わります	to end	終(お)わり	the end
手伝(てつだ)います	to help out	手伝(てつだ)い	help; helper
楽(たの)しみます	to enjoy (oneself)	楽(たの)しみ	enjoyment; pleasure

EXAMPLE SENTENCES

1. 疲れが出ないように、よく休んで下さいね。

   Rest well so the <u>fatigue</u> doesn't come out.

2. 愛犬との別れは辛かったけど、またもう一匹、犬を飼おうと思っています。

   The <u>separation</u> with my pet dog was hard, but I'm considering raising another dog again.

3. みんなが「ハッピーバースデー」と叫んだ時、お父さんは驚きを隠せなかった。

   When everyone yelled, "happy birthday", my father couldn't hide his surprise.

11 | Practice and Review 練習と復習

● 1. Mini Conversation ミニ会話 J → E

1. Polite conversation between friends

A: 今日の晩ご飯は和風と洋風と、どちらがいいですか。

B: そうですね。どちらかと言うと、和風がいいです。

A: どこかにいい和食のレストランがありますか。

B: 分かりません。グーグルで調べてみましょう。

A: What (which one) do you want for dinner today, Japanese style or western style?

B: Let me see. If you ask me which one I prefer (is good), it's Japanese style.

A: Where is a good Japanese-style restaurant?

B: I'm not sure. Let's check Google.

2. Casual conversation between classmates

A: トーマス、漢字テストで 100点、取ったの？

B: うん。驚きだったよ。

A: どうやって勉強したの？

B: どうやってしたかと言うと、漢字アプリを使ったり、何回もノートに書いたりしたんだ。

A: Thomas, did you get 100 points on your kanji test?

B: Yeah. It was a surprise.

A: How did you study for it?

B: If you ask how I did it, I did things like use kanji apps, and write them in my notes many times.

3. Informal conversation between friends

A: さっき電話で、田中さんと佐々木さんがパーティーに遅れるって。

B: そう。本田さんは、ちゃんと来てくれるかな。

A: あ、本田さんはパーティーが明日だと勘違いしてたんだって。

B: ええ！じゃあ、本田さんは来ないつもり？信じられない。

> The って ending (she said, he said) was introduced in lesson 3.

A: Just now on the phone, Tanaka-san and Sasaki-san said they will be late to the party.

B: I see. I wonder if Honda-san will actually (properly) come.

A: Ah, Honda-san said he thought the party was tomorrow.

B: What?! Well is it Honda-san's intention not to come? Unbelievable.

● 2. Mini Conversation ミニ会話 E → J

1. Casual conversation between two female friends

A: Wow, what a pretty ring? You have it on your left hand! Who bought it for you?

B: Well... if you want to know who bought it for me...

A: Yes, yes, who?

B: Actually, I bought it by myself. Don't tell anyone, ok.

A: あ〜、きれいな指輪！左手にしてる！誰に買ってもらったの？

B: 誰に買ってもらったかと言うと。。。

A: うん、うん。誰？

B: 実は自分で買ったの。ばらさないでね。

> うん、うん is just an acknowledgment that they were listing and are waiting for the person to continue.

2. Polite conversation between co-workers after a party

A: It's already time to go home. But I might be drunk due to the wine.

B: Well then, we should call a taxi.

A: Yes right. What are you going to do, Tanaka-san?

B: I plan on walking home. Since I ate a bit too much, I'll get some exercise.

A: もう帰る時間ですね。でも、ワインで酔ってしまったかも知れません。

B: じゃあ、タクシーを呼んだほうがいいですよ。

A: そうですね。田中さんはどうしますか。

B: 私は歩いて帰るつもりです。ちょっと食べ過ぎたので、運動します。

3. Polite conversation between neighbors

A: Tagami-san, you always seem so cheerful.
B: Is that so? I'll be turning 65 this year.
A: You really don't look like it! Are you doing some sort of sports?
B: Yes, during the week, I walk 5 days. I am also planning on starting tennis.
A: That's amazing. Please do your best.

A: 田上さんは、いつもお元気そうですね。

B: そうですか。今年65歳になるんですよ。

A: そう見えませんね！何かスポーツをしていますか。

B: はい。一週間のうち、五日はウォーキングをしています。テニスも始めるつもりです。

A: すごいですね。頑張ってください。

● 3. Short Dialogue

A wife is trying to make her husband confess his secret.

奥さん	「あなた、何か隠してることがあるでしょう？」
旦那さん	「え？何も隠してないよ。何でそんなこと言うの？」
奥さん	「おととい、近所の奥さんがあなたを駅の近くのモールで見たそうよ。」
旦那さん	「それは僕じゃないよ。」
奥さん	「高そうな指輪を買ってたって。」
旦那さん	「どうしてそれが僕だと言えるの？」
奥さん	「どうしてそう言えるかと言うと、あなたには指輪を買う理由があるから。」
旦那さん	「どんな理由？」
奥さん	「私の誕生日！それ、私に買ってくれたんでしょう？」
旦那さん	「え・・・？ そ、そうなんだ！誕生日に渡すつもりだった。」

11 Kanji Lesson 11:
工理算図社科

From the teacher...
For this lesson, we have gathered kanji that are related to school subjects.

11 | New Kanji 新しい漢字

223	工	3 画	artisan; work; craft

くんよみ	none
おんよみ	コウ、ク

大工 (だい・く) carpenter　　工夫 (く・ふう) scheme, device
工作 (こう・さく) handicraft　　工業 (こう・ぎょう) (manufacturing) industry
工場 (こう・じょう) factory　　工面 (く・めん) managing (to raise money)

工

224	王	11 画	reason; justice

くんよみ	none
おんよみ	リ

修理 (しゅう・り) repair　　理科 (り・か) science
地理 (ち・り) geography　　理解 (り・かい) understanding; sympathy
理由 (り・ゆう) reason, cause　　理想 (り・そう) ideal

理

225	竹	14 画	count; calculation

くんよみ	none
おんよみ	サン

決算 (けっ・さん) balance sheet　　計算 (けい・さん) calculation
算数 (さん・すう) arithmetic　　予算 (よ・さん) budget, estimate
精算 (せい・さん) adjustment　　決算 (けっ・さん) financial results

算

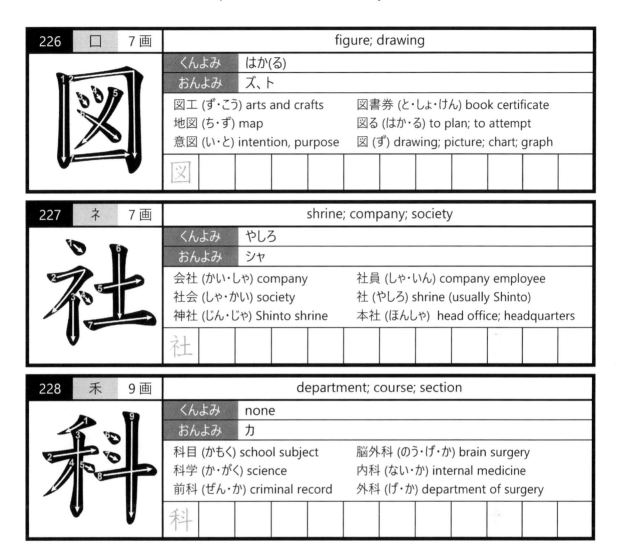

226	口	7 画	figure; drawing

くんよみ　はか(る)
おんよみ　ズ、ト

図工 (ず・こう) arts and crafts　　図書券 (と・しょ・けん) book certificate
地図 (ち・ず) map　　図る (はか・る) to plan; to attempt
意図 (い・と) intention, purpose　　図 (ず) drawing; picture; chart; graph

227	ネ	7 画	shrine; company; society

くんよみ　やしろ
おんよみ　シャ

会社 (かい・しゃ) company　　社員 (しゃ・いん) company employee
社会 (しゃ・かい) society　　社 (やしろ) shrine (usually Shinto)
神社 (じん・じゃ) Shinto shrine　　本社 (ほん・しゃ) head office; headquarters

228	禾	9 画	department; course; section

くんよみ　none
おんよみ　カ

科目 (かもく) school subject　　脳外科 (のう・げ・か) brain surgery
科学 (か・がく) science　　内科 (ない・か) internal medicine
前科 (ぜん・か) criminal record　　外科 (げ・か) department of surgery

11 Kanji Culture 漢字の文化

● 4 ways to write はかる?

There are four different ways to write はかる. They mostly mean, "to measure", or something close to that, but use different kanji depending on what is measured.

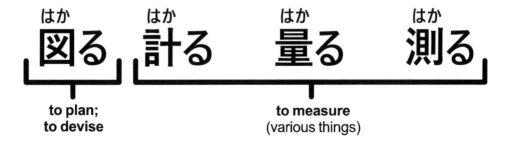

図る — to plan; to devise　　計る 量る 測る — to measure (various things)

1. 図る (はか)　to plan; to devise
   解決を図る (かいけつ はか)　to devise a resolution
   合理化を図る (ごうりか はか)　to streamline; to rationalize

2. 計る (はか)　to measure (time)
   時間を計る (じかん はか)　to time
   体温を計る (たいおん はか)　to measure body temperature

3. 量る (はか)　to measure (weight)
   分量を量る (ぶんりょう はか)　to weigh
   容積を量る (ようせき はか)　to measure capacity/volume

4. 測る (はか)　to measure (lengths)
   身長を測る (しんちょう はか)　to measure one's height
   距離を測る (きょり はか)　to measure distance

11 | Words You Can Write かける言葉

大工 (だいく) carpenter

大	工								

工作 (こうさく) handicraft

工	作								

地理 (ちり) geography

地	理								

理科 (りか) science

理	科								

計算 (けいさん) calculation

計	算									

算数 (さんすう) arithmetic; math

算	数									

図る (はかる) to plan

図	る									

合図 (あいず) sign; signal

合	図									

地図 (ちず) map

地	図									

会社 (かいしゃ) company

会	社									

社会 (しゃかい) society

社	会									

科学 (かがく) science

科	学									

科目 (かもく) subject

科	目									

11 Workbook 11:
Workbook Activities

11 | Kanji Drills 漢字ドリル

● 1. Reading practice
Write FURIGANA above the underlined kanji words.

1. 息子は工作が好きで、大きくなったら大工になるそうです。

2. 小学校では、理科より図工のクラスのほうが楽しかったです。

3. ぼくは社会に出たら、東京の会社で働きたいです。

4. 高校では、数学が好きな科目の一つでした。

5. 体の調子が悪かったので、内科の先生にみてもらいました。

● 2. Fill in the kanji
Fill in the appropriate kanji in the blanks for each sentence.

1.
だい　く　　　あめ　　ひ
___ ___ は ___ の___に しごとが できません。
Carpenters can't work on rainy days.

2.
か　もく　　り　か　しゃ　かい　か
わたしがすきな ___ ___ は___ ___と___ ___ ___です。
My favorite subjects are science and social studies.

3. ___ ___ より___ ___のほうが かんたんです。

けい さん　　さく ぶん

Essays are easier than calculations.

---

4. ___ く、___ ___に ___たほうが いいですよ。

はや　しゃ かい　で

You should enter society soon.

---

5. わたしが ___ ___ をするまで、まって___ さい。

あい　ず　　　　　　　　　くだ

Please wait until I make a signal.

---

6. ___ ___ ___の___ は、___ ___が すきでした。

しょう がく せい　とき　　ず こう

When I was an elementary school student, I liked arts and crafts.

---

7. ___ ___は ___ ___ で はたらいています。

ゆう じん　　こう じょう

My friend works at a factory.

---

11 Usage Activities 文法アクティビティー

● 3. Reading comprehension

Translate the following on a separate piece of paper or type in an electronic device.

| 可愛い彼女 | *Some people try too hard. Some people learn from their mistakes and others do not. What do you think of this person?* |

かわい　かの じょ

❶ 私は去年、初めて彼氏ができました。
わたし きょ ねん　はじ　　かれ し

❷ かわいい彼女になりたくて、デートのために今風の服をたくさん買いました。
かの じょ　　　　　　　　　　　いま ふう ふく　　　　　　か

❸ 彼はタバコが嫌いなので、彼の前では吸わないで、隠れて吸っていました。
かれ　　　　きら　　　　　　かれ まえ　す　　　　　かく　　す

❹ アルバイトの時に彼に呼ばれたら、店長に頭が痛いと嘘をついて、彼の所へ行ったりしました。
とき かれ よ　　　　てん ちょう あたま いた　うそ　　　　かれ ところ い

❺ 料理が下手な事がばれないように、どこかでテイクアウトをして、家で食べてもらいました。
りょう り へ た こと　　　　　　　　　　　　　　　　　　　　うち た

❻ 彼が好きで好きで、しょうがなかったんです。
かれ す　　す

❼ でも、ちょっと頑張りすぎたかも知れません。

~すぎる means "doing something in excess."

❽ アルバイトを休んだり、買い物をしてばかりで、お金がなくなってしまったんです。

❾ すると、ある日突然、彼に別れたいと言われました。

❿ 彼と結婚するつもりだったのに。。。私のどこが悪いの？！

⓫ 彼に理由を聞くと、「君は完璧なんだよ。それが重いんだ。」と言われました。

⓬ 「きれいで、料理ができるのはいいけど、いつもそばにいるから疲れるんだ」って。

⓭ そうなんです。完璧な彼女のふりをしていたのが悪かったんです。

⓮ 私はこの恋愛で色々教えられて、一つかしこくなった気がします。

⓯ だから今度はきれいだけど、料理ができない彼女になるつもりです。

● 4. Reading comprehension questions

Translate the questions about the reading comprehension then answer in Japanese.

1. この人は、彼のためにタバコを止めましたか。

Translation: _____

Answer: _____

2. どうして店長にうそをつくんですか。

Translation: _____

Answer: _____

3. 「彼が大好きだった」というのを、違う言い方で何と言っていますか。

Translation: _____

Answer: _____

4.　彼_{かれ}が彼女_{かのじょ}と別_{わか}れた理由_{りゆう}は何_{なん}でしたか。

Translation: _____

Answer: _____

5.　この人_{ひと}はどんな女性_{じょせい}になったほうがいいと思_{おも}いますか。

Translation: _____

Answer: _____

● 5. Fill in the blanks
Fill in the missing part based on the English sentence.

1.　息子_{むすこ}が_____、見_みつけられないんです。

My son is hiding somewhere, and I can't find him.

2.　私_{わたし}はいつも_____。

I always end up getting sick in a car.

3.　_____を買_かいたいけど、_____です。

I want to buy fashionable clothes, but I plan on holding back.

4.　私_{わたし}は_____、宿題_{しゅくだい}を_____。

I had planned on doing my homework while it's still morning.

5.　どうして_____、_____からです。

If you ask why I don't eat anything, it's because I have a stomachache.

● **6. Question and Answer**
Answer the following questions as if you were directly asked.

1. 両親に言えない秘密がありますか。

_____

2. 今風の洋服を集めていますか。

_____

3. レストランの店長に文句を言ったことがありますか。

_____

4. 来年、何をするつもりですか。

_____

5. 洋食はおいしいけど、どっちかと言うと、和食の方が好きです。あなたはどうですか？

_____

● **7. Practice 1**
In each ( ) write the letter of the sentence that makes the most sense.

1. その秘密がばれたら、（　　）

2. 何か隠しているなら、（　　）

3. 子供はどちらかと言うと、（　　）

4. 私の頭の中は、（　　）

5. 買い物をするつもりだったけど、（　　）

a. 男の子のほうがほしいです。

b. 明日の試験のことでいっぱいです。

c. もうみんなに顔を見せられません。

d. 間に合ってよかったです。

e. 正直に言ってほしいです。

f. 疲れてるから、家にいます。

● 8. Translation
Translate the following sentences into Japanese.

1. I am planning to go to Japan next year.

   _____

2. I had intended to call you, but I fell asleep (before I knew it).

   _____

3. If you ask what I'm doing now, I'm making salad.

   _____

4. You should take a break while you can.

   _____

5. My room is filled with things I don't need.

   _____

● 9. Practice 2
Translate the following dialogue into English and change it into the informal form.

小川さん：　❶「田中くん。テストのために勉強するつもりですが、一緒にしませんか。」

Translation: _____

Informal: _____

田中くん：　❷「えっ？　何のテストですか。」

Translation: _____

Informal: _____

小川さん　❸「英語のテストですよ。先生が明日の一時間目にすると言っていました。」

Translation: _____

Informal: _____

田中くん　❹「聞いていませんでした・・・。どこからどこまでですか。」

Translation: _____

Informal: _____

小川さん　❺「10 ページから 45 ページまでだと言いましたよ。」

Translation: _____

Informal: _____

田中くん　❻「そんなにたくさんあるんですか。どうしましょう・・・。」

Translation: _____

Informal: _____

11 Answer Key 答え合わせ

Short Dialogue (translation)

Wife	There's something you are hiding, isn't there?
Husband	What? I'm not hiding anything. Why do you say such things?
Wife	I heard a neighborhood wife saw you at the mall near the station the day before yesterday.
Husband	That wasn't me.
Wife	She said you were buying an expensive looking ring.
Husband	How can she say that's me?
Wife	If you want to know why she can say it, it's because you have a reason to buy a ring.
Husband	What reason?
Wife	My birthday! You bought it for me, right?
Husband	What? Oh yeah! I was planning on giving it to you on your birthday.

1. Reading practice (answers)

1. 息子は工作が好きで、大きくなったら大工になるそうです。
2. 小学校では、理科より図工のクラスのほうが楽しかったです。
3. ぼくは社会に出たら、東京の会社で働きたいです。
4. 高校では、数学が好きな科目の一つでした。
5. 体の調子が悪かったので、内科の先生にみてもらいました。

2. Fill in the kanji (answers)

1. 大工は雨の日にしごとができません。
2. わたしがすきな科目は理科と社会科です。
3. 計算より作文のほうがかんたんです。
4. 早く社会に出たほうがいいですよ。
5. わたしが合図をするまで、まって下さい。
6. 小学生の時は、図工がすきでした。
7. 友人は工場ではたらいています。

3. Reading comprehension (translation)

❶ I made my first boyfriend last year.
❷ Wanting to be a cute girlfriend, I bought a lot of trendy clothing for our dates.
❸ Since he doesn't like cigarettes, I didn't smoke in front of him and hid and smoked.
❹ When he called me when I was working, I lied to my manager, saying I had a headache, and went to where he was.
❺ I would get takeout somewhere and had him eat it at home, so I wouldn't get found out that I am bad at cooking.
❻ I really liked him so much and it couldn't be helped.
❼ But I might have tried too hard.
❽ Taking time off work, and constantly buying things, I ended up running out of money.
❾ Whereupon, one day all of a sudden, I was told by him that he wants to break up.
❿ Even though I was planning on marrying him... what part of me is bad?!
⓫ When I asked him the reason, he told me, "You are perfect, and that is heavy."
⓬ He said, "It's good that you are pretty, and you can cook, but because you are always next to me, I get exhausted."

⑬ That's right. Me acting like the perfect girlfriend was bad.
⑭ I was taught a bunch of things with this love and I feel like I have gotten a bit smarter.
⑮ So next time, I'm pretty, but I plan on being a girlfriend that can't cook.

4. Reading comprehension questions (answers)

1. Translation: Did this person stop smoking for her boyfriend?

   Answer(s):   いいえ、止めませんでした。

   いいえ、隠れて吸っていました。

2. Translation: Why does she lie to her manager?

   Answer(s):   彼に会いたいから、仕事を休むと言えないからです。

   病気だったら、仕事が休めるからです。

3. Translation: In what different way does she say, "I like him a lot"?

   Answer(s):   彼が好きで好きで、しょうがなかったんです。

4. Translation: What was the reason that he broke up with her?

   Answer(s):   彼女が完璧すぎるからです。

   いつもそばにいて疲れるからです。

5. Translation: What kind of woman do you think this person should be?

   Answer(s):   完璧な女性にならないほうがいいです。

   正直な女性になったほうがいいです。

5. Fill in the blank (answers)

1. 息子がどこかに隠れていて、見つけられないんです。

2. 私はいつも車に酔ってしまいます。／私はいつも車の中で気持ちが悪くなってしまいます。

3. 今風の洋服を買いたいけど、我慢するつもりです。

4. 私は午前中のうちに、宿題をするつもりでした。／私は朝のうちに、宿題をするつもりだった。

5. どうして何も食べない(の)かと言うと、お腹が痛いからです。

6. Question and Answer (answers)

(answers may vary)

1. Do you have any secrets that you can't tell your parents?

   はい、あります。/ いいえ、全然ありません。

2. Are you collecting trendy clothing?

   はい、集めています。/　いいえ、集めていません。/ いいえ、興味がありません (I am not interested.)

3. Have you ever complained to the manager of a restaurant?

   はい、あります。/ いいえ、ありません。/ 言おうと思ったことはあるけど、止めました。

4. What do you plan on doing next year?
   日本に行くつもりです。 / 大学に戻って勉強するつもりです。

5. Western food is good, but if you ask me which one, I like Japanese food more. How about you?
   私も和食の方が好きです。 / 洋食の方が好きです。

7. Practice 1 (answers)

1. (c) その秘密がばれたら、もうみんなに顔を見せられません。

2. (e) 何か隠しているなら、正直に言ってほしいです。

3. (a) 子供はどちらかと言うと、男の子のほうがほしいです。

4. (b) 私の頭の中は、明日の試験のことでいっぱいです。

5. (f) 買い物をするつもりだったけど、疲れてるから、家にいます。

8. Translation (answers)

1. 来年、日本に行くつもりです。

2. 電話をするつもりだったけど、寝てしまいました。

3. 今、何をしてるかと言うと、サラダを作っています。

4. 今のうちに、休んだほうがいいですよ。

5. 私の部屋は、要らない物でいっぱいです。

9. Practice 2 (answers)

1. Tanaka-kun. I'm planning on studying for the test. Won't you do it with me?
   田中君。テストのために勉強するつもりだけど、一緒にしない？

2. What? What test?
   えっ？何のテスト？

3. An English test. The teacher said, we are doing it during the first period tomorrow.
   英語のテストだよ。先生が明日の一時間目にするって。

4. I hadn't heard it. From where until where is it?
   聞いてなかった。。。どこからどこまで？

5. She said it's from page 10 to page 45.
   10 ページから 45 ページまでだって。

6. There's that much? What shall I do...
   そんなにたくさんあるの。どうしよう。。。

Vocabulary Builder:
Group P

■ Group P: Things around Japanese houses

押し入れ	Japanese-style closet
物干し(場)	laundry drying area
空気清浄機	air purifier
乾燥機	drying machine; dryer
布団乾燥機	futon dryer
掃除機	vacuum cleaner
炊飯器	rice cooker
洗濯機	washing machine

掃除機

物干し場

洗濯機

12

| 14 PAGES | 6 USAGE SECTIONS | 18 NEW WORDS |

Lesson 12:
Causative and Permissive

12 | New Words 新しい言葉

Nouns etc.

日常会話	daily conversation	不安	anxiety; fear; unrest
当たり前	natural; common; reasonable	和式	Japanese style
同じように	in the same way	洋式	Western style
土日	Saturday and Sunday	筋トレ	weight (muscle) training

Adjectives

| 伝統的(な) | traditional |

Verbs

慣れる	to get used to; to get accustomed to	脱ぐ	to take off clothes/shoes
揃える	to gather; to put in order; to match	敷く	to spread; to lay
しゃがむ	to squat; to crouch; to keep down	干す	to dry; to hang out
苦労する	to make great effort; to suffer	向ける	to turn towards; to point
くつろぐ	to relax; to feel at home		

12 | Word Usage   言葉の使い方

W-1 | どの〜も／どんな〜も | Every 〜; Any 〜 |

Combining どの and どんな with a noun+も, we can say "any" or "every" of that noun.

> **EXAMPLES**
> どの店も (any/every store)
> どの学校も (any/every school)
> どの国も (any/every country)
>
> どんな人も (any/every person)
> どんな時も (at any time/no matter when)
> どんな言語も (any language)

Even though どの (which) and どんな (what type of) are question words, when used in this way they are not part of a question, but part of a statement.

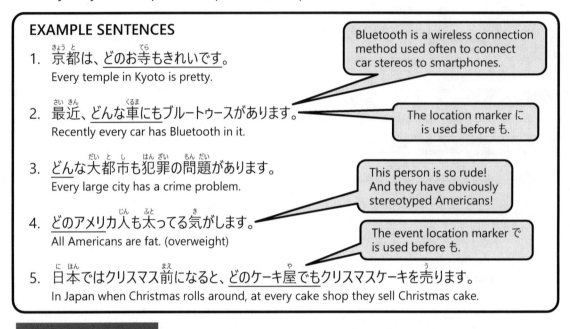

EXAMPLE SENTENCES

1. 京都は、どのお寺もきれいです。
Every temple in Kyoto is pretty.

2. 最近、どんな車にもブルートゥースがあります。
Recently every car has Bluetooth in it.

3. どんな大都市も犯罪の問題があります。
Every large city has a crime problem.

4. どのアメリカ人も太ってる気がします。
All Americans are fat. (overweight)

5. 日本ではクリスマス前になると、どのケーキ屋でもクリスマスケーキを売ります。
In Japan when Christmas rolls around, at every cake shop they sell Christmas cake.

> Bluetooth is a wireless connection method used often to connect car stereos to smartphones.

> The location marker に is used before も.

> This person is so rude! And they have obviously stereotyped Americans!

> The event location marker で is used before も.

RELATED GRAMMAR

Japanese From Zero! ⑤ Section 7-3. Question word extensions か、も、でも

W-2

土日   **Saturday and Sunday**

Days of the week can be shortened and combined. You can't say 土 or 日 alone, but you can say, "Saturday and Sunday" by dropping the 曜日 from both. Days that follow each other, or are one day apart, are commonly combined.

EXAMPLE SENTENCES

1. 今週の休みは月水金になります。
The days off this week will be Monday, Wednesday, and Friday.

2. 毎週の火木にジムで筋トレをやっています。
I do weight training every Tuesday and Thursday.

3. 来週の木金か金土に温泉に一緒に行きませんか。
How about we go to a hot spring next week on Thursday-Friday, or Friday-Saturday?

> げつようび becomes げっ with a small つ.

> かようび adds an あ to lengthen it. Without it you might not be understood.

> Thursday-Friday can be either もっきん or もくきん.

12 | Verb Usage 動詞の使い方

V-1	慣れる な	to get used to; to grow accustomed to	いる/える

1. (something) に慣れる	to get used to (something)

EXAMPLE SENTENCES
1. もう日本の生活に慣れましたか。
   にほん　せいかつ　な
   Have you gotten used to living in Japan? (a Japanese lifestyle)

2. 私はいつもお母さんに怒られるのに慣れています。
   わたし　かあ　おこ　な
   I am used to my mother always getting mad at me.

V-2	しゃがむ	to squat; to crouch	regular

しゃがむ is a common verb in Japan because of the Japanese-style toilets. If you can't しゃがむ, then you might have a hard time using them!

EXAMPLE SENTENCES
1. 今日はお腹が痛かったから、ずっと しゃがんでいました。
   きょう　なか　いた
   I had a stomachache today, so I have been crouching the whole time.

2. 和式のトイレを使う時は、しゃがまないといけません。
   わ しき　つか　とき
   You have to squat when you use the Japanese-style toilet.

   > Or you might need to wash your pants afterwards.

V-3	揃える そろ	to gather; to put in order; to match	いる/える

1. (something) を揃える	to put (something) in order; to collect (something)

EXAMPLE SENTENCES
1. 教室を出る前に、机をそろえて下さい。
   きょう しつ　で　まえ　つくえ　くだ
   Please line up the desks before you leave the classroom.

2. 家を買ったので、家具をそろえようと思っています。
   いえ　か　か ぐ　おも
   Since I bought a house, I think I'm going to match up the furniture.

V-4	脱ぐ	to take off (clothes, shoes etc.)	regular
	1. (item) を脱ぐ	to take off (item)	

Even though putting on clothing in Japanese uses various verbs such as はく、きる、かぶる etc., 脱ぐ can be used for shoes, socks, shirts, skirts, pants etc. However, when taking off hats, 取る is used. As for accessories, it's either 取る or はずす.

EXAMPLE SENTENCES

1. 暑いから、コートを脱ぎます。
   It's hot, so I am going to take off my coat.

2. 玄関で靴を脱いで下さい。
   Please take off your shoes at the entrance.

RELATED VERB(S)

Japanese From Zero! ④ V3-4. Verbs for wearing things

V-5	苦労する	to experience hardships; to struggle	する
	1. (something) に苦労する	to struggle with (something)	

EXAMPLE SENTENCES

1. 今の仕事が見つかるまで、車の支払いに苦労しました。
   I struggled with my car payment until I found my current job.

> This のに isn't "even though",
> It's an action + に.
> (taught more in Lesson 13)

2. 台風のせいで飛行機に乗れなくて、帰るのに苦労しました。
   Not being able to take an airplane due to the typhoon, I had a hard time returning home.

V-6	向ける	to face; to turn; to point toward	いる/える
	1. (somewhere) に(something) を向ける	to face (something) at (somewhere)	

EXAMPLE SENTENCES

1. 私が話してる時は、私に目を向けてください。
   Please turn your eyes towards me when I am talking.

> ～ないと (if you don't) +
> だめです (not good) =
> ～ないとだめです
> (you must, you should)

2. このリモコンの電池は弱いから、テレビにちゃんと向けて押さないとだめです。
   Because this remote's batteries are weak, you must properly point it toward the TV and push.

V-7	敷<ruby>く<rt>し</rt></ruby>	to spread; to lay out	regular

1. (something) を敷く	to spread, to lay out (something)

敷く is used for laying out a futon or blanket etc. It's also used to put something underneath something else, such as a napkin laid under candy on a table etc.

EXAMPLE SENTENCES

1. <ruby>母<rt>はは</rt></ruby>に<ruby>布団<rt>ふとん</rt></ruby>を<ruby>敷<rt>し</rt></ruby>いてもらいました。
   I had my mother lay out a futon for me.

2. <ruby>日本<rt>にほん</rt></ruby>の<ruby>旅館<rt>りょかん</rt></ruby>では、お<ruby>客<rt>きゃく</rt></ruby>さんのために<ruby>布団<rt>ふとん</rt></ruby>を<ruby>敷<rt>し</rt></ruby>きます。
   At Japanese-style hotels, they lay out futons for their customers.

3. <ruby>明日<rt>あした</rt></ruby>はパーティーだから、<ruby>新<rt>あたら</rt></ruby>しいテーブルクロスを<ruby>敷<rt>し</rt></ruby>きましょう。
   Tomorrow is our party, so let's spread the new tablecloth.

V-8	干<ruby>す<rt>ほ</rt></ruby>	to hang out; to dry	regular

1. (something) を干す	to hang out (something)

Japanese hang out their futons to dry due to Japan's high humidity. Even homes with a clothing dryer often don't use it to save money. So, it's common to see clothing on a clothesline and futons hanging on a balcony in Japan.

EXAMPLE SENTENCES

1. <ruby>家<rt>うち</rt></ruby>はいつも<ruby>外<rt>そと</rt></ruby>で<ruby>洗濯物<rt>せんたくもの</rt></ruby>を<ruby>干<rt>ほ</rt></ruby>します。
   Our family always hangs laundry out to dry.

   > Japanese often use 「うち」 to mean "my family".

2. <ruby>雨<rt>あめ</rt></ruby>が<ruby>降<rt>ふ</rt></ruby>っているから、<ruby>今日<rt>きょう</rt></ruby>は<ruby>布団<rt>ふとん</rt></ruby>が<ruby>干<rt>ほ</rt></ruby>せませんね。
   We can't put out the futons to dry since it's raining today.

V-9	くつろぐ	to relax; to get comfortable	regular

EXAMPLE SENTENCES

1. <ruby>洋室<rt>ようしつ</rt></ruby>より<ruby>和室<rt>わしつ</rt></ruby>のほうが、くつろげますね。
   You can relax more in a Japanese-style room than a western style room.

2. くつろぎたい<ruby>時<rt>とき</rt></ruby>は、<ruby>猫<rt>ねこ</rt></ruby>と<ruby>遊<rt>あそ</rt></ruby>びます。
   When I want to relax, I play with my cat.

12 | Grammar and Usage 文法と使い方

● 12-1. Making, letting someone do with ～させる form

させる is the causative/permissive form for する (to do). させる form
(causative/permissive) means "let~ / make~ / have~ do" depending on the context.

Situation #1

A mother is told that her son, Ren, said mean things to another boy named Shogo. She wants her
son to apologize, and tells Shogo's mother:

1. 将伍君に電話をさせる。 ← Here させる is "soft prodding".
    I will <u>have him</u> call Shogo.

Situation #2

Ren's mother has taken away his phone for 3 days as a punishment, but he needs his phone to ask
a classmate about homework. His mother says:

2. 一回だけ電話をさせる。 ← Here させる is "permission".
    I will <u>let you</u> call just one time.

Situation #3

Ren promised to apologize to Shogo, but he didn't. When his mother found out, she was very
angry with Ren and told Shogo's mother on the phone.

3. 今すぐ電話をさせる。 ← Here させる is "forcing".
    I will <u>make him</u> call right now.

All verb types can become causative/permissive form using the following patterns:

Verb type	Plain form		させる form	
Regular verbs (あ form + せる)	怒る	to be mad	怒らせる	to make someone mad
	聞く	to listen; to ask	聞かせる	to make someone listen
	笑う	to laugh	笑わせる	to make someone laugh
いる/える verbs (minus る + させる)	見る	to see; to watch	見させる	to make someone watch
	食べる	to eat	食べさせる	to make someone eat
	忘れる	to forget	忘れさせる	to make someone forget
Irregular verbs	する	to do	させる	to make someone do
	来る	to come	来させる	to make someone come

● 12-2. Using appropriate particles with させる

When using a verb with させる, the person being allowed or made to do the action, can be marked with に or を. However, the particle used can change the meaning.

For forcing and compulsion, use を

1. 私は娘を歩かせました。
   I <u>made</u> my daughter walk.

2. 先生は生徒を座らせました。
   The teacher <u>made</u> the student sit down.

3. 母は子供を学校に行かせました。
   The mother <u>made</u> her child go to school.

4. コーチは選手を練習させます。
   The coach <u>made</u> the player practice.

For allowing and permission, use に

1. 私は娘に歩かせました。
   I <u>let</u> my daughter walk.

2. 先生は生徒に座らせました。
   The teacher <u>let</u> the student sit down.

3. 母は子供に学校に行かせました。
   The mother <u>let</u> her child go to school.

4. コーチは選手に練習させます。
   The coach <u>let</u> the player practice.

に and を don't change the meaning if the action is considered negative. In Japan, overtime is mostly considered a bad thing. So, 上司はいつも私(に or を)残業させる would mean, "My boss always <u>makes</u> me work overtime." If the speaker wanted to relay to the listener that they were happy to get overtime then the speaker would change the final verb to 残業させて<u>くれる</u> to show that the manager did them a favor by "giving" them overtime.

For inanimate objects that can be controlled or automated, use に

1. 私はロボットに掃除させます。
   I let the robot clean.

2. 兄はアレクサに家の電気を付けさせます。
   My older brother makes Alexa turn on the house lights.

3. 計算機ばかりに計算させると、自分で計算できなくなってしまいます。
   If you only let calculators do calculations, you'll end up being unable to calculate on your own.

For things without intention or that occur naturally, use を

1. 冷蔵庫に入れなかったせいで、ミルクを腐らせました。
   Because I didn't put it in the refrigerator, I let the milk spoil.

When feelings are triggered, use を

1. 先生は生徒を笑わせました。
   The teacher made the students laugh.

2. 弟 は母を怒らせました。
   My younger brother made my mother mad.

3. 家の子は私を驚かせました。
   My kid surprised me.

● 12-3. Review of similar verb forms

Just for a sanity check, let's look at some forms that might seem similar in sound.

Verb type	Potential form	Passive form	させる form
Regular	言える to be able to say	言われる to be told	言わせる to make someone say
	消せる to be able to turn off	消される to be turned off	消させる to make someone turn off
いる・える	食べられる to be able to eat	食べられる to be eaten	食べさせる to make someone eat
	捨てられる to be able to throw away	捨てられる to be thrown away	捨てさせる to make someone throw away
Irregular	できる to be able to do	される to have done to	させる to make someone do
	来られる to be able to come	来られる to be visited	来させる to make someone come

RELATED GRAMMAR

Japanese From Zero! ⑤ Section 6-5. Passive verb form 〜られる
Japanese From Zero! ③ Section 13-6. Changing regular verbs into the potential verb form
Japanese From Zero! ③ Section 13-7. Changing いるえる verbs into the potential verb form

● 12-4. Can we use を twice in a sentence? (NO)

When using a verb that takes an object (such as 飲む、買う、取る), the particle に must be used after the recipient of the action to avoid overlapping を in a sentence. The context of the sentence determines if someone is "letting" or "making" an action happen.

1. 私は赤ちゃんにミルクを飲ませた。	I let/made my baby drink milk.
2. 先生は私に本を読ませた。	The teacher let/made me read a book.
3. 母は僕に人参を食べさせた。	My mother made me eat carrots.

● 12-5. Combination of させる with other grammar

させる form can be treated as a new verb and used with other grammar.

させる + られる (passive) ➡ させられる
(to be made/forced to do something)

1. 母に家事をさせられた。
   I was made to do housework by my mother. (My mother made me do housework.)

2. 上司に仕事を辞めさせられた。
   My boss made me leave my job. (I got fired by my boss.)

3. 彼女の一言に考えさせられた。
   Her short comment made me think. (Her words caused me to think.)

4. 小さい時は息子に苦労させられました。
   When he was small, my son really made it hard for me.

させる + てください ➡ させてください
(Please let me do something)

1. 私に運転させてください。
   Please let me drive.

3. 今日中に終わらせてください。
   Please finish it by the end of the day.

2. 暑いので、窓を開けさせて下さい。
   Let me open the window since it's hot.

4. あなたのことを「ひろちゃん」と呼ばせて下さい。
   Please let me call you "Hiro-chan".

させる + ないでください ➡ させないでください
(Please don't make me do something)

1. 急がせないでください。
Please don't make me rush.

2. 後悔させないで下さい。
Please don't make me regret.

3. あんまり怖がらせないでください。
Please don't make me scared.

4. これ以上、怒らせないで下さい。
Please don't make me angrier than this.

させる + たい form ➡ させたい、たくない
(I want/don't want to make/let someone do something)

1. あなたを両親に会わせたいです。
I want to introduce you to my parents.

2. 母に苦労させたくないです。
I don't want to make my mother suffer.

3. びっくりさせたいことがあります。
There is something I want to surprise you with.

4. 主人に今の仕事を続けさせたくないです。
I don't want to let my husband continue his current job.

させる + other grammar

1. 明日試合に勝つために、チームをもっと練習させないといけません。
In order to win the match, we must make the team practice more.

2. なぜか分からないけど、私はいつも彼女を怒らせてしまいます。
I don't know why, but I always end up making my girlfriend mad.

3. お母さんは赤ちゃんを食べさせながら、お兄ちゃんの宿題を見ています。
My mother is looking at my older brother's homework while feeding the baby.

4. 勉強したくない人を無理やり勉強させられません。
させる＋られる
(causative + potential)
You can't forcibly make someone study who doesn't want to study.

5. 子供には、何でも好きなことをさせてあげたいです。
させる＋てあげる (giving the benefit of the action)
I want to allow my children to do what they like.

● 12-6. Understanding double particles

You have seen double particles such as には、にも and では in previous books.

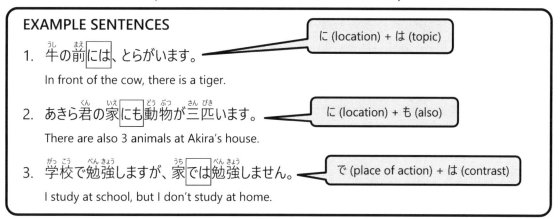

EXAMPLE SENTENCES

1. 牛の前には、とらがいます。　　に (location) + は (topic)

   In front of the cow, there is a tiger.

2. あきら君の家にも動物が三匹います。　　に (location) + も (also)

   There are also 3 animals at Akira's house.

3. 学校で勉強しますが、家では勉強しません。　　で (place of action) + は (contrast)

   I study at school, but I don't study at home.

We can link a noun and its particle to another noun with の to have a very powerful noun phrase that we can ask a question about or make a statement.

EXAMPLES

A. 都会で (in a city) + の + 一人暮らし (living alone)

   都会での一人暮らしは寂しいです。　　Living alone in a city is lonely.

B. 友達から (from my friend) + の + メール (email)

   友達からのメールを削除しました。　　I deleted e-mail from my friend.

C. 日本へ (to Japan) + の + 航空券 (airline ticket)

   日本への航空券は時々安いです。　　Sometimes airline tickets to Japan are cheap.

You could argue that the following three sentences below are similar. But the third sentence is not possible without the double particle.

1. お父さんから手紙が届きました。　　From my father, a letter arrived.
2. お父さんからの手紙が届きました。　　A letter from my father arrived.
3. お父さんからの手紙を読みました。　　I read the letter from my father.

MORE EXAMPLE SENTENCES

1. 彼女からの電話を待っています。　　2. ビーチでのプロポーズは、うまく行きました。

   I'm waiting for a call from her.　　My marriage proposal at the beach went well.

12 | Practice and Review 練習と復習

● 1. Mini Conversation ミニ会話 J → E

1. Casual conversation between mother and her daughter

A: お母さんは、どうしていつも私に勉強させるの？

B: どの家でも同じだよ。子供は勉強するの。

A みおちゃんのお母さんは、学校が終わってから、みおちゃんにゲームさせてるよ。

B: そうか。じゃあ、土日だけだったら、ゲームしてもいいよ。

A: How come you always make me study?

B: Every house (family) is the same. Children study.

A: Mio's mother let's Mio play games when school is over.

B: I see. Well then, you can play games on Saturday and Sunday.

> おかあさん = "you" since Japanese often use names and titles instead of "you".

2. Polite conversation between friends

> での is not a typo, we are modifying "living alone" with 東京で (in Tokyo).

A: 森田さん、東京での一人暮らしはどうですか。

B: う～ん。部屋が狭いのに物でいっぱいだから、くつろげないですね。

A: 今度、遊びに行ってもいいですか。

> こんど translates as, "soon", "this time", "shortly", and even "next time".

B: いいえ、だめです！ 洋服が脱ぎっぱなしになっていますから。

A: How is living alone in Tokyo Morita-san?

B: Hmmm. I can't relax, because my room is filled with things despite it being small.

A: Can we go hang out soon?

B: No way! Because my clothes are strewn all over the place.

3. Mixed conversation between friends

A: この間、姉の赤ちゃんにミルクを飲ませたら。。。

B: 吐かれたの？

A: いいえ、げっぷをされてしまいました。くさかった。。。

B: それは当たり前だよ。げっぷをさせないと、赤ちゃんは苦しくなるよ。

A: The other day when I was feeding (allowing to drink) my older sister's baby...

B: Were you thrown up on?

A: No, I got burped on. It was smelly...

B: Of course! If you don't let them burp, babies will become distressed.

● 2. Mini Conversation ミニ会話 E → J

1. Casual conversation in a house with home automation

A: It's time to sleep now. Can you make Alexa turn off the lights?
B: Yeah. Alexa, turn off the lights.
A: You didn't lay out the futon yet. Can you make Alexa do it?
B: That's impossible! Ah... your intent is to make me do it.

A: もう寝る時間だね。アレクサに電気を消させてくれる？

B: うん。アレクサ、電気を消して。

A: 布団をまだ敷いてなかったね。アレクサにさせてくれる？

B: それは無理でしょう！あ、僕にさせるつもりだね。

2. Polite conversation between two parents

A: It seems my son started a business on his own.
B: Is that so. That's a good thing.
A: I want to make him quit. Because it's not easy to succeed with a business alone.
B: It's true that he might suffer. But I want him to work hard and succeed.

A: 息子が自分でビジネスを始めたそうです。

B: そうですか。それはいい事ですね。

A: 私は辞めさせたいんです。一人でビジネスを成功させるのは簡単じゃないですから。

B: 確かに苦労するかも知れませんね。でも、私は頑張って、成功してほしいです。

3. Polite conversation between two old women in a waiting room

A: Um, excuse me please let me sit here.
B: Of course, go ahead.
A: Thank you. Since your knees get bad when you age, standing the whole time is rough.
B: That's true. It takes time for me to crouch also.

A: あのう、すみませんが、ちょっとここに座らせてください。

B: もちろん、どうぞ。

A: ありがとう。年を取ると、ひざが悪くなるから、ずっと立っているのが辛いですね。

B: そうですね。私はしゃがむのも時間がかかるんですよ。

● **3. Short Dialogue**

Mr. Iwata's co-worker is asking about his engagement.

同僚	「岩田さん、聞いたよ！ゆかりさんと結婚するんでしょう？」
岩田さん	「え！何で知ってるの？！ゆかりから聞いたの？」
同僚	「ううん、ゆかりさんから聞いてないよ。何で知ってるかと言うと、それはゆかりさんの友達の千穂さんから聞いたの。」
岩田さん	「ええ！千穂ちゃんと知り合いだったの？」
同僚	「ううん。知り合いじゃないよ。おととい、レストランで食べている時に、千穂さんが僕の近くに座っていて、大きい声でゆかりさんの結婚の話をしてたから。」
岩田さん	「そうか。ばれたら、しょうがないね。実は、日曜日に公園でプロポーズしたんだ。皆の前で泣かれて困ったよ〜。結婚式は、半年後にすることにした。」
同僚	「よかったね。結婚式の時はスピーチさせてね。」
岩田さん	「うん、よろしく頼むよ。」

12 Kanji Lesson 12:
電船汽弓矢形

Some of the following kanji characters are related to vehicles & transportation.

12 New Kanji 新しい漢字

229	雨	13 画	electricity; lightning	
		くんよみ	none	
		おんよみ	デン	

電気 (でん・き) electricity　　　　停電 (てい・でん) power outage, blackout
電話 (でん・わ) telephone　　　　電球 (でん・きゅう) light bulb
電車 (でん・しゃ) electric train　　充電 (じゅう・でん) charging (electrically)

電

230	舟	11 画	ship; boat	
		くんよみ	ふね、ふな	
		おんよみ	セン	

漁船 (ぎょ・せん) fishing boat　　船長 (せん・ちょう) captain
船 (ふね) ship, boat　　　　　　船員 (せん・いん) sailor
船旅 (ふな・たび) trip by boat　　船便 (ふな・びん) surface mail; sea mail

船

231	氵	7 画	steam; vapor	
		くんよみ	none	
		おんよみ	キ	

汽笛 (き・てき) steam whistle　　汽車賃 (き・しゃ・ちん) train fare
汽船 (き・せん) steamboat　　　　夜汽車 (よ・ぎ・しゃ) night train
汽車 (き・しゃ) train (steam)　　汽水 (き・すい) brackish water

汽

232	弓	3画	bow; bow-shaped		

	くんよみ	ゆみ
	おんよみ	キュウ

弓 (ゆみ) bow　　　　　　弓道 (きゅう・どう) Japanese archery
弓矢 (ゆみ・や) bow and arrow　　弓具 (きゅう・ぐ) archery equipment
弓なり (ゆみ・なり) arched　　弓術 (きゅう・じゅつ) the art of archery

233	矢	5画	arrow		

	くんよみ	や
	おんよみ	シ

投げ矢 (な・げ・や) dart　　　　矢先 (や・さき) arrowhead, moment
矢 (や) arrow　　　　　　矢車 (や・ぐるま) arrow wheel
矢印 (や・じるし) arrow (symbol)　無理矢理 (む・り・や・り) against one's will

234	彡	7画	form; shape; type; figure		

	くんよみ	かた、かたち
	おんよみ	ケイ、ギョウ

人形 (にん・ぎょう) doll　　　　形見 (かた・み) memento
図形 (ず・けい) figure　　　　形容詞 (けい・よう・し) adjective
形 (かたち) shape　　　　　手形 (て・がた) handprint; promissory note

12 Kanji Culture 漢字の文化

● Names of Shapes using 形

There is sometimes more than one way to say shape names. But at least of the names often includes the kanji for shape 形.

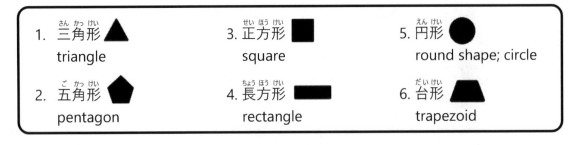

1. 三角形 ▲ triangle
3. 正方形 ■ square
5. 円形 ● round shape; circle
2. 五角形 ⬠ pentagon
4. 長方形 ▬ rectangle
6. 台形 ⏢ trapezoid

12 Words You Can Write かける言葉

電池 (でんち) battery

電	池										

電車 (でんしゃ) electric train

電	車										

船長 (せんちょう) captain

船	長										

汽車 (きしゃ) steam train

汽	車										

汽水 (きすい) brackish water

汽	水										

弓矢 (ゆみや) bow and arrow

弓	矢										

弓道 (きゅうどう) Japanese archery

弓	道										

矢先 (やさき) arrowhead; moment

矢	先										

形見 (かたみ) memento

形	見										

人形 (にんぎょう) doll

人	形										

風船 (ふうせん) balloon

風	船										

12 Workbook 12: Workbook Activities

12 Kanji Drills 漢字ドリル

● 1. Reading practice
Write FURIGANA above the underlined kanji words.

1.　ぼくは昔、弓道クラブに入っていました。
<small>むかし</small>

2.　この人形は、母の形見です。

3.　この矢印の通りに、歩いて行きましょう。
<small>じるし</small>

4　旅行するなら、汽車と船と どちらが いいですか。
<small>りょ こう</small>

5.　船長さんは今、電話中ですよ。
<small>ちゅう</small>

● 2. Fill in the kanji
Fill in the appropriate kanji in the blanks for each sentence.

1.　___ ___ で___ ___に ___ っています。
<small>でん しゃ　　がっ こう　　かよ</small>
I commute to (go to and from) school by train.

2.　___ がすきだから、___ ___みに___でりょ___します。
<small>うみ　　　　　　なつ やす　　ふね　　　こう</small>
Because I like the ocean, I will take a trip by boat on summer break.

3.　あの ___ ___ は ___ きくて、___いです。
<small>き しゃ　　おお　　　ふる</small>
That steam train (over there) is big and old.

4. わたしの<ruby>友<rt>とも</rt></ruby>___だちは ___ ___を<ruby>弓<rt>ゆみ</rt></ruby><ruby>矢<rt>や</rt></ruby>つかうのが___ ___<ruby>上<rt>じょう</rt></ruby><ruby>手<rt>ず</rt></ruby>です。

My friend is skilled at using a bow and arrow.

---

5. <ruby>今<rt>いま</rt></ruby>___ でも、おじいさんの___ ___<ruby>形<rt>かた</rt></ruby><ruby>見<rt>み</rt></ruby>を___<ruby>持<rt>も</rt></ruby>っています。

Even now, I have mementos of my grandfather.

---

6. <ruby>高<rt>こう</rt></ruby><ruby>校<rt>こう</rt></ruby>___ ___の<ruby>時<rt>とき</rt></ruby>___は、<ruby>弓<rt>きゅう</rt></ruby><ruby>道<rt>どう</rt></ruby>___ ___をしていました。

When I was in high school, I did Japanese archery.

---

7. <ruby>電<rt>でん</rt></ruby><ruby>池<rt>ち</rt></ruby>___ ___が <ruby>切<rt>き</rt></ruby>___れたから、<ruby>買<rt>か</rt></ruby>___いに<ruby>行<rt>い</rt></ruby>___きましょう。

Let's go and buy some when the batteries run out.

---

12 | Usage Activities 文法アクティビティー

● 3. Reading comprehension

Translate the following on a separate piece of paper or type in an electronic device.

<ruby>日<rt>に</rt></ruby><ruby>本<rt>ほん</rt></ruby>のホームステイ

Japan and America share many similarities, but if you ever are able to homestay in a Japanese home, you will find many peculiarities.

❶ <ruby>今年<rt>ことし</rt></ruby>の<ruby>夏休<rt>なつやす</rt></ruby>みに<ruby>初<rt>はじ</rt></ruby>めて<ruby>日本<rt>にほん</rt></ruby>でホームステイをしました。

❷ <ruby>大学<rt>だいがく</rt></ruby>で<ruby>日本語<rt>にほんご</rt></ruby>を<ruby>勉強<rt>べんきょう</rt></ruby>しているので、<ruby>日常会話<rt>にちじょうかいわ</rt></ruby>には<ruby>自信<rt>じしん</rt></ruby>がありましたが、ホストファミリーと一<ruby>緒<rt>しょ</rt></ruby>にうまく<ruby>生活<rt>せいかつ</rt></ruby>できるかどうかは<ruby>不安<rt>ふあん</rt></ruby>でした。

❸ ホストファミリーの<ruby>池田<rt>いけだ</rt></ruby>さんの<ruby>家<rt>いえ</rt></ruby>は、<ruby>田舎<rt>いなか</rt></ruby>にある<ruby>伝統的<rt>でんとうてき</rt></ruby>な<ruby>日本<rt>にほん</rt></ruby>の<ruby>家<rt>いえ</rt></ruby>でした。

❹ <ruby>玄関<rt>げんかん</rt></ruby>で<ruby>靴<rt>くつ</rt></ruby>を<ruby>脱<rt>ぬ</rt></ruby>ぐことは<ruby>知<rt>し</rt></ruby>っていましたが、<ruby>靴<rt>くつ</rt></ruby>の<ruby>先<rt>さき</rt></ruby>をドアに<ruby>向<rt>む</rt></ruby>けて<ruby>揃<rt>そろ</rt></ruby>えないといけないことは<ruby>知<rt>し</rt></ruby>りませんでした。

❺ どうして<ruby>靴<rt>くつ</rt></ruby>を<ruby>揃<rt>そろ</rt></ruby>えるかと<ruby>言<rt>い</rt></ruby>うと、それは<ruby>玄関<rt>げんかん</rt></ruby>をいつもきれいに<ruby>見<rt>み</rt></ruby>せるためです。

❻ そして、<ruby>外<rt>そと</rt></ruby>に<ruby>出<rt>で</rt></ruby>る<ruby>時<rt>とき</rt></ruby>すぐに<ruby>靴<rt>くつ</rt></ruby>を<ruby>履<rt>は</rt></ruby>けるようにするためです。

❼ びっくりしたのは、<ruby>池田<rt>いけだ</rt></ruby>さんの<ruby>家<rt>いえ</rt></ruby>のトイレが<ruby>和式<rt>わしき</rt></ruby>だったことです。

Western Style　Japanese Style

❽ 和式のトイレは座る所がないから、しゃがまないといけません。

❾ これだけは、すぐに慣れませんでした。

❿ また、部屋は全部たたみで、寝る時はいつも押し入れから布団を出して敷きました。

⓫ 池田さんのおばあちゃんが私の布団をいつも敷いてくれました。

⓬ 「私に布団を敷かせて下さい」と頼んだけど、「だめだめ。これは私がやるの。」と言われてしまいました。

⓭ 池田さんのお母さんが、外で洗濯物を干そうとしていたので、「私にさせて下さい」と言ったけど、「いいの、いいの。こんな事、トム君にさせられないよ。」と言われました。

⓮ 僕は手伝いたかっただけなのに。。。誰も僕を手伝わせてくれませんでした。

⓯ 池田さんのおじいちゃんはいつも居間で新聞を読んでいて、お父さんは休みの日はずっとテレビから離れません。

⓰ 他の家のお母さんも同じように忙しく家事をしていて、お父さんはくつろいでいました。

⓱ 日本のどの家族も、そうなんでしょうか。

⓲ 私の家では、父と母は家事を二人でやっています。

● 4. Reading comprehension questions

Translate the questions about the reading comprehension then answer in Japanese.

1. 日本の家に入る時、何をしなければなりませんか。

   Translation: _____

   Answer: _____

2. どうして玄関で靴を揃えないといけないですか。（２つ書きましょう。）

   Translation: _____

   Answer: _____

3. トムさんが池田さんの家ですぐに慣れなかったことは何ですか。

   Translation: _____

   Answer: _____

4. トムさんは、どうして家の手伝いができませんでしたか。

   Translation: _____

   Answer: _____

5. あなたは池田さんの家に住みたいと思いますか。それはどうしてですか。

   Translation: _____

   Answer: _____

● 5. Fill in the blanks

Fill in the missing part based on the English sentence.

1.　お母さんは私＿＿＿＿＿＿＿＿＿＿＿＿＿＿＿＿＿＿＿＿＿。

My mother makes me eat vegetables.

2.　先生は＿＿＿＿＿＿＿＿＿家に＿＿＿＿＿＿＿＿＿＿＿＿＿＿＿＿＿。

My teacher let me go home.

3.　＿＿＿＿＿＿＿レストラン＿＿＿＿、＿＿＿＿＿＿＿＿＿＿そうです。

Every restaurant looks good.

4.　＿＿＿＿＿＿＿＿＿＿＿＿＿＿＿＿＿、私の犬といっしょに＿＿＿＿＿＿＿＿＿です。

I want to be with my dog at any time (always).

5.　中に＿＿＿＿＿＿＿＿＿時、靴を＿＿＿＿＿＿＿＿＿＿＿＿＿＿＿＿＿。

Please take off your shoes when you get inside.

● 6. Question & Answer

Answer the following questions as if you were directly asked.

1.　伝統的な家と今風の家と、どちらに住みたいですか。

＿＿＿＿＿＿＿＿＿＿＿＿＿＿＿＿＿＿＿＿＿＿＿＿＿＿＿＿＿＿＿＿＿

2.　玄関でいつも靴をそろえますか。

＿＿＿＿＿＿＿＿＿＿＿＿＿＿＿＿＿＿＿＿＿＿＿＿＿＿＿＿＿＿＿＿＿

3.　小さい時、ご両親に何をさせられましたか。

＿＿＿＿＿＿＿＿＿＿＿＿＿＿＿＿＿＿＿＿＿＿＿＿＿＿＿＿＿＿＿＿＿

4. 誰^{だれ}があなたを笑^{わら}わせてくれますか。

_____

5. 学校^{がっこう}で先生^{せんせい}に何^{なに}をさせられましたか。

_____

● **7. Translation**

Translate the following sentences into Japanese.

1. I want to let/make you eat healthy food.

_____

2. My head hurts, so don't make me laugh.

_____

3. Please let me decide who to marry or not marry.

_____

4. I will have my wife call you when she comes home.

_____

5. The coach made the players practice in order to win tomorrow's game.

_____

● **8. Practice**

Underline the correct item, then translate the resulting sentence into English.

1. 冷蔵庫^{れいぞうこ}にあったケーキを弟^{おとうと}に (食^たべられて・食^たべさせて)、私^{わたし}は怒^{おこ}りました。

Translation: _____

2. 娘^{むすめ}を今^{いま}、学校^{がっこう}に (行^いかれた・行^いかせた) ので、もうすぐ着^つくと思^{おも}います。

Translation: _____

3. 息子の部屋はおもちゃでいっぱいだから、要らない物は (捨てられ・捨てさせ) ようと思います。

Translation: _____

4. 傘を持っていなかったから、雨に (降られて・降らせて) 大変でした。

Translation: _____

5. 私の彼は面白い人なので、私はいつも (笑われて・笑わされて) います。

Translation: _____

12 | Answer Key 答え合わせ

Short Dialogue (translation)

Co-worker	Iwata, I heard! You're getting married to Yukari, right?
Iwata	What! How come you know?! Did you hear it from Yukari?
Co-worker	No, I didn't hear it from Yukari. The reason why I know is because I heard it from Yukari's friend, Chiho.
Iwata	What? Was Chiho your acquaintance?
Co-worker	No. She isn't an acquaintance. It's because when I was eating at a restaurant the day before yesterday, Chiho was sitting near me and was talking loud about Yukari's marriage.
Iwata	I see. If it has been found out, it can't be helped. Actually, I proposed to her at the park on Sunday. I was troubled because she cried on me in front of everyone. We decided to have our wedding ceremony half a year from now.
Co-worker	That's great. Let me give a speech at your wedding ceremony, okay?
Iwata	Yeah, please. (I request well.)

1. Reading practice (answers)

1. ぼくは昔、弓道クラブに入っていました。
2. この人形は、母の形見です。
3. この矢印の通りに、歩いて行きましょう。
4. 旅行するなら、汽車と船と どちらが いいですか。
5. 船長さんは今、電話中ですよ。

2. Fill in the kanji (answers)

1. 電車で学校に通っています。
2. 海がすきだから、夏休みに船でりょ行します。
3. あの汽車は大きくて、古いです。
4. わたしの友だちは弓矢をつかうのが上手です。
5. 今でも、おじいさんの形見を持っています。

6. 高校の時は、弓道をしていました。
7. 電池が切れたから、買いに行きましょう。

3. Reading comprehension (translation)

❶ On summer vacation this year, I homestayed in Japan for the first time.

❷ Because I'm studying Japanese in college, I had confidence in my everyday conversations, but I wasn't sure if I could live well with my host family.

❸ My host family Ikeda's house was a traditional Japanese house in the countryside.

❹ I knew about taking off shoes in the entrance of the home, but I didn't know I had to line them up and face the tips of the shoes towards the door.

❺ The reason why you line up the shoes is in order to always cleanly display the entrance of the home.

❻ And it's also to be able to put on your shoes right away when you go out.

❼ What surprised me was that Ikeda-san's house toilet was Japanese-style.

❽ There isn't a place to sit on a Japanese-style toilet, so you need to squat.

❾ This is the only thing I didn't immediately get used to.

❿ Also, all the rooms were tatami-mats, so you always take the futon out from the closet and lay it out when you went to bed.

⓫ Ikeda-san's grandmother always laid out the futon for me.

⓬ I asked, "Let me lay out the futon, please", but I was told, "No, no, I will do this".

⓭ Since Ikeda-san's mother was trying to hang laundry outside, I said, "Please allow me to do it", but I was told, "It's okay, It's okay, I can't let you (Tom) do this sort of thing."

⓮ Even though I just wanted to help, nobody let me help.

⓯ Ikeda-san's grandfather is always in the living room reading the newspaper, and his father never separates from the TV on his days off.

⓰ Mothers of other homes also busily did housework in the same way and the fathers relaxed.

⓱ I wonder if all Japanese families are this way.

⓲ At my house, my father and mother do the housework together.

4. Reading comprehension questions (answers)

1. Translation: What must you do when you enter a Japanese home?

   Answer(s): 玄関で靴を脱がないといけません。／玄関で靴を脱いで、そろえないといけません。

2. Translation: Why must you line up your shows at the entrance. (Write 2)

   Answer(s): 玄関をいつもきれいにして、すぐに靴がはけるようにするためです。

   玄関をきれいに見せるためです。そして、外に出る時にすぐに靴がはけるようにするためです。

3. Translation: What was the thing that Tom didn't get used to right away at Ikeda's house?

   Answer(s): 和式のトイレです。／和式のトイレを使うことです。

4. Translation: How come Tom wasn't able to help around the house?

   Answer(s): おばあちゃんとお母さんが手伝わせてくれなかったからです。

   おばあちゃんとお母さんにだめと言われたからです。

5. Translation: Do you think you want to live in Ikeda's home? Why is that?

Answer(s):　はい、思います。なぜかと言うと、おばあさんとお母さんが何でもしてくれるからです。

いいえ、思いません。和式のトイレを使いたくないからです。

5. Fill in the blanks (answers)

1. お母さんは私に野菜を食べさせます。

2. 先生は僕を家に帰らせました。

3. どのレストランも、よさそうです。／どのレストランも、おいしそうです。

4. どんな時も、私の犬といっしょにいたいです。

5. 中に入る時、靴を脱いで下さい。

6. Question and Answer (answers may vary)

1. Which house do you want to live in, a traditional house or modern-style house?
伝統的な家に住みたいです。／今風の家がいいです。

2. Do you always line up your shoes at your home's entrance?
はい、そろえます。／いいえ、そろえません。／日本の友達の家では、そろえます。

3. What were you made to do by your parents when you were small?
家の手伝いをさせられました。／勉強させられました。／全然、覚えていません。

4. Who makes you laugh?
友達です。／子供が笑わせてくれます。

5. What were you made to do in school?
宿題をやらされました。／授業中に本を読まされました。／何もさせられませんでした。

7. Translation (answers)

1. あなたにヘルシーな食べ物を食べさせたい。／あなたに健康的な物を食べさせてあげたい。

2. 頭が痛いから、笑わせないで。

3. 誰と結婚するか、しないか決めさせてください。

4. 妻が帰ったら、電話をさせます。／妻が家に帰ってきたら、電話をさせます。

5. 明日の試合に勝つために、コーチは選手を練習させました。

8. Practice (answers)

1. 冷蔵庫にあったケーキを弟に食べられて、私は怒りました。
Translation: I got mad because the cake that was in the refrigerator got eaten by my little brother.

2. 娘を今、学校に行かせたので、もうすぐ着くと思います。

Translation: I made my daughter go to school, so I think she will arrive soon.

3. 息子の部屋はおもちゃでいっぱいだから、要らない物は捨てさせようと思います。

Translation: Since my son's room is filled with toys, I'm thinking of making him throw away unneeded things.

4. 傘を持っていなかったから、雨に降られて大変でした。

Translation: Since I didn't bring an umbrella, I got rained on and it was rough.

5. 私の彼は面白い人なので、私はいつも笑わされています。

Translation: Since my boyfriend is funny, I'm always made to laugh. (He always makes me laugh)

13

| 19 PAGES | 8 USAGE SECTIONS | 33 NEW WORDS |

Lesson 13:
Even if...

13 New Words 新しい言葉

Nouns etc.

はっ しゃ			
発車	departure of a vehicle	しわ	wrinkle; crease
定期券	commuter's ticket; pass	十円玉	ten yen coin
料金	fee; charge	最悪	the worst
改札	ticket gate; wicket	足元	under one's feet
動画	video; movie; moving picture	保存	saving (e.g. to disk); storage
参加	participation	満員	full (of people); crowded
ガタン	with a bang; with a jolt	券売機	ticket sales machine
お礼	thanks; gratitude	〜ずつ	each; at a time
しおり	bookmark		

> ガタン is an onomatopoeia

Adjective

は		うらや	
恥ずかしい	embarrassing; embarrassed; shy	羨ましい	envious
涼しい	cool (air)		

Adverb

おも			
思わず	accidentally; unintentionally	そのうち	sooner or later; someday
そのまま	as it is; without change; just like	丁寧に	carefully; politely
ゆっくりと	slowly		

Verbs

はさ		き	
挟む	to hold between; to pinch	切れる	to run down; to expire
気が付く	to notice; to become aware of	開く	to open; to be open
汚れる	to get dirty; to become dirty	閉まる	to close; to be closed
動かす	to move; to set in motion	保存する	to save (file etc.)

13 | New Expressions 新しい表現

There are phrases you might never use yourself, but might hear every day in Japan.

1. 発車いたします。
はっしゃ

We are departing.

いたす is 謙譲語 (けんじょうご / humble language) made into 丁寧語 (ていねいご / polite) when in the ます forms. けんじょうご is only used for the actions of the speaker to show respect and never used for the actions of the people being spoken to.

> **MORE EXAMPLES USING いたす**
>
> The following examples are commonly used when a store clerk or company staff is communicating with a customer or client.
>
> | 丁寧語 (POLITE LANGUAGE) | | 謙譲語 (HUMBLE LANGUAGE) |
> |---|---|---|
> | 1. 連絡します (I will contact you.) | ➡ | ご連絡いたします |
> | 2. 電話します (I will call.) | ➡ | お電話いたします |
> | 3. 調べます (I will search.) | ➡ | お調べいたします |

When using けんじょうご, a prefix of ご or お is often added. These can be used to raise the level of respect toward the person being spoken to.

2. ご注意下さい。
ちゅう い くだ

Please be careful.

ください is the command form of くださる which itself is the 尊敬語 (そんけいご / respectful language) version of the verb くれる (to give). ください can sound strong even when used with polite ご prefix. The following phrases are not used casually but are often used to warn the public of nearby dangers OR in formal situations.

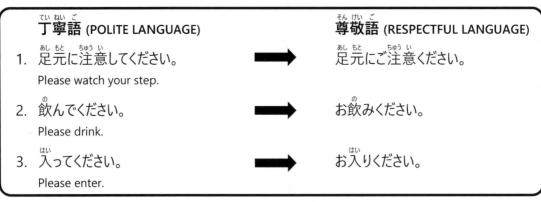

丁寧語 (POLITE LANGUAGE)		尊敬語 (RESPECTFUL LANGUAGE)
1. 足元に注意してください。 Please watch your step.	➡	足元にご注意ください。
2. 飲んでください。 Please drink.	➡	お飲みください。
3. 入ってください。 Please enter.	➡	お入りください。

13 | Japanese Living 日本の暮らし

● Local Trains in Japan

Japan is crisscrossed with thousands of kilometers of train tracks run by many national and local train companies. There are several different types of trains running across these tracks.

The naming convention of train routes differs from company to company depending on how many stops a train makes on its route. Skipping stations means faster arrival times. Here are some of the meanings behind the train names:

普通（local）

Short for 普通列車 (normal train), these trains stop at every station on the route.

Depending on where you want to go, this can add much time to your trip.

急行（express）

Short for 急行列車 (express train), these trains don't stop at less popular or smaller stations and only stop at major stations.

特急（limited express）

Short for 特別急行列車 (special express train), these trains are faster than trains designated as 急行 since they stop at even less stations along the route.

快速（rapid express）

Short for 快速列車 (rapid express train), these trains are similar to 急行 as they only stop at major stations, but are not as fast as 特急 due to stopping at more stations.

準急（semi express）

Short for 準急列車 (semi express train), these stop at more stations than 急行 and 快速, but less than trains designated 普通. JR (Japan Rail) lines have no 準急 trains.

13 | Word Usage 言葉の使い方

W-1 | 〜ずつ | each; at a time

〜ずつ is a suffix that comes after a counter or quantity.

EXAMPLES

二つずつ (two each)

三回ずつ (three times each)

五ドルずつ (5 dollars each)

一語ずつ (word for word)

半分ずつ (half and half)

少しずつ (little by little)

EXAMPLE SENTENCES

1. 体調は少しずつよくなっています。
   My condition is getting better little by little.

2. 一語ずつ、丁寧に言いましょう。
   Carefully say word for word.

   > 〜ましょう form can be used like a soft command.

3. 明日は面接に三十人来ますが、一人ずつ話をしなければなりません。
   Tomorrow 30 people are coming for an interview, they have to be talked to one by one.

13 | Verb Usage 動詞の使い方

V-1 | 気が付く | to notice; to become aware of | regular

1. (something) に気が付く	to notice (something)

EXAMPLE SENTENCES

1. 雨が降っていることに気が付かなかった。
   I wasn't aware it was raining.

2. 大人になってから、父の優しさに気が付きました。
   After becoming an adult, I realized the kindness of my father.

3. 私が落ち込んでいる時、愛犬のポチはいつも気が付いてくれます。
   When I am feeling down, my pet dog Pochi always realizes it.

4. 遠藤さんは、よく気が付く人で、仕事がたまっている人を助けます。
   Endo-san, being a very perceptive person, always helps people who have a lot of work.

V-2	挟<ruby>む<rt>はさ</rt></ruby>	to hold between, to pinch, to put in between	regular
	1. (thing) に挟む	to pinch or hold in a (thing)	
	2. (thing) を挟む	to pinch a (thing)	

A good way to remember はさむ is to recognize that the word "scissors" in Japanese (はさみ) is based on this verb. はさむ can translate to "put in" for natural English.

EXAMPLE SENTENCES

1. 電車のドアに指を挟まないでください。

   Please don't get your fingers caught in the door of the train.

2. 私は読んでいる本にいつもしおりを挟みます。

   I always put a bookmark in the book I am reading.

3. パンにハムと玉子を挟んで食べると、おいしいですね。

   If you put ham and egg between (two slices of) bread, it's delicious.

V-3	切<ruby>れる<rt>き</rt></ruby>	to run down; to expire; to run out	regular

This verb can be written in katakana as キレる when it means "to get angry" or "to lose one's temper."

EXAMPLE SENTENCES

1. 定期券が切れてしまいました。

   My commuter's pass expired (before I knew it).

2. 電池が切れた。新しいのはある？

   The battery is dead. Do you have a new one?

3. 携帯のバッテリーが切れる前に充電したほうがいいよ。

   You should charge before your cell phone battery dies.

4. 私の彼女はすぐキレるから別れたいです。

   I want to break up because my girlfriend loses her temper right away.

V-4	開 あ く	to open; to be empty (DESCRIPTIVE)	regular
	1. (something) が開く	(something) opens	

	閉 し まる	to close; to shut (DESCRIPTIVE)	regular
	1. (something) が閉まる	(something) closes	

EXAMPLE SENTENCES

1. もう夜の11時ですが、コンビニならまだ開いていますよ。
   It's already 11 at night, but the convenience store is still open.

2. すみません。この席は開いていますか。
   Excuse me. Is this seat empty?

3. 後15分で銀行が閉まるから、急ぎましょう。
   Let's hurry since the bank will close in 15 minutes.

4. あの店はずっと閉まっていましたが、最近また営業していますね。
   That store had been closed the whole time, but recently, it's been open for business again.

RELATED VERB(S)

Japanese From Zero! ⑤ V3-3. あける and しめる (ACTION)

V-5	動 うご かす	to move; to shift; to set in motion (ACTION)	regular
	1. (something) を動かす	to move (something)	

EXAMPLE SENTENCES

1. すみませんが、そのテーブルをちょっと動かして下さい。
   Excuse me, can you please move that table?

   > ちょっと softens the request.

2. 車を動かしたいんですが、横の自転車のせいで動かせません。
   I want to move my car, but I can't move it because of the bicycle next to it.

RELATED VERB(S)

Japanese From Zero!⑤ V2-4. うごく (to move)

V-6	汚れる よご	to get dirty; to become dirty (DESCRIPTIVE)	いる/える
	1. (something) が汚れる	(something) gets dirty	

EXAMPLE SENTENCES

1. 手が汚れているから、洗ってきます。
   I'm going to go wash my hands because they're dirty.

2. 僕の車は汚れていますが、明日雨が降るから大丈夫です。
   My car is dirty, but it's raining tomorrow so it's okay.

V-7	保存する ほ ぞん	to save (data etc.); to store; to conserve	する
	1. (place) に保存する	to save at a (place)	
	2. (things) を保存する	to save (files, information, messages etc.)	

EXAMPLE SENTENCES

1. お客様からのメールは、このフォルダーに保存して下さい。
   Please save mail from customers in this folder.

2. 今日買った牛肉を冷凍庫に保存しました。
   I stored the beef I bought today in the refrigerator.

13 | Grammar and Usage 文法と使い方

● 13-1. The hardest working particle in Japanese (に)

Let's take a moment to reflect on how many different ways に is used in Japanese and how many different ways it can be translated into English. Reviewing the "Direct VS Natural Translation" section in Lesson B will help you better understand how one particle can be translated in so many ways.

EXAMPLE SENTENCES (VARIOUS ENGLISH TRANSLATIONS)

1. 田中さんは部屋にいます。　　　　　Tanaka-san is <u>in</u> the room.
2. 田中さんの眼鏡はテーブルにあります。　Tanaka-san's glasses are <u>on</u> the table.
3. 田中さんは3時に行きます。　　　　Tanaka-san will go <u>at</u> three.
4. 田中さんは東京に行きます。　　　　Tanaka-san will go <u>to</u> Tokyo.
5. 田中さんに「かわいい」と言われました。　I was called "cute" <u>by</u> Tanaka-san.
6. 田中さんにもらいました。　　　　　I got this <u>from</u> Tanaka-san.
7. 田中さんがプールに飛び込んだ。　　Tanaka-san jumped <u>into</u> the pool.

Sometimes it isn't even translated into English.

---

8. 田中さんは買い物に行きます。　　　Tanaka-san is going shopping.
9. 田中さんはお父さんになります。　　Tanaka-san will be a father.
10. 田中さんは左に曲がりました。　　　Tanaka-san turned left.

Is there any limit to what に can be translated to? NOPE! Keep reading!

● 13-2. When particle に can translate as "for"

Depending on the requirements of English に can also translate to "for". Even simple sentences with one に, but different verbs, can have different translations for に.

お父さんに買いました。　　　　I bought it <u>for</u> my father.
Here any other translation of に would be unnatural or plain wrong in English, so に becomes "for".

お父さんにあげました。　　　　I gave it <u>to</u> my father.
In this very similar sentence just changing the verb makes に become "to" simply because the English would sound unnatural if we said "for".

For natural sounding English, when に is used after occasions, it can be translated as "for". This に isn't a "time marker", but is marking the event or occasion.

EXAMPLE SENTENCES

1. 父の誕生日に、セーターを買うつもりです。
   I plan on buying a sweater for my father's birthday.

> The sweater isn't bought "on" the birthday, but bought "for" it.

2. 朝ご飯に、何が食べたいですか。
   What do you want to eat for breakfast?

● 13-3. When のに doesn't mean "even though"

Before we start, we need to remember that any verb can be a noun by adding の to the end of its plain form. Once it's a noun, we can talk about it like any other noun.

食べるの (eating)   → 食べるのが好き。(I like eating.)
泳ぐの (swimming)   → 泳ぐのが難しい。(Swimming is hard.)
読むの (reading)   → 読むのが大切。(Reading is important.)

のに (even though) is taught in Lesson 1. But there is a のに that doesn't mean "even though". This のに is a verb changed into a noun with の, followed by に, creating a different grammar. With this のに the に means, "for", "to", or "in order to".

EXAMPLE SENTENCES (NOUN PHRASE の + に)

1. ここは学校に通うのに、便利です。
   This place is convenient for attending school.

2. 音楽を聴くのに、スマホを使います。
   I use a smartphone to listen to music. / I use a smartphone for listening to music.

3. パーティーに参加するのに、五千円要ります。
   In order to participate in the party, you need 5,000 yen.

4. このSDカードは動画を保存するのに容量が十分あると思います。
   I think this SD card has adequate space to store videos.

5. この本は漢字を勉強するのに、いいです。
   This book is good for studying kanji.

6. パスポートを取るのに、2週間必要です。
   2 weeks is required to get a passport.

RELATED GRAMMAR

Japanese From Zero! ④ Section 8-4. Making a verb into a noun with の and こと

● 13-4. How to distinguish のに (in order to) from のに (even though)

"How can I know which のに is being used?" The answer is.... CONTEXT.
It should be easy to know which is being used if you read the entire sentence first.

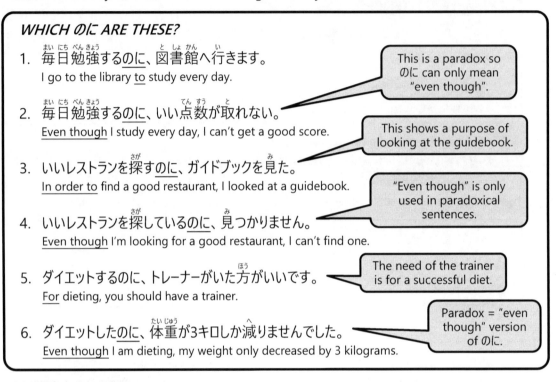

WHICH のに ARE THESE?

1. 毎日勉強するのに、図書館へ行きます。
   I go to the library <u>to</u> study every day.

   > This is a paradox so のに can only mean "even though".

2. 毎日勉強するのに、いい点数が取れない。
   <u>Even though</u> I study every day, I can't get a good score.

   > This shows a purpose of looking at the guidebook.

3. いいレストランを探すのに、ガイドブックを見た。
   <u>In order to</u> find a good restaurant, I looked at a guidebook.

   > "Even though" is only used in paradoxical sentences.

4. いいレストランを探しているのに、見つかりません。
   <u>Even though</u> I'm looking for a good restaurant, I can't find one.

   > The need of the trainer is for a successful diet.

5. ダイエットするのに、トレーナーがいた方がいいです。
   <u>For</u> dieting, you should have a trainer.

   > Paradox = "even though" version of のに.

6. ダイエットしたのに、体重が3キロしか減りませんでした。
   <u>Even though</u> I am dieting, my weight only decreased by 3 kilograms.

RELATED GRAMMAR

Japanese From Zero! ⑤ Section 1-2. Using のに (even though) with verbs and い adjectives

📖 もっと詳しく… More Details ⓘ

The difference between のに and ために
Both のに and ために can be translated to "for" or "in order to" and there are times when either can be used.

> Both sentences sound good.

EXAMPLE SENTENCES

1. 飲み物を買うために、コンビニに行った。　2. 飲み物を買うのに、コンビニに行った。
   BOTH SENTENCES: In order to buy drinks, I went to the convenience store.

ために is perfect for when your purpose or goal is lofty or has weight.
A quick way to think about ために is this guide sentence:

> (goal worth accomplishing) ために (action to accomplish it)

のに sometimes doesn't sound natural or somehow wrong when used with big or important goals.

> The goal feels light.

CORRECT	SOUNDS WRONG

1. 医者になるために、勉強しています。　2. 医者になるのに、勉強しています。
   BOTH SENTENCES: I am studying in order to be a doctor.

3. 家を買うために、貯金するつもりだ。　4. 家を買うのに、貯金するつもりだ。
   BOTH SENTENCES: In order to buy a house, I am saving money.

When talking about one's benefit, ために is more appropriate to use.

CORRECT	SOUNDS WRONG

1. 5キロやせるために、ジョギングします。　2. 5キロやせるのに、ジョギングします。
   BOTH SENTENCES: I jog so I can lose 5 kilograms.

3. 健康になるために、ビタミンをとります。　4. 健康になるのに、ビタミンをとります。
   BOTH SENTENCES: I take vitamins in order to become healthy.

RELATED GRAMMAR

Japanese From Zero! ⑤ Section 8-5. Using ため with verbs

● 13-5. でも after a noun to mean "even if~ / even though~"

でも directly after nouns or な adjectives means "even if~ / even though~". It's used in statements where the result is paradoxical or contrary to the norm.

> **EXAMPLE SENTENCES**
>
> 1. 新しい車が必要でも、お金がないから、今は買えません。
>   Even though I need a car, I can't buy one now because I don't have money.
>
>   *(callout: Buying a new car is expected.)*
>
> 2. ユニバーサル・スタジオは、平日でも人でいっぱいです。
>   Even though it's a weekday, Universal Studios is filled with people.
>
>   *(callout: You would expect few people on a weekday.)*

● 13-6. Using ても (even though, even if) with verbs

〜ても is used to say "even if" and "even though" to represent that the facts or assumptions are contrary to the outcome of a situation or action.

> **EXAMPLES**
>
> 行く (I go)   → 行っても (even if/though I go)
> 行かない (I don't go)   → 行かなくても (even if/though I don't go)
> 行きたい (I want to go)   → 行きたくても (even if/though I want to go)
> 行っている (I am going / I go) → 行っていても (even if/though I am going)
>
> **EXAMPLE SENTENCES**
>
> 1. 恵理子さんは毎日ピザを食べても、太らないです。羨ましいです！
>   Eriko doesn't gain weight <u>even though she eats</u> pizza every day. I'm envious!
>
> 2. 日本に行きたくても、休みがないから行けません。
>   <u>Even though I want to go</u> to Japan, I can't go because I don't have days off.
>
> 3. 私は勉強しなくても、このテストに合格します。
>   I will pass this test <u>even if I don't study</u>. / I will pass this test <u>even though I don't study</u>.
>
> 4. 雨が降っても、野球の試合はあります。
>   <u>Even if it rains</u>, I have a baseball game. / <u>Even if it rains</u>, there will be a baseball game.
>
> 5. お父さんに頼んでも、自転車は買ってもらえないよ。
>   <u>Even if I ask</u> my father, he won't buy me a bicycle.
>
> 6. ホテルの部屋を予約しようとしても、もう無理だと思いますよ。
>   <u>Even if we try to book</u> a hotel room, I think it's already impossible.

📖 もっと詳しく… More Details ℹ

What is the difference between ても and のに?

～ても can be used for "even if" and "even though" sentences. In other words, it can be used for <u>assumptions</u> (even if) and <u>facts</u> (even though).

～のに is only used for "even if" sentences based on facts and **NOT** assumptions.

ても VS のに COMPARISONS

1. 勉強<u>しても</u>、テストで100点が取れません。(ASSUMPTION)
   <u>Even if I study</u>, I won't get 100 points on the test.

2. 勉強<u>したのに</u>、テストで100点が取れませんでした。(FACT)
   <u>Even though I studied</u>, I didn't get 100 points on the test.

3. 社長は<u>熱があっても</u>、会社に来ると思います。(ASSUMPTION)
   <u>Even if</u> the president <u>has a fever</u>, I think she will come to work.

4. 社長は<u>熱があるのに</u>、会社に来ました。(FACT)
   <u>Even though</u> the president <u>has a fever</u>, she came to the work.

As stated above, ～ても can be used for ASSUMPTIONS and FACTS, which is why it's different from ～のに which is only used with FACTS.

5. クーラーを<u>つけていても</u>、全然涼しくならない。(FACT)
   <u>Even though</u> the cooler <u>is on</u>, it isn't cooling down at all.

6. クーラーを<u>つけているのに</u>、全然涼しくならない。(FACT)
   <u>Even though</u> the cooler <u>is on</u>, it isn't cooling down at all.

7. クーラーを<u>つけても</u>、涼しくならないと思う。(ASSUMPTION)
   <u>Even if I turn</u> the cooler <u>on</u>, I don't think it will cool down.

RELATED GRAMMAR

Japanese From Zero! ⑤ Section 1-2. Using のに (even though)

● 13-7. Using ても with い adjectives

The same rules apply to い adjectives with 〜ても as apply to the verbs.

EXAMPLES (い ADJECTIVES)

恥ずかしい (embarrassed) → 恥ずかしくても (even if I am embarrassed)

辛い (hard; painful) → 辛くても (even if it is hard)

危なくない (not dangerous) → 危なくなくても (even if it isn't dangerous)

背が低くない (not short in height) → 背が低くなくても (even if I am not short)

EXAMPLE SENTENCES

1. 子供は寒くても、外で遊びたがります。
   Children want to play outside even if it's cold.

   > 〜たがる is used when talking about 3rd person's feelings and desires.

2. 母は何かほしくても、いつも我慢しています。
   Even though (even when) my mother wants something, she always holds back.

   > Mothers put family first, so they won't buy something even if wanted.

3. 彼女が作ったものなら、おいしくなくても、食べます。
   If it's something my girlfriend made (cooked), I will eat it even if it isn't delicious.

RELATED GRAMMAR

Japanese From Zero! ⑤ Section 3-5. What someone else wants 〜がる (たい form verbs)

● 13-8. Listing facts and conditions 〜し〜し

〜し is used to support or emphasize an opinion or fact. It can be used for one fact, or several in succession.

EXAMPLE SENTENCES

1. 頭がいたいし、咳がでるし、つらいです。
   My head hurts... I'm coughing... it's hard for me.

2. 時間はないし、宿題は終わっていないし、困っています。
   I have no time... I haven't finished my homework... I'm in a fix (troubled).

When used with nouns and な adjectives it must be proceeded with です or だ.

3. 今日は休みだし、天気もいいし、何をしようか。
   Today's our day off... the weather's good... what shall we do?

～し can be used when saying a fact, which leads to a conclusion or a decision.

> **EXAMPLE SENTENCES**
> 1. 雨も降ってきたし、帰りましょう。
>   It started to rain... let's go home.
>
> 2. もう7時だし、起きないといけませんね。
>   It's already 7 o'clock... I have to get up.

When ending a statement with a し fact, in English you could add the word "plus" or "and also" to make the English sound more natural.

> **EXAMPLE SENTENCES**
> 3. 今日は風邪で仕事に行かなかった。眠かったし。
>   Today, due to a cold, I didn't go to work. Plus, I was tired!
>
> 4. 今晩は料理したくないからピザにしよう。皆も好きだし。
>   Tonight, since I don't want to cook, let's eat pizza. Plus, everyone likes it.

～し can also be used to avoid directly saying a reason. Perhaps to avoid hurting someone's feelings by being direct, or to avoid self-embarrassment.

> **EXAMPLE SENTENCES**
> 1. 外国に住みたいけど、親がいいと言わないし...
>   I want to live abroad, but my parents won't let me...
>
>   > The reason might be they can't speak English, but they blame their parents.
>
> 2. お金を貸してあげたいけど、私も貯金がないし...
>   I want to loan you money, but I don't have any savings either...
>
>   > Maybe they think the person won't pay them back, but that is harsh to say.
>
> **EXAMPLE CONVERSATION**
> 1. **INFORMAL CONVERSATION BETWEEN HAYAKAWA-SAN AND A FRIEND**
>   A: 早川さんは、頭がいいし、スポーツもできるし、完璧だね。
>   B: そんなことないよ。苦手なこともあるよ。
>   A: え？何？
>   B: 英語が全然話せないし、料理もできないし...
>
>   > "So, I am not perfect." The last half of the sentence is omitted.
>
>   ---
>   A: You are smart... you can also play sports... you are perfect.
>   B: That's not the case. There are things I'm not good at.
>   A: What? What are they?
>   B: I can't speak English... I can't cook either...

📖 もっと詳_わしく… More Details

Can I use the て form instead of し?

You can use both て and し when listing facts or conditions (#1). However, when telling a reason (#2 and #3), し and から are better options to use than て.

1. て and し are similar when listing facts or conditions.

   You can shop in Akihabara… you can go to Disneyland… Tokyo is fun.

   ○ 東京_{とうきょう}は、秋葉原_{あきはばら}で買_かい物_{もの}ができる[し]、ディズニーランドにも行_いける[し]、楽_{たの}しいですよ。

   ○ 東京_{とうきょう}は、秋葉原_{あきはばら}で買_かい物_{もの}ができ[て]、ディズニーランドにも行_いけ[て]、楽_{たの}しいですよ。

2. When saying a fact leading to a conclusion or decision, て isn't used.

   It's already gotten dark, (so) let's go home.

   ○ もう暗_{くら}くなった[し]、家_{うち}に帰_{かえ}りましょう。

   ○ もう暗_{くら}くなった[から]、家_{うち}に帰_{かえ}りましょう。

   ✕ もう暗_{くら}くなっ[て]、家_{うち}に帰_{かえ}りましょう。

   > This doesn't make any sense.

3. When avoiding direct or embarrassing conclusions, て isn't used.

   I want to go out with everyone, but I'm tired…

   ○ みんなと出_でかけたいけど、疲_{つか}れてる[し]…

   ○ みんなと出_でかけたいけど、疲_{つか}れてる[から]…

   ✕ みんなと出_でかけたいけど、疲_{つか}れてい[て]…

   > て here is weak. More information is expected after て.

13 | Practice and Review 練習と復習

● 1. Mini Conversation ミニ会話 J → E

Try translating the entire conversation before looking at the translation below.

1. Casual conversation between friends

A: 10時の電車に間に合わないかもしれない。急ごう！

B: 人が多くて走れないし、切符も買ってないし、無理だよ。

A: まだ分からないよ。あ、電車が見えた。

B: もうドアが閉まりそうだよ。次のにしよう。危ないし。

> Informal "Let's" form is a soft command.

A: I might not make the 10 o'clock train. Hurry!

B: There's so many people, we can't run... we haven't bought a ticket yet... it's impossible.

A: You don't know that yet. Ah, I see the train.

B: It looks like the door is closing already. Let's take the next one. Plus, it's dangerous.

2. Casual conversation between a mother and her son

A: ひろし、おじいちゃんの部屋のたんすを動かしたいんだけど、手伝ってくれる？

B: なんで？

A: 地震でたんすが倒れたら、おじいちゃんが怪我するかも知れないから。

B: 分かったけど、動かしても、おじいちゃんはきっと気が付かないね。

> たおれる = to fall over

A: Hiroshi, I want to move the dresser in grandpa's room, can you help me?

B: Why?

A: Because, if it falls over due to an earthquake, Grandpa might get injured.

B: Ok but, even if we move it Grandpa probably (surely) wouldn't even notice.

3. Polite conversation between friends

A: ぼく、中島さんのことが好きになってしまったかも知れません。

B: そうですか。中島さんのどんなところがいいんですか。

A: そうですね。きれいだし、頭がいいし、足が長いし。。。

B: 彼女のことを好きな人は多いですよ。頑張ってください。

A: I might have fallen for Nakajima-san.

B: Is that so? What do you like about Nakajima-san?

A: Let me think... She's pretty... she's smart... plus, she has long legs.

B: A lot of people like her. Good luck.

● 2. Mini Conversation ミニ会話 E → J

Try translating the entire conversation before looking at the translation below.

1. Polite conversation between friends

A: I got caught in the department store elevator door today.

B: What? Didn't you get hurt? (Did you get hurt?)

A: It was okay. But it was so embarrassing that my face turned pure red.

A: 今日、デパートでエレベーターのドアに挟まれてしまいました。

B: ええ！怪我をしませんでしたか。

A: 大丈夫でした。でも、恥ずかしくて、顔が真っ赤になりましたよ。

2. Casual conversation between a mother and her child

A: I might go all night long today since I have a ton of homework. (built-up homework)

B: When homework has built up, It's hard later on.

A: I know. But I have my part time job... I want to go hang out with friends... I have no time.

B: Using time well is also a part of studying.

A: 宿題がたまってるから、今日は夜更かしするかもしれない。

B: 宿題をためたら、後が大変だよ。

A: 分かってる。でも、アルバイトはあるし、友達と遊びにも行きたいし、時間がないんだ。

B: 時間をうまく使うのも、勉強の一つだよ。

3. Polite conversation between moms

A: Even though his clothes are dirty, my son continues wearing them.

B: That's boys for you.

A: But, he's already a junior high student... I want him to properly change his clothes.

B: Certainly, he will eventually change.

> きがえる = to change clothes

A: うちの息子は服が汚れていても、そのまま着ているんです。

B: それが男の子なんですよ。

A: でも、もう中学生だし、ちゃんと着替えてほしい。

B: きっと、そのうち変わりますよ。

● 3. Short Dialogue

Tom is asking a station worker how to get to Nara station.

トム	「すみません。ここから奈良駅まで、どうやって行ったらいいですか。」
駅員	「ここからなら、特急電車に乗って30分で行けますよ。」
トム	「切符はどこで買うんでしょうか。」
駅員	「あそこです。特急は一番速いですが、特急料金がかかりますよ。快速か急行なら、かかりません。」
トム	「分かりました。じゃあ、特急には乗らないようにします。」
駅員	「あ、快速が来ましたよ。後2分で出ますから、急いでください。」
トム	「はい、ありがとうございます。」

13 Kanji Lesson 13:
万戸室刀何同

13 | New Kanji 新しい漢字

From the teacher...

This lesson is random kanji that weren't easy to group but are all used quite often.

235	一	3画	ten thousand; myriad

くんよみ	none
おんよみ	マン、バン

万能 (ばん・のう) all-purpose	万全 (ばん・ぜん) thorough, flawless
万人 (ばん・にん) everyone	一万円 (いち・まん・えん) 10,000 yen
万病 (まん・びょう) all ills	万が一 (まん・が・いち) if by any chance

万

236	戸	4画	door

くんよみ	と
おんよみ	コ

引き戸 (ひ・き・ど) sliding door	戸籍 (こ・せき) official family registry
戸口 (と・ぐち) door	戸数 (こ・すう) number of houses
戸棚 (と・だな) cupboard	網戸 (あみ・ど) netted door; screen door

戸

237	宀	9画	room

くんよみ	むろ
おんよみ	シツ

地下室 (ち・か・しつ) basement	室温 (しつ・おん) room temperature
教室 (きょう・しつ) classroom	室内 (しつ・ない) inside the room
氷室 (ひ・むろ) ice room	洋室 (よう・しつ) western-style room

室

238	刀	2 画	sword; blade; knife								
		くんよみ	かたな								
		おんよみ	トウ								
		刀 (かたな) sword		日本刀 (に･ほん･とう) Japanese sword							
		小刀 (こ･がたな) small knife		短刀 (たん･とう) dagger							
		木刀 (ぼく･とう) wooden sword		大刀 (だい･とう) bearing sword							
		刀									

239	イ	7 画	what?								
		くんよみ	なに、なん								
		おんよみ	カ								
		何か (なに･か) something		何日 (なん･にち) what day (of the month)?							
		何時 (なん･じ) what time?		何円 (なん･えん) how many yen? how much?							
		何色 (なに･いろ) what color?		何本 (なん･ぼん) how many (long objects)?							
		何									

240	口/冂	6 画	same; similar								
		くんよみ	おな(じ)								
		おんよみ	ドウ								
		同じ (おな･じ) same		同級生 (どう･きゅう･せい) classmate							
		同居 (どう･きょ) living together		同時 (どう･じ) the same time							
		同情 (どう･じょう) sympathy		同感 (どう･かん) feeling the same way							
		同									

13 Kanji Culture 漢字の文化

● Types of rooms using 室

There are many types of rooms.

EXAMPLES

1. 客室 (きゃく しつ)
guest room

2. 個室 (こ しつ)
private room

3. 寝室 (しん しつ)
bedroom

4. 病室 (びょう しつ)
patient's room

5. 浴室 (よく しつ)
bathroom

6. 暗室 (あん しつ)
darkroom

13 | Words You Can Write かける言葉

十万 (じゅうまん) hundred thousand

十	万								

万人 (ばんにん) everyone; all people; universal

万	人								

戸口 (とぐち) door; doorway

戸	口								

戸数 (こすう) number of houses

戸	数								

茶室 (ちゃしつ) tea house; tea-ceremony house (room)

茶	室								

同行 (どうこう) accompany; traveling with

同	行								

教室 (きょうしつ) classroom

教	室								

小刀 (こがたな) small knife

小	刀								

竹刀 (しない) bamboo sword (not common reading)

竹	刀								

何月 (なんがつ) what month?

何	月								

何日 (なんにち) what day of the month?

何	日								

同じ (おなじ) same

同	じ								

合同 (ごうどう) joint; combination

合	同								

引き戸 (ひきど) sliding door

引	き	戸					

地下室 (ちかしつ) basement

地	下	室					

日本刀 (にほんとう) Japanese sword

日	本	刀					

13 Workbook 13:
Workbook Activities

13 | Kanji Drills 漢字ドリル

● **1. Reading practice**
Write FURIGANA above the underlined kanji words.

1.   いつも<u>何時</u>に<u>教室</u>に<u>行</u>っていますか。

2.   <u>午後</u>のミーティングの^{じゅん び}<u>準備</u>は、<u>万全</u>です。

3.   この<u>引</u>き<u>戸</u>がかたくて、なかなか^あ<u>開</u>きません。

4.   ^{りょ こう}<u>旅行</u>するなら、<u>汽車</u>と<u>船</u>とどちらがいいですか。

5.   ^{えい が}<u>映画</u>に<u>出</u>ている^{さむらい}<u>侍</u>と<u>同</u>じ<u>日本刀</u>がほしいです。

● **2. Fill in the kanji**
Fill in the appropriate kanji in the blanks for each sentence.

1.   このけいたい^{でん}___ ^わ___ は、^{さん}___ ^{まん}___ ^{えん}___ しました。
   This cell phone costs 30,000 yen.

2.   この ___ ^ひき ___ ^どは ___ ^{ふる}いですか。
   Is this sliding door old?

3.   ^{きょう}___ ^{しつ}___ で ___ ^て___ ^{がみ}を ___ ^かきました。
   I wrote a letter in the classroom.

4.   ^{きょ}___ ^う___ は ___ ^{なん}___ ^{がつ}___ ^{なん}___ ^{にち}ですか。
   What is the date (what month what day) today?

5. いつも＿＿じ＿＿で ＿＿べるのは、あきました。
   <ruby>同<rt>おな</rt></ruby> <ruby>店<rt>みせ</rt></ruby> <ruby>食<rt>た</rt></ruby>

   I am sick of always eating at the same place (store).

6. この ＿＿ 、＿＿ ＿＿ ＿＿ を＿＿いました。
   <ruby>間<rt>あいだ</rt></ruby> <ruby>日<rt>に</rt></ruby> <ruby>本<rt>ほん</rt></ruby> <ruby>刀<rt>とう</rt></ruby> <ruby>買<rt>か</rt></ruby>

   The other day, I bought a Japanese sword.

7. ＿＿ ＿＿に、＿＿ ＿＿ ＿＿ で＿＿いましょうか。
   <ruby>何<rt>なん</rt></ruby> <ruby>時<rt>じ</rt></ruby> <ruby>図<rt>と</rt></ruby> <ruby>書<rt>しょ</rt></ruby> <ruby>室<rt>しつ</rt></ruby> <ruby>会<rt>あ</rt></ruby>

   At what time shall me meet in the library room?

13 ｜ Usage Activities 文法アクティビティー

● 3. Reading comprehension

Translate the following on a separate piece of paper or type in an electronic device.

たったの５<ruby>分<rt>ふん</rt></ruby>　　*When it rains it pours! Often bad things occur one after another. What small change can you make to stop the first bad thing in the chain?*

① 「<ruby>発車<rt>はっしゃ</rt></ruby>いたします。ドアにご<ruby>注意<rt>ちゅうい</rt></ruby>ください。」
② <ruby>駅員<rt>えきいん</rt></ruby>さんがそう<ruby>言<rt>い</rt></ruby>って、ドアがガタンと<ruby>閉<rt>し</rt></ruby>まった<ruby>時<rt>とき</rt></ruby>、<ruby>自分<rt>じぶん</rt></ruby>のコートがドアに<ruby>挟<rt>はさ</rt></ruby>まったのが<ruby>分<rt>わ</rt></ruby>かりました。
③ 「ちょっと、どうしよう。<ruby>引<rt>ひ</rt></ruby>っ<ruby>張<rt>ば</rt></ruby>っても、だめだ。。。」
④ <ruby>満員電車<rt>まんいんでんしゃ</rt></ruby>は、そのまま<ruby>出発<rt>しゅっぱつ</rt></ruby>してしまいました。
⑤ すると、<ruby>隣<rt>となり</rt></ruby>に<ruby>立<rt>た</rt></ruby>っていた<ruby>男性<rt>だんせい</rt></ruby>が、<ruby>私<rt>わたし</rt></ruby>が<ruby>困<rt>こま</rt></ruby>っている<ruby>事<rt>こと</rt></ruby>に<ruby>気<rt>き</rt></ruby>が<ruby>付<rt>つ</rt></ruby>いて、<ruby>助<rt>たす</rt></ruby>けてくれました。
⑥ <ruby>先週<rt>せんしゅう</rt></ruby><ruby>買<rt>か</rt></ruby>ったばかりのコートなのに、<ruby>汚<rt>よご</rt></ruby>れたし、しわになったし、<ruby>最悪<rt>さいあく</rt></ruby>です。
⑦ <ruby>私<rt>わたし</rt></ruby>はその<ruby>男性<rt>だんせい</rt></ruby>にお<ruby>礼<rt>れい</rt></ruby>を<ruby>言<rt>い</rt></ruby>って、<ruby>自分<rt>じぶん</rt></ruby>の<ruby>駅<rt>えき</rt></ruby>で<ruby>降<rt>お</rt></ruby>りました。
⑧ <ruby>改札<rt>かいさつ</rt></ruby>を<ruby>通<rt>とお</rt></ruby>ろうとした<ruby>時<rt>とき</rt></ruby>、<ruby>突然<rt>とつぜん</rt></ruby>ブザーが<ruby>鳴<rt>な</rt></ruby>って、<ruby>私<rt>わたし</rt></ruby>の<ruby>所<rt>ところ</rt></ruby>だけ<ruby>通<rt>とお</rt></ruby>れなくなりました。
⑨ 「どうして？<ruby>何<rt>なん</rt></ruby>で？」と<ruby>頭<rt>あたま</rt></ruby>の<ruby>中<rt>なか</rt></ruby>で<ruby>考<rt>かんが</rt></ruby>えましたが、<ruby>分<rt>わ</rt></ruby>かりません。
⑩ そうしたら、<ruby>怖<rt>こわ</rt></ruby>そうな<ruby>駅員<rt>えきいん</rt></ruby>さんが<ruby>来<rt>き</rt></ruby>て、わたしの<ruby>定期券<rt>ていきけん</rt></ruby>を<ruby>見<rt>み</rt></ruby>ました。
⑪ 「お<ruby>客<rt>きゃく</rt></ruby>さん。この<ruby>定期券<rt>ていきけん</rt></ruby>はもう<ruby>切<rt>き</rt></ruby>れてますよ。<ruby>新<rt>あたら</rt></ruby>しいのを<ruby>買<rt>か</rt></ruby>って<ruby>下<rt>くだ</rt></ruby>さい。」と<ruby>言<rt>い</rt></ruby>われました。
⑫ 「そうでしたか。すみません。」と<ruby>言<rt>い</rt></ruby>って、<ruby>急<rt>いそ</rt></ruby>いで<ruby>切符<rt>きっぷ</rt></ruby>を<ruby>買<rt>か</rt></ruby>いに<ruby>行<rt>い</rt></ruby>きました。

⑬ 券売機では、一人のおばあさんが切符を買おうとしていました。

⑭ 私がおばあさんの後ろに行くと、おばあさんが「新宿駅に行くのに、いくらかかるの？」と私に聞いたので、「260円ですよ。」と答えました。

⑮ すると、そのおばあさんは、かばんの中から財布を出して、ゆっくりと 10円玉を一枚ずつ入れ始めたんです。

⑯ あまりにも遅くて、私はキレそうになりました。

⑰ 「10円玉を 26枚出すつもり？！100円玉を使ってよ！私は急いでるの！」

⑱ そう言いたかったけど、もちろん言えませんでした。

⑲ 結局、そのおばあさんのせいで、仕事に遅れてしまいました。

⑳ 上司から冷たい目で見られるし、残業させられるし、くたくたです。

㉑ 明日からは、5分早く家を出ようと思っています。

● 4. Reading comprehension questions

Translate the questions about the reading comprehension then answer in Japanese.

1. 電車が発車した時、この人はどこに立っていましたか。

Translation: _____

Answer: _____

2. この人はどうして「最悪」だと思ったんですか。

Translation: _____

Answer: _____

3. 改札を通る時、何が必要ですか。

Translation: _____

Answer: _____

4. この人はどうして、おばあさんに怒っていましたか。

Translation: _____

Answer: _____

5. この人はこれから、どんな事に気を付けないといけませんか。

Translation: _____

Answer: _____

● 5. Fill in the blanks
Fill in the missing part based on the English sentence.

1. 漢字を_____。
Let's write the kanji 5 times each.

2. ノートパソコンを_____前に、データを_____。
Please save your data before closing your laptop.

3. いいレストランを_____、ネットで_____。
In order to find a good restaurant, I searched on the net.

4. 雨が_____、テニスの練習を_____です。
Even if it rains, I intend to practice tennis.

5. 彼女は_____し、_____し、親切です。
She is smart, pretty, and kind.

● 6. Question and Answer
Answer the following questions as if you were directly asked.

1. 病気でも、しなければならない事は何ですか。

_____

2. 頑張っても、できない事はありますか。

_____

3. 雨の日でも、楽しめる場所はどこですか。

_____

4. あなたのお友達は、どんな人ですか。 (use 〜し、〜し pattern.)

_____

5. どうして日本語を勉強しているんですか。(use 〜し、〜し pattern.)

_____

● 7. Translation

Translate the following sentences into Japanese.

1. I went to a nearby shop in order to buy a birthday present for my mother. (use のに)

_____

2. I searched everywhere (here and there) in order to find my cat. (use のに)

_____

3. Even though I had a fever, I went to school.

_____

4. Even though I am continuing exercises, I don't lose weight.

_____

5. Today is Sunday and we have nothing to do, so let's go out somewhere. (use 〜し、〜し)

_____

● 8. Word Review
Select the appropriate words from the box below and complete the sentences.

へそくり　大_{だい}都_と市_し　自_じ信_{しん}　量_{りょう}　観_{かん}光_{こう}客_{きゃく}　通_{つう}学_{がく}
最_{さい}新_{しん}　田_{いなか}舎　予_よ約_{やく}　工_{こう}事_じ　外_{がい}出_{しゅつ}　決_きまり
将_{しょう}来_{らい}　真_まっ青_{さお}　真_まっ赤_か　泥_{どろ}棒_{ぼう}　秘_ひ密_{みつ}　今_{いま}風_{ふう}

1. ヘアサロンで(　　　　)したのに、すぐに髪_{かみ}の毛_けを切_きってもらえませんでした。

2. 昨_{きのう}日のお昼_{ひる}ごろ、近_{きん}所_{じょ}の家_{いえ}に(　　　　)が入_{はい}ったそうです。

3. 東_{とうきょう}京や京_{きょう}都_とは、外_{がいこくじん}国人の(　　　　)でいっぱいです。

4. 大_{おお}雨_{あめ}のせいで、(　　　　)できませんでした。

5. (　　　　)に住_すんでいるから、電_{でん}車_{しゃ}はあるし、お店_{みせ}も近_{ちか}くにたくさんあるし、とても便_{べん}利_りです。

6. 彼_{かれ}は殺_{さつ}人_{じん}事_じ件_{けん}を見_みて、顔_{かお}が(　　　　)になりました。

7. 押_おし入_いれに(　　　　)を隠_{かく}していたのに、見_みつかってしまいました。

8. 外_{そと}は(　　　　)の音_{おと}がして、毎_{まい}日_{にち}うるさいんです。

13 | Answer Key 答え合わせ

Short Dialogue (translation)

Tom	Excuse me. How do you go from here to Nara station?
Station worker	If it's from here, you can get there in 30 minutes on the limited express train.
Tom	Where do I buy tickets?
Station worker	Over there. The limited express is the fastest, but it'll cost you the limited express fare. If you take the rapid or the express, it won't cost you.
Tom	I see. Well then, I'll make sure to not ride the limited express.
Station worker	Ah, the rapid has arrived (come). Hurry up since it departs (leaves) in 2 more minutes.
Tom	Ok, thank you.

1. Reading practice (answers)

1. いつも何時に教室に行っていますか。
2. 午後のミーティングの準備は、万全です。
3. この引き戸がかたくて、なかなか開きません。
4. 旅行するなら、汽車と船とどちらがいいですか。
5. 映画に出ている侍と同じ日本刀がほしいです。

2. Fill in the kanji (answers)

1. このけいたい電話は、三万円しました。
2. この引き戸は古いですか。
3. 教室で手紙を書きました。
4. 今日は何月何日ですか。
5. いつも同じ店で食べるのは、あきました。
6. この間、日本刀を買いました。
7. 何時に図書室で会いましょうか。

3. Reading comprehension (translation)

① "We are departing. Beware of the door."
② The train staff said this, and when the door closed with a bang, I realized (understood) that my own coat was caught in the door.
③ "Argh, what should I do? Pulling it doesn't work."
④ The filled to capacity train departed without haste.
⑤ Whereupon, the man that was standing next to me realized I was in a bind and helped me.
⑥ Even though this is a coat I just bought last week, it got dirty... it got wrinkled... this is horrible.
⑦ I said thanks to the man and got off at my station.
⑧ Just as I was going through the ticket gate, a buzzer sounded suddenly, and only my spot became unable to pass through.
⑨ In my head I thought, "Why? Why?", but I don't know.
⑩ Then, a scary looking station staff came and looked at my commuter pass.
⑪ I was told, "Customer. This commuter pass is already expired. Please buy a new one."
⑫ I said, "Really? Sorry." and hurriedly went to buy a ticket.
⑬ At the ticket sales machine, an old woman was trying to buy a ticket.

⑭ Upon getting behind the old lady, she asked me, "How much does it cost to go to Shinjuku station?" so I answered, "It's 260 yen."

⑮ Whereupon, that old lady took out her wallet from her bag and slowly began putting in 10-yen coins one at a time.

⑯ It was so slow that I almost lost my temper.

⑰ "Do you intend to put (all) twenty six 10-yen coins in?! Use some 100-yen coins! I'm in a hurry!"

⑱ This is what I wanted to say, but of course I couldn't say it.

⑲ In the end, because (of the fault) of this old lady, I ended up being late for work.

⑳ I got looked at with cold eyes by my boss... I was made to work overtime... I'm exhausted.

㉑ Starting tomorrow, I'm thinking to leave the house 5 minutes earlier.

4. Reading comprehension questions (answers)

1. Translation: Where was this person standing when the train departed?
   Answer(s): ドアの近くに立っていました。／ドアの前か横に立っていたと思います。

2. Translation: Why did this person think it was "the worst"?
   Answer(s): 買ったばかりのコートが汚れて、しわになったからです。／新しいコートがドアに挟まったからです。

3. Translation: What is needed when you go through the ticket gate?
   Answer(s): 定期券か切符が必要です。

4. Translation: Why was this person mad at the old lady?
   Answer(s): おばあさんがゆっくりお金を出すからです。／おばあさんが遅いからです。

5. Translation: From now on, what thing does this person need to be careful about?
   Answer(s): 電車に乗る時は服をドアに挟まないことと、定期券が切れないようにすることです。
   家をもう少し早く出るようにしないといけません。

5. Fill in the blanks (answers)

1. 漢字を5回ずつ書きましょう。

2. ノートパソコンを閉じる前に、データを保存して下さい。

3. いいレストランを見つけるのに、ネットで探しました。／いいレストランを見つけるために、ネットで調べました。

4. 雨が降っても、テニスの練習をするつもりです。

5. 彼女は頭がいいし、きれいだし、親切です。／彼女はかしこいし、美人だし、親切です。

6. Question and Answer (answers may vary)

1. What is something you need to do even when you are sick?
   仕事や家事です。／宿題です。／歯をみがくことです。／トイレに行くことです。

2. Is there something that you can't do even if you try hard?
   多分、ないと思います。／彼女を見つける事です。／スポーツが全然できません。

3. Where is a place that you can have fun even on a rainy day?
映画館だと思います。／ショッピング・モールでしょう。／家が一番です。

4. What type of person is your friend? / What type of people are your friends?
背が高いし、やさしいし、いい人です。／頭がいいし、元気だし、かっこいいです。／友達がいないし。。。

5. Why are you studying Japanese?
日本語は楽しいし、アニメが好きだからです。／難しいけど、面白いし、日本人の友達もいるし、好きだから。

7. Translation (answers may vary)

1. 母に(の)誕生日プレゼントを買うのに、近くのお店へ行きました。

2. 猫を見つけるのに、あちこち探しました。

3. 熱があっても、学校へ行きました。／熱があったのに、学校に行きました。

4. 運動を続けているのに、体重が減りません。／運動を続けていても、やせません。

5. 今日は日曜日だし、(何も)することがないし、どこかに出かけましょう。

8. Word Review (answers)

1. ヘアサロンで(予約)したのに、すぐに髪の毛を切ってもらえませんでした。

2. 昨日のお昼ごろ、近所の家に(泥棒)が入ったそうです。

3. 東京や京都は、外国人の(観光客)でいっぱいです。

4. 大雨のせいで、(外出)できませんでした。

5. (大都市)に住んでいるから、電車はあるし、お店も近くにたくさんあるし、とても便利です。

6. 彼は殺人事件を見て、顔が(真っ青)になりました。

7. 押し入れに(へそくり)を隠していたのに、見つかってしまいました。

8. 外は(工事)の音がして、毎日うるさいんです。

GLOSSARY

English-Japanese

A

accidentally　おもわず　思わず	401
accordingly　そこで	96
act as (to)　ふりをする	34
action　おこない　行い	193
actually　じつは　実は	256
addicted (to be)　はまる	318
address　じゅうしょ　住所	161
adulterous lover　うわきあいて　浮気相手	286
afraid (to be)　こわがる　怖がる	65
agricultural produce　のうさくぶつ　農作物	193
aid　(お)せわ　(お)世話	34
air temperature　きおん　気温	34
all in all　やっぱり	343
all of a sudden　とつぜん　突然	193
all of the members　ぜんいん　全員	256
all over the place　あちこち	96
all right　へいき　平気	227
alternatively　そのかわり　その代わり	161
ambulance　きゅうきゅうしゃ　救急車	96
amenable　すなお(な)　素直(な)	193
amount　りょう　量	65
an idea　かんがえ　考え	227
and then　そうしたら	34
anticipate (to)　きたいする　期待する	132
anxiety　ふあん　不安	373
apart　べつべつに　別々に	227
apart (to be)　はなれる　離れる	96
appear (to)　でてくる　出てくる	34
apply (to)　ぬる　塗る	286
appointment　よやく　予約	132
arise (to)　おきる　起きる	65
aroma　におい　匂い	96
arrive (to)　つく　着く	286
as a matter of fact　じつは　実は	256
as it is　そのまま	401
as suspected　やっぱり	343
as was expected　やっぱり	343
ask (to)　たずねる　尋ねる	256
assistance　(お)せわ　(お)世話	34
at a time　〜ずつ	401
at once　さっそく　早速	318
attached (to be)　つく　付く	286
awhile　しばらく	65

B

back-country　いなか　田舎	96
backup　おうえん　応援	318
bag　ふくろ　袋	96
bank　つつみ　堤	193
be just like　そっくり（な）	256
because　せい	132
because　なぜなら	96
become aware of (to)　きがつく　気が付く	401
become dirty (to)　よごれる　汚れる	401

become intoxicated (to)　よう　酔う	343
become sick　よう　酔う	343
behavior　おこない　行い	193
believe (to)　しんじる　信じる	286
beside　そば	343
big city　だいとし　大都市	34
bite off (to)　かみきる　噛み切る	161
booking　よやく　予約	132
bookmark　しおり	401
boost　おうえん　応援	318
bread crust　パンのみみ　パンの耳	161
break up (to)　わかれる　別れる	34
bring back memories　なつかしい　懐かしい	96
burn (to)　もやす　燃やす	227
burn (to)　もえる　燃える	227

C

call (to)　よぶ　呼ぶ	343
cancer　がん　癌	256
can't be helped　しょうがない	34
cap　ふた	96
careful (to be)　ちゅういする　注意する	65
carefully　ていねいに　丁寧に	401
casually　さりげなく　さり気なく	193
certain day　あるひ　ある日	161
certainly　きっと	34
certainly　たしかに　確かに	318
charge　りょうきん　料金	401
chase down (to)　おいかける　追いかける	256
chase game　おいかけっこ　追いかけっこ	161
check out　しらべる　調べる	286
cheering　おうえん　応援	318
clever　かしこい　賢い	161
close　そば	343
close (to)　しまる　閉まる	401
close (to)　しめる　閉める	96
close (to)　とじる　閉じる	96
closed (to be)　しまる　閉まる	401
collect (to)　あつめる　集める	227
collect (to)　あつまる　集まる	227
collect (to)　たまる	96
column　れつ　列	65
come out (to)　でてくる　出てくる	34
common　あたりまえ　当たり前	373
commuter's ticket　ていきけん　定期券	401
companion　あいて　相手	34
complain (to)　もんくをいう　文句を言う	343
complete　かんぺき　完璧	343
conceal (to)　かくす　隠す	343
conceal oneself (to)　かくれる　隠れる	343
conduct　おこない　行い	193
confess one's love (to)　こくはくする　告白する	318
confidence　じしん　自信	34
considerably　かなり	227
construction　こうじ　工事	132
continue (to)　つづける　続ける	318
convey (to)　つたえる　伝える	318
cool (air)　すずしい　涼しい	401
countermeasure, step　たいさく　対策	132
countryside　いなか　田舎	96
cover　ふた	96

here and there　あちこち　96
hide something (to)　かくす　隠す　343
hit (active) (to)　なぐる　殴る　286
hold between (to)　はさむ　挟む　401
honest　しょうじき(な)　正直(な)　193
hopeless　しょうがない　34
human resources　じんざい　人材　96
human(s)　にんげん　人間　193

I
immediately　さっそく　早速　318
impossible　むり(な)　無理(な)　96
in exchange for　かわりに　代わりに　256
in particular　とくに　特に　65
in return　かわりに　代わりに　256
in return　そのかわり　その代わり　161
in the same way　おなじように　同じように　373
in the years to come　しょうらい　将来　256
incidentally　さりげなく　さり気なく　193
included (to be)　つく　付く　286
increase (to)　ふす　増やすす　65
increase (to)　ふえる　増える　65
influence　えいきょう　影響　65
injury　ひがい　被害　65
inquire (to)　たずねる　尋ねる　256
instead　そのかわり　その代わり　161
instead of　かわりに　代わりに　256
intense　きびしい　厳しい　227
investigate (to)　しらべる　調べる　286
invite (to)　よぶ　呼ぶ　343

J
Japanese folding fan　せんす　扇子　96
Japanese food　にほんしょく　日本食　318
Japanese style　わしき　和式　373
jump in (to)　とびこむ　飛び込む　193
junk　がらくた　343
just like　そのまま　401

K
keep down (to)　しゃがむ　373
kill (to)　ころす　殺す　286

L
large city　だいとし　大都市　34
lay (to)　しく　敷く　373
leak out information (to)　ばらす　343
leave behind (to)　のこす　残す　132
left (to be)　のこる　残る　132
liar　うそつき　嘘つき　286
lid　ふた　96
like　～みたい　286
line　れつ　列　65
little while ago　さっき　96
living　くらし　暮らし　96
look like (to)　にる　似る　256
looking after　(お)せわ　(お)世話　34
love　れんあい　恋愛　343
low　ひくい　低い　343

M
make a mistake (to)　しっぱいする　失敗する　132
make a sound (to)　おとをたてる　音を立てる　193
make great effort (to)　くろうする　苦労する　373
make it in time (to)　まにあう　間に合う　318
manner　ほうほう　方法　65
manpower　じんざい　人材　96
mark　てん　点　34
match (to)　そろえる　揃える　373
mess up (to)　しっぱいする　失敗する　132
metal　きんぞく　金属　193
method　ほうほう　方法　65
mill　こうじょう　工場　65
mischief　いたずら　193
miss getting on train etc. (to)　のりおくれる　乗り遅れる　256
mistaken (to be)　かんちがいする　勘違いする　318
modern　いまふう　今風　343
more than anyone　だれよりも　誰よりも　286
more than one deserves　もったいない　227
mosquito　か　蚊　96
most likely　きっと　34
move (to)　うごかす　動かす　401
move (to)　うごく　動く　65
movie　どうが　動画　401
moving picture　どうが　動画　401
murder case　さつじんじけん　殺人事件　286
murderer　さつじんはん　殺人犯　286

N
natural　あたりまえ　当たり前　373
natural resources　しげん　資源　227
near　そば　343
never again　にどと　二度と　161
nostalgic　なつかしい　懐かしい　96
not even once　いちども　一度も　34
notice (to)　きがつく　気が付く　401
notice (to)　みかける　見かける　256
now　そこで　96
number　てんすう　点数　343

O
obedient　すなお(な)　素直(な)　193
occur (to)　おきる　起きる　65
odor　におい　匂い　96
OK　へいき　平気　227
old person　おとしより　お年寄り　343
older in age　としうえ　年上　286
on (electrically) (to be)　つく　286
one day　あるひ　ある日　161
one way or another　なんとか　何とか　34
one's parents' home　じっか　実家　96
open (stores etc.) (to be)　えいぎょうする　営業する　65
open (to be)　あく　開く　401
open (to)　あく　開く　401
open (to)　あける　開ける　96
open (to)　ひらく　開く　96
opponent　あいて　相手　34
or perhaps　それとも　34
or something　～など　227
order of things　じゅんばん　順番　132

GLOSSARY

Japanese-English

あ

あたりまえ　当たり前　natural; common; reasonable	373
あいて　相手　companion; partner; opponent	34
あきかん　空き缶　empty can	227
あく　開く　to open; to be open	401
あくびをする　to yawn	161
あける　開ける　to open	96
あさはやく　朝早く　early in the morning	34
あしもと　足元　under one's feet	401
あせがでる　汗が出る　to sweat	34
あせをかく　汗をかく　to sweat	34
あたまがいい　頭がいい　smart	193
あちこち　here and there; all over the place	96
あつまる　集まる　to collect	227
あつめる　集める　to collect	227
あまりにも　too much; excessive; too	34
あるひ　ある日　one day; a certain day	161

い

いけ　池　a pond	193
いたずら　trick; mischief	193
いちども　一度も　not even once	34
いなか　田舎　countryside; back-country	96
いまのうち　今のうち　while you can	343
いまふう　今風　fashionable; modern	343
いれる　入れる　to put into; to put inside	161

う

うごかす　動かす　to move; to set in motion	401
うごく　動く　to move; to run	65
うそつき　嘘つき　a liar	286
うそをつく　嘘をつく　to tell a lie	286
うらやましい　羨ましい　envious	401
うわきあいて　浮気相手　adulterous lover	286
うわさばなし　噂話　gossip	318

え

えいきょう　影響　influence; effect	65
えいぎょうする　営業する　to do business; to be open (stores etc.)	65
えらい　偉い　good! great!	161

お

おいかけっこ　追いかけっこ　chase game; game of tag	161
おいかける　追いかける　to pursue; to chase down	256
おうえん　応援　cheering; backup; boost; rooting	318
おきる　起きる　to occur; to happen; to arise	65
おく　置く　to place; to put	96
おこない　行い　action; behavior; conduct	193
おせわ　お世話　looking after; help; aid; assistance	34
おちこむ　落ち込む　to feel down	34
おとしより　お年寄り　old person; senior citizen	343
おとをたてる　音を立てる　to make a sound	193
おどろく　驚く　to be surprised	193

おなじように　同じように　in the same way	373
おなべ　お鍋　a pan; a pot	96
おひゃくしょう　お百姓　farmer	161
おもわず　思わず　accidentally; unintentionally	401
おれい　お礼　thanks; gratitude	401

か

か　蚊　mosquito	96
かいさつ　改札　ticket gate; wicket	401
かくす　隠す　to hide something; to conceal	343
かくれる　隠れる　to conceal oneself	343
かぐ　家具　furniture	227
かしこい　賢い　wise; clever; smart	161
かなり　considerably; quite	227
かみきる　噛み切る　to bite off	161
かわりに　代わりに　instead of; in exchange for; in return	256
かんがえ　考え　an idea	227
かんきょう　環境　environment	227
かんこうきゃく　観光客　tourist; visitor	65
かんちがいする　勘違いする　to be mistaken	318
かんぺき　完璧　perfect; complete	343

が

がいしゃ　外車　foreign car	132
がいしゅつ　外出　outing; trip; going out	193
がめん　画面　screen; picture	161
がらくた　junk; rubbish; garbage	343
がん　癌　cancer	256

き

きえる　消える　to disappear; to go out	256
きおん　気温　air temperature	34
きがつく　気が付く　to notice; to become aware of	401
きたいする　期待する　to expect; to anticipate	132
きっと　surely; certainly; most likely	34
きびしい　厳しい　strict; severe; rigid; intense	227
きまり　決まり　a rule	227
きゅうきゅうしゃ　救急車　ambulance	96
きれる　切れる　to run down; to expire	401
きん　筋トレ　weight (muscle) training	373
きんぞく　金属　metal	193

く

くさる　腐る　to spoil; to turn rotten	161
くつろぐ　to relax; to feel at home	373
くらし　暮らし　living; day-to-day life	96
くろうする　苦労する　to make great effort; to suffer	373

け

けっか　結果　results	286
けっこんきねんび　結婚記念日　wedding anniversary	286
けんばいき　券売機　ticket sales machine	401

こ

こうかいする　後悔する　to regret	318
こうじ　工事　construction	132
こうじょう　工場　factory; plant; mill; workshop	65
こくはくする　告白する　to confess one's love	318

こまかい　細かい　small; fine; detailed		227
こまる　困る　to be troubled/bothered		34
ころす　殺す　to kill		286
こわがる　怖がる　to be afraid		65

ご

ごうかく　合格　pass		343

さ

さいあく　最悪　the worst		401
さいしん　最新　the newest; the latest		96
さっき　a little while ago		96
さっそく　早速　immediately; right away; at once		318
さつじんじけん　殺人事件　murder case		286
さつじんはん　殺人犯　murderer		286
さりげなく　さり気なく　casually; incidentally		193
さんか　参加　participation		401

ざ

ざんぎょうする　残業する　to work overtime		132

し

しおり　bookmark		401
しく　敷く　to spread; to lay		373
しげん　資源　natural resources		227
したい　死体　dead body		286
しっぱいする　失敗する　to mess up; to make a mistake		132
しなぎれ　品切れ　out of stock		65
しばらく　for a while; awhile		65
しぼうじこく　死亡時刻　time of death		286
しまう　to put away; put an end to		161
しまる　閉まる　to close; to be closed		401
しめる　閉める　to close; to shut		96
しゃがむ　to squat; to crouch; to keep down		373
しゃくようしょ　借用書　proof of debt document		286
しゃっきん　借金　debt		286
しょうがない　hopeless; can't be helped		34
しょうじきな　正直な　honest		193
しょうらい　将来　future; in the years to come		256
しらべる　調べる　to investigate; check out		286
しわ　wrinkle; crease		401
しんけんに　真剣に　seriously; earnestly		34
しんじる　信じる　to believe; to trust		286
しんせんな　新鮮な　fresh		193

じ

じしん　自信　confidence; self-assurance		34
じっか　実家　one's parents' home		96
じつは　実は　as a matter of fact; actually		256
じゃくてん　弱点　a weak point; weakness		193
じゅう　銃　gun; pistol		286
じゅうえんだま　十円玉　ten yen coin		401
じゅうしょ　住所　address		161
じゅく　塾　cramming school		227
じゅんばん　順番　turn (in line); order of things		132
じょうきゃく　乗客　passengers		256
じんざい　人材　manpower; human resources		96

す

すずしい　涼しい　cool (air)		401
すなおな　素直な　obedient; amenable; straightforward	193
すると　thereupon; with that		161

ず

ずつ　each; at a time		401

せ

せい　fault; because; due to		132
せいこうする　成功する　to succeed		132
せつやく　節約　savings; economizing		34
せつやくする　節約する　to economize; to save		227
せんす　扇子　Japanese folding fan		96

ぜ

ぜんいん　全員　all of the members; everybody		256

そ

そうしたら　and then		34
そこで　so; accordingly; now; therefore		96
そだいごみ　粗大ごみ　oversized or bulky trash		227
そっくり（な）　spitting image; be just like		256
そつぎょうしき　卒業式　graduation ceremony		34
そのうち　sooner or later; someday		401
そのかわり　その代わり　instead; in return; alternatively	161
そのまま　as it is; without change; just like		401
そば　near; close; beside		343
それとも　or perhaps		34
そろえる　揃える　to gather; to put in order; to match	373

た

たいさく　対策　countermeasure, step		132
たいじゅう　体重　weight (for body)		227
たしかに　確かに　surely; certainly; for sure		318
たすける　助ける　to help; to save		256
たずねる　尋ねる　to ask; to inquire		256
たまる　to collect; to save; to pile up		96
たんぼ　田んぼ　a rice field		193

だ

だいとし　大都市　big city; large city		34
だいぶ　大分　fairly; quite; pretty		318
だまされる　騙される　to be fooled; tricked; deceived	193
だます　騙す　to fool; trick; deceive		193
だれよりも　誰よりも　more than anyone		286

ち

ちかてつ　地下鉄　underground train; subway		132
ちがい　違い　difference		34
ちゅういする　注意する　to be careful; to pay attention; to warn	65

つ

つうがく　通学　school commute		65
つかれる　疲れる　to get tired; to tire		318
つく　to be on (electrically)		286

Other From Zero! Books

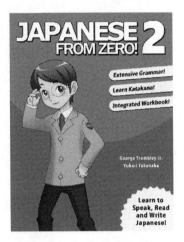

出力日：2019-12-02

Made in the USA
Columbia, SC
25 April 2024

34693706R00241